NATIONALISM AND TERRITORY

NATIONALISM AND TERRITORY

Constructing Group Identity
in Southeastern Europe

GEORGE W. WHITE

ROWMAN & LITTLEFIELD PUBLISHERS, INC.
Lanham • Boulder • New York • Oxford

ROWMAN & LITTLEFIELD PUBLISHERS, INC.

Published in the United States of America
by Rowman & Littlefield Publishers, Inc.
4720 Boston Way, Lanham, Maryland 20706
http://www.rowmanlittlefield.com

12 Hid's Copse Road
Cumnor Hill, Oxford OX2 9JJ, England

British Library Cataloguing in Publication Information Available

Library of Congress Cataloging-in-Publication Data

White, George W., 1963–
    Nationalism and territory : constructing group identity in Southeastern Europe / George W. White.
        p.   cm. — (Geographical perspectives on the human past)
    Includes bibliographical references and index.
    ISBN 0-8476-9808-4 (c. : alk. paper). — ISBN 0-8476-9809-2 (pbk. : alk. paper)
        1. Balkan Peninsula—Politics and government.   2. Nationalism—Balkan Peninsula.   3. Territory, National—Balkan Peninsula.   4. Hungary—Politics and government.   5. Nationalism—Hungary.   6. Territory, National—Hungary.   I. Title.   II. Series.
    DR38.2.W48   1999
    323.1'496—dc21   99-39940
                                                                                                        CIP

Printed in the United States of America

♾ ™ The paper used in this publication meets the minimum requirements of American National Standard for information Sciences—Permanence of Paper for Printed Library Materials, ANSI/NISO Z39.48–1992.

To my mother,
Yvonne Lea White,
who has given her love and support all along

How does one describe and measure that which is invisible?
By the shadow it casts and the footprints it leaves behind.

Contents

Figures

Acknowledgments

I would like to extend my appreciation to those who have helped me since the beginning. I express my sincere appreciation to Professors Alexander B. Murphy, Ronald Wixman, Everett G. Smith, and Carol Silverman, all of whom helped me to refine my ideas on this subject. Their expertise and thoughtful comments were invaluable. A crucial year of this research was supported in large part by an International Trade and Development Fellowship, provided by the Sasakawa Foundation of Japan. This research also was supported in part by a National Science Foundation Grant to Alexander B. Murphy. Special thanks also go to Emily Linholm, who completed the lion's share of the cartographic work and in an unreasonably short amount of time. Additional thanks to Lorna Baldwin, John and Susan Dolan, Nancy Leeper, Cindy Mendoza, Dana Hudson, Tracy Edwards, Tonya Buckmaster, Sean Triplett, Todd Taylor, Mathew Habersack, Christopher Robinson, Stacy Talmadge, and Frederick Baker for their assistance in the preparation of the maps, and to N. Kirk Lucas and Professor Glynn Baugher for their thoughtful and careful editing. Finally, I would like to express my appreciation to Shannon B. Dawson for her friendship and encouragement during the latter part of this project and for her eleventh-hour proofreading of the manuscript.

Place-Name Terminology

As a general rule, English equivalents are used for many of the place-names in this study, but the forms used by the nations themselves are provided. In many cases, no clear consensus exists concerning the appropriate English equivalent. Since this study seeks to understand place and territory from the perspective of the nation in question, the choice of an English equivalent is closely related to the spelling employed by the nation examined. For example, "Walachia" is used instead of "Wallachia" because the former is the same as the Romanian. However, "Moldavia" is used in place of "Moldova" so as not to confuse the territory with the former Soviet Republic of Moldova, itself formerly called Besarabia.

In many cases, places important to a nation lie outside the nation's modern state territory and are commonly known by the names of the nations that currently possess them. Again, since this study seeks to understand place and territory from the perspective of the nation in question, these place-names are spelled according to the respective national perspectives. For example, the name "Timişoara" is used in the Romanian chapter while "Temesvár" is used in the Hungarian and "Temišvar" is used in the Serbian chapter. Since the city is now in Romania and generally known by its Romanian name, the Romanian name Timişoara is provided in parentheses in the Hungarian and Serbian chapters. In some cases, particularly in the periphery, the local name or English equivalent of a place is used although the nation being examined may have its own name for the place. The local or English equivalent is chosen to show that the place is only of peripheral importance to the nation. For example, Vienna is used instead of Bécs in the Hungarian section. While Vienna was an important city in the development of modern Hungarian national identity, using the term Bécs would suggest that the Hungarians consider the city to be Hungarian.

1

Introduction

In recent years the world's political map has undergone significant changes as countries such as the Soviet Union and Yugoslavia simply have ceased to exist as we once knew them. As these states disintegrated, violence between ethnic groups and nations increased to a level not seen since the Second World War. Even in places such as Somalia and Rwanda, where the existence of the state was not in question, intergroup conflict was horrific. Although many people around the world had welcomed the end of tensions associated with the Cold War, the emerging new world order of interethnic violence seemed chaotic, perilous, and downright incomprehensible.

To fully comprehend the underpinnings of the world's new and continually-changing political map, however, we must realize that the recent and ever-increasing number of conflicts is not simply caused by chaos. Although nationalism is a contributing factor, its corollary—the nation-state ideal—has been and continues to be at the root of the violence. The nation-state ideal is premised on the belief that human beings are fundamentally and naturally divided into social groupings known as nations. It follows that nations can be free and the world at peace only when all nations are able to govern themselves. Self-governance, however, implies sovereignty over a piece of the earth's territory, for how can a nation govern itself without control over a territory of its own? Hence, the dissolution of the Soviet Union and of Yugoslavia was driven by nations within these states who felt that their rights had been violated and that the only way to protect their rights and to cultivate national identities was to proclaim political, and therefore territorial, independence.

Nations' striving for control of their own territories is by no means a recent phenomenon. Indeed, since the rise of modern nationalism more than two hundred years ago, many of history's great conflicts have been marked by it. In the twentieth century alone, the dissolution of empires in Europe after the First World War, the rise of fascism (an extreme

1

variation of nationalism), and European decolonization following the Second World War all were driven by the need of nations to control their own territories. The dissolution of the Soviet Union, Yugoslavia, and Czechoslovakia, among others, has been merely a new incarnation of this nationalist principle.

Because most of humanity subscribes to the nation-state ideal by belonging to one of the world's nations, the recent struggles of some nations to control their own territories with their own sovereign governments have elicited some sympathy from those in independent and secure nations. Yet the disparity between the number of nations and the number of states in turn creates a major disjunction between the spatial distribution of nations and the spatial distribution of states. The earth contains as many as five thousand nations yet is divided into only approximately two hundred states! Because international relations are already very complicated with two hundred states, the prospect of some five thousand nations is forbidding. Moreover, because the earth's entire land surface already is allotted, new states would have to be carved out of current ones. Therefore, in spite of any underlying sympathies for those nations wishing to have their own states, the independent and secure nations have a vested interest in maintaining the status quo concerning the world's political map. Witness the initial refusal of various national governments to recognize the declarations of independence by many of the substate units of both the Soviet Union and Yugoslavia. The U.S. government even refused to recognize the declarations of independence by the Baltic states—although the United States had never acknowledged their absorption into the Soviet Union in the 1940s. When the German government finally broke ranks more recently and recognized the independence of Slovenia and Croatia, it was condemned by other governments.

The prospect of a world with five thousand states, accompanied by the inevitable loss of territory of current states, are just two of the reasons why political leaders are reluctant to recognize independence movements of subjugated nations. In fact, the recognition of another nation's right to independence may not in principle be the issue; recognition is withheld to forestall an even more difficult question: Which nation receives which territory as part of an independence declaration? When governments were forced to accept the dissolution of the Soviet Union and Yugoslavia, they took the position that former republic boundaries within these states should serve as the boundaries of the new independent states. Because most of these boundaries were unjust or flawed representations of the nation-state ideal, this response was not an answer to the question but an attempt to stave it off.

The question of territory is so complicated and delicate that if the right answer is not given, violence will erupt. Yet in some cases, there may be no right answer. Not surprisingly, most political leaders avoid at all costs the issue of drawing new political boundaries. Nonetheless, it can be the only path to peace. Hence policy makers often find themselves staring at maps and facing a near-impossible task: reordering the political map in such a way to please everyone involved while at the same time keeping at bay the biased participants and their often unreasonable demands.

A brief survey of new boundary proposals in regions such as the former Yugoslavia and the Middle East demonstrates that the diplomats charged with the tasks were unequipped to handle their assignments. Their approach typically tried to provide objective solutions for subjective problems. Because conflicts often are characterized by emotionalism and subjectivity, objectivity is embraced in the false belief that it will solve conflict.

Some disputes certainly could use an infusion of objectivity, but the desire to treat all issues in an objective manner has led to unfortunate consequences. The first and most dangerous mistake that any political leader can make is to believe that ethnic groups and/or nations can be defined objectively. Indeed, the illusion of objectivity can be so strong that mediators begin from the assumption that group identities are clear and unchanging; therefore, it is easy to identify the number and locations of members of a group simply by taking a census. A census is a favorite tool of diplomats because objective criteria such as language use and religious affiliation are tallied. Moreover, since this data can be mapped, diplomats believe that they can use this information to determine "appropriate" boundaries for nation-states. This process seems straightforward and objective, and hence is believed to be appropriate. Unfortunately, it fails to identify all members of ethnic groups and nations. Using the "objective" characteristics of an ethnic group or a nation to map out the distribution of such groups often excludes individuals who consider themselves to be members of a particular group, and includes individuals who do not consider themselves to be members of a specific group. Not all French speakers consider themselves to be French, even in Europe. By the same token, not all who consider themselves to be French actually speak French. This may be less true today than in the past, but groups such as the Alsatians preferred to be part of the French nation rather than the German one when they spoke their native Germanic language.

Despite relentless attempts to objectively define ethnic groups and nations, such efforts are doomed to failure because ethnic and national identities are not objective phenomena. Ethnic groups and nations are composed of human beings, and the human condition is not an objective one. Feelings and emotions are major components of what it is to be human and thus are key components of any form of human identity as well. Therefore, any examination of human beings, from the individual to large social formations such as nations, must take into account the subjective nature of human identity. The scholar Frederick Barth recognized this aspect of human identity when he argued that we must understand the way in which each group defines itself because a group's identity is derived largely from its self-perception (Barth 1969, 14). Others have agreed, noting that ethnic and national identities are more subjective than objective (Kohn 1955; Smith 1983; Symmons-Symonolewicz 1985; Williams 1985). There is growing consensus that those who consider subjective components are closer to capturing the nature and dynamics of ethnicity and nationalism than those who have focused exclusively on objective criteria (Murphy 1988, 15). Therefore, our understanding of ethnicity and nationalism can best be enhanced by a further refinement of our understanding of their subjective components.

Place and territory are two key subjective components of identity that have been considered separate and distinct from human identity. Beyond the fact that human beings occupy places and territories, little acknowledgment has been given to the relationships, even strong emotional bonds, that we have with particular places. This lack of recognition has persisted though our vocabularies contain words and expressions that illustrate these strong passionate attachments. "Homesickness," for example, is a word that expresses a depression through a longing for one's home; home can be a place as small as an individual dwelling or as large as an entire country. In a similar vein, "territoriality" describes the protective attitude that humans exhibit toward places; like homesickness, it is a very emotional and subjective human expression. If places and territories were separate and distinct from the human condition, and thus outside the realm of human identity, then they would be meaningless to us. We would move from place to place without ever feeling the loss of separation from or the need to protect certain places, and we would not have any concept of homesickness or territoriality. Clearly this is not the case, indeed, quite the opposite is true. Places and territories have deep meaning for us, indicating that human identity is in some way derived from them.

Place and territory also are qualities of group identities as well as individual ones. If an individual can feel a homesickness for an entire country, it follows that this feeling will exist in large numbers as well. The same is true of territoriality. Groups can express a collective need or desire to protect "their" portion of the earth's surface. Both of these phenomena illustrate that group identities also derive from place and territory.

These strong emotional bonds that connect individuals and groups to places and territories may be nonrational but are not irrational. At the most basic level, places and territories contain the natural resources that people need to sustain themselves. Economic analyses measure the amount of actual or potential resources contained around the world. However, the importance of place and territory goes much further. Human beings are diverse; we are differentiated by culture, and culture varies from region to region. It does not exist independently of place. Groups organize and shape the places and territories they inhabit to reflect their attitudes, values, sense of history—in essence their cultures. This expression of group culture in the landscape is daily reinforced in the individual members of the group. Hence places and their unique cultural landscapes in turn influence and mold the attitudes and values of their inhabitants (Relph 1976; Tuan 1974). This continual process of action and reaction represents a significant aspect of human identity at all levels. Hence "place" has become as much a part of human identity as language, religion, or shared history, and likewise we often feel as passionate about protecting our "place" as we do about our language, our religion, or our history.

This protectiveness of place, expressed in the term *territoriality*, manifests itself forcefully within groups, and in sometimes unpredictable ways. Keeping in mind that places and territories contain not only natural resources but also the cultural landscapes of group identity, then the expression of territoriality is moreover the expression of a group's need to protect its language, its religion, its essential identity. Understanding this aspect of territoriality makes its virulent and often violent expressions less unpredictable.

Because we as human beings simultaneously subscribe to many levels of identity—as an individual, a member of a community, and part of a nation—place and territory have meaning for us at all of these levels. Likewise, we express territoriality at all of these levels, but to varying degrees. The nation-state era in which we currently live has had a tremendous impact on the nature of human identity and the way in which we express territoriality. Because the nation-state ideal professes the belief that humanity is fundamentally divided into nations, our national identities have come to take precedence in our lives. While we obviously have not abandoned our individual, community, or ethnic identities, we often sacrifice our individual, community, and ethnic needs to those of the nation.

The world's current state system, composed primarily of nation-states, exists to ensure that our national identities take precedence in our lives, particularly when it serves the needs of the state. This state system allows us to negotiate, arbitrate, and even litigate territorial spaces at smaller scales of identity—at the individual, community, and ethnic levels; hence transgressions of territorial spaces at these levels of identity tend to be less violent. On the other hand, the world's state system has no higher level of government that can effectively compel a given nation to act against its own best interest, even for the benefit of all nations. Nations are free to exert their control over territories but are limited to the resources that they can marshal to accomplish this. Because many nations identify with territories that overlap one another, their attempts to assert control of a territory as they define it often result in discord, and sometimes lead to armed conflict. Armed confrontation may seem futile, but nations often feel that they must have sovereignty over their territories if they are to preserve and maintain their national identity. In southeastern Europe, many nations feel that their identities have been violated because their territories have been continually transgressed by other nations. Not surprisingly, conflict has been persistent in this region.

Nations being territorial or having other subjective qualities is not new. Nevertheless, the subjective components of national identity frequently are not addressed because they are difficult to measure, whereas it is easier to grasp objective criteria. Measuring something more concrete, such as language use or religious affiliation, is attractive because it is seemingly easier to accomplish and less controversial than analyzing the emotional bonds that nations have with particular places and territories. Geographers too have great difficulty "mapping" these subjective components and likewise prefer to map more tangible criteria.

Despite the inherent problems in trying to map a subjective component of national identity like emotional attachment to place, we must endeavor to do so in order to truly understand the nature of nationalism and thereby be able to resolve territorial disputes between nations. One of the intended contributions of this book is to propose a method for accomplishing this task. The emotional attachments to and the significance of places and territories can be judged by the roles that they play for a nation, by the feelings a nation expresses toward them, and by the efforts a nation undertakes to protect them. In a more systematic manner, the significance of places and territories can be judged by looking at three indicators: site identification, landscape description, and the "tenacity factor." Site identification denotes the locations of institutions (e.g., seats of government, printing presses, educational and religious centers) and historic sites (e.g., battles, birthplaces). Landscape description identifies important places as expressed in literature, poetry, art, and music. Besides specific sites, landscape description can refer to broad categories of places such as mountain ranges, valleys, and rivers. Both site identification and landscape description create a spatial distribution of places important to a nation. In other words, they help to define and thus delineate a nation's territory. In order to ascertain just how significant particular places are for a nation, the "tenacity factor" is employed. The tenacity factor looks at the history of a group's determination to protect or seize individual places or pieces of territory. Southeastern Europe is a region of continual conflict; numerous wars, alliances, and proclamations by national governments demonstrate the zeal of nations in protecting or seizing particular places or territories.

The identification and mapping of significant places are intended to elucidate the place component of national identity. When complete, however, it will provide another benefit by contributing to our understanding of the nature of territorial disputes. In short, territorial conflicts and their level of intensity between nations are in direct proportion to the significance of the contested territories to the nations' identities. This should not be surprising, but current methods of analyzing territorial disputes have not been able to draw this conclusion because they do not take into account the significance of place. As a partial consequence, many analyses also have not been able to predict the locations and intensities of territorial conflicts. The identification and mapping of significant places will help to accomplish these goals.

Recognizing that place and territory represent significant aspects of national identity helps to explain the cause and intensity of territorial conflicts; however, this is only a start. Beyond merely identifying significant places and territories, we must address why they come to be significant, and what can be done to solve or even prevent these conflicts. To address these issues, we must discuss, in its proper historical context, the very idea of what it is to have a national identity. The concept of the modern nation is a very recent phenomenon in human history, and many places become significant upon being recast in a nationalist framework. Understanding how this recasting takes place gets at the very heart of any national identity and thus explains why certain places and territories become significant.

When modern nationalism emerged some two hundred years ago, it began with the premise that humanity was fundamentally divided into nations. A few corollaries soon followed, culminating in the idea that every nation must have its own state if the world is to enjoy everlasting peace—thus formulating the nation-state ideal. These fundamental ideas still characterize the doctrine of nationalist ideology, but they cannot stand alone, either now or when first formulated. Myriad ancillary concepts had to accompany these simple ideas to make the nation-state ideal a viable socio-political system. Some of the crucial issues that still needed to be addressed were how a nation was to be defined and how a nation's territory was to be delineated. As nationalism grew, however, many of the accompanying concepts did not grow directly out of the original doctrine. Instead, the basic concept of the nation crystallized around many ideas from the past, from previous ideological systems. Thus these earlier ideas became enmeshed in the concept of nation, serving as many of the ancillary concepts to make the nation-state ideal a reality.

Many of the prenationalist ideas embedded within the nation-state ideal relate to the meaning of place and the political organization of territory. The nation-state ideal has logical implications here, but the actual attitudes that nations hold toward place and territory deviate considerably. These attitudes are holdovers from the time that imperialism reigned supreme but persisted into the era of nationalism and even provided a trunk onto which the nation-state could firmly graft itself. These attitudes differ around the world, resulting in many regional variations. In general terms, the conception of territory and its political arrangement emerged differently in the empires of Western Europe than it did in the empires of Central and Eastern Europe.

When nationalism emerged in Western Europe, it was within the context of the Enlightenment, which was noteworthy for the emphasis it placed on rational thought and the rights of the individual. In contrast to the imperial order of states and their territories, the nationalist ideal in the context of Enlightenment philosophy implied a reordering of political control over territories to create numerous small states. Small territories ensure the rights of the individual better than huge and sprawling empires. The actual delineation of such territories is irrelevant because individuals have rights no matter where they live or what their individual cultural characteristics may be. This conclusion, however, was rarely discussed as a serious issue for nationalists at the time. Instead, the concept of nation was framed directly within the existing territorial order that was accepted as a given. Thus empires were simply redefined as nation-states. The French empire, for example, became redefined as the French Republic, with no call to redraw its boundaries as implied by the new ideology of nationalism expressed in the context of Enlightenment philosophy.

When nationalism spread to Central and Eastern Europe, this process could not be replicated easily. First of all, individual rights did not have a strong tradition in these regions. Instead, more emphasis was placed on the collective group, which came to be defined by common cultural characteristics such as language and religion. This idea implied a philosophy much different than that of the Enlightenment. In fact, it developed into a system that became known as Romantic philosophy and it called for a much different territorial arrangement of states than Enlightenment philosophy. In short, Romanticism implied the redrawing of boundaries according to the distribution of nations, supposedly defined by language and religion. This task may seem simple today because many national identities have evolved to the point that they clearly are distinguishable from one another. At the time, however, national identities based on shared cultural characteristics was more a notion than a reality. Cultural characteristics continually changed across the landscape with few obvious and neat breaks that could serve as political boundaries. Therefore, the practice of drawing political boundaries was not a straightforward one.

Some Central and Eastern Europeans, such as the Germans and Russians, could define their new national territories in the same manner as Western Europeans, by redefining their imperial states as new nation-states. Unfortunately, circumstances did not allow this process to take place for most in either region. Quite simply, most did not have existing imperial states of their own that could be recast as new nation-states. Yet imperialism and its political ordering of the landscape was just as much a legacy for these peoples as it was for Western Europeans. Central and Eastern Europeans even experienced the process of redefining imperial territories as national ones; they lived in imperial states under the control of groups that were developing policies to do just that. Consequently, many Central and Eastern Europeans found themselves persecuted and treated as unwanted minorities. As they experienced discrimination, they began to develop a national consciousness and in turn also began to feel alien to the empires in which they lived. Not all developed a national consciousness through discrimination. Some developed group awareness simply through the diffusion of the nationalist idea from Western Europe. Nevertheless, they too could no longer identify with the empires in which they lived.

The need for secession was becoming obvious. Yet the choice of territory for such an act was not obvious because Central and Eastern Europeans lacked their own imperial states to redefine as their new national states. This was a problem that their Western European counterparts never had to confront. The philosophy of Romanticism, however, provided a means for solving this; in addition to language and religion, Romanticism emphasized "shared history" as a unique characteristic of peoples. This emphasis on history allowed those who were developing a national consciousness to reach into the past, to times of great empires of their ancestors. Those empires were then resurrected so that their territories could serve as the bases for modern nation-states. In other words, in contrast to Western Europeans who had existing empires that they could redefine, many Central and Eastern Europeans had to add one step to the process of defining national territories by resurrecting defunct empires. This process also avoided the problems associated with drawing political boundaries according to cultural characteristics when the cultural landscape was in constant transition. It also avoided addressing the fact that imperial governments had manipulated people's identities for so long and to such a degree that language use and religious adherence were not an accurate measure of an individual's or a group's identity.

Analyzing a phenomenon such as nationalism tempts us to examine it in its pure ideological form. Doing so, however, presents the danger that previous ideological structures and institutions will be mistakenly de-emphasized or even disregarded. This error must be avoided, for nationalism did not arise out of a temporal and spatial vacuum. What preceded it was imperialism, which had been a strong force in shaping the world's political and social landscape. Despite the sudden and fervent ascent of nationalism and its disdain for imperialism, the latter's political structures and institutions were not easily swept aside. One look at Europe's political map in the early twentieth century illustrates that imperialism was still a powerful force despite more than a century of nationalist agitation against it (see Figure 1.1). Imperialism did collapse, but it would be a gross oversimplification to say that nationalism wholly supplanted it. During the struggle against imperialism, nationalism was still in its formative years. Many facets of its ideology were not yet formulated, and historical circumstances did not allow it to develop logically and purely from its own premises. Elements of previous cultural and ideological systems were taken up by it and enmeshed within it. For instance, imperialism's territorial order remained meaningful and largely intact in the minds of people, and served as an important link to the past, which even nationalists could not reject. Nationalism did triumph, but describing its victory as one in which it deposed imperialism is not accurate. A more apt analogy would be the petrification process: in the end the new material of stone comes into being as the old wood vanishes; however, this new material is in the form of the old. Such was the case with nationalism's triumph over imperialism. It was a new material in the form of the old, and that form was the territorial order.

The concepts presented in this book are not a rejection of, or a radical departure from, current ideas. Rather they grow out of and extend existing concepts. What has been lacking in studies on nationalism is the strong recognition that nations derive their identities to a large degree from particular places and territories, and that control of these is often essential to maintaining a healthy sense of national identity. Failure to give full recognition to this aspect of nationhood has prevented a thorough understanding of the nature of many territorial conflicts. To address these deficiencies, Chapter 2 begins by laying out what is already known about forms of human identity, with greatest emphasis placed on that of the nation. From there, the place and territorial components of identity are discussed. These are significant for several reasons. First, they provide groups with the natural resources necessary for basic human survival. In addition, they are essential from a cultural perspective because they enable groups to express their identities in landscape. This expression plays an important role in transmitting group characteristics to individuals and to succeeding generations. Groups also must have the ability to enact laws to maintain and cultivate their identities. Laws, however,

Figure 1.1 Europe on the Eve of the First World War.

are effective only within certain geographical spaces, and territory is a form of geographical space that enables groups to formulate the laws and policies necessary to their identities. The significance of territory is underscored by a phenomenon known as territoriality, which exists at all levels of identity but is strongest at the national level—not surprisingly, considering that we live in the nation-state era. The significance of place and territory reflects this phenomenon, but it is a difficult thing to measure and map. The chapter ends with a discussion of indicators that can be used to accomplish this task.

Chapter 3 takes up the historical dimensions of nationalism in an effort to understand how certain places and territories came to be significant to particular nations in southeastern Europe. These historical dimensions are vital to consider because nationalism did not evolve independently of what came before. On the contrary, it grew out of previous ideologies and consequently has embedded within it many ideas from its predecessors, particularly imperialism. Imperialism's political arrangement of territory is most noteworthy because it persisted and even became integral to nationalism's understanding of territorial arrangements. Although imperialism's view of territory became that of nationalism, that view expressed itself differently in Western Europe than in Central and Eastern Europe. In Western Europe, nationalism emerged in the context of the Enlightenment, the ideas of which should therefore be elucidated. In brief, this brand of nationalism redefined imperial territories as national ones. This process often was not possible in Central and Eastern Europe because many peoples of these regions simply did not have existing empires that could be converted into nation-states. Because the nationalist idea reached Central and Eastern Europe during the Romantic period, Chapter 3 proceeds with the key ideas of that period. In short, the veneration of history allowed Central and Eastern Europeans to reach back into the past and resurrect the memory of previous empires. Subsequently, though with this added step, they also used imperial territories to define their national territories.

Chapters 4, 5, and 6 are an attempt to elucidate and spatially delineate the sense of territory of three ethnonational groups in southeastern Europe: the Hungarian, Romanian, and Serbian nations. These nations have been chosen as case studies because substantial spatial disjunctions exist or have existed between their modern state territories and the territories from which they derived much of their identities. The mapping of language and religion does not adequately identify the full extent of the territories to which these nations have strong emotional attachments. Individually, each offers specific advantages as a case study. The Hungarian nation has had a well-defined territory that has remained relatively intact over the last thousand years. As such, it shows how a nation has redefined an old imperial territory as a new national one. The Hungarian nation, however, has had difficulty maintaining control of its territory because Hungarians have barely constituted a majority in it. The Romanian nation stands in sharp contrast to the Hungarian nation because it has had many small, discreet, and relatively stable territorial units through time, but rarely has it had a single state that encompasses them all—a state that could be used as the basis for a modern Romanian nation-state. The Romanian nation shows how a modern nation has struggled to find historical precedent to justify the unification of these small territorial units. The Serbian nation is the most complex case and in many ways the most illustrative. It has never had a stable territorial unit. Consequently, it has had great difficulty in identifying a national territory for itself. The Serbian struggle to delineate a national territory and its effort to establish some sort of historical precedent for controlling that territory show how important places are to a nation. Significantly, the Serbian nation has focused on ethnic distributions as a means of protecting and controlling its national territory rather than as a means of defining its national territory.

The task of delineating the Hungarian, Romanian, and Serbian senses of territory is accomplished by the application of three indicators: site identification, landscape description, and the tenacity factor. Before attempting to portray or understand a group's sense of territory, we must place each group into its proper historical context. Therefore, each chapter begins with a brief historical overview of the group in question. These overviews are then followed by the application of the three indicators of a nation's sense of territory. This reveals a core, semi-core, and periphery of significant places. These categories are based on the degrees of importance of the places in them. All three categories are discussed first in relation to site identification and landscape description, then in relation to the tenacity factor.

Sense of territory and emotional attachment to place are integral components of national identity. It is often important for nations to control the places that define this identity. In those cases where effective control is achieved, a healthy and peaceful national psychology will emerge; in cases where that control is not achieved, conflict with neighboring ethnic groups and nations will persist. Therefore, knowing the place component of group identity tells us much about national identity and helps us to understand many of the conflicts that arise between nations.

2

The Nation in Its Spatial Context

Because nations exist in time, they are shaped by temporal processes and thus have temporal components. Because nations also exist in space, they are shaped by spatial processes and thus have spatial components as well. While it would be ludicrous to argue that nations do not exist in either time or space, the second axiom is virtually ignored in most studies of nations. The tacit recognition given to the fact that nations occupy spaces does not qualify as genuine inquiry into the spatiality of nations. To truly recognize that nations have spatial qualities is to recognize that spatial processes and interactions contribute to the development of national identities (Deutsch 1969; Soja 1971). While general principles underlie spatial relationships, the exact nature and intensity of these relationships differ geographically, making the character of places and territories unique. The uniqueness of places and territories in turn contributes to the uniqueness of national identities.

In a broad sense, "place" and "territory" are spatial components of nationhood because they both shape and are shaped by their human inhabitants. More specifically, place and territory, however, have many important nuances as well. Of these is the notion that certain places and territories become significant to nations, that nations develop strong emotional bonds to these places and territories,[1] and that nations can become very protective of these places and territories—a phenomenon known as territoriality. Thus the spatiality of nations is multiplex. This chapter focuses on and elucidates the spatial components of nationhood in detail. Unfortunately, the term *nation* often is used with a lack of clarity, making it too difficult to discuss it in a spatial context without first clarifying the concept of *nation* in its entirety. Therefore, this chapter begins with some clarification of the term *nation* so that the concepts of place and territory can be understood more easily.

Definitions of Nation

The concept of nation is poorly understood by those who use it, including those in the media, government and politics, and even in education
and academia—excluding those who specifically research it. That the term
nation is frequently used interchangeably with terms such as *ethnic group,*
tribe, and *race* is an indication that the concept of nation is poorly understood. This lack of understanding is even more poignantly illustrated
whenever the term *nation* is used as a synonym for words like *country,*
nation-state, and *state.* The misuse of the term *nation,* and terms related to
it, occurs because few objective criteria underlie it. While popular perception places considerable weight on language and religion as defining
characteristics, a one-to-one correlation does not exist between language
and/or religion and national identities around the world. English, for
example, is the mother tongue for a number of nations, with not all
English speakers considering themselves to be part of a single English
nation; the same situation exists for a number of other languages, such as
French, Spanish,[2] and German. By the same token, not all nations have a
single language. Belgians, Swiss, and Americans, for example, are poly-
glot nations.

The lack of objective criteria certainly has led to confusion, and continues to do so, but does not invalidate the concept of nation. Defining
criteria exist but lie almost exclusively in the subjective realm. Numerous
attempts have been made to create a definition of nationhood that takes
into account its subjective qualities. Of the definitions that exist, one
created by Konstantin Symmons-Symonolewicz seems to be the most all-
encompassing and, therefore, the most accurate when applied to the
nations of the world. Symmons-Symonolewicz defines a nation as

> a territorially-based community of human beings sharing a distinct variant
> of modern culture, bound together by a strong sentiment of unity and sol-
> idarity, marked by a clear historically-rooted consciousness of national
> identity, and possessing, or striving to possess, a genuine political self-gov-
> ernment. (1985, 221)

This definition illustrates that nationhood is largely self-perceived.
Benedict Anderson poignantly illustrates the self-perceived nature of
nationhood with the term "imagined community" (Anderson 1991). Thus
nations are defined by any number of cultural characteristics. The key to
understanding any particular nation's identity is an appreciation of the
entire set of traits and how a nation conceives of them, not in a preoccupation with individual cultural traits. Even though nations share many
similar attributes, the meaning and significance of individual attributes
vary from nation to nation. Even when nations latch onto phenomena

such as language and religion, language and religion become significant only because individual nations have perceived them to be so. Therefore, studies that narrowly focus on these measurable cultural attributes completely miss the point of language and religion as a characteristic of nationhood, that is for those nations which hold these phenomena meaningful.

Ethnic groups are similar to nations in the sense that they too are distinct variants of modern culture. Because ethnic groups often have their own languages, religious beliefs, social customs, etc., they are frequently confused with nations. Any such similarities notwithstanding, ethnic groups are not nations. First, ethnic groups do not always have self-awareness (Connor 1978, 390). Ethnic groups are often conceived of and defined by outside observers, such as academics or even nations. Second, ethnic groups do not possess, or strive to possess, a genuine political self-government. Therefore, ethnic groups do not have their own states or struggle to establish them for themselves. Consequently, while "national struggle for independence" and "nation-state" are necessary conditions of nationhood, the concept of ethnic group has not spawned the same corollary concepts of "ethnic struggle for independence" and "ethnic group-state." Indeed, when an ethnic group develops the desire for political self-government, it has by definition become a nation.

Because ethnic groups do not desire political self-government, they exist as subgroups within nations. Some nations, such as the Americans, are composed of many ethnic groups. By the same token, a number of ethnic groups, such as the Jews and the Arabs, can even be found within many different nations. Ethnic groups have their own distinct variant of modern culture, but they also have many of the characteristics of the nation they are a part of, and they share with the other members of the nation a sense of belonging and the desire for political self-government.

If an ethnic group does not have the same sense of belonging or the desire for self-government as the host nation, tensions will arise, often resulting in the rise of a separate national consciousness among members of the ethnic group. The tensions that arise between ethnic groups and nations often come about because the dominant national group redefines the national identity in a way that contradicts the identity of one or more of its ethnic groups. This situation, for example, occurred with the rise of Nazi Germany. Most ethnic Jews within Germany accepted German national identity and did not feel that their religious beliefs and cultural practices disqualified them from being part of the German nation. The Nazis, however, redefined German identity, and conflict resulted. It is important to note that the Jews did not exclude themselves but were, in fact, excluded. Moreover, the continual exclusion of Jews in Europe led to the rise of a Jewish national consciousness among many Jews, known as Zionism.

The Jewish case is poignant but not unique. The redefinition of national identities by dominant groups and the resultant exclusion of ethnic minorities continue to serve as an important catalyst for the development of new national identities today. French speakers within Canada do not believe that their language disqualifies them from being Canadian. The poor treatment that they have received from English-speaking Canadians, however, has led to the emergence of a national consciousness among many French speakers. The rise of national consciousness in turn is leading to demands for political self-government. Similarly, some English speakers within the United States are trying to make English a necessary characteristic of American nationhood. While Spanish speakers do not feel disqualified from being American because they may not speak English, continued exclusionary treatment, particularly in the form of legislation, may cause Spanish speakers to reject American identity and develop a new national consciousness.

These three cases illustrate that ethnic and national identities are not simple, unchanging givens. Both forms of identity are very dynamic, with ethnic groups existing within nations, among nations, and often evolving into nations. Nations even contribute to the changing character of ethnic identities because national identities are ever-changing themselves. As national identities change, they cause reevaluations of identities within ethnic groups.

That ethnic groups and nations are closely related is illustrated by the interchangeable use of the terms without clear recognition of their distinct differences. Ironically, adherence to either form of identity on the part of an entire population is often treated as excluding the other. Consequently, arguments arise, for example, as to whether the Jews, Scots, Catalans, etc., are ethnic groups or nations. Evidence is collected to support either argument, but no recognition is given to the possibility that some Jews, Scots, Catalans, etc., have a corresponding national consciousness while others have an ethnic identity within another nation. For example, individual Jews with a national consciousness (i.e., Zionists) want their own nation-state (i.e., Israel), while ethnic Jews who accept another national identity want to be in the nation-state of their appropriate national identity (e.g., Jewish-Americans want to be in the American nation-state). By the same token, Scots with a national consciousness want an independent Scottish nation-state but ethnic Scots are content to stay within Great Britain. In other words, an entire population does not have to be classified as exclusively an ethnic group or a nation. Moreover, the numbers within a population that subscribe to either an ethnic or a national identity are likely to be ever-changing, depending on the evolving political, economic, and social circumstances that affect them.[3]

As ethnic groups develop national consciousness, they are confronted with being within the states of other nations. Before long members of these emerging nations realize that full nationhood cannot be achieved without political independence, a condition which can be achieved only with sovereignty over territory. When this realization occurs, the struggle for an independent nation-state begins. At any given moment in modern history, the world has fully developed nations with political self-rule and territorial sovereignty, nations striving for it, and nations still in their embryonic state. The world's nations are not static and fixed, but evolutionary, with some nations being very mature and new ones being born before our eyes.

Some researchers do not recognize that the desire for political self-rule and territorial sovereignty are necessary conditions for nationhood (Gallagher 1995, 717–18; Seton-Watson 1977, 1; Shafer 1972, 18). They point to multi-national states such as Great Britain and Spain. These examples, however, do not refute the aforementioned characteristics of the term *nation* but, in fact, confirm them. To simply point out that Scots, Welsh, and English coexist within Great Britain, and that Basques and Catalans live with the Spanish in the same state, is to paper over the tensions that exist among these peoples. Such a conclusion also ignores that the most discontent among these peoples (i.e., Scots, Welsh, Irish, Basque, and Catalans), and the ones calling for political self-rule and territorial sovereignty, are the ones who call themselves nationalists. The attempt to use Great Britain or Spain as a refutation likewise fails to take into account that not every individual among the Scots, Welsh, Irish, Basque, and Catalans has expressed national consciousness, though these peoples are collectively dubbed nations. Moreover, looking at the political map and pointing out that Great Britain and Spain are multinational is treating nationhood as a static concept and not recognizing that an evolutionary process is unfolding which, in fact, may require a redrawing of the political map to accommodate the nationalist aspirations of these peoples, thus proving that the desire for political self-rule and territorial sovereignty are necessary conditions for nationhood.

Because the terms *nation* and *ethnic group* refer to forms of group identity, unsurprisingly they are used interchangeably despite the important differences distinguishing the two concepts. On the other hand, *nation* also is used as a synonym for words such as *country, nation-state*, and *state*. *Nation* and these other words greatly differ, making their substitution highly inappropriate. *Nation* and *ethnic group* are significant terms because they refer to groups of *people*. On the other hand, *country, nation-state*, and *state* refer to politically organized *places and territories*. Therefore, the people-rooted concept of *nation* is fundamentally different in meaning than the place-rooted concept of *country, nation-state*, and *state*. Nevertheless, despite the obvious and significant differences between the two types of terms, people-rooted terms are chronically interchanged with place-rooted terms (Connor 1978). In other words, the term *nation* is frequently and mistakenly used to refer to a place. Spain, France, Poland, and Bulgaria often are called nations when, in fact, they are nation-states. The Spanish, the French, the Poles, and the Bulgarians are nations.

That people-rooted terms, like *nation*, are used so casually and freely as synonyms for place-rooted terms should not be regarded as simple ignorance. The casual interchange of these words should be taken as an indication that people and place are closely linked, that identity is derived from places and, therefore, people-rooted terms can be justifiably exchanged with place-rooted terms. After all, most peoples, especially nations, receive their names from places, thus indicating the close link. The French, Swiss, and Germans nations, for example, derive their names from places (e.g., France, Switzerland, and Germany), not languages.[4]

The inappropriate substitution of people-rooted terms with place-rooted terms also stems from the ideology of nationalism. Modern nationalism advocates a world in which the spatial extent of political units is coterminous with the spatial distributions of nations (Connor 1978, 381–82). Reality does not conform to this principle of nationalist ideology because many political units contain multiple nations (albeit with tension), and a number of nations are distributed across two or more political units. Nevertheless, the belief in "one people—one state" leads many to assume that the existence of a state implies the existence of a people with a similar name. Because the world's political map, for example, contains a Somalia, a Zaire, and at one time a Yugoslavia, many would assume that there are or were Somalian, Zairian, and Yugoslavian nations. People and place become linked so closely together that they essentially become indistinguishable and, therefore, are used interchangeably. Some of the best examples are the names of organizations such as the International Monetary Fund, the International Court of Justice, and the United Nations. The presence of the term *nation* in the names of these organizations implies that the basic building blocks of these organizations are peoples, and that these organizations are to serve peoples. On the contrary, members of these organizations are states, not nations. While it is true that the member states nominally represent nations,[5] nations without states are not represented. Describing these organizations for what they are, their names should be the "Interstate Monetary Fund," the "Interstate Court of Justice," and the "United States"! Governments of multi-national states also encourage the interchange of the terms *nation* and *state*. Such substitutions promote the idea that the government and state exist to serve a single nation with the same name. This gives legitimacy to the governments of states with diverse and disunited populations, thereby helping such governments to perpetuate themselves.

Misapplications of place-rooted terms and people-rooted terms only lead to greater errors and prevent situations from being properly understood. For example, if it were to be reported that Hungary occupied part of Czechoslovakia, that would suggest that one place is occupying another place—a physical impossibility. Of course, many would not interpret it this way; instead, they would see it as the statement was intended. Nevertheless, the statement carries with it the implication that the Hungarians took something that did not belong to them. Consequently, anyone who heard such a statement without knowing much about the situation might be inclined to oppose the Hungarian action. However, if the statement were made by using the terms correctly, a different reaction might well result. Thus a statement to the effect that Hungarian troops had occupied territories of Czechoslovakia over which the Hungarian government claimed rightful dominion could well send a different message. Anyone hearing this statement who knew little about the situation would likely want to know if the Hungarian claims were legitimate before making a judgment.

The inappropriate use of the terms *nation* and *nation-state* actually illustrates the close link between people and place. While many researchers consider the temporal development of nations, few realize that nations develop spatially as well. Nevertheless, the concept of place and territory manifests itself in some form in many definitions of nation (Alter 1994, 18; Anderson 1991, 7; Stalin 1994, 19–20; van den Berghe 1981, 61). Konstantin Symmons-Symonolewicz's definition of the modern nation, which begins with the phrase "territorially-based community," is just one example.

The Significance of Place and Territory

Place and territory are significant to nations for two major reasons. First, they contain within them the natural resources that contribute to the particularities of human culture. The emphasis here is on quality, not quantity, which often leads us to unsubstantiated conclusions about self-sufficiency and security. Quality of natural resources focuses more on the spatial variations within nature and how they in turn contribute to the varying character of human identity from region to region. Second, place and territory are important from the cultural perspective as well. Nations express their identities in the cultural landscape of places and territories. In turn, identities are reinforced in the members of the nation and passed on from generation to generation through the cultural landscape. Because nations derive their identities from the natural and cultural environments, nations need to have sovereign political control over place and territory. Sovereignty means the ability to enact and enforce laws to protect and cultivate national identity. Because laws need to be tied to place and territory to be effective, nations need place and territory to enact and enforce laws that protect their natural and cultural environments.

Natural Resources

At one level, place and territory are significant because they contain the natural resources that sustain human life. We obviously cannot survive without air, water, and food. Because place and territory provide us with these necessities, our lives are connected to place and territory to such a degree that we are dependent on them. This dependency, however, is not limited to mere survival, for our luxuries are likewise derived from the resources of place and territory. Resources then are a common denominator for all societies, from the most primitive to the most extravagant.

Resources are not the same everywhere. Some places and territories obviously contain more than others, and the kinds of resources vary as well. Human beings have been acutely aware of the areal differences in the quality and quantity of resources for time immemorial. The uneven distribution of the earth's resources is at the source of many conflicts that have arisen between and within human societies. Not surprisingly, modern analysts, including many geographers, have become preoccupied with the location of resources. Resource location is certainly significant, but locational analysis of resources is often pursued on the assumption that humans, whether individuals or societies, struggle for resources simply to improve material conditions, usually characterized as basic human greed when not directly related to survival.

The conclusion that human beings struggle for resources out of greed has overshadowed the other significant attributes of resources. What is forgotten is that the particular resources of places and territories fundamentally shape human culture. We human beings, of course, have the ability to use resources any way we choose, resulting in groups with varying cultural characteristics despite similar availability of resources. Therefore, the argument here is not for environmental determinism but for cultural possibilism. Nevertheless, despite the ability of human beings to interpret their natural environments differently, they can create material cultures only from the possibilities that particular natural environments offer in each place and territory. This means that the spatial variations that exist in culture are partially tied to the spatial variations of natural resources. So from the perspective of natural resources, the uniqueness of place and territory is an attribute of ethnic and national identities.

That each place and territory contains within it different resources is seemingly more important prior to the rise of advanced technology that characterizes modern society. Nevertheless, while modern technologies may allow human beings to break free from the restrictions presented by the limited resources found in each place and territory, the uneven and varied distribution of resources in the world has not become insignificant to human culture. Many cultures, despite their modernity, still reflect the characteristics of particular natural environments. David Sopher points out that Jewish culture, for example, is largely derived from the natural environment of the Eastern Mediterranean. He shows that Jewish holidays are tied to the seasonal rhythms of the Eastern Mediterranean environment, which in turn resulted in particular agricultural practices, diets, and lifestyles (Sopher 1967, 5, 19–21). In other words, if Judaism had originated in another place in the world, it would have developed into something much different than it is today. Furthermore, even though Jews are found all over the world, they still have many cultural characteristics that are derived from the Eastern Mediterranean environment. No wonder then that modern Zionists chose the Eastern Mediterranean for a modern Jewish nation-state. The nation-state ideal requires only an independent state with sovereignty over territory; a specific territory is not required. Zionists even had offers of territory in other countries but rejected them in favor of the territory of ancient Israel (Glassner 1993, 14). The Eastern Mediterranean region obviously continued to have meaning for Zionists, even though their ancestors had been separated from it for many centuries. Not to recognize this meaning requires one to ask why Zionists chose the resource-poor and politically hostile Eastern Mediterranean for a modern Jewish state.

The significance of place and territory for the natural resources they provide plays a key role in modern societies. Take the French, Swiss, and Japanese for example, three of the wealthiest and most technologically advanced nations in the world. All three of these nations have the ability to import just about any product they desire, thereby having the ability to reshape their cultures in any way they choose. Despite this ability, however, these nations continue using the products that were originally developed in their national territories. In cuisine alone, the French, the Swiss, and the Japanese have not given up their traditional foods for more globally consumed products like Coca-Cola, hamburgers, and pizza. Even though these nations certainly have increased their consumption of these products, it is still difficult to imagine these nations without their traditional foods that they developed in their national territories. Moreover, even though these nations can import many of their traditional foods from other areas of the world more cheaply than they can produce them at home, they tend not to. These nations, as well as others, show a preference for the types of products that have been traditionally grown in the home territory; they even show a bias for the actual products that they grow at home. Not only is wine a part of French culture, the French prefer to drink wines from France instead of buying cheaper wines from other countries.

Nations often profess that the products grown at home are superior to similar ones grown abroad, in foreign places and territories. Such beliefs can be attributed only to cultural particularities because they cannot be substantiated by rational scientific means. Nevertheless, nations subsequently will subsidize their home producers at great economic expense to protect them from foreign competition. Such subsidies are not rational from an economic perspective, yet even the wealthiest and most capitalistic nations subsidize certain home industries. Often it is in the name of protecting jobs, but the money could be more wisely spent developing competitive industries. Moreover, such subsidies are directed at industries producing goods in the home territory that are fundamentally a part of the national culture.

Emphasizing traditional foods is a concrete way of illustrating the importance of place and territory for the natural resources they provide. Other material traits in national cultures demonstrate linkages to the natural resources of particular places and territories. Many festivals and other celebrations may be tied to the natural environment. Combining diet with the myriad material traits of a nation, one sees the importance of place and territory: it becomes hard to imagine how the various nations of the world could be as they are if they had developed in places other than the ones where they have had a long-standing relationship with the natural world. Would French national identity still be what it is if it had developed in the tropical rain forests of South America? Would the Swiss nation still have the same character if it had developed on an island archipelago in the South Pacific? Would Japanese culture be what it is if it had developed in the deserts of North Africa? It is impossible to say exactly how the identities of these nations would have developed if they were born and had matured in these other natural environments. Only an environmental determinist would pretend to know how. Yet it is clear that these national identities would have developed differently in different natural environments. Therefore, from the perspective of natural resources alone, because place and territory shape the material traits of national cultures, they must be components of national identities as well.

Cultural Landscapes

Place and territory are significant to human identity beyond providing the natural resources that sustain human life and shape culture. They are crucial from a purely cultural perspective as well. As Edward Relph notes, places are profound centres of human experience. There is for everyone a deep association with the consciousness of the places where we were born and grew up, where we live now, or where we have had particularly moving experiences. This association seems to constitute a vital source of both individual and cultural identity and security, a point of departure from which we orient ourselves in the world. (Relph 1976, 430)

Place and territory as cultural phenomena are not passive, however. They contain the idea of the cultural landscape, which is an important medium for human beings "to embody their feelings, images, and thoughts in tangible material" (Tuan 1977, 17). This means that cultural identity is expressed and even invested in the landscape, making the cultural landscape a basis for common identity for members of a group. It is even possible to gain important insight into the characteristics of a cultural group by examining the group's landscape. The amount of space that a cultural group allocates to activities (e.g., economic, political, social, religious), as well as the locations assigned to these activities, reveals much about a cultural group's values and beliefs. Investigations of the cultural landscape illustrate that "place" is not separate and detached from the human condition but actually "an organized world of meaning" (Tuan 1977, 179) that is very much a part of human identity.

Reading the cultural landscape is an important means of understanding the character of a nation's identity; however, the cultural landscape has even greater significance: it plays a key role in the development of a common national consciousness among individuals. The particular spatial arrangements within the cultural landscape of a nation's territory dictate the movements and interactions of individuals, making such movements and interactions unique to the members of a nation, thus the basis of a common identity. In other words, as Peter Taylor notes, "Every social organization has its created space so that the spatiality is part of their being" (Taylor 1993, 84). Thus, the assertion "America is an automobile society" implies that the distinctive spatial arrangements found within the United States have led to social interactions and relationships that separate Americans from other nations.

In addition to contributing to the rise of a national identity with a certain character, the cultural landscapes of a nation's territory serve to maintain the national identity among individual members and to transmit the national identity to succeeding generations. Donald Meinig illustrates this aspect very well with the following: "Every mature nation has its symbolic landscapes. They are part of the shared set of ideas and memories which bind people together" (Meinig 1979, 164). Therefore, although language, religion, shared history, and even common ideology are often touted as common ingredients for a national identity, these national characteristics must be expressed in the cultural landscape.

Nations that base their identity on a particular language need to be able to write their language in the cultural landscape: on street signs, on buildings, on billboards, etc. Nations cultivate their languages partly through this medium. Not to be able to do so, implying that a foreign language must be used, would be too repressive to the nation. Nations that have their own religious beliefs must be able to build places of worship and mourning, erect monuments of religious significance, and express their religious beliefs in myriad subtle ways in the landscape. Nations that cannot express their religious beliefs in the landscape and create landscapes to practice their religion's beliefs likewise are repressed. A sense of shared history and political ideology is also reflected and invested in the cultural landscape. Monuments are the obvious examples, but names of streets, buildings, plazas, parks, and even cities are also an important part of a nation's cultural landscape of history and ideology. Although individuals learn the history and ideology of their nation when they are young, the expressions of history and ideology in the landscape serve as constant reminders of specific histories and ideologies and even make historical events and figures and ideological figures and beliefs more concrete, thus more real.[6] A nation unable to express its history and ideology in the landscape is in danger of losing these aspects of its identity. Territory then, with its cultural landscapes, "comes to be viewed as the repository of shared collective consciousness, the place wherein memory is rooted" (Williams and Smith 1983, 503). Moreover, the landscape of a nation's beliefs plays an important role in inculcating the national identity into individuals long after the formal educational experience of youth. As a constant three-dimensional, visual reminder, the cultural landscape reinforces the shared national identity within the psyche of every individual on a daily basis, even transmitting the nation's characteristics from generation to generation.

The significance of place and territory is illustrated every time a dispute arises concerning the placement or treatment of some element in the cultural landscape. The inhabitants of a city can become incensed if a public place receives a name or becomes the location of a monument or art work that does not reflect their identity. Likewise, the shift in identity requires the reconstruction of the cultural landscape before the identity shift can become complete. The world has witnessed this process over the last few years as Communism was rejected in the former Soviet Union and Eastern Europe. Monuments to the Communist ideology were systematically destroyed, and street names, plaza names, and even city names that reflected Communist beliefs were changed immediately. Additionally, in non-Russian countries of the former Soviet Union and Eastern Europe, the landscape was filled not only with elements of Communism but also with reminders of foreign domination. Vast sums of money were spent in destroying these landscapes, and much more was invested in building new monuments and other elements in the landscape that reflected the new sense of national pride. From the rational economic perspective, such behavior was, and is, perplexing. The economies of these countries were in shambles, and huge investments were needed to correct the situation, making the investments in monuments seem frivolous. For these nations, however, the Communist landscapes did not reflect their identities. For some, these landscapes were constant reminders of past oppression. Thus East Europeans put great effort into destroying the Communist and other landscapes because it was necessary to eradicate Communism and foreign domination from their national identities. At the same time, these peoples spent vast sums of money constructing new landscapes as a necessary means of building new national identities. The energy that East Europeans have put into reconstructing their cultural landscapes illustrates how people and place are closely linked, even intertwined.

Both Natural and Cultural

Place and territory are significant and form a part of human identity, including national identity, because they provide the natural resources that sustain human life and they contain the cultural landscapes that both express human identity and reinforce various forms of group identity within individuals. Even though natural resources and cultural landscapes are two different phenomena that can be discussed separately, only a fine line separates them.[7] Aside from natural resources, human beings become very accustomed to the natural landscapes of places and territories, each with its own seasonal rhythms, climates, geomorphologies, and vegetation. These natural elements become engrained in the human psyche. In turn, human beings, including nations, begin to appreciate these natural landscapes not just for their resources but for their aesthetic beauty and begin to incorporate this sense of aesthetic beauty into poetry, art, and literature. Natural landscapes then become much like cultural landscapes in that we as human beings become very accustomed to them, and they in turn become meaningful to us, to such a degree that we begin to identify with them. Place then is composed of both culturally created and natural elements, intertwined and inseparable for human identity:

> [Place] is made up of experiences, mostly fleeting and undramatic, repeated day after day and over the span of years. It is a unique blend of sights, sounds, and smells, a unique harmony of natural and artificial rhythms such as times of sunset, of work and play. The feel of a place is registered in one's muscles and bones. (Tuan 1977, 183–84)

The belief that place and territory are inextricably linked with human identity is reflected in human speech in a number of ways. One of the most illustrative examples of this link is the adage "You can take the boy out of the country but you cannot take the country out of the boy." This adage, and its many variations which name specific places and territories, gives tacit recognition that we as human beings derive much of our identity from particular places. The influence that place has on our beliefs and personalities becomes obvious when we go to new places. We often behave awkwardly because we do not know the people or the course of events in these new places. We fit into new social groupings only when we have lived in new places long enough to have developed a full appreciation for the qualities of these new places, meaning that our identities have been reshaped by these new places.

A second example of human speech illustrating that place and territory are qualities of human identity is the first question usually put to a stranger: "Where are you from?" The answer to this question often reveals more about a person than the answer to any other question, a multitude of images and information. To say that one is from California, New York, or Mississippi (or Germany, India, or China on another scale) reveals much about one's identity. Even in places like Northern Ireland, where religious adherence seems to be the primary means of group identification, young children in the Protestant and Catholic ghettos also pose this same question first. While the children are interested in religious affiliation, they determine it by identifying place of residence. On the other hand, if the answer to this question is a place or territory outside of Northern Ireland, then religious affiliation becomes unimportant, and volunteering one's religious belief is treated as a non sequitur. The children prefer to hear about other characteristics of the stranger's place of origin.[8]

Basic human vocabulary also reveals strong emotional bonds that we humans have for particular places and territories, in turn illustrating that human identity is partially derived from place and territory. On the positive side, we have words like *home* and its derivations, such as *hometown* and *homeland*. In contrast to the word *house,* which simply connotes a physical structure, home has deeper meaning, referring to the experiences, memories, and people that make up such a place. Personified terms such as *motherland* and *fatherland* recognize that places and territories give us life, nurture and provide for us, and even protect us, making us who we are. In turn, we refer to places and territories with our strongest words of endearment. In fact, "to die for one's country"[9] is one of the most noble and heroic sacrifices that one can make. To evade military service is treated with intense scorn, not only by governments but by members of the nation who believe it necessary to risk one's life to protect one's country.

On the negative side, we have words such as *homesickness*, which refers to a deep emotional longing for places and territories from which we are separated. This separation often results in profound feelings of despair and despondency. Even those of us who move and eventually adjust to new places and territories often feel that there is still "no place like home." Permanent separation from homeland makes one an *exile*, which most of us would consider a dreaded fate. The trauma of separation has molded exiled literary writers who have provided humanity with great works which eloquently express the significance of place to the human condition. As Andrew Gurr points out:

> In consequence of this separation from home in space as well as time, the writer characteristically centres his attention not so much on his sense of history (that was the preoccupation of the stay-at-homes of whom Yeats is perhaps the greatest example), as on his sense of home as a unit in space and time together. For the colonial exiles the search for identity and the construction of a vision of home amount to the same thing. (1981, 11)

> Alienation from a cultural or physical home has radical effects on the writer's mind as well as his choice of theme. Joyce's life and art, inseparable as they are, make a kind of paradigm for the non-metropolitan writer in this century. Exiled by what might be called the mutual consent of the exile and the society sending him into exile, he spent his life obsessively rebuilding his home in his art. The characters in *Dubliners*, . . . reappear in *A Portrait* and *Ulysses*. The geography is narrow and exact. . . . With Joyce, as with many other writers, the distance of exile only intensified the faithful minuteness with which the home was recorded. (1981, 15)

The power of place and the preoccupation that exiled writers have with their homelands as they attempt to hold on to their identities is echoed by Jan Vladislav as well:

> With some effort, or nostalgia, we can evoke our country's true geography. Slowly but correctly, we can redraw its faded contours. . . .
> Our home is the place from which we originate, and toward which we turn to look from an ever-increasing distance. Our home is a point in time which we have lost, but can always rediscover, along with details which we would not even have noticed *then, on the spot*. . . . This is not only a question of individual memory but, for a man's home, fixed in time, is shaped not only by his own history, but also by the histories of those who surround him, by his family and his tribe, and by the palpable history of tilled fields, of ancient villages and new cities, and above all by that changeable, unfathomable, mythic reservoir of his native language.
> A man's native village can be engulfed by the waters of a dam, a city can be razed to the ground by bombs, a landscape can be rendered unrecogniz-

able by the creative as well as the destructive activity of man. But one thing never changes. We never stop carrying within us this meeting place with ourselves, with all our successive and abandoned selves, this place of recognition, of acceptance or rejection of ourselves and the rest of the world. Perhaps that is the hell which each of us is said to carry in his heart. But if our hell is there, so too is our paradise.

. . . *To live one's own life* means to protect a home within oneself, an elusive yet real home. It means to provide a refuge for one's personal history, one's family traditions, one's language, one's ideas, *one's native land.* To live an alien life, even if only a few feet from his place of birth, is to lose all of this. To accept an alien life is to accept an alien death—and that is notably the lot of those forced into exile.

. . . The state has at its disposal only one means of imposing a foreign existence on a man who wants to lead his own life: exile is a death penalty in effigy which aims at destroying everything that makes up man's life, his history, his particular language, in brief, his *home,* and makes a foreigner of him everywhere. Only the man who is determined to refuse to live an alien, imaginary life is immunized against such a sentence, for it cannot reach his world. This path may lead to self-deception, suffering, and tragedy, but it will not destroy him. His native land, which has made him and which allows him to live his own life to the end, cannot be stolen from him. This native land, which a man cannot abandon and which even more cannot be stolen from him, is not a hope, but a certainty, on which each one of us can rely, wherever we may be, whether in our home town or ten thousand miles away. (1990, 14–16)

Just as negative as exile and one of the greatest fears of individuals is *homelessness*, a form of placelessness. Homelessness not only represents a total loss of power within society, it even represents a total loss of identity: homeless people are treated as if they do not exist. Often such people are even stripped of the word *people* and simply referred to as *the homeless*. Without places of their own, homeless people have "no place in society."[10]

Territoriality

Because human identity is derived, expressed, and even invested in place and territory, it logically follows that we as human beings become very protective of the places and territories that define our identities. Indeed, we need to be able to exert some degree of political control over place and territory if we are to obtain and exploit natural resources and maintain the natural and cultural landscapes that shape and define our identities. Place and territory are necessary even for governance, which entails the ability to enact and execute laws. Because all laws have to be tied to place and territory to be effective and meaningful, the possession of place and territory is necessary for governance. This need we have to exert some degree of control over and to protect place and territory is referred to as *territoriality*.[11]

Territoriality exists at all levels of human identity, from that of the individual to that of the nation. At the individual level, territoriality is commonly called personal space. Personal space includes the envelope of air surrounding our bodies as well as the places that we require for our various activities (workplaces, living spaces, etc.). Because our individual identities are tied to the small spaces that we occupy while going about our daily lives, it is not surprising that we exhibit a protectiveness over our personal spaces, cautioning others not to violate them. Our protectiveness is often demonstrated by nameplates, signs, and other markings that make it clear to others that a particular space belongs to us or is under our control. The need for individuals to occupy and use places, often exclusively, is protected by laws within societies. Trespassing, assault, theft, and vandalism, all related to the transgression of personal space, are all treated as serious crimes within societies. Even though theft and vandalism seem to apply to inanimate objects, we as individuals feel personally violated when our personal spaces have been transgressed by such acts. The importance of personal space is illustrated even by social, economic, and political status, those with high status occupying the largest spaces in the most desirable locations.[12]

Territoriality is an expression not only of individuality, but of group identity as well. Families, communities, and even nations exhibit the need to protect the places and territories that they use to define their identities. Similar to individuals, social groups demonstrate their territoriality by posting signs and erecting boundary markers, walls, fences, etc. Fraternities and sororities congregate in houses and explicitly decorate them with symbols and banners to declare their presence and control over a particular space. Furthermore, the spaces that fraternities and sororities establish control over are necessary for the healthy functioning of these social groups. Likewise, retired people often express the need to congregate in retirement communities where they can erect fences and gates. This practice preserves a way of life by keeping children and others away. Even illegal social groupings such as gangs feel the need to protect themselves by establishing control over space; graffiti marks the limits of a gang's territory, contributing to the protection of a gang by warning others to stay out. These examples illustrate that territoriality is related to the concept of segregation, which also involves the control of space, often requiring its reorganization. What group can segregate itself or others without reassigning geographic space?

Once social groups are able to establish control over demarcated spaces and territories, they are then able to enact rules and enforce them to protect and cultivate the group's identity. At higher levels of identity, rules become laws, and more formalized policing agencies are formed. At the national level, in addition to a national police, a military exists to protect the nation's territory from transgression. Protecting a group's territory and protecting a group's identity go hand in hand and are inseparable. For small social groups that see themselves as part of a larger society, political independence is not necessary to exercise control over their social spaces. Only a small degree of autonomy is necessary to express territoriality. On the other hand, nations express a territoriality that requires independent statehood by virtue of the fact that nations have a strong sense of self-awareness and a desire for self-rule. Nations can achieve self-rule only by having complete sovereign control over a given territory. Nations sharing a territory with other nations inevitably will feel that their rights are impinged upon by the other nations, as these other nations attempt to enact and enforce laws within the common territory to cultivate and protect their identities.

Territoriality seems fundamental to the human condition; consequently, many have argued that it is a biological need, genetically ingrained (Ardrey 1996; Malmberg 1980). On the other hand, territoriality is expressed with considerable variation from individual to individual and social group to social group, suggesting that it is a cultural phenomenon rather than a biological one. Some researchers who believe that territoriality is a cultural phenomenon have noted that hunter-gatherer societies—a social form most closely tied to the land—demonstrate the weakest forms of territoriality (Alland 1972; Rosenberg 1990). The varying expressions of territoriality and the weak expressions of territoriality demonstrated by hunter-gatherer societies certainly suggest that territoriality is more cultural than biological. Nevertheless, it is noteworthy that social groups demonstrating weak forms of territoriality have been systematically destroyed by social groups expressing strong forms of territoriality.

Of these latter groups, the nation has the strongest form of territoriality. Not surprisingly, we live in an era known as the nation-state era, the name of which indicates that the nation and its form of identity hold primacy over all other social groups and levels of identity. The primacy of nationhood is shown by the earth's surface having been divided into territories nominally defined by nations. Ultimate sovereign authority rests with national governments; larger political organizations such as the United Nations have very little authority without the consent of national governments. Moreover, almost all human beings, regardless of their social groupings, have voluntarily chosen a national identity or have had one forced upon them by national governments. Even though individuals and more localized communities may exercise autonomy vis-à-vis the nation, such autonomy is possible only with the consent of the nation. The nation has the ability to compel individuals and communities, with force if necessary, to conform to the desires and needs of the nation. Individuals and communities may have rights, but these rights can be revoked by national governments. Individuals and communities do not have the same ability in regard to the nation. Therefore, unlike nations, individuals and communities often have to sacrifice their needs to the nation, compromising and even altering their identities.

Because we live in the nation-state era, and nations express a strong sense of territoriality, territoriality must be addressed as part of the idea of the nation, and even incorporated within the definition of the term. Nevertheless, as noted, territoriality is not exclusively expressed by the nation but by other forms of human identity as well. Territoriality then is multilayered, exactly like the general concept of identity itself. Every person has not only an individual identity but some sense of a familial, community, and national identity, all at the same time. These levels of identity do not act independently but interdependently. The national identity influences and shapes smaller scale identities, including individual ones. At the same time, individual and familial identities shape and influence broader levels of identity, such as the nation. A continual interplay of characteristics exists between the various levels of identity, both within individuals and between individuals and their social groups. A changed characteristic at one level of identity necessarily reverberates through all levels, requiring a reevaluation of identity at all other levels. As a characteristic of human identity, territoriality exists at all levels of identity and is part of the interplay between levels of identity. In a manner of speaking, a given nation's sense of territoriality is the product of many personal spaces interacting, and personal spaces are shaped by the nation's sense of territoriality.

A Nation's Territory

National territoriality is more than large-scale personal space. Individuals have an intimate knowledge of their personal spaces; they create them and live within them. In contrast, individuals, although belonging to larger social groups, do not know every individual within their large social groups and likewise do not know the larger group territories intimately. In fact, most individuals have never even visited many areas within the territories of their social groupings, especially at the national level. Nevertheless, individuals, as members of nations, have strong emotional attachments to their nation's territory[13] and even express a clear sense of the areal extent of their nation's territory. Lacking intimate experience, one gets the sense of the national territory via the interplay of ideas between the various levels of identity. Quite simply, the emergence of a national identity and the sense of a particular national territory come through social interaction. In other words, individuals depend on their social groups to define their broader levels of identity, including the territorialities of these broader levels.

Identity is a dynamic phenomenon, with much of the dynamism deriving from the interplay between the various levels of identity, from that of the individual to that of the nation. The dynamic aspect of identity means that national identities evolve over time. Conceptions of national territories also evolve over time. In fact, they evolve concurrently because place and terrritory are components of national identity. Of course, events, politics, and innovations are active in the interplay between the various levels of identity and, therefore, influence the development of national identities. For example, when an innovation like the computer is introduced, people in each region will evaluate it differently; a national consensus will be worked out, and then each regional group will reevaluate it. Innovations do not need to be earth-shattering in their implications. Individually, their impact may be minor, yet cumulatively they are very significant. Subtle yet continual changes in farming practices, industrial technologies, and business methods often have a profound influence on culture over time. As a result of these changes, a people's understanding of itself and its place in the world changes as well. Additionally, a new stimulus seldom occurs uniformly throughout a national territory. A war, for example, may result in the partial occupation of the national territory. Such an occupation has differing implications for those who experience the occupation and for those who do not. Again, a national consensus has to develop concerning the meaning of such an occupation; a national consensus in turn causes a reevaluation at the regional and local levels.

Because individuals develop their broader levels of identity and territorialities through social interaction, individuals' sense of identity and senses of territory can be manipulated; individuals can even be inculcated with particular ideas concerning their identity and territoriality,[14] all because individuals of a nation lack personal knowledge of all their fellow members and the nation's supposed territory. Individuals, small groups, and even governments with agendas can take advantage of social dynamics to inject particular ideas into society with the intent of shaping a national identity with certain cultural characteristics and a specific sense of territoriality. For example, the Ecuadoran government issued a postage stamp with a map of Ecuador showing Ecuador's boundaries extending deep into Peru (Glassner 1993, 86).[15] Governments in particular have the ability to make sure that the histories of certain places and territories are learned, with a prescribed emphasis placed on the value and significance of certain places and territories. Governments also have the ability to organize the cultural landscape in a particular way. The Argentine government, for example, has erected signs with a map of the Malvinas (Falklands) and a slogan that claims that the islands are Argentine, not British (Glassner 1993, 85).[16] Governments also have the ability to promote the use of particular symbols, images, religions, and languages.[17] Finally, and just as important to consider, governments can suppress ideas and beliefs as well as repress and persecute those who promote unwanted ideas that may cause the nation to reevaluate itself.

The continual reconciliation of identities at their various scales, coupled with the broad and generalized characteristics of national identities, makes national identities very complex and prone to manipulation by nationalists, political leaders, and governments. Modern nationalists often place a greater emphasis on language, religion, and shared history as the primary elements of national identity, even though individual and group identity is intimately tied to place. For example, at one time people who lived in Prussia considered themselves to be Prussian first, and then German or Polish. However, after the rise of modern nationalism, German nationalists focused on language as the crucial, unifying factor of German identity. In response, Polish nationalists did the same (Herb 1993, 14; Holborn 1969, 294). Prussian identity, as a common identity of those living in Prussia, was eventually shunted aside by what it was to be German or Polish (Davies 1982, 2:131–32). While language became the defining characteristic for German and Polish national identities—and the national identities of many other Central and East Europeans—the meaning of place and territory evolved as well at the broader levels. After all, the Germans and the Poles needed a Germany and a Poland. Simply considering the distribution of German speakers and Polish speakers would not and will not satisfy either group. The conceptions of place and territory of both of these groups must be considered.

Although sense of territory is a fundamental component of group identity, the actual delimitation of a group's sense of territory changes depending on the emphasis placed on other components of identity. For example, as Prussian identity changed, the concept of Prussia changed as well. The Prussian case is a typical example of group identities as they evolved in Central and Eastern Europe. Over the last few centuries, imperial ideologies have been replaced by nationalist ideologies. Imperial ideologies were primarily concerned with religious affiliation; language was generally considered to be an unimportant issue. With the rise of nationalism, language became paramount. Prussian leaders and hence Prussians shifted from being the protectors and propagators of Protestantism to the protectors and propagators of Germanism as defined by language. The shift in identity altered conceptions of place and territory. When language did not matter to Prussians, Prussia was an independent, sovereign unit and, most of all, a bulwark of Protestantism. However, when language became an issue, Prussians rechanneled their religious fervor and developed the need to act and speak as exemplary Germans and be advocates for all of Germany. As a result, Prussia eventually became a subunit of Germany—a Germany with strong Prussian characteristics.

Despite changing identities for large-scale groups (e.g., nations) and the resulting changes in how place and territory became understood, people who live together in a place tend to develop a common identity through their shared experience of that place. In other words, place and territory can be a defining characteristic of a nation as much as language or religion. In fact, emotional attachments to place can take precedence over other characteristics despite any nationalist rhetoric. For example, many inhabitants of Bosnia see themselves as Bosnian first, then as Croats, Serbs, or Muslims. Religion is not the basis of Bosnian identity. However, as stated, national identity is very complex and easily manipulated by political leaders. By emphasizing certain components of group identity such as language or religion, political leaders are able to redefine a situation to their advantage and fulfill their ambitions. In the case of Bosnia, political leaders in Serbia and Croatia have not accepted a Bosnian identity and thus have tried to prevent the rest of the world from accepting one as well. They have forced the issue of religion in an attempt to delegitimize any sense of Bosnian identity. When a new version of group identity is created, a new group territory is likewise required. Often, of course, and by political design, the new national territory expands beyond the current boundaries of the political state. Political leaders then can claim restitution of national territories through military force. In most cases, political leaders claim historical territories that actually existed (Murphy 1990). In other cases, they claim "restitution" of fabricated historical territories.

Possession of territories has changed continually in Central Europe and Eastern Europe for many centuries (see Figure 2.1) and, therefore, large-scale group identities have changed as well.[18] Consequently, modern nationalists have had to try to sew together regions that often were isolated from one another (even when in close geographical proximity). The task is monumental because many of the nations' territories were not focused on the modern national core areas. Moreover, many of the territories were divided among and manipulated by outside empires with foreign ideologies. Even under normal circumstances, members living in different regions have different ideas regarding the boundaries of the national territory. The boundaries of the national territory may even be somewhat unclear to its members. Even so, the territory is usually discussed as something whole and inviolable. Varied historical pasts and differing regional perceptions of a nation's members give political leaders the ability to manipulate a nation's sense of identity, including, of course, the nation's sense of place and territory.

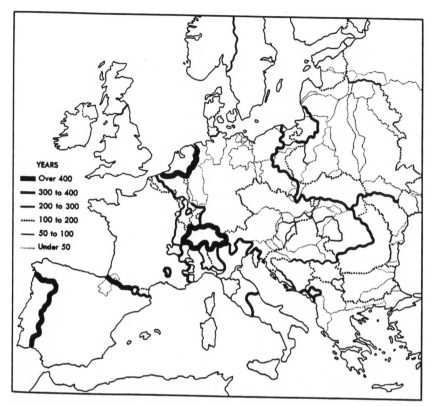

Figure 2.1 Map Showing the Permanence of European Boundaries (Pounds 1963, 29).

The dynamics of social interaction, and the evolution of subjective ideas and conceptions that arise from it, provide a better explanation for actual nations' identities than any attempt to objectively map spatial patterns of language, religion, or any other cultural characteristic. In fact, the emphasis placed on language, religion, and many of the other cultural characteristics that modern nations may have is unwarranted when the evolution of social groups is taken into account. When nationalism began to be a potent socio-political force a mere few hundred years ago, cultural characteristics were in constant transition across the landscape, providing no obvious means for drawing lines on maps that could identify nations. In the case of language, what became designated as either a language or a dialect had more to do with conceptions that arose in the human mind than with linguistics. The common but mistaken belief that those who speak the same language consider themselves to be one people did not conform to reality. In an attempt to make reality conform to human conceptions, many mutually intelligible forms of

Chapter Two

communication—what linguists would classify as dialects within a single language—instead were treated as separate and distinct languages; the reverse was done as well. The case of Serbian and Croatian illustrates this situation very well. Serbian and Croatian often were considered to be separate languages until these two peoples attempted to form a single Yugoslav nation. During the attempt to unify, Serbo-Croatian was the designated language, and the varying forms of communication of those involved were classified as dialects of the Serbo-Croatian language. Because the people who spoke the varying forms of communication were grouped together in a single territory, the varying forms of communication began to grow together. Following the break-up of the Yugoslav state, Serbian and Croatian now are considered to be separate languages by the people involved, despite any designation by linguists (Asher 1995, 18). Moreover, conscious efforts have been made by those involved to make Serbian and Croatian separate and distinct languages (Woodward 1996). These actions are being taken to make language conform to the perceived number of nations that exist. In other words, language does not determine national identity; national identity determines language.[19]

In addition to language, religion and other cultural characteristics are defined by human conceptions as well, making them not only unreliable as national determinants but also unreliable in delineating a nation's territory as it defines it. How a nation comes to understand and define its cultural characteristics has to do with the interplay of all of these characteristics with one another; outside forces often influence this interplay. Until now, language and religion have been treated as constants which shape other national characteristics, including a nation's understanding and identification with a particular territory. Languages and religions may be objectively described, but a nation's understanding and identification with a language or a religion are not nearly so objective and concrete. Such understandings and identifications are not constants but instead are shaped by understandings and conceptions of other cultural characteristics. Territoriality is a cultural characteristic and is just as likely to shape and define other cultural characteristics as it is to be shaped by the other characteristics. In other words, territoriality is just as likely to shape a nation's understanding and definition of its language and religion as it is to be shaped by the nation's language and religion. The question then arises as to how nations have come to conceive of and define their territories. Before addressing this question (in Chapter 3), however, we must find a means of locating the places and territories with which nations develop strong emotional bonds and hence come to identify.

Indicators of a Nation's Sense of Territory

Although nations may express a deep emotional attachment to particular places, the spatial delimitation of a national territory as the nation itself conceptualizes it is not a simple matter. Competing regional identities, manipulative political leaders, and fervent nationalists, not to mention wars and the migrations of people, make the task of understanding the spatial extent of a nation's "place" very difficult. Nevertheless, some insights can be gained by looking at the spatial distribution of three major indicators: (1) the sites identified by the locations of important institutions and of historical events; (2) the landscapes described in nationally renowned literature, poetry, art, and music; and (3) the historical willingness to use force to hold onto a particular territory—the "tenacity factor."

Site is perhaps the most tangible and easiest to identify. As mentioned earlier, elements in the landscape become symbols and as such serve as "repositories of memories" (Tuan 1974, 145) and concrete evidence and expressions of accomplishments. Seats of government, printing centers,[20] theaters, educational centers (e.g., schools, universities, research institutes) and religious centers (e.g., houses of worship, monasteries, and pilgrimage sites) are the most common examples. Historic sites of battles and birthplaces are just as important, especially if monuments are erected to remind future generations—or even the current one—of who they are. Individual sites, especially those with institutions, not only can hold the cultural artifacts of a nation but can house those individuals who preserve, protect, and cultivate these artifacts as well as the less tangible characteristics of the nation's identity.[21] Because institutions and historic events are instrumental in defining a given nation's identity and who adopts that national identity, then studying the locations of institutions and historic events is not only valuable but necessary in understanding how and where particular national identities emerge and develop.[22] Therefore, locating institutions and historic sites is an important first step in delineating a nation's territory as the nation itself conceives of and understands it.

Site identification serves well for describing the built landscape, but landscape description is the most useful for identifying those elements in the natural landscape to which a nation becomes emotionally bonded, and thus fall within a nation's sense of territory. Landscape descriptions typically refer to misty mountains, rolling blue rivers, and golden fields of grain. Such references usually are interwoven with strong feelings of reverence and sanctity. Nationalist writers often put more effort into describing the nation's territory than the social and cultural characteristics of the nation itself. Many national anthems typically make more references to the national territory than to the nation itself. In essence, the nation is depicted through descriptions of place and territory; small wonder then that the term *nation* so often is mistakenly used to refer to a place. Thus, by examining literature, poetry, music, and the visual arts, we can highlight and map the important and meaningful elements of the physical landscape for a given nation.

The value of poetry, storytelling, music, and the visual arts (especially folk and popular forms of all four) is difficult to overestimate. Nationalism emerged at a time when most people were illiterate. The primary means of transmitting ideas and beliefs was through the oral tradition, supplemented through visual arts. Even in today's world, with its advanced technologies and the concomitant need for high levels of literacy, many significant ideas and beliefs are still transmitted in the informal settings of the pub, the sports field, houses of worship, and over the airwaves of radio and television. In fact, most people do not continue with a formal education into adulthood, and the few of us who do usually do not pursue a higher education for more than a small fraction of our adult lives. Therefore, folk and popular forms of communication are still the primary means for most to receive and transmit ideas and beliefs. In other words, the oral tradition is alive and well, continuing to play a vital role in most societies. In order to understand how nations feel about and conceive of their national territories, it is crucial to examine these forms of communication, summarized as landscape description in this work.

The last means of identifying a nation's sense of territory is through an examination of the "tenacity factor." The tenacity factor is the measure of a nation's willingness and determination to protect or seize a piece of territory. While the first two indicators are a means of identifying significant places, the tenacity factor demonstrates the degree of importance a group ascribes to a given place. Although nations use places to define their identity, each place has a varying degree of significance. Therefore, only by examining the political-geographic history of a nation can we determine the significance of place. Specifically, this can be achieved by looking at attempts of national movements or national governments to seize or protect territory through declarations, policies, agreements, military actions, and alliances. In some cases, if a nation is unable to maintain or obtain control of a territory of minor significance the national identity is redefined to exclude that place. In other cases, a territory may be so significant that the nation finds it very difficult to redefine its identity. In these circumstances, military action may continue even if the costs in human life are great.

Because place and territory vary in degree of significance, it is then possible to categorize them accordingly. For this research, three levels have been chosen: core, semi-core, and periphery. The core contains territories with places of greatest national significance, and with the greatest variety of places of importance (e.g., religious, political, cultural). The core also is distinguished by maintaining significance over long periods and by being struggled for very tenaciously. Political control of core territories is crucial to a nation's ability to maintain its sense of identity. The semi-core is characterized by territories with some places of primary importance but mostly by places of secondary importance. The semi-core tends to represent one aspect of the nation's identity and was important at one time or another but not continuously throughout history. For example, Bosnia-Herzegovina was an important refuge for the Serbian nation during its struggles with the Ottoman Empire. The semi-core is significant enough that a nation usually feels the need to politically control it. Indeed, a nation will struggle very intensely to maintain or gain control of a semi-core territory. Loss of control requires a nation to seriously reevaluate its sense of identity, but such loss does not permanently endanger the nation. The periphery contains places of some national significance, but not to the degree that possession is necessary. In fact, possession may not even be desired. The periphery is important because it ties the nation to the greater world around it, and provides examples of the nation's greatness by illustrating an extended spatial stretch of the nation's involvement in regional, even global, concerns.

The search for all three of the indicators that illustrate a nation's sense of territory has to be undertaken on a nation-by-nation basis. Emotional attachments to place are a highly subjective matter; a nation's territory is understood and delineated only through the eyes and emotions of the nation itself. In Central and Eastern Europe, many nations have had their sense of identity violated by the continual redistribution of territories. In an attempt to create stability and strengthen claims, many nationalist writers have written a great deal about their nation's territory. Many Central and Eastern European nationalists have tried to solicit aid from Western Europe and North America as a means of maintaining and preserving the integrity of national territories. Many of these works can be more articulate expressions of a nation's emotional attachment to place than works written for domestic consumption.

Notes

1. The idea that human beings become emotionally attached to places and territories is not a new one. Yi-Fu Tuan considers the phenomenon to be so significant that he has coined a term to represent it—*Topophilia*—which he defines as "the affective bond between people and place or setting" (Tuan 1974, 4). Tuan has not only written a book about it but has devoted much of his academic career to exploring it.

2. In the Spanish case, for example, why did New Spain separate itself from the Spanish Empire when those in control spoke Spanish and were Roman Catholic like those in the motherland? Not insignificant was that the break-away

occurred during, and even as a result of, a heightened period of nationalism. Why too, did all of these Spanish-speaking Roman Catholics not identify with one another and thus stay together in a single unified New Spanish state? Moreover, why did many Spanish-speaking Roman Catholics form common bonds with the indigenous peoples instead of with one another as part of the rise in national consciousness (Anderson 1991, 50–54)?

3. The Scots, for example, voted for their own parliament in a recent referendum. The overwhelming victory for greater self-rule stands in sharp contrast to the failure of a similar referendum in 1979 (Glauber 1997, 17a). Clearly more Scots today think of themselves as a nation than previously. The rise in national consciousness has been attributed to a perceived "indifference and even scorn from England" (Lyall 1997, A3). This perception came about in the 1980s "when many Scots found the Tory Government of Prime Minister Margaret Thatcher cold and unresponsive to Scotland's demands" (Lyall 1997, A3).

4. French and German speakers from places outside of France and Germany are not called French and Germans—definitely not the French and German speakers of Switzerland or the German speakers of Austria. At the same time, those native peoples from France and Germany who do not have French or German as a mother tongue still are considered to be French and German respectively because they are from France and Germany respectively.

5. While states do represent nations, they only represent those members of a nation that live within the state's boundaries. Members of a nation living outside the state's boundaries are represented by other state governments. Therefore, many nations are not represented by a single state government. Some are even represented by opposing governments.

6. No wonder then that schools try to bear the expense of taking children on field trips to museums and historical sites. Even adults eagerly spend their vacations going to historical places of national significance.

7. The close, inseparable connection between human beings and the physical world is best illustrated by Simon Schama: "Even the landscapes that we suppose to be most free of our culture may turn out, on closer inspection, to be its product" (1996, 9). He made this statement while discussing the natural, pristine beauty of Yosemite.

8. This information was gained through fieldwork of the author while in Northern Ireland.

9. Notice that the place-rooted term *country* is used in the expression, not the people-rooted term *nation*. We as humans obviously must have strong emotional attachments to place and territory if we are willing to sacrifice our lives for them.

10. Furthermore, homeless people obviously have to occupy space somewhere. Those who do for a while begin to create places by filling them with belongings, thus organizing them to reflect their identity. This is an important step in reentering society. Not surprisingly, homeless people become protective of these places. Unfortunately, having no rights, homeless people often are unable to prevent authorities or others from transgressing and even destroying their places. When their places are transgressed, intense emotional duress follows.

11. Robert Sack defines territoriality as "the attempt by an individual or group to affect, influence, or control people, phenomena, and relationships, by delimiting and asserting control over a geographic area" (1986, 19).

Edward Soja defines territoriality as "a behavioral phenomenon associated with the organization of space into spheres of influence or clearly demarcated territories which are made distinctive and considered at least partially exclusive by their occupants or definers" (1971, 19).

12. The organization of personal space and what it signifies is integral to a phenomenon that Philip Wagner calls *Geltung* (Wagner 1996).

13. "It is characteristic of the symbol-making human species that its members can become passionately attached to places of enormous size, such as a nation-state, of which they have limited direct experience" (Tuan 1977, 18).

14. "Maps in school atlases and history books show nation-states as sharply bounded units. Small scale maps encourage people to think of their counties as self-sufficient entities. Visible limits to a nation's sovereignty, such as a row of hills or a stretch of river, support the sense of the nation as place. From the air, however, mountains and rivers are merely elements of physical geography, and man-made markers like fences and guard posts are invisible. Aerial photographs are useless in history books. Maps, which also present the vertical view, are another matter. Cartography can clearly be made to serve a political end. In a school atlas the world's nations appear as a mosaic of clashing colors. Pink Canada looms large over butter-tinted United States; there can be no doubt about where one ends and another begins, nor of their sharply contrasting identities" (Tuan 1977, 178).

15. Being that postage stamps are an item that millions of people see on a regular basis, governments have decided that they are an appropriate medium for inculcating particular understandings of territorial arrangements into the minds of their citizens. The Ecuadoran example is merely one in a long list of postage stamp examples that Martin Glassner depicts in his book *Political Geography* (1993, 86).

16. Signs are a popularly used device in the cultural landscape. In addition to the Argentine case, the Polish government has erected signs stating that the territories taken from Germany after the Second World War are really Polish (Glassner 1993, 85); signs in Japan state that the Sakhalin Islands, now part of Russia, are really Japanese.

17. Thus explaining Eric J. Hobsbawn's statement that "languages multiply with states; not the other way around" (1990, 63).

18. This statement is based on the recognition that boundaries are active, not passive, in regard to human identity. Boundaries simply do not encapsulate and summarize what exists across the landscape even though they are treated as if their function is just that. On the contrary, boundaries shape and alter the flow of trade, people, and ideas. The location of boundaries often determines the languages that people speak and the religions they practice. Likewise, human identities are often altered when boundaries change locations as individuals find themselves in new streams of movement and under the jurisdiction of a new government.

19. The case of the Irish language serves as an excellent example as well. The Irish language almost died out completely while the Irish people remained firmly in *place*. It was not a resurgence in the use of the Irish language that led to a rise in Irish national identity but a rise in Irish national consciousness that brought about the revival of the Irish language. Even today, only a small percentage of

Irish speak Irish as if it were their mother tongue, yet no one questions the fact that millions more are Irish. In fact, the Irish nation is defined by the territory called Ireland, not the Irish language. No one agrees with this statement more than Irish nationalists, whose primary obsession is to drive foreigners (i.e., British) and Irish traitors out of Northern Ireland.

20. Benedict Anderson argues throughout much of his book (*Imagined Communities*) that "print-capitalism" was a major factor in the rise of modern nationalism (Anderson 1991). If this is true, then certainly the locations of printing centers are significant.

21. What would the English language be without Oxford, or even Cambridge and London? What would the French language be without the Sorbonne or the government in Paris? What would any language be without its place of cultivation?

22. To ignore geography, particularly the meaning of place and territory, one would have to argue, for example, that the English language would be the same today even if it had developed in a place like Newcastle or even Beijing. One also would have to argue that French would be the same if the Sorbonne were in Marseille or even Calcutta.

3

Southeastern European Nationalism in Its Temporal and Spatial Context

In Chapter 2, the concept of nation was highlighted as a spatial phenomenon. Nationalism, however, is just as much a temporal phenomenon, a product of historical processes. Indeed, historical processes have worked as powerful instruments in molding nations into what they are today. Moreover, geographical inquiry needs to factor in historical processes in order to identify the particular places and territories that become significant to nations. Nations differ from one another because places and territories differ from one another, but differences exist in part because historical processes vary over space. Because history cannot be divorced from geography, this chapter examines those historical circumstances under which nationalism developed, thus providing the means for identifying the specific places and territories that have become significant to the nations of southeastern Europe.

History shows that nationalism is a rather recent development in human social formation. Characteristics of nationalism can be traced back further but the concept of nation, as we know it today, dates back little more than two hundred years[1] (Anderson 1991, 4; Kemiläinen 1964, 48–49). More important, history shows us that nationalism did not emerge in isolation from the ideologies that preceded it. It may seem that nationalism was such a pervasive force when it arose that it destroyed everything in its path, including the dominant socio-political force at the time—imperialism. Imperialism did eventually succumb to nationalism but fought against it bitterly, surviving well into the twentieth century (see Figure 1.1). Although imperialism as a whole was rejected, many imperialist ideas persisted through the struggle that lasted more than a hundred years and became part of and even inseparable from the new nationalist ideology. Imperialist ideas, for example, determined membership in nations and identified the boundaries of nation-states.

The way in which many imperialist concepts became rearticulated as modern nationalist ones varied from region to region, depending on the evolution of ideas and events within each region. In Western Europe, modern nationalism was shaped by Enlightenment thinking, but in Central and Eastern Europe it was molded by Romantic philosophy. Because modern nationalism developed first in Western Europe and then spread to Central and Eastern Europe, and because Enlightenment thought evolved into Romantic philosophy, it is necessary to begin with the Enlightenment in Western Europe.

The Enlightenment

Up until the advent of the Enlightenment, the idea that the ruler was a Divine Right Monarch was fundamental to imperialism (Anderson 1991, 19). In other words, the ruler was chosen by God to rule, meaning that the subject had no right to question the authority of the ruler. This dynastic-imperialist philosophy allowed rulers to claim any territories that they wished because they would be governing in the name of God. In fact, spreading of the word and expanding the empire were synonymous. Ethnicity was not relevant in determining boundaries, and nationalism was yet unknown. The primary concern of rulers was religious adherence because the legitimacy of rulers was tied to specific faiths. Consequently, any concern that rulers had concerning ethnic groups was limited to religious affiliation. Those with the same affiliation would be more receptive to the ruler's authority than those with another belief. Other than religious affiliation, rulers were unconcerned about ethnicity and left ethnic groups in peace as long as the ethnic groups recognized the authority of their ruler. Indeed, most empires were multiethnic (Anderson 1991, 83), and rulers did little to homogenize the populations of their empires before the rise of modern nationalism.[2]

With the rise of the Enlightenment at the end of the seventeenth century, the legitimacy of sovereignty was questioned. This questioning of authority followed from a series of new scientific discoveries that changed the way people thought about the world. An important idea was the realization that the universe was heliocentric, not geocentric (Greer 1977, 359). The heliocentric universe operated under the force of gravity, not by God's hand. In fact, God was not even necessary to the functioning of the solar system. This new scientific view of the universe had profound socio-political implications. Rulers derived their legitimacy from the belief that they were agents of God, helping God run the universe. When God was removed from the equation, the legitimacy of imperial leaders immediately evaporated.

A new legitimacy of governance obviously had to be found, and the new scientific philosophy provided an answer. Because the new science of the Enlightenment placed great emphasis on mathematical and mechanical laws, the idea emerged that all things were bound by universal laws and truths, no matter who or what they were. In social terms, this idea implied that an equality existed between all individuals, with no basis for preference or favoritism.[3] Therefore, the governance and functioning of states should be geared to protecting the rights of individuals. This new idea that the individual was the basic building block of society was expressed first in England by figures such as John Locke (1632–1704) and John Milton (1608–1674). Locke, for example, believed

the [individual's] liberty, dignity, and happiness remain the basic elements of national life, and that the government of a nation is a moral trust dependent upon the free consent of the governed. (Kohn 1955, 18)

The new social ideas of the Enlightenment, with its emphasis on the rights of the individual, implied a restructuring of the politico-territorial order. If the sovereignty by divine right was rejected, then certainly the territorial ordering of Divine Right Monarchs had to be rejected as well. Indeed, the large, sprawling territories of empires could not adequately serve individuals, or protect their rights. With administrative centers at great distances from many inhabitants, administrators were separated from those that they served, making it impossible to provide for the needs of individuals. To serve individuals, states need to have small territories. Small states facilitate the participation of individuals in government because the ratio between the governing and governed is much smaller than in large states. This situation existed even in the classical Greek city-state, which, by virtue of its small size, maximized the participation of individuals in their own governance. Enlightenment thinkers were well aware of the classical Greeks. They admired them greatly and emulated much of their thinking.[4]

Although Enlightenment thinking implied a spatial reordering of the world's states to create a political map of many small states, a movement to bring this about never materialized. Such a movement would have had difficulty because the existing territorial order had a weighty inertia. Imperial leaders could easily be disposed of, but entrenched bureaucracies were much more difficult to eliminate. Bureaucracies have a life of their own; even though they can change to serve new needs, they strongly resist being abolished.

Imperial bureaucracies were indeed a formidable force, but the conceptions of the human mind proved to be insurmountable. Although Enlightenment thinkers were intrigued with every little detail of classical Greek culture, to the point of blatant imitation, Enlightenment thinkers could not bring themselves to start a movement to replicate the classical Greek city-state. The existing politico-territorial order of the eighteenth century had too much meaning for them to question it. Indeed, even though Enlightenment philosophy implied small states, it did not provide a logical means of areally delineating small states. In other words, if individuals were the basic building block of society with all having the same rights regardless of cultural characteristics, then where should boundaries be drawn? No particular answer was implied; in fact, boundary location was irrelevant to Enlightenment philosophy because all individuals had the same rights no matter what state they lived in. Beyond the implied need to create small states, the lack of a particular conception of where boundaries should be drawn precluded Enlightenment thinkers from ever challenging the existing imperial-territorial order, or their own acceptance of it. Instead, Enlightenment thinkers accepted the existing states and their territories, attempting only to bring about democratic reforms within them.[5] Thus Great Britain was pushed from the pathway of imperialism to a pathway that would make it evolve into a nation-state, without any call to change its political boundaries.[6]

In one sense, the questioning of the imperial-territorial order was hindered even more as Enlightenment philosophy evolved. When Locke's ideas spread to France, they influenced people such as François-Marie Arouet Voltaire (1694–1778) and Jean-Jacques Rousseau (1712–1778). Rousseau, however, did not place as much emphasis on the individual as did Locke. In fact, as Hans Kohn points out,

> with the old dynastic and religious authority in the state breaking down [Rousseau] saw the necessity of establishing the collective personality of the nation as the new center and justification of society and social order. . . . [He believed that] the whole people must be united in the closest possible feeling of affinity, of common destiny and common responsibility. . . . [Furthermore] the true political community could be based only on the virtue of its citizens and their ardent love of the fatherland. Public education had to implant those feelings in the hearts of all children. (Kohn 1955, 20–21)

This new emphasis on the whole people rather than the individual certainly precluded the creation of small states. The new thinking implied a redrawing of boundaries based on the distribution of peoples. But what defined a people? National consciousness had not fully emerged but was still in its infancy. The only mechanisms in place that could cultivate a common identity among a group were the imperial bureaucracies. The imperial bureaucracies had not been cultivating a common national identity among subjects, only a sense of common loyalty to the state.[7] This common loyalty, however, became the basis of a common national identity. Because common loyalty was defined by the imperial-territorial order, the new national identities were defined by the imperial-territorial order as well. Indeed, "the people," as Rousseau defined them, were determined by "their ardent love of the fatherland" (see block quote above), not by common cultural characteristics like language and religion. The fatherland, however, was defined by the existing territorial structure. Therefore, membership in nations was determined by the map of imperial states. So, despite the radical reforms brought about by the French Revolution in 1789, not even modest calls were made to change France's boundaries to correspond to the new radical ideas. Territorially, the French Republic was exactly the same as the French Empire (see Figure 3.1), and membership in the French nation was defined by the French Republic's boundaries.

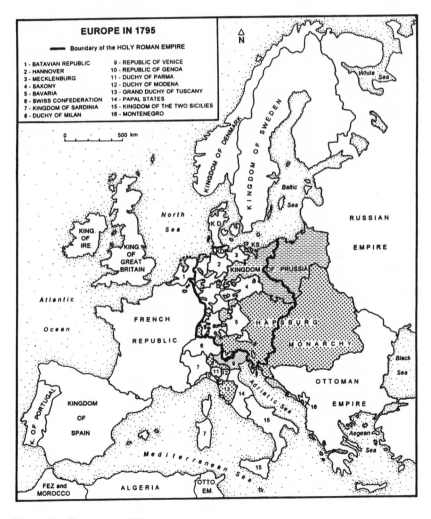

Figure 3.1 Europe in 1795.

The Romantic Period

Enlightenment ideas spread eastward and influenced thinking but were modified heavily and even rejected to a large degree. What emerged was a new way of thinking, known as Romantic philosophy. One of the more noteworthy Romantic philosophers was Johann Gottfried Herder (1744–1803). Herder rejected the sterile nature of the Enlightenment view with its emphasis on rational scientific thinking and the rights of the individual. Instead, he focused on the irrational and creative force of the people as a collective, *das Volk* (Wilson 1973, 829). Herder believed that

> humanity was something man could achieve only as a member of a nation and that nations could arrive at humanity only if they remained true to their national characters, or souls. Each nation, then, by developing its language, art, literature, religion, customs, and laws—all of which were expressions of the national soul—would be working not only for its own strength and unity, but for the well-being of civilization as a whole. Each nation had a special "mission" to perform in the progress of man toward humanity—the cultivation of one's own characteristics. (Wilson 1973, 823–24)

In fact, the contemporary emphasis placed on language as a defining characteristic of a nation can be traced back to Herder. According to Herder,

> every language has its definite national character, and therefore nature obliges us to learn only our native tongue, which is the most appropriate to our character, and which is most commensurate with our way of thought. (Kohn 1967, 432–33)

By rejecting the idea of universalism, Herder advocated a view of nature and history as organic processes: "an endless creative process in which attention should be centered not on the general and common but on the individual and unique" (Kohn 1955, 31). Because history was no longer viewed as cyclical but organic, the study of history received new attention.

Fused together with the new emphasis on history was a new regard for nature. Nature was seen as being unique from place to place and perceived as a molding force in the development of nations. As Herder wrote, nature

> has sketched with the mountain ranges she formed and with the rivers she made flow for them the rough but definite outline of the entire history of man. . . . One height created a nation of hunters, thus supporting and necessitating a savage state; another, more spread out and mild, provided a field for shepherd peoples and supplied them with tame animals; another made agriculture easy and essential; and still another began with navigation and

fishing and finally to trade. . . . In many regions the customs and ways of life have continued for millennia; in others they have changed, . . . but always in harmony with the terrain from which the change came. . . . Oceans, mountain chains, and rivers are the most natural boundaries not only of lands, but also of peoples, customs, languages, and empires; and even in the greatest revolutions of human affairs they have been the guiding lines and the limits of world history. (Wilson 1973, 821–22; Ergang 1966, 37–38)

These ideas reflect the prevailing influence of environmental determinism on thinking. In political-geographic terms, for example, the idea emerged that natural (or physiographic) regions were the "natural" territories of states. Therefore, natural features could be used to identify the appropriate political boundaries of states and were thus called natural political boundaries.[8] The French, for example, saw the natural boundaries for their state as the Atlantic Ocean, Mediterranean Sea, the Pyrenees Mountains, and the Rhine River.[9] By the end of the nineteenth century, the idea that natural regions were the basis of political states developed into the theory of the "Organic State," which viewed the state as a living organism fixed to the soil[10] (Pearcy 1948, 14).

Although Herder was a German-speaking Prussian, he can hardly be called a German nationalist. "Each nation was to him a manifestation of the Divine, and, therefore, something sacred which should not be destroyed but cultivated" (Kohn 1955, 31). He despised Prussian militarism and believed that a healthy and prosperous nation could best develop among peaceful peasant peoples such as the Slavs. In fact, Herder greatly admired the lifestyles and folk traditions of the Slavs. He predicted a glorious future for the Slavic peoples and encouraged them and others to collect Slavic folk poetry and information on Slavic traditions and customs. Herder's writings were published in many Slavic languages as well as German, and they were instrumental in stimulating national consciousness among Slavs (Wilson 1973, 830–31).

The ideas of Romanticism stimulated a great interest in the past among Europe's educated classes (Craig 1972, 7). Unfortunately, a major problem arose: no one had kept a detailed record of the history of European nations, especially not in Eastern Europe. The only history known was that of dynasties and of ancient Greek and Roman scholars. History, therefore, had to be reconstructed, and Herder believed that it could only be done through folk poetry (Wilson 1973, 825). To Herder and his mentors, folk poets were really historians who spoke in a metaphorical language that reflected the very essence of the national soul. Although folklore and folk poetry provided a means for reconstructing history, it was itself very problematic. It was often very ambiguous, and various interpretations could be made of it. In an attempt to provide meaning for the past and also fill in the past's numerous gaps, Romantic historicists reconstructed many histories and mythologies that were essentially fabricated. Romantics were not bothered by the lack of hard evidence. Meaningful continuity was more important than unexplained facts. As Anthony D. Smith points out,

> Their aim is to retail the "past," in such a way as to "explain" the lot of their community and prescribe remedies for its ills. To this end, historicists must collate different versions and strands of communal traditions and produce a single, unified "past" which gives a convincing and emotionally satisfying account of the present situation of their ethnic kinsmen. There must be no loose ends, no doubts or conflicting versions, which can blur and erode the "native hue of resolution." (Smith 1986b, 191–92)

Smith goes on to outline a series of eight elements that are found in any national mythology or myth of ethnic descent:

1) a myth of origins in time; i.e. when the community was "born";
2) a myth of origins in space; i.e. where the community was "born";
3) a myth of ancestry; i.e. who bore us, and how we descended from him/her;
4) a myth of migration; whither we wandered;
5) a myth of liberation; i.e. how we were freed;
6) a myth of a golden age; i.e. how we became great and heroic;
7) a myth of decline; i.e. how we decayed and were conquered/exiled; and
8) a myth of rebirth; i.e. how we shall be restored to our former glory. (Smith 1986b, 192)

In summary then, Romanticism stood in sharp contrast to Enlightenment philosophy. Where the Enlightenment stressed universal truths and the rights of the individual, Romanticism emphasized unique truths and the rights of the group. While Enlightenment thinkers valued universal languages of Latin and Greek, Romantics promoted the use of native, vernacular languages. While Enlightenment philosophers insisted on rational, intellectual thought, Romantics cherished the irrational, emotional spirit. While Enlightenment thinkers preferred urban settings—known for great social interaction and stimulating intellectual environments, Romantics idolized bucolic settings with their close connections with nature. Moreover, unlike cities, rural areas were preserves of folk cultures, which in turn provided a means for Romantics to write "histories" for their peoples.

Subsequently, Romantic philosophy has given rise to a number of terms and phrases, which in turn can be employed to identify Romantic thinking. Romantics, for example, speak of "national awakening," as if nations always existed but did not know it. Not surprising then, Romantics use the term "historical continuity" to prove that nations have always existed, ignoring that they have to fabricate history to demonstrate its continuity. Historical continuity implies "destiny," and a "glorious" one at that. After all, a linear past, especially a well-constructed one, implies a particular future. Not surprisingly then, Romantics heavily employ the terms "natural" and "artificial," implying that some historical acts and events, or even current policies and situations, are unnatural.[11]

Romanticism implied a different spatial ordering for nationalism in Central and Eastern Europe than did the Enlightenment in Western Europe. As the idea of the nation evolved, so did the ideas relating to the spatial extent of a nation's territory. The emphasis placed on language, for example, suggests that nationalists might have defined the national territory on the basis of the spatial distribution of language speakers. However, this was not the case. Language was not as simple and as straightforward an issue as it may seem. First of all, until the rise of Romanticism, language was not thought of as it is today. In particular, language was not considered to be the basis of identity. Thus individuals did not feel as strongly attached to certain languages and were more willing to change their language practices. The educated and privileged, for example, routinely learned and spoke many languages. As a result, some were multilingual while others, although speaking only one language, did not speak the language of their ancestors and felt no qualms about it. In fact, modern standard languages had not been thoroughly in use yet, so language was in constant transition across the landscape.[12] Therefore, language was a very problematic issue for those who wanted to use it as a national determinant.

Romantics were even aware of the fluidity of language and tried to rectify the situation by encouraging individuals to "relearn" their native languages. By doing so, individuals could discover their true national identities. This belief, however, led to other problems: How could individuals identify their proper national languages so that they could learn them, speak them, and thus realize their true national identities? Moreover, if many did not actually speak their true national languages, then how could language be used to map out the spatial distribution of nations? The latter question must be answered before national territories could be mapped out, at least if language was to be used as Romantic philosophy implied. The answer to this question was not easy because it involved an inherent contradiction. Romantics insisted that language was a national determinant, yet many Romantics could not accept that many then must have changed their national identities when they adopted a new language. Instead, Romantics insisted these individuals not speaking their true native languages were oppressed, and could realize their true national identities only when they relearned their native languages. But again, who were these people—these Russified Poles, Belarussians,

Ukrainians, etc., these Germanized Poles, Czechs, Slovenes, etc., these Magyarized Slovaks, Romanians, Croats, etc.? And where did they live?

Language and shared history were not the concrete issues that they seemed to be and, therefore, were not dependable in delimiting the territories of nations though Romantic philosophy implied that they should be used for such a purpose. Romantics, nevertheless, were able to identify members of nations and national territories through the existing imperial-territorial order. Indeed, Romantic philosophers were no more able to reject the existing imperial-territorial order than the Enlightenment thinkers who preceded them. With the rise of Romantic nationalism in Central and Eastern Europe at the beginning of the nineteenth century, the Germans, Austrians, Russians,[13] and even the Hungarians began viewing their imperial states as their new national states. The Germans had more of a problem in this process because they did not have a single imperial state, but many small dynastic states. Nevertheless, the modern Romantic conception was not simply a welding together of German peoples based on the notion of a common German language. Such a description would be an oversimplification of the process. Modern national Germany came about from the welding together of numerous German states (Herb 1997, 8–12), identified to a significant degree by larger territorial configurations.[14]

As imperial territories were being redefined into nation-states, a new emphasis was indeed placed on language as a defining national characteristic, thanks to Romantic philosophy. Consequently, many new group identities emerged, and many peoples in Central and Eastern Europe found themselves to be defined as a new class of minorities. In imperial times these peoples were simply part of the underclass that labored for the imperial leaders. During the period of growing nationalism, however, some joined the ranks of the ruling group while others were viewed as unwanted minorities who increasingly were seen as outsiders and a threat to the ruling nation.

The minority peoples of Central and Eastern Europe were likewise influenced by the ideas of nationalism. Herder, for example, glorified the Slavs in his writings and encouraged them to cultivate their national identities. However, the newly emerging minorities found that the Germans, the Austrians, the Russians, and the Hungarians increasingly were discriminating against them.[15] In many ways, such discrimination only encouraged these minority peoples to develop their own group identities— national identities. The growing sense of nationalism among the minority peoples of Central and Eastern Europe was also spurred on by Napoleon. Napoleon demonstrated the power of nationalism every time his national army defeated an imperialist army. Napoleon's victories were swift and decisive, and every one eroded the legitimacy of the imperialist idea. By 1812, Napoleon had completely redrawn the map of Europe (see Figure 3.2). In addition to success on the battlefield, Napoleon's achievements were partly attributed to his ability to appeal to the national sentiments of peoples within the empires of Central and Eastern Europe. The Poles, the Slovenes, and the Croats were particularly receptive to Napoleon, and in return for their help, Napoleon created states for them.

By 1815, Napoleon was defeated. The victors—the old dynastic forces—obviously were threatened by the ideas of nationalism. They sought to

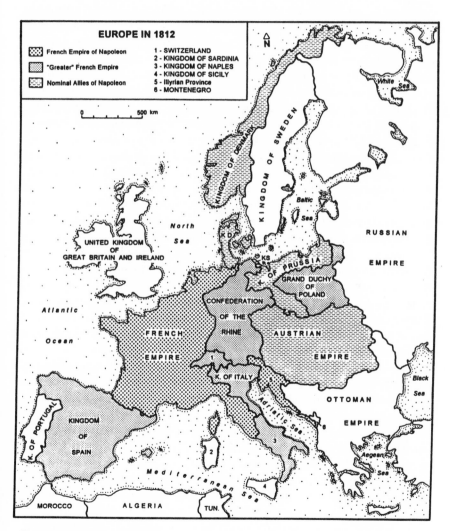

Figure 3.2 Europe in 1812.

extinguish national sentiments completely and reestablish the old imperial order (see Figure 3.3). At first, it seemed that the old dynastic forces
would be successful. However, the seeds of nationalism were sown, even
among the dominant peoples. Napoleon had shown that a national army
could be raised and such a force could defeat an imperial army; such concrete achievements brought into question the legitimacy of Divine Right
Monarchs in the minds of the masses, much more than the abstract
rhetoric of Enlightenment philosophers. Even though the imperialist ideas
reigned supreme again, the nationalist idea continued to smolder, and
even ignited in 1848 with widespread national revolutions throughout
Europe. The imperialist forces were able to put down the revolutions, but
nationalism was on the rise. In fact, European imperial leaders began
manipulating nationalistic sentiments in opposing empires, including the
Ottoman Empire, as a means of extending their own influence and power.
In doing so, imperial leaders found that they often had to foster the creation of nation-states instead of simply annexing territories to their
empires as they desired. Nation-states began to emerge in the Balkans as
the waning Ottoman Empire withdrew from Europe (see Figure 3.4).
Encouraging nationalism abroad only fanned the flames of nationalism
at home, and only further undermined the idea of imperialism. The multiethnic Hapsburg Empire was particularly vulnerable to the centrifugal
forces of nationalism. Eventually, imperial leaders had to manipulate
nationalistic sentiments just to stay in power. In the end, nationalism
became too strong a force to suppress. By 1918, at the end of a disastrous
war, many of the European dynasties were obliterated, and most of the
European empires collapsed; from their ruins, nation-states were created
(see Figure 3.5).

Despite nationalism's rise, imperialism's territorial and bureaucratic structure remained firmly intact throughout the nineteenth century and the early
part of the twentieth century. Thus imperialism was not simply swept aside
by nationalism, but instead became the mold for nationalism to grow
within. This mold was most significant in terms of the conception of territory and how it should be organized. In Western Europe, the imperial states
simply became conceptualized as the new nation-states, with almost no call
for changes in political boundaries. In Central and Eastern Europe, a similar process occurred for the dominant peoples such as the Russians,
Hungarians, and even the Germans and Austrians, although with some
modifications for these latter groups. The minority peoples had a problem,
however, because most of them did not have an existing state to use as the
basis from which a national territory could be defined. However, the
emphasis that Romanticism placed on history allowed these peoples to
reach back into the past, to the "Golden Age" of the nation (see Smith quote,
page 52), and choose the territory of the nation's ancestors. Because the

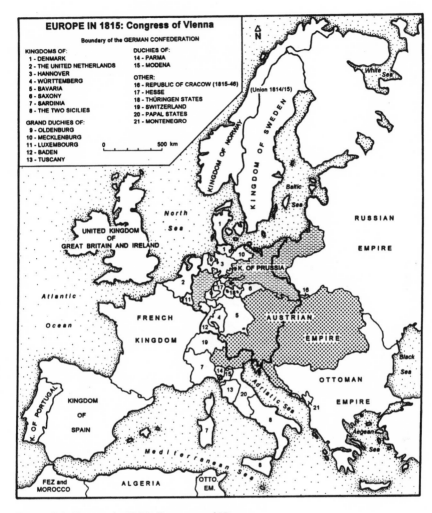

Figure 3.3 Europe in 1815: Congress of Vienna.

ancestors of the past were empire builders, not nation builders, the minority nations of Central and Eastern Europe often chose territories that had little relationship to contemporary ethnic distributions. Nevertheless, reaching back into the past gave East Europeans the ability to do what the West Europeans were doing—redefine an imperial territory as a national territory.[16] Considering that most of Eastern Europe's educated elite received its education in the West, it is no surprise that many Eastern European thinkers would try to emulate Western Europeans. Looking back into the past to a "Golden Age" of a great empire also gave Eastern Europeans parity with

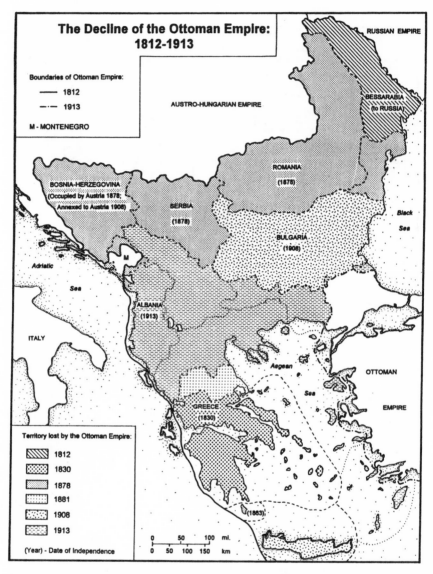

Figure 3.4 The Decline of the Ottoman Empire: 1812–1913. Note that these nation-states were not defined and created by the peoples they were intended for. The nations in question conceptualized their nation-state territories differently and only considered the establishment of political control over these territories as a step in obtaining their rightful territories, a step in achieving full nationhood.

Western Europeans by showing that Eastern Europeans had achieved greatness as well.

Using the imperial territories as the new national territories created two major problems. First, the existing imperial territories and the recreated

Figure 3.5 Territorial Changes after the First World War.

imperial territories overlapped considerably. Consequently, many areas have been hotly contested because they were once part of two different empires. In addition, empires characteristically have boundary zones instead of clearly defined borders. As a result, controversies have arisen concerning the control that a particular imperial government or leader had over certain areas. Second, unlike nation-states, empires are by definition multiethnic. Consequently, many of the nations in Central and Eastern Europe had to deal with having numerous minorities in their newly defined nation-states.

The existence of ethnic minorities became a direct challenge and eventually a threat to the legitimacy of the nation-state and, by extension, to the legitimacy of the nation. Dominant groups had to explain why minorities were present in their territories. Through Romantic revisionism of history, minorities were described as outsiders who migrated into national territories. In some cases, they were said to have been invited in, but they always had to respect the legitimacy of the ruling nation and the integrity of its territory. The ruling nation, therefore, had the right to evict or assimilate minorities as it saw fit.

Such an explanation is actually inaccurate in many cases. Many ethnic minorities are remnant populations of older groups (e.g., Basques, Celts, Serbs) that inhabited an area long before the ancestors of the modern national groups arrived. Nevertheless, in the nineteenth century, ruling nations instituted ever stronger policies of assimilation (e.g. Germanization, Russification, and Magyarization). Minorities reacted by creating secret literary and historical societies to preserve their national culture. Ever stronger actions and reactions only exacerbated poor relations among nations. By the mid-twentieth century, ruling nations were resorting to the practice of forced deportations and annihilation—often called "ethnic cleansing."

Wars, rigid assimilation policies, forced deportations, massacres, the rhetoric of fervent nationalists, historical revisionism, manipulative political leaders, and overlapping territorial claims convolute and even obscure that nations derive their identities from particular places and territories, thus having a strong emotional attachment to them. Consequently, significance of place and territory and emotional attachment to place and territory rarely have been recognized as an integral component of national identity. Instead, the concept of "place" sometimes has been reduced to nothing more than a mere commodity—an object to be bartered (Williams and Smith 1983, 502); consequently, territorial claims are seen as the a result of attempts to procure more resources—natural or strategic. Yet such is not often the case. Nations, like individuals, use place to define their identity. In the cases of Central and Eastern Europe, modern nations choose past imperial territories to define their national identity. Unfortunately, it is not always clear which of these past empires a particular nation is claiming. The Poles, the Czechs, the Bulgarians, just to name a few examples, had many. Moreover, empires typically had unclear boundaries. Individual nationalists then have ample opportunity to offer their personal interpretations of history; personal interpretations of history are influenced not only by an individual's biases and ambitions but also by the context of the individual's own time period.

Structure of the Case Studies

Because historical process is fundamental to the development of any national identity, it is important to understand the history of a nation before its sense of territory can be understood fully. Many of the places significant for a nation are closely tied to historical events. In fact, place and history work hand in hand as places are glorified and even constructed in order to pass on a sense of shared historical experience from generation to generation. Therefore, before beginning immediately with an analysis of the significant places of the three nations in the following chapters, each chapter contains a historical overview of the nation in question. The historical overviews are very brief, even crude by the standards of historians. Nonetheless, they sufficiently establish the proper temporal limits for identifying and discussing the significant places and territories for each nation.

Knowledge of history, even a cursory one, is particularly important for understanding the national identities of Eastern Europeans because their national identities have been strongly influenced by the ideas of Romantic philosophy, which emphasizes particular historical events. Romantic thinkers believe that it is important to write histories that describe a coherent and continuous past, a past that points to an inevitable future. Consequently, the nations of Eastern Europe have written histories for themselves that are not necessarily in agreement with scholarly accounts. However, because the purpose of this book is to understand how nations define themselves, particularly their territories, the historical overviews in the case studies are presented primarily from the perspective of the nations in question.

The process of "writing" histories for a nation shows that nations are not the inevitable product of the past. In fact, nations did not exist before the emergence of modern nationalism at the end of the eighteenth century. Because the nation is not a given throughout history, the territory of a nation is not a given either. National identities and hence national territories form out of the fusion of regional identities and territories. The process is complicated, because regional identities often develop out of local identities, and local identities are composed of familial and individual identities. The fusion of all of these identities with their place components into a clearly defined national identity and territory is not always a harmonious process. Each regional identity, for example, has a different conception of what the national identity should be. Regional relationships can become quite volatile when some regional identities assert their agenda and try to make them the national agenda.

In essence, national identities are created (Anderson 1991); they are not simply there waiting to be "awakened" as Romantic thinkers would argue. Romantic nationalists contribute to the creation of national identities by emphasizing certain common characteristics of the various regional identities that they desire to fuse together. They write—sometimes even fabricate—histories that demonstrate a unified past and emphasize an inevitable common destiny (Hobsbawn, 1983). These "national characteristics and histories," of course, are defined and written by individuals who have a particular notion of what the nation should be. Consequently, the course of national development is very much influenced by the ideas and actions of many individuals. In order to understand the "place" component of a national identity, it is thus not only important to look for important places but also to examine the places that have become significant through the ideas and efforts of particularly prominent nationalist figures. In fact, many of these prominent nationalist figures are identified in the case studies where appropriate.

Once a group has been set in its historical context, the process of delineating a nation's sense of territory proceeds by the application of site identification and landscape description (the first two of the three indicators of a nation's sense of territory). The places identified in conjunction with these indicators were drawn from a survey of sources which identify nationally known works in history, literature, poetry, art, and music. The sources surveyed would normally be considered secondary sources; however, they served as the primary sources for this study. Because this study focuses on the meaning and perceptions of place, the study could not base its results on a survey of original data. Original data do not convey the perceptions of the people who consider them to be meaningful and significant. To decipher and understand perceptions, one has to examine sources written about original data. Thus these sources, which would normally be labeled secondary sources, served as the primary sources for this study. Additionally, because the more influential works of Hungarian, Romanian, and Serbian nationalists have been made available to an English-speaking audience, English-language sources were as useful as those written in the respective native languages. In fact, English-language sources were more useful. First, they more explicitly expressed emotional attachments to place and territory than did the native-language sources. Authors of such sources felt the strong need to unequivocally explain the importance of places and territories to the English-speaking world, which often has been responsible for redrawing boundaries in Central and Eastern Europe. Second, English-language sources serve as a better summary of significant places and territories, filtering out many of the smaller works in the native languages that do not fully represent an entire nation's perceptions. Broader surveys written in English, therefore, were the most useful for a study of this nature. Important places were identified by their continual recurrence in the corpus of work consulted and by their continual recurrence in different contexts. For example, when a place was not only emphasized again and again in works on history but also again and again in other fields, such as literature, poetry, art, and music, then that place was considered significant. Places occurring less frequently, and in fewer contexts, were considered less important.

After the most significant places were noted, maps were constructed showing their locations. The "tenacity factor" (the historical determination of a nation to protect or seize particular places or territories) was then employed to gain a deeper understanding of just how important some of these places are and have been. Included in the tenacity factor was a consideration of past territorial configurations of empires that Romantic nationalists have used to define "appropriate" boundaries of the modern nation-state.

Despite everything that overshadows the strong emotional-psychological bonds that nations develop with places and territories, places and territories are, nevertheless, significant. In fact, they are so significant that they are important components of national identity. The application of the three indicators of a nation's sense of territory (site identification, landscape description, and the "tenacity factor") does much to elucidate this component of national identity as well as spatially delineate a nation's sense of territory. By doing so, this study also yields a deeper understanding of current ethnic and national conflicts in these regions.

Notes

1. For a more detailed discussion on the origins of nationalism, see Anthony D. Smith, "The problem of national identity: ancient, medieval and modern?" *Ethnic and Racial Studies* 17 (July 1994): 375–99.

2. The Prussian case illustrates this point. At the turn of the eighteenth century, foreigners outnumbered middle-class Prussians in the Prussian army (Anderson 1991, 22; Vagts 1959, 64, 85)—hardly a nationalist army as we would conceive of one today.

3. The idea of equality had linguistic implications as well. In Europe, in particular, Enlightenment philosophy could not recognize the special status that Latin, or even Greek and Hebrew, had long enjoyed in the Christian realm up until that point (Anderson 1991, 70–71). All languages were equal.

4. The political landscape that Enlightenment thinkers created, and still in existence today, demonstrates that Enlightenment thinkers venerated Greek social and political philosophy greatly. Examples are readily seen in the United States where many federal government buildings and state capitols have a distinct Greco-Roman architectural style.

5. Benedict Anderson makes a very similar argument in the beginning of his book *Imagined Communities* (Anderson 1991, 2). Anderson, however, goes on to explore the historical dimensions of this process, while this book explores the geographical dimensions.

6. Benedict Anderson argues that territorial framework created by the great European colonial empires defined the states and nations in Latin America, Africa, and Asia: "In considering the origins of recent 'colonial nationalism,' one central similarity with the colonial nationalisms of an earlier age immediately strikes the eye: the isomorphism between each nationalism's territorial stretch and that of the previous imperial administrative unit" (Anderson 1991, 114). This process occurred first in New Spain. As noted earlier, the Spanish-speaking Roman Catholics did not band together to create a new Spanish state but instead banded together with the indigenous peoples in a number of smaller states. The Spanish administrative-territorial units defined the number and areal extent of the new states (Anderson 1991, 52–53), and with them, the new national identities. In other words, individuals transcended, actually ignored, their linguistic and religious similarities and differences and developed national identities with one another based on the shared experiences of living together in the same places and territories.

7. Following the fall of Latin as a favored language, imperial bureaucracies adopted many vernacular languages to promote state loyalty. Ironically, individuals began to identify more strongly with these vernacular languages than they did with their imperial states (Anderson 1991, 42–43, 77–78).

8. The potency of this idea is still with us today and is exemplified with the continued application of the term "natural political boundary" to certain political boundaries. The term "natural" relates to anything created by nature, or God, depending on one's belief system. Because all political boundaries are created by human beings, there are no natural political boundaries, only artificial ones. Some political boundaries do follow natural features, and they appropriately are called physiographic political boundaries. Many nationalists, particularly Romantic nationalists, perpetuate the use of the term "natural political boundary" because it bolsters their arguments. Irish nationalists, for example, argue that the shores of the island of Ireland are the natural political boundaries of the Irish state. By using the term "natural" in this manner, Irish nationalists are claiming that they are conforming to the will of nature and God. Therefore, to disagree with them is to disagree with the laws of nature and God. Certainly no one would want to do that!

9. As further examples, the Hungarians chose the Carpathian Basin (Birinyi 1924, 94–95), the Italians, Spanish, and the Scandinavians chose peninsulas. The Irish chose an island, and so did the British. However, the correlation between nations and physiographic regions was not a simple one. Was Great Britain one island or a chain of islands? Also, the French people did not extend all the way to the Rhine River, or the Hungarians to the ridges of the Carpathian Mountains. And these were the easy cases! In most cases, physiographic regions do not have sharp boundaries. Most are in constant transition. Where, for example, is the natural territory of Germany, Belgium, or China?

10. *Lebensraum* ("Living Space") is a corollary to Organic State Theory, a more commonly known term thanks to the Nazis.

11. Turning to the Irish case again, because Irish nationalists believe that the political boundaries of the Irish state should naturally coincide with the shores of the island of Ireland, then British control over any part of Ireland is (or was), therefore, artificial and unnatural—that is going against the will of nature and God!

12. For a more detailed discussion on this issue, see Eric J. Hobsbawn, *Nations and Nationalism since 1780: Programme, Myth, and Reality* (1990), pages 51–53. Hobsbawn points out for example that "even though in 1789 50% of Frenchmen [sic] did not speak it [French] at all, 12–13% spoke it 'correctly'. . . at the moment of unification [of Italy] (1860) only [2.5%] of the population used the language [Italian] for everyday purposes" (pages 60–61). These two examples, along with others that Hobsbawn discusses, demonstrate that language was not the primordial essence of nationhood.

For the French case, which is often touted as one of the first modern nations, Eugen Weber produced a study in 1976 which showed that most people in rural areas of France did not think of themselves as members of the French nation in 1870 and did not adopt French identity until the First World War (Connor 1994, 220).

13. Benedict Anderson eloquently describes the process for the Russians in the following manner: ". . . stretching the short, tight, skin of the nation over the gigantic body of the empire. 'Russification' of the heterogeneous population of the Czar's subjects thus represented a violent, conscious welding of two opposing political orders, one ancient, one quite new. . . . 'official nationalism' [was a] willed merger of nation and dynastic empire" (1991, 86).

The significance of existing or previously existing territorial configurations is also illustrated in the rise of socialism. Most socialists also conceived of the political-territorial order of the world in terms of the imperialist order (Anderson 1991, 108). In contrast to the Austrian socialists, the Bolsheviks of Russia were more successful in reestablishing the boundaries of the Czarist empire for the new Communist state (Schöpflin 1991, 7).

14. The German case excellently illustrates the power that previous territorial configurations hold in people's minds. In the early years of German nationalism, German nationalists defined the German national state in terms of the German Confederation and even spoke of the Holy Roman Empire (Alter 1994, 74–77; Seton-Watson 1977, 94–97). In fact, the very name of the modern German national state—the Second German Empire—demonstrates the power of previous territorial configurations. Although the state came about as a result of the emergence of nationalism, the state was called an empire; indeed, it had many imperial characteristics. The word *empire*, however, not only illustrated the persistence of imperialist thinking, it gave legitimacy to the new state by claiming to be the reincarnation of the Holy Roman Empire, which itself derived legitimacy from an earlier territorial configuration—the Roman Empire. Terms such as Kaiser, which was a reincarnation of the term Caesar, serve as further illustrations. Thus legitimacy was found in previous territorial configurations, not just the German people, despite the new nationalist idea. The Nazis also legitimized themselves by crafting a name for their state—The Third Reich (meaning the Third German Empire)—based on prior territorial configurations. Such a name was chosen despite all of the nationalist fervor and rhetoric of Nazism.

15. Benedict Anderson argues in the Austrian and Russian cases, however, that nationalism emerged among the minority peoples before it did among the dominant ones (Anderson 1991, 84–88). In these cases then, the minority peoples developed a new sense of alienation towards their empires before they were persecuted for not being members of the dominant groups. Nevertheless, even though the Austrians and Russians were late in developing national consciousness, they

implemented nationalist policies against their minorities as voraciously as the other dominant groups of Europe.

16. On the surface, the minority peoples of Central and Eastern Europe seemed to be challenging the imperial order by their attempts to carve nation-states out of the existing empires. This challenge was nonexistent from the perspective that they defined their national territories on the basis of previously existing empires.

4

Hungary and the Hungarians

Culturally the Hungarians are differentiated from their fellow Europeans by some noteworthy Asiatic characteristics, such as their language, which is Ural-Altaic instead of Indo-European. Because Hungarian (Magyar) is so different from the languages around it, it would be very tempting to try to argue that the Hungarian nation is an outgrowth of the Hungarian language, especially because Hungarians show an intense pride in their language and its uniqueness. Such an argument, however, can be made only by projecting the present back into the past and rewriting history. Romantics, of course, insist that language is the primordial essence of nationhood and, therefore, try to argue that the Hungarian nation was born of the Hungarian language. Fortunately for them, rewriting the past is a particular talent they possess, and they have employed it quite readily to show, or at least imply, that the genesis of the Hungarian nation lies in the Hungarian language.

To support their belief, Romantics like to point out that the Hungarian nobility staunchly opposed the introduction of German as the official language within the Hapsburg realm by Joseph II in the 1780s. Unfortunately, they cut the story short here, allowing it to be assumed that the upper echelons of Hungarian society were too proud of Magyar to allow it to be swept aside by the German language. The facts, however, paint a much different picture, particularly because "the high [Hungarian] aristocracy, acclimatized to the court in Vienna, spoke alternately French or German, diluted with some Spanish or Italian and, later, English. The lesser nobility or, precisely, the men of middle-nobility, the office holders in the counties and the like, conversed in dog-Latin strewn with Magyar, but also with Slovak, Serb, and Romanian expressions and vernacular German" (Ignotus 1972, 45).[1] It also should be noted that the Hungarian ruling classes defended Latin as the state language and did not attempt to make Magyar the official language of the Hungarian Kingdom until 1844 (Ignotus 1972, 48).[2] Because of these two facts, other reasons must have underlain the position of the Hungarian ruling classes in regard to Magyar. It is more likely that Hungarian leaders feared that the Germanization policies would marginalize their authority in the Hapsburg monarchy (Anderson 1991, 102);[3] this explains why they initially defended Latin. However, with the rise of Romanticism and its emphasis on native languages, Magyar became popular in the land where only a third of the inhabitants spoke the language (Ignotus 1972, 46). The growing popularity of Magyar, however, soon gained the attention of Hungary's nobility, who concluded that they could use Magyar as a political tool to secure their authority. Indeed, they may have even had the opportunity to use Magyar to free the Hungarian Kingdom from Hapsburg rule.[4] All they had to do was learn Magyar and identify with it the way the peasants were beginning to do so.[5] They then could portray themselves as the true leaders of the Hungarian people and thus wean the peasantry away from the Hapsburgs to create their own independent state where they could exercise full sovereign authority.

The situation of Magyar as the language of the Hungarians shows that Hungarian national identity emerged prior to the widespread use of the language. Therefore, Magyar was not a national determinant, and furthermore could not reliably be mapped to delimit the appropriate boundaries of the Hungarian national state. If language mapping was not dependable, then what defined the areal extent of the Hungarian national state? For the Hungarians, the answer was quite simple. It was the Kingdom of Hungary, a relatively stable state in terms of boundaries over the previous thousand years. Of course, the Kingdom of Hungary was not a national state, indicated by its very name, but a dynastic one. Hungary's leaders did not derive their legitimacy from some sense that they were Hungarian, and they were not concerned about the multiethnic character of their subjects, only their loyalty. Witness the total lack of Magyarization policies and that many Hungarians did not even bother to speak Magyar until the mid-nineteenth century, well after the rise of Romantic nationalism.

When Hungarian national identity was in its infancy in the eighteenth century, it grafted itself onto, indeed defined itself in terms of, the Hungarian Kingdom—an entity of enduring quality. The Hungarian Kingdom was a territorial configuration that had long served as a framework for understanding the world, the stage on which a particular social, economic, and political order played out. It had become so firmly ingrained within the minds of its inhabitants that it was not possible for most of them to conceive of their lives in the context of a different territorial ordering. The meaning of the imperial territorial order was rooted so deeply that the contradiction of defining the Hungarian nation in terms of dynastic-imperialist understanding of territory was not even recognized. Without qualms, the Hungarian nation defined itself in terms of the Hungarian Kingdom and took for itself the history of this territorial entity. Historical figures and events of this territorial configuration were recast as the figures and events in the history of the Hungarian people. This reformulation of history and identity was confirmed not only in the tangible existence of the territory as a whole but in the local places associated with these individual figures and events that became significant to the nation.

The purpose of this chapter is to map out the Hungarian Kingdom and all the significant places within it that define Hungarian national identity. Site identification and landscape description are employed to bring these places to light. Because dozens of places exist, they are presented in regional groupings for the sake of clarity, and even regrouped more broadly into a core, semi-core, and periphery categorization. The depth of their importance is revealed by the application of the tenacity factor, which is presented as the latter part of each of the broader classification presentations (i.e., that of the core, semi-core, and periphery). Because modern Hungarian national identity is only about two hundred years old, the tenacity factor is applied to only the last two centuries. Of course, peoples fought over territory through history. However, because identity existed in a different context prior to the late eighteenth century, the meaning of place and territory was likewise much different as well. It would be anachronistic to apply the tenacity factor to such struggles as if they were nationalist ones, even though Romantic nationalists do so as a matter of habit.

That the tenacity factor cannot be applied much earlier than the end of the eighteenth century does not mean that the course of events before this time is insignificant. On the contrary, in terms of site identification and landscape description, many places highlighted are associated with figures and events of much earlier periods. It always must be remembered, however, that places are brought to light not for the significance of their time but for their importance to the modern Hungarian nation. In fact, many of the places identified became memorialized with monuments, shrines, and the such only since the rise of nationalism, some only in the last few years even though they signify an event that may have taken place a thousand years ago. Therefore, all places and territories are identified in terms of their current significance, even though many represent something much older.

Because Hungarian national identity contains within it many Romantic elements, history cannot be ignored. On the contrary, the Hungarian nation has developed emotional-psychological bonds to a long list of places that it now considers to be historically significant. An understanding of Hungarian history facilitates an appreciation of Hungarian sense of territory. Therefore, while the purpose of this book is not to retell Hungarian history, it is, nevertheless, necessary to make a few notations of history, no matter how crude and generalized, in order to set the territorial component of Hungarian national identity in its proper context.

Brief Overview of Hungarian History

In 1996, the Hungarian nation celebrated the eleven-hundredth anniversary of the founding of the Hungarian Kingdom. The anniversary was marked by a series of festivals, exhibitions, and other programs that took place around the current Hungarian state over the course of the year. The nature and magnitude of the celebrations summarize the historical and geographical dimensions of Hungarian national identity quite succinctly.[6] Indeed, essentially all the places and territories that are significant to the Hungarian nation fall both within the boundaries of the Hungarian Kingdom and within an eleven-hundred-year time frame.

The early years of the kingdom centered on the loose confederation of nomadic warriors who swept in from the east in the ninth century. The nomads generally were known as Magyars but probably had others (e.g., Kabars) in their ranks as well (Ignotus 1972, 22). Indeed, even though Hungarians trace their lineage through the Magyars, earlier nomadic groups (e.g., Huns, Avars, Khazars) who settled in the Carpathian Basin often get caught up and incorporated within Hungarian genealogy.[7] The settling of these nomadic peoples and their subsequent consolidation of power over the Carpathian Basin was a process that took time. No single date is clearly identifiable as a watershed moment, and quite frankly most Hungarians throughout history had not considered a founding date to be of any significance. However, when modern Hungarian nationalism began exerting itself forcefully at the end of the nineteenth century, the idea of a founding date suddenly became significant. Subsequently, the year 896 was chosen.[8]

In the centuries that followed the founding of the Hungarian Kingdom in the ninth century, Hungary's leaders consolidated their power over their new territory and even exerted control beyond its boundaries. The "golden age" of the Hungarian Kingdom came to an abrupt end following a disastrous defeat by Ottoman armies in 1526. Ceasing to exist as a single territorial unit, the central part of the kingdom was integrated into the Ottoman Empire, the western and northern portions became domains of the Hapsburgs, and Transylvania pursued a path of quasi-independence—usually under Ottoman suzerainty (see Figure 4.1). The division of the Hungarian Kingdom following the Ottoman invasion had a tremendous impact on how Hungarian sense of territory later developed in the context of nationalism. The division and occupation forced Hungarian leaders and intellectuals to flee to the fringes of their kingdom. As a result, many of Hungary's great institutions were also transferred to the fringes of the kingdom. As the modern era unfolded, many new institutions were founded on the edges of the kingdom's territories as well. Subsequently, these territories became very significant. Despite such significance, however, conflict emerged in the era of nationalism when many of the inhabitants of these important territories did not develop a Hungarian national identity.

At the end of the seventeenth century, the Ottomans were driven out of the kingdom's territory with Hapsburg aid, only to have the entire kingdom incorporated within the Hapsburg monarchy. With the rise of Hungarian nationalism, which first manifested rudiments of its own existence at the end of the eighteenth century, Hungarians eventually developed the desire to free their kingdom from the Hapsburgs. In the ensuing decades a struggle for independence began. Military campaigns in 1848–49 resulted in defeat; however, on the political front, Hungary's leaders were eventually able to gain some autonomy for the kingdom with the Compromise of 1867. The compromise turned the Hapsburg Monarchy into a dual monarchy, which also became known as the Austro-Hungarian Empire.

Hungary's leaders continued to press for full sovereignty but failed to gain it by the outbreak of the First World War. For Hungary's political association with Austria, the Hungarians found themselves on the side of the defeated at the conclusion of the war. In terms of territory, the Hungarians were dealt the severest punishment of all the defeated. Two-thirds of the Hungarian Kingdom was stripped away and awarded to the victors. This action dealt a psychologically devastating blow to the Hungarian nation. In the years that followed, Hungarians supported leaders—from communists to fascists—who promised to restore the territorial integrity of the kingdom, but no one was able to implement any actions with lasting effect. The imposition of Soviet control after the Second World War suppressed even attempts to change the situation. Hungary and the Hungarians were freed from Soviet domination in the 1990s, but no irredentist policies have been pursued. Yet the Kingdom of Hungary and its full territory remain at the root of Hungarian national identity, illustrated by the celebration of its eleven hundredth anniversary in 1996 and an endless stream of new maps and images of the Kingdom that appear frequently throughout the country in private and public places alike.

This whirlwind review of history is very crude, but sufficient to set the stage for understanding the territorial component of Hungarian national identity.

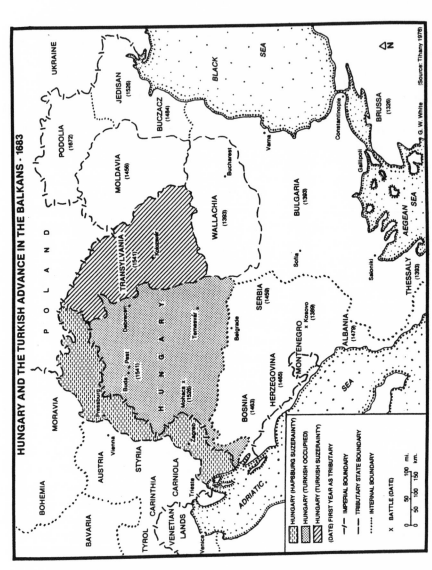

Figure 4.1 Hungary and the Turkish Advance in the Balkans—1683.

Places and Territories Significant to Hungarian National Identity

The three indicators of a nation's sense of territory (site identification, landscape description, and the tenacity factor) show that Hungarian national identity is tied to a number of places throughout the Carpathian Basin (see Figure 4.2). The varied locations of these significant places and the roles that they have played through history have facilitated the perception among many Hungarians that their territory is a natural, integrated, physiographic unit. Before discussing any of the individual regions and the specific places within them, we must understand the nature of this "integrated" Hungarian territory which Hungarians call Historic Hungary—formerly known as the Kingdom of Hungary. With this foundation, we can then examine the component regions of Hungarian territoriality by dividing them into a core, semi-core, and periphery. The core includes Transdanubia, southern Slovakia and southwestern Ruthenia, the Great Alföld, and Transylvania; the semi-core encompasses Burgenland, Muravidék, and Muraköz, northern Slovakia and northeastern Ruthenia, and Bácska and Bánság; the periphery consists of Croatia, Bosnia, Bukovina, and a number of other places in East Central Europe and the Balkans.

Treating Hungary as a series of discrete regions that neatly fit into a core, semi-core, and periphery is a difficult proposition. Over time, some regions have been divided politically, and consequently the divided parts have evolved differently in their degree of significance. For example, Burgenland, Muravidék, and Muraköz were integrated areas of Transdanubia; Bácska and Bánság were part of the Great Alföld; and Slovakia and Ruthenia were simply considered to be Upper Hungary before the end of the First World War. Separation has resulted in differing perceptions and degrees of emotional attachment to these newer territories and other such territories that have been divided over time.

The identification of places significant to Hungarian national identity is accomplished by looking at the locations of important cultural and political institutions and by examining music and art inspired by nationalist sentiments. In contrast to the Romanians and the Serbs, Hungarians have exercised a greater amount of control over their territory through history. As a result, Hungarians have created a number of cultural and political institutions over time; these institutions include the seats of government, colleges and universities, printing houses, ecclesiastical centers, etc. The locations of these institutions are very important. Specifically, the buildings of these institutions stand as monuments, elements in the landscape, that testify not only to the greatness of the Hungarian nation but also to the legitimacy of Hungarian national identity. In addition to important institutions, music and art illustrate Hungarian sense of territory and

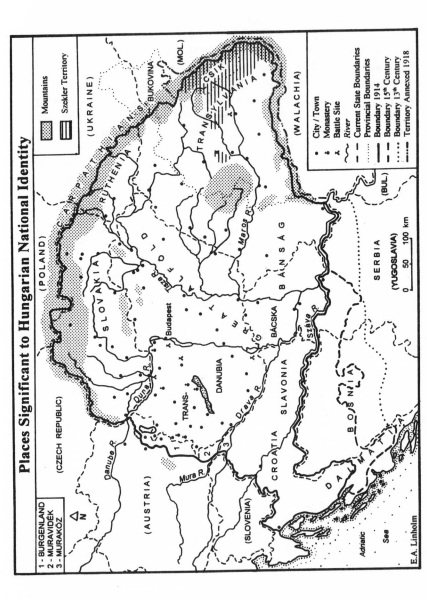

Figure 4.2 Places Significant to Hungarian National Identity.

hence modern Hungarian national identity. Therefore, music and art are examined to identify many of the other kinds of places that are important to modern Hungarian national identity.

Historic Hungary

> Peaks of high Carpathian hills
>   Thou didst give our sires;
> Sons of Bendeguz receiv'd
>   Thus their fair hearth-fires
> Where the waves of Tisza glide,
>   Where the Danube rages,
> Valiant seed of Árpád grew,
>   Flourished through the ages.
>   (*Hymnuz* [Hungarian National Anthem] by Ferenc Kölcsey;
>   quoted from Kirkconnell 1947, 26)

> O Magyar, by thy native land
> With faithful heart abide!
> Thy cradle first, thy grave at last,
> It nurs'd thee, and shall hide.

> For thee the spacious world affords
> As home no other spot,
> Here must thou live and must die,
> Be weal or woe thy lot.

> Upon this soil thy father's blood
> Flow'd to redeem thy claims,
> Upon this ten centuries
> Engrave immortal names.

> Here struggled Árpád's gallant crew
> To win our fatherland,
> And here the yoke of slavery
> Was snapt by Hunyad's hand.

> Here freedom's banner, dyed with blood,
> Shone proudly from afar,
> Here fell the braves of our brave
> In long protracted war.

> It cannot be that all in vain
> Have countless tears been shed;
> Or vainly for the fatherland
> Unnumbered hearts have bled.

O Magyar, for thy country play
A firm and faithful part;
She gives thee strength, and if thou fall
She hides thee in her heart.

The spacious world doth offer thee
For home no other spot;
Here must thou live, and here must die,
Be weal or woe thy lot.
    (*Szózat [Appeal]* [1836] by Mihály Vörösmarty;
    quoted from The Eighty Club 1907, 412)

The idea that political units should be coterminous with natural regions clearly expressed itself in the attitude that Hungarians held in regard to the Hungarian Kingdom. Hungarians believed that their kingdom was a natural integrated, physical-political unit, and this belief was expressed often in writing:

From the end of the 9th century to 1920, the Carpathian Ranges, which are in an arc, were the natural border of Hungary for a distance of over 1,000 miles. With few exceptions, all the rivers on the southern and western side of the Carpathians run into the Danube or Tisza, the two main rivers of the Great Plain. All the valleys, waterways, roads, or rails lead there. This closed-in territory has determined the creation of a unified state. The Carpathian Basin was called by the French Geographer, Himly, as "the Magyar System."
    For thousands of years, the mountains' natural products, timber and minerals were exchanged for the products of the Hungarian Plain: wheat, foods and fruits. The economical unity of the Carpathian Basin is much emphasized by geographers, since the products of the different regions supplement one another. (Konnyu 1971, 9)

The *naturalness* of the Hungarian Kingdom was the main defense that Hungarian diplomats used after the First World War to prevent the Allied powers from dismantling their country.[9] The naturalness defense is illustrated poignantly by a statement sent to the American Peace Delegation in Paris by an American professor named Archibald Coolidge while he was on a diplomatic mission in Hungary after the First World War (Deák 1972, 363). Coolidge wrote that the Hungarians:

Point to the historic unity of their state, and say that it could never have been preserved through all the ups and downs of its history of a thousand years, despite the variety of nationalities that have lived in it, if its continuity had not been in the nature of things in obedience to geographic law.

This belief did not simply derive from an understanding of laws of spatial interaction. Its roots were much deeper and clearly a product of Organic State Theory. The Kingdom of Hungary was seen as a living organism, even created by God:

> Hence, the various sections of the country are interdependent. Separately they cannot exist; while together they form a self-supporting organism. It would seem that the Creator had purposely intended the territory of Hungary [i.e. the Kingdom of] to be one inseparable geographical and organic unit. It would therefore, appear nothing less than a desecration and sacrilege to attempt to cut apart and tear asunder this beautiful creation of God. (Birinyi 1924, 94–95)

Most of the best illustrations of the Hungarian belief in the territorial integrity of the Kingdom of Hungary come from the 1920s, the period immediately following the partition of the country and the creation of the current state territory. An irredentist movement arose and adopted the slogan "No, No, Never" (Bauler 1923, 7). The slogan was typically written across maps of the Kingdom of Hungary, usually depicted as being brutally ripped apart (Lázár 1996a, 112). The organic unity is shown in many illustrations produced by the irredentists. A particularly noteworthy illustration is one that shows the Hungarian Kingdom as a tree (Bauler 1923, 29). The trunk and the branches of the tree are the rivers of the Hungarian Kingdom: the Danube, Tisza, Drava, Sava, Vág, Nyitra, Garam, Körös, Maros, etc. A caterpillar symbolizing the Italians is shown attacking a flower representing Fiume; another caterpillar symbolizing the Serbs is shown attacking Temesvár, while a third symbolizing Romania is shown approaching Kolozsvár and Brassó; birds hovering over and attacking the top of the tree represent Czechs and Slovaks. A number of illustrations produced by the irredentists also underscore the close bond that Hungarians have with their *place*. One particularly interesting postcard shows a Hungarian clutching the Hungarian Kingdom close to his chest while he tries to fend off four birds of prey that represent Italy, Yugoslavia, Romania, and Czechoslovakia (Bauler 1923, 34). One of the best examples of the close, inextricable bond that people develop with a place is an illustration that shows the territory of the Hungarian Kingdom being crucified on a Christian cross (Bauler 1923, 39: Légrády Brothers 1930, 2).

These examples come from the period immediately following the dismantling of the Hungarian Kingdom, a time of national distress. However, the power of the Hungarian Kingdom has not lost its potency. Since the fall of Communism, Hungarians have more of an opportunity to express themselves openly. Subsequently, maps and illustrations of the Hungarian Kingdom have appeared all over Hungary. One work in particular is noteworthy for its depictions. It has two maps and one illustration. One map shows the physical features of the kingdom, emphasizing its natural unity. The other map shows the historic counties, the ones with which Hungarians have identified on a more local level. Across the top is an illustration with multiple figures. In the center is an angel, possibly the archangel Gabriel himself, who is seen as having delivered the message from God many centuries ago that God had designated the Hungarian Kingdom as the rightful homeland of the Hungarians. The angel is holding the scales of justice with a small map of the Hungarian Kingdom on one side and paper representing the Treaty of Trianon on the other.[10] The scale is tipped strongly in favor of the Kingdom of Hungary, obviously meaning that the will of God outweighs the desires of humans.

From this overall perspective of the Hungarian Kingdom, we can now turn to its parts: its individual places and territories.

The Core: Site Identification and Landscape Description

The core area of modern Hungarian national identity is centered on four regions: Transdanubia, southern Slovakia and southwestern Ruthenia, the Great Alföld, and Transylvania. Politically and culturally, all four regions have shared in the molding of modern Hungarian national identity, though not to the same degree.

Transdanubia (Dunatúl)

Transdanubia *(Dunatúl)*, the former Roman province of Pannonia, is the region that lies south and west of the Danube River and north of the Drava River (see Figures 4.2 and 4.3). Transdanubia is important because it contains many of the historic capitals of Hungary. These places testify not only to the long and coherent history of Hungary, but also to the greatness of the Hungarian people and the legitimacy of Historic Hungary. The oldest of these capitals are Székesfehérvár (formerly Alba Regia) and Esztergom (Erdei 1968, 182). István (Stephen) I made Székesfehérvár his capital, and it remained an important political center where many Hungarian kings were crowned and buried until the sixteenth century when the Ottoman threat arose (Dercsényi 1969, 31). István, however, was born in Esztergom and had himself crowned king there in the year 1000. Little remains in Székesfehérvár today, but Esztergom is still an important city. Its archbishopric dates back to 1189. Although many of Hungary's great institutions were moved from the city during the Ottoman period, many of these institutions moved back in the nineteenth century. Esztergom continues to be a major religious center for Hungarians today. The great cathedral, built between 1822 and 1860 and modeled after Saint Peter's in Rome, provides a tangible element in the landscape that

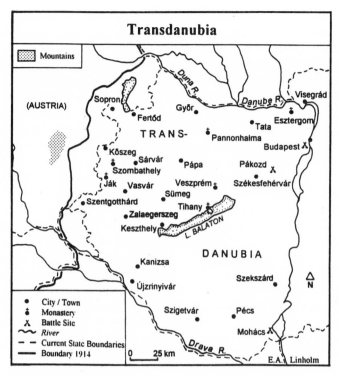

Figure 4.3 Transdanubia.

testifies to the cultural link that Hungarians believe they have with West European civilization. Another early capital of Hungary is Visegrád. The importance of Visegrád to modern Hungarian national identity is underscored by its being one of the first places to be restored during the modern restoration movement (Erdei 1968, 167). It is noteworthy that the modern restoration took place in the nineteenth century, approximately coinciding with the rise of Romantic nationalism. In other words, many historical sites fell into disrepair because they were meaningless to the people around them. With the rise of Romantic nationalism, however, the past became meaningful to people's identity. Thus restoration of landscapes of history increased as nationalism developed. Indeed, landscapes needed to be *restored*, that is landscapes of nationalism needed to be created or recreated, for individuals to develop a sense of Hungarian national identity.

Budapest, the modern capital of Hungary, is understandably the best known of Hungary's cities. The cultural, economic, and political roles that it has played and continues to play unquestionably make the city a significant place. Budapest also contributes greatly to the core status of

Transdanubia. Lying on the west bank of the Danube River, the old town of Buda historically served as the political center of Hungary. Buda Castle is a prominent feature in the city and contains many historical features in its landscape. Among these features, Mátyás (Matthias) Church served as the coronation church for many of Hungary's kings. As an important symbol of Hungarian power and prestige, the Mátyás Church was also restored during the early restoration movement (Erdei 1968, 69, 167). Located across the river in Pest is the Parliament building with its grandiose architectural design, making the structure a prominent feature in the city's landscape and a powerful symbol of Hungarian democratic convictions. Impressive also is the Basilica of St. Stephen (Wiebenson and Sisa 1998, 188), which is also significant because contains the hand of St. Stephen. A number of bridges currently link Buda with Pest; however, the first one, the Chain Bridge, is the most noteworthy (Sisa 1990, 137). When it was built, the bridge was considered to be a monumental accomplishment, not just in Hungary but by world engineering standards (Erdei 1968, 911). In fact, all three elements in Budapest's landscape—Buda Castle, the Parliament building, and the Chain Bridge—all situated along one of Europe's greatest rivers and all of which can be viewed together, testify to the greatness of the Hungarian nation. Added to this, of course, is the aesthetic value of Budapest's cityscape, which is ingrained in the psyches of Hungarians and can be found nowhere else.

One of the most notable features in Budapest's landscape is the Millennium Monument, located on Heroes' Square. It was constructed in 1896 to celebrate the thousand-year anniversary of the Hungarian Kingdom. In a semicircle on the perimeter are statues of great Hungarian leaders. Statues of the great Magyar horsemen stand at the monument's center. A column rises from the center of the Magyar horsemen and dominates the square. On the column is a statue of the archangel Gabriel, who symbolizes God's blessing of the Hungarian Kingdom. The Millennium Monument is a classic example of how the cultural landscape is used to inculcate a particular sense of history into the minds of the individual members of a nation. In simple terms, the monument and all of its individual elements continually remind individuals of all the significant figures, events, and struggles in Hungarian history. The monument, however, is not just a reminder, but a teacher, for both parents and their children alike. Some parents use the monument to teach their children about Hungarian history, values, and beliefs. Others who do not intend to use the monument for such purpose find, however, that they cannot ignore the structure. The monument is a dominating feature in the city's landscape and must be passed through even to reach the city park. When parents take their children to the city park, they find that they are queried about the meaning of the place. As parents struggle to answer their children's questions, they find that they likewise give themselves a refresher in Hungarian history and culture.[11]

Behind the Millennium Monument is the agricultural museum, also constructed for the millennium celebration. A prominent section of the building's facade is a reproduction of Vajdahunyad Castle (Sisa 1990, 176; Wiebenson and Sisa 1998, 225), the home of one of Hungary's greatest leaders—János Hunyadi, who successfully fought against the Ottomans, considered to be a menace by many Europeans. The replica of Vajdahunyad Castle underscores the determination that Hungarians had to overcome what they saw as a threat to world civilization, and their eventual success in so doing. Because the original Vajdahunyad Castle is in southern Transylvania, the replica in Budapest helps to reinforce and cultivate the emotional bond that many Hungarians have with Transylvania by serving as a reminder of just how important a role Transylvania has played in the preservation of Hungarian civilization.

In addition to the capitals, two other places are clearly part of Hungary's core territory because they are associated with the advanced character of Hungarian civilization in early times: Ják (Sisa 1990, 330) and Pannonhalma. Both towns are known for their Benedictine abbeys, but Pannonhalma is also known for its library, which dates back to the eleventh century, the oldest in Hungary (Dercsényi 1969, at end; Erdei 1968, 99, 587). In fact, national celebrations were held in 1996 to honor the millennium anniversary of Pannonhalma. In conjunction with the historic capitals, these abbeys serve as tangible elements in the landscape that testify to the long and continuous history of the Hungarian people.

Pécs is another important political-cultural center of Transdanubia. The location of some of Hungary's oldest and most influential religious and educational institutions, Pécs not only is significant to Hungarian sense of place but contributes greatly to the core status of Transdanubia. István I made Pécs an archbishopric in 1009. The immense four-towered cathedral, restored between 1888 and 1891, is a famous landmark (Hootz and Genthon 1974, 220) and very much in the psyches of Hungarians. Pécs is also the location of Hungary's first university, founded in 1367 by Louis I. Hungarian scholars at Pécs' university were the ones who expressed the belief that the Huns and Magyars were closely related; it later turned out that they were mistaken (Hanák 1988, 45). While the university continued for some time, it was closed by the Ottomans during their rule. Nevertheless, after the Ottomans were driven out of Hungary, Pécs regained much of its influence and status and is seen as one of Hungary's great cities.

Just to the southeast of Pécs, not far from the Danube, is Mohács. The Battle of Mohács in 1526, which resulted in a great Ottoman victory, marked the end of Hungarian supremacy in Central and southeastern Europe. Viewed as a national tragedy and as an explanation of why the Hungarian nation is not currently one of the great nations of the world, the battle and the battle site receive great emphasis in Hungarian history, literature, and poetry:

> Sighing I greet thee and mourn thee, thou meadow of burial, Mohács—
> Grave of our national life, redden'd with blood of the brave!
> . . .
> Over the battlefield, musing, the serious traveler trudges,
> Brooding on the human distress, struck by the blindness of fate.
> Pausing he gazes and sighs, and goes onward with eyes of dejection;
> Wounds that are centuries old open again in his heart.
> There where the mists of the twilight are shed on the marsh and the river,
> Cloaking their green from our sight, shrouding their gloom from our eyes,
> Yonder fought Louis, ill-fated, a monarch of ghastly ill-fortune,
> Yonder his battle-horse plung'd, stumbling all arm'd in the fen.
> . . .
> Many a virgin died slowly in lustful embraces of tyrants,
> Many a prisoner sank, deep in the Danube's dark stream!
> Nothing was ours any more, with our home in the hands of the stranger,
> Only the crescent was flown, flaunting from tower and wall—
> . . .
> Magyars yet live; Buda stands, and the pangs of the past are a lesson;
> Burning with patriot zeal, forwards our vision is turn'd,
> Yet do thou bloom, field of sorrow! May peace brood at last on thy bosom,
> Grave of our national life, Mohács, the tomb of our past!
> (From *Mohács* by Károlyi Kisfaludy;
> quoted from Kirkconnell 1947, 15–19)

Many places in Transdanubia illustrate the core status of Transdanubia by the role that they played during the threat of Ottoman power. These places testify to the valiant struggle of the Hungarians against the Ottomans. They also are seen as the physical refuge of the Hungarians. As a result, these places are closely associated with the survival of the Hungarian people. Buda, Fehérvár (now Székesfehérvár), Szekszárd, and Szigetvár were the places of the earliest struggles. Szigetvár in particular is known as one of earliest places of stiff resistance. Miklós Zrinyi was able to halt the Ottoman advance in 1566 when he refused to surrender Szigetvár (Sisa 1990, 94). After a prolonged siege, the castle was finally set afire. Zrinyi and his troops hurled themselves at the Ottoman forces rather than surrender. Through the efforts of Zrinyi's grandson, who wrote the epic poem *The Disaster at Sziget*, the memory of this event survived long enough to become a national tragedy for modern Hungarians. The event has subsequently been immortalized in a painting (Lázár 1996a, 69) as well; a museum in the castle depicts the heroic actions of the event.

By the beginning of the seventeenth century, the Ottoman advance had been brought to almost a standstill as the Hungarians were able to establish a defensive line that ran from Kanizsa in the southeast along a line that ran northeast through Lake Balaton to a point on the Danube River between Győr and Esztergom. This line of defense was known as the *Végvárak* or "frontierland" (Czigány 1984, 546). With the establishment of the defensive line, many places behind the line grew in importance: Győr, Kőszeg, Pápa, Sárvár, Sümeg, Szombathely, Tata, Újzrinyivár ("New Zrinyi Castle"), Veszprém, and Zalaegerszeg. Kőszeg was actually the scene of one the earliest Ottoman attacks on Hungary (Sisa 1990, 84). The repelling of the attack is seen as an heroic act (Hanák 1988, 49). Szentgotthárd is known for a decisive military victory over the Ottomans in 1664, and Vasvár is known for the subsequent treaty that was signed with the Ottomans in the same year (Erdei 1968, 222). All of these great fortresses are places that have come to illustrate and testify to the great sacrifices that Hungarians have made over time in Transdanubia to preserve and protect Western civilization. They thus inextricably link Transdanubia with Hungarian national identity.

In addition to the places associated with the Hungarian struggles against the Ottomans, places exist that demonstrate the added burden that Hungarians had in preserving their uniqueness and right of "self-determination" in the face of other hostile forces. For example, in the Revolution of 1848, the first battle took place at Pákozd and resulted in a victory for the Hungarians. The battle, as well as others that took place in Transdanubia, is immortalized in a number of paintings (Deák 1979, between pages 168 and 169).

Many of these places just mentioned, however, did not simply serve in a military capacity but were cultural centers as well. Sopron has been the most diverse and persistent cultural center over time, but Veszprém and Szombathely have long been great religious centers, underscored by their great cathedrals. The Protestant college in Pápa made the town an educational center. Many cathedrals, palaces, and museums are located in Győr. Győr also contains many of the treasures of one of Hungary's great kings, King Ladislas (1040–95) (Konnyu 1971, 48). Sárvár had a printing press as early as 1537 and printed the first book in Hungarian in 1541 (Hanák 1988, 54). All of these places contribute to the writing of a

Hungarian history that shows centuries of achievement, even in the face of the Ottoman menace.

Some of these places have been important in modern times as well. Sopron is known as "Hungary's most loyal city" (Légrády Brothers 1930, 103). It is the only place in Historic Hungary where a plebiscite was held after the First World War. The city earned its title when its inhabitants expressed their desire to be included in the Hungarian state rather than be annexed to Austria. Fertőd (formerly Eszterháza) is the site of the Esterházy Palace, built by a famous Hungarian family of the same name (Gates-Coon 1994, 147–50; Sisa 1990, 222, 296). Joseph Haydn, one of the few great European composers who lived and worked in Hungary, produced much of his work in this palace. Currently many concerts are held there in his honor (Hanák 1988, 247). The concerts held in honor of Haydn in Esterházy Palace help to establish and affirm the Hungarian belief that Hungarians are a part of West European civilization.

Lake Balaton and the places around it are also important. Tihany, on a peninsula of the lake, is known for its abbey, the oldest in Hungary. The museum in it contains the first document written in Hungarian (Erdei 1968, 616). Keszthely is known for its agricultural institute, which dates back to 1797, the first one in Europe (Hanák 1988, 100, 196). The first institute of its kind in Europe, it serves as a place that indicates to Hungarians that they are just as accomplished as the great nations of Western Europe.

Southern Slovakia and Southwestern Ruthenia (Felvidék and Kárpátalja)

In Historic Hungary, Slovakia and Ruthenia generally are known as Upper Hungary *(Felvidék)*; Ruthenia *(Kárpátalja)* became differentiated as a subregion of Upper Hungary during the time of the Second World War. Although not formerly divided into northern and southern regions, only the southern areas are significant enough to be considered part of the core territories of Hungarian national identity (see Figures 4.2 and 4.4). Southern Slovakia and southwestern Ruthenia have core status because they played decisive roles in Hungarian history. When the Ottoman armies penetrated Hungary in the sixteenth century, most of Hungary's great institutions moved into southern Slovakia. Subsequently, many Hungarians developed a strong emotional attachment to this part of the Hungarian Kingdom as southern Slovakia developed into the political and cultural center of Hungary during a 300-year period.

The city of Pozsony (now Bratislava; Pressburg) became the capital and main political center. Although the Ottomans were driven out of Hungary at the end of the seventeenth century, Pozsony remained important because the Hungarian Parliament continued to meet there until 1848. It even continued to be the city where Hungarian kings were crowned. The

Figure 4.4 Southern Slovakia and Southwestern Ruthenia.

university in Pozsony, founded by King Mátyás, was the preeminent educational center in Hungary for almost four hundred years.[12] The prestigious Hungarian Academy of Sciences was also founded in the city (Erdei 1968, 704). The significance of Pozsony to Hungarian national identity cannot be overemphasized: "Pozsony is inseparably connected with the Hungarian people and Hungarian history" (Légrády Brothers 1930, 112).[13]

During the same time period that Pozsony became the capital of Hungary, the Hungarian church moved its center from Esztergom to Nagyszombat (now Trnava). Nyitra (now Nitra) became an important religious center as well. While Nagyszombat was the main religious center of Hungary, other important institutions were established as well that illustrate the importance of this town. For example, a university was founded in 1635. The prestige of Nagyszombat's university is underscored by its later becoming the college of arts and sciences at the university in Budapest (Hanák 1988, 65).

The important places just mentioned lie in the western areas of southern Slovakia. Noteworthy centers also lie in the eastern areas as well. Kassa (now Košice) was the main regional center in the east. In addition to its role as an important trading center, the university (founded in 1674) made the town an important educational center too. The first Hungarian literary periodical, *Magyar Museum*, was published in Kassa (Barany 1990, 186). Kassa is also the location of Saint Elizabeth Cathedral (Sisa 1990, 331), considered one of Hungary's greatest churches and tangible evidence in the landscape of the greatness of the Hungarian nation. One of Hungary's popular leaders who struggled for Hungary's independence— Ferenc Rákóczi II—is buried in the cathedral. In fact, the Rákóczi family is from the area around Kassa. Eastern Slovakia in general is significant because it is seen as the home of one of the nation's greatest families, the Rákóczis.

Southwestern Ruthenia is a core territory of Hungarian sense of identity because it played an important role in the struggle for Hungarian independence. The towns of Munkács (now Mukačevo) and Ungvár (now Užhorod) are particularly noteworthy. The castles in these towns held out the longest in the struggle for independence in the late seventeenth to early eighteenth centuries (Kann and David 1984, 179). Both towns are also closely associated with three great Hungarian families: the Rákóczis, the Thökölys, and the Zrinyis (Sisa 1990, 111). All three of these families fought for Hungarian independence.

The cultural-political centers of Slovakia were protected by a number of fortresses. Of these, Érsekújvár (now Nové Zámky), Komárom (now Komárno on the Slovak side of the Danube), Léva (now Levice), and Gömör (now Gemer) are the most important. Of the four, Komárom is the place of greatest significance. As one of the places that held out against the Austrian and Russian armies in the Revolution of 1848–49, Komárom is seen as a place that demonstrates Hungarian bravery and valor (Légrády Brothers 1930, 99). The strong emotional attachment that many Hungarians have to Komárom is illustrated in a number of paintings (Deák 1979, between pages 168 and 169).

As the political-cultural center of the Hungarian Kingdom for centuries, southern Slovakia became important to Hungarian national identity in another context, more specifically in music and folk culture. Pozsony[14] and Nagyszombat were centers of music (Dobszay 1993, 70–71). When Hungarian Romantics collected folk songs and noted folk customs as a means of emphasizing the uniqueness and historical continuity of the Hungarian nation, they used southern Slovakia as one of their primary source areas (Manga 1969); Zoltán Kodály's *Dances from Galanta* is one of the most notable works (Konnyu 1971, 21). Gömör, although an old medieval fortress, remains in the national consciousness with the poem *King Mátyás in Gömör*:

> By old Hungarian custom after his royal assize,
> He held a feast in Gömör, to crown his high emprise;
> The tides of banquet ebbed and flowed from serious to gay,
> As flowed the gold of Maros or the vintage of Tokay.
>   (Quoted from Kirkconnell 1947, 11)

In other words, many cultural elements of Hungarian identity are derived from the southern Slovakian region (Dobszay 1993, 176). Subsequently, many Hungarians developed a strong emotional attachment to this territory, which they see as one of their cultural hearths.

Great Alföld (Nagy Alföld)

What, O ye wild Carpathians,[15] to me
Are your romantic eyries, bold with pine?
Ye win my admiration, not my love;
Your lofty valleys lure no dreams of mine.

Down where the prairies billow like a sea,
Here is my world, my home, my heart's true fane.
My eagle spirit soars, from chains released,
When I behold the unhorizoned plain.

Upwards I mount in ecstasies of thought
Above the earth, to cloud-heights still more near,
And see, beneath, the image of the plain,
From Danube on to Tisza smiling clear.

Twinkling beneath a sky mirage-possessed
Kis-Kunság's fatted herds by hundreds stray;
At noon beside the well's long windlass waits
The double trough to which they make their way.

Stampeding herds of horses, as they run,
Thunder across the wind with trampling hoof,
As lusty herdsmen's whoops resound again
And noisy whips crack out in sharp reproof.

Across the gentle bosom of the farm
Soft breezes hold the swaying wheat enthrall'd
And crown the pleasant beauty of the place
With myriad gleams of living emerald.

Here from the neighboring reeds, the wild ducks come
In evening dusk a resting-place to find:
Frighten'd they rise on an aerial path
If reeds begin to flutter in the wind.

Still farther on, deep in the plain, there stands
A lonely inn, whose chimney needs repair;
The thirsty farm-hands sometimes visit it
For goat's milk as they journey to the fair.

Beside that tavern's stunted poplar grove
The caltrop grows up yellow in the sand;
Near by, the screaming kestrel makes its home,
Its nest untouched by any urchin's hand.

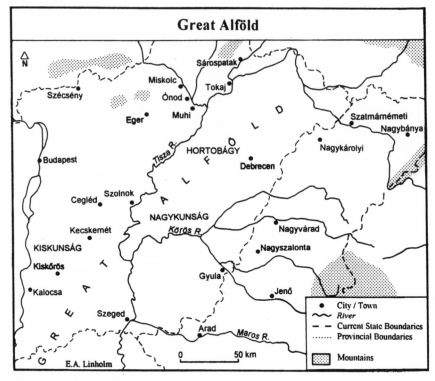

Figure 4.5 Great Alföld.

And there the feathery grasses sigh unmarked,
The hardy thistle spreads its purple flower,
And there the mottled lizards turn to rest
By cooling stems in noon-tide's burning hour.

Far, far away, where heaven touches earth,
Blue tree-tops of dim orchards tower higher
Like some pale fog-bank, and beyond them still
A village church projects a simple spire.

Fair art thou, Alföld, fair at least to me!
Here was I born, and in my cradle lay.
God grant I may be buried 'neath its sod,
And mix my mouldering cerements with its clay!
　　　(*Alföld* by Sándor Petöfi; quoted from Kirkconnell 1947, 39–40)

The Great Alföld (or Plain) probably illustrates modern Hungarian national identity more than any other region in Historic Hungary (see Figures 4.2 and 4.5). Hungarians see themselves as the descendants of a nomadic people who originated in the plains of Central Eurasia, and they continue to emphasize their nomadic past and identity today. The ancestors of the Hungarians were obviously attracted to the natural landscapes of the Great Alföld because it would allow them to continue their way of life, and thus preserve their sense of identity. Today, the Great Alföld represents the connection that modern Hungarians have with their ancestors and traditional way of life. Many modern Hungarians have strong emotional bonds to this place which has shaped and continues to shape their sense of national identity. In short, the Hungarian nation would not be what it is without the natural landscapes of the Great Alföld.[16]

A term often used in conjunction with the Alföld is *puszta*, meaning steppe, desert, or wasteland. While the term *puszta* is used to refer to the Alföld or places within it, the *puszta* actually has no geographical limits. The Alföld, on the other hand, is geographically defined and has many subregions within it. The Great Alföld stretches from the Danube River in the west and south to the northern mountains near Miskolc in the north, to the Carpathians in Ruthenia in the northeast, and to the Bihor Mountains of modern Romania in the east. Noteworthy subregions of the Alföld are the Kunság and Hortobágy. The Kunság, meaning Cumania, is the home of the Cumans, an early tribe that was similar to the Magyars when they arrived in the Carpathian Basin. The Kunság is divided into the Kiskunság (Little Cumania), lying between the Danube and Tisza Rivers, and Nagykunság (Greater Cumania), lying east of the Tisza River. The Hortobágy lies between the Tisza River and the city of Debrecen. As one of the undeveloped areas of the Alföld in modern times, the Hortobágy, with its untouched environment and traditional forms of horse and stock-breeding, best represents the nomadic component of Hungarian national identity in its true Romantic form (Burant 1990, 68; Erdei 1968, 128–29). One of the human constructs in the Hortobágy is a very old nine-spanned bridge (Erdei 1968, 127); it is captured in a painting titled *Storm on the Hortobágy* (Egri 1988, at end).

Szeged, Debrecen, and Miskolc have been instrumental in shaping modern Hungarian national identity. Serving as the major centers of the Great Alföld, all three towns contribute to the territory's core status. Szeged is an important market town and educational center. The twin-towered Votive Church with its open-air theater has come to symbolize the greatness of the town. The church is also one of the few great cultural features in the landscape of the Great Alföld. Miskolc is an important mining center for modern Hungary, and it is the location of one of the first Hungarian-language theaters (Hanák 1988, 108). Debrecen, however, is probably the greatest Hungarian city of the Great Alföld. Known as "the Calvinist Rome," Debrecen was the center of the Calvinist movement in Hungary. The Great Reformed Church in the city is a testament to this movement. A center of Protestantism, Debrecen had one of Hungary's first printing presses. With a printing press and the founding of a Protestant university, Debrecen became a major center in the shaping of Hungarian history and identity. Debrecen's influence increased with the subsequent founding of two more universities. During the rise of nationalism, Debrecen played a large role. Lajos Kossuth proclaimed the independence of Hungary from the Austrian Empire in this city and made it the capital of a free Hungary (Deák 1979, 216). Memory of that event is preserved in Debrecen's main square, named Kossuth Square, dominated by a statue of Kossuth. In more recent history, Debrecen became the temporary capital of anti-fascist Hungary in 1944. The provisional government of 1944 deliberately convened in the building that was used by the revolutionary government of 1849 (Deák 1979, 216). The significance of place is demonstrated by governments choosing places of earlier events to justify themselves or their actions. Place then is a means of legitimizing oneself or one's actions.

A number of important smaller towns of the Great Alföld illustrate the core status of the territory. They include places such as Eger, Kecskemét, Kiskörös, Nagybánya, Nagykárolyi, and Tokaj. In addition to castles, Eger and Tokaj are famous for their wines. The Tokay wines are the most known internationally and mentioned most in song and poetry:

> The fish loves water for its part,
>   No fish's shape is mine!
> For me the wine that warms the heart
>   Born beside Tokay's vine.
> What's water unto me?
> Whoever drinks not wine
> No Magyar can be.
>   (From *The Wine Song*; quoted from Mitton 1915, 50)

Eger is known for a famous red wine known as the Bull's Blood (Konnyu 1971, 50). International recognition of these wines is a source of national pride for Hungarians.

Kecskemét is important to Hungarian sense of territory for a couple of reasons. First, it serves as one of the market towns on the Great Alföld. Many of the cherished agricultural products[17] of the Hungarians are collected and distributed from here. Second, Kecskemét is important for an artist colony that began in the late eighteenth century. Subsequently, the town became the location of one of Hungary's first language theaters. Kecskemét was also the home of dramatist Jószef Katona and Zoltán Kodály. Currently, the Kodály Seminar is held in Kecskemét (Hanák 1988, 247). To no surprise, Kecskemét and the area around it is brought to national attention by descriptions in literature and poetry:

Where were you born, shepherd lad?
The famous land of the Cumans, Kecskemét is my country.
My dear mother gave me birth there.
I was born in the hilly land of Kecskemét,
I had no mother, yet I was raised.
I grew up as mushrooms in the woods.
(From *My Bell-Wether Does Not Want to Graze*;
quoted from Vargyas 1983, 2: 851)

Kiskörös is the birthplace of Hungary's greatest poet, Sándor Petöfi. A museum in the town honors his work (Erdei 1968, 616). Nagybánya (now Baia Mare) became a cultural center with the founding of a school of painting in 1896; an artist colony soon developed as Hungarian artists began to migrate there. Even before the artist colony developed, Nagybánya had been an important place. In the fourteenth century, Nagybánya was an important gold mining town, a source of Hungary's wealth (Hanák 1988, 31, 161, 168). Nagykárolyi (now Carei), with its castle, is the home of Károlyi family (The Eighty Club 1907, 296–301). Mihály Károlyi was the first leader to establish a democracy in Hungary. The birth of democracy in Hungary is associated with Károlyi and his estate.

In addition to Debrecen, other towns in the Great Alföld played roles during the struggles to liberate Hungary and thereby have contributed to the region's core status in Hungarian sense of territory. During the Revolution of 1848–49, Kossuth inspired many Hungarians to rise up against the Austrians in a speech he made in the town of Cegléd (also Czeglód). Cegléd and Kossuth are captured in a popular drawing (Deák 1979, between pages 168 and 169). The town is the location of the Lajos Kossuth Museum. Cegléd was also the town where György Dózsa, the leader of a peasant movement, gave a speech in 1514 and where a statue of him was unveiled in 1908 (Hanák 1988, 170). One of the final acts of the revolution took place in Arad (now in Romania), the final headquarters for the revolution. Thirteen Hungarian generals were executed on October 6, 1849, by orders of the Austrian commander Baron Ludwig Haynau. The Hungarian generals, who became known as the "Martyrs of Arad," were immortalized in a statue in the city (Légrády Brothers 1930, 98). Arad subsequently was viewed as an important place of Hungarian perseverance and resistance.

Other places in the Great Alföld illustrate the attempts of Hungary's leaders to obtain Hungary's independence from the Austrian Empire. Hungary's War of Independence (1704–11), led by Ferenc Rákóczi, is marked by several declarations that identify an important area that facilitated the struggle for Hungarian independence. For example, Rákóczi obtained the title of Prince of Hungary at the Diet of Szécsény in 1705. The Hapsburgs were dethroned in the Diet of Ónod in 1707. Serfs fighting in the War of Independence were freed in the Diet of Sárospatak in 1708; Sárospatak is now the location of the Rákóczi Museum. The war ended when Hungarian forces surrendered in 1711, following the signing of the Treaty of Szatmár; Szatmár became Szátmarnémeti but is now known as Satu-Mare, Romania (Hanák 1988, 78–80).

Many places in the Great Alföld testify to the struggles of the Hungarians in earlier times. Muhi, for example, was the site of a battle between the Hungarians and the Mongols in 1241. The Hungarians lost the battle, but the event was forgotten, if perhaps held meaningless for centuries—until the rise of nationalism. In fact, a memorial was built on the site of the battle in 1991, to commemorate the 750th anniversary of the event (Lázár 1996a, 45). Because the memorial was just recently built, it was designed according to modern Hungarian national understanding of the event. What the battle meant to the Hungarians of the time is lost to written history. Yet this place is obviously significant to the Hungarian sense of national identity, and its power is underscored by modern Hungarians' feeling the need to erect such a memorial. The newly constructed cultural landscape of this place provides tangible evidence of Hungarian heroism and cements the bond that modern Hungarians have with their ancestors.

Many of the places that represent Hungarian struggles are associated with the Ottoman period. Some of the most important strongholds that resisted the Ottomans were Eger, Gyula, Jenő, Nagyszalonta, Szolnok, and Nagyvárad. Eger is particularly known for a heroic defense against an Ottoman assault in 1552 (Lázár 1996b, 1552; Sisa 1990, 92–93). The resistance of this city is a source of great pride for modern Hungarians. A dramatic statue in the center of the city, just below the castle, depicts the commander of the castle flanked by Hungarian soldiers and a Hungarian woman aiding the cause by hurling a rock at the Turks. Not surprisingly, Eger is a top tourist destination for Hungarians. Obviously, many want to see the place which represents Hungarian devotion and determination. Later in history, when Ottoman power began to wane, Rákóczi routed the Ottoman army at Nagyszalonta (now Salonta, Romania) in 1636. Victories against the Ottomans were few. Yet Nagyszalonta exemplifies the ability of Hungarians to overcome such a menacing enemy. Nagyszalonta is also the hometown of János Arany (1817–1882), one of the greatest Hungarian poets of the nineteenth century. Arany wrote many of his works in the town, and Sándor Petőfi spent time with him there (Erdei 1968, 753–54).

Nagyvárad (formerly just Várad but now Oradea, Romania) is one of the most significant places of the Great Alföld for Hungarian national identity. Called the "Little Paris on the Körös," the town was important as early as the eleventh century, when King Ladislas built a cathedral and made the town an important political center in the Hungarian Kingdom. Later, Ladislas was buried there. A statue of Ladislas as well as statues of many other kings stood in the town until the Turks finally captured it in 1660. When the Ottomans were driven out of Nagyvárad, the importance of the town was confirmed by a decision to erect a new statue of Ladislas (Hanák 1988, 44; Légrády Brothers 1930, 109). In more recent times, Nagyvárad, as the center of the western literary movement, became an important cultural center in Hungary (Erdei 1968, 766, 772).

Transylvania (Erdély)

Autumn no longer rends the orphan'd leaf,
Drifting in myriad cries of fright and grief.

By day I roam'd, at evening did not rest:
And greet the morning from the mountain's crest.

Below, a cauldron boils with murk and mist
Beneath this timeless crag of amethyst;

While on the naked peak the sunlight throws
The solemn crystal splendors of the rose.

A fever stirs the valley far below;
Here shepherds eat their cheese, serene and slow.

Their quiet tongues speak few but peaceful words;
Their quiet hands protect their peaceful herds.

Still upward, where the snow-peaks soar, there fly
The far, eternal banners of the sky.

My questing, bird-like glance unsated seeks
The infinite horizon's billowing peaks;

A hundred, nay a thousand crests I saw,
And breathed thy name, my Transylvania!
   (From *On the Summit* by Lajos Áprily;
   quoted from Kirkconnell 1947, 42)

The emotional attachment that many Hungarians have for Transylvania *(Erdély)* is represented by the phrase *"két haza,"* which means two home-lands (Czigány 1984, 537) (see Figures 4.2 and 4.6). The view that Transylvania is the other homeland of the Hungarians stems in part from the role that the territory has played in history. During the period of Ottoman occupation, Transylvania preserved the highest degree of inde-pendence of any of the territories of the Hungarian Kingdom. In fact, Transylvania even experienced a "golden age" of its own in the seven-

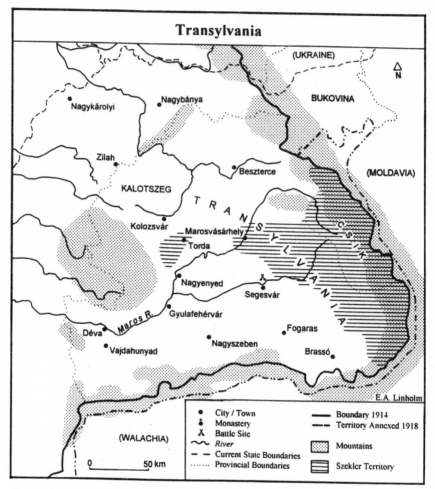

Figure 4.6 Transylvania.

teenth century.[18] As a result, Transylvania is seen as a refuge of Hungarian culture, largely untainted by either the Ottomans or the Austrians.

Transylvania's political strength in the seventeenth century reinforces ideas about the historical continuity of the Hungarian nation. The argument is made that Hungarian civilization initially emerged in the central part of the Carpathian Basin, transferred itself to Transylvania (and Slovakia) during the Ottoman occupation, and then reestablished itself in the central part of the basin afterward. Such a view also illustrates the belief that the various territories of the Hungarian Kingdom work in harmony with one another and are even mutually dependent on one another. Thanks to all the political and cultural accomplishments in Transylvania in the seventeenth century, Hungarian culture can be described as having continuous vitality throughout history.

The significance of many places within Transylvania, and the associated strong emotional bonds that Hungarians have developed for the territory, derives in part from many great leaders of Hungary who came from Transylvania. Indeed, it is difficult to think of great Hungarians without thinking of Transylvania. The memory of these great Hungarians is preserved in Transylvania, where the castles, palaces, churches, universities, and libraries associated with them are found, as well as statues and other memorials that were erected to honor these people and their accomplishments.

The role that Transylvania has played in Hungarian history is also illustrated by the lack of a clear defining of Transylvania's western boundary. While a historical boundary in the west exists, the jurisdictions of Transylvanian leaders have fluctuated greatly. For example, during Transylvania's golden age, Transylvania's leaders extended their power to Várad, often considered to be a great Transylvanian city. Also, Mihály Károlyi (from Nagykárolyi) is called a Transylvanian. Actually, all of the territory lost to Romania after the First World War has come to be referred to as Transylvania, even though a substantial part of it, including the two towns just mentioned, was in the Great Alföld or in other regions. The lack of a distinct boundary between Transylvania and the rest of Hungary reinforces the belief that Transylvania is truly Hungarian. Many places are alternately referred to as either Hungarian or Transylvanian because they have been alternately in Hungary and Transylvania. In fact, because Transylvania is seen as an integral part of Hungary, anything Transylvanian is by definition Hungarian as well, although not necessarily vice versa.

Hungarian national identity is intimately tied to a number of political-cultural centers within Transylvania. The most important are Gyulafehérvár (now Alba Iulia; Karlsburg or Weissenburg), Nagyenyed (now Aiud), and Marosvásárhely (now Târgu Mureş): ". . . all these towns—the staples of the ancient Hungarian civilization and strongholds of European civilization . . ." (Légrády Brothers 1930, 111). However, Beszterce (now Bistriţa), Déva, and Nagyszeben (formerly just Szeben; Sibiu; Hermannstadt) also were important fortresses that contributed to Transylvania's role as the preserver and protector of Hungarian culture.

Kolozsvár (now Cluj-Napoca; Klausenburg) is one of the most important. Beyond being the major city of Transylvania, Kolozsvár is thought of as the birthplace of one of Hungary's great kings, Mátyás (or Matthias Corvinus). The statue of him in front of the great Hungarian Gothic church has come to symbolize the city. The Hungarian university, before being merged with the Romanian one, was one of the most prestigious in

Hungary. The state theater and many of the museums and other institutions are regarded among the greatest cultural institutions produced by the Hungarian nation in modern times (Erdei 1968, 212, 556, 560, 569, 590, 618, 677, 679, 732, 792, 804, 809–10, 919). Recent events in Kolozsvár illustrate how national identity is tied to the cultural landscape. Tensions have arisen as individuals have tried to reshape the cultural landscape of the city. Because these actions have been initiated by Romanians, they will primarily be dealt with in Chapter 5. Nevertheless, it is important to note at this point that excavations of Daco-Roman ruins in front of the Matthias Corvinus statue have left an unsightly mess in the main city square, which is not just coincidentally a place of distinct Hungarian character. The Hungarians of the city have reacted to the excavations as a direct affront to their identity and have launched bitter protests in response.

When the capital of Transylvania was not in Kolozsvár, it was usually in Gyulafehérvár. As the home of one of Hungary's ruling families, the Bethlens, the town contains the Bethlen Palace, the university that Gábor Bethlen founded. As much as the Bethlens are Hungarian, Gyulafehérvár is Hungarian. Similarly, Nagyenyed (now Aiud), the location where Gábor Bethlen moved his college, is an important place as well.

Marosvásárhely is the other great cultural center of Transylvania. Its university represents many great achievements in Hungarian science. Marosvásárhely also is associated with many great Hungarian leaders such as the Telekis, General Bem, and Lajos Kossuth (Légrády Brothers 1930, 99). The Teleki library was one of the finest libraries in the Kingdom of Hungary (Erdei 1968, 590). In the Palace of Culture is a stained-glass window that depicts *The Ballad of Kata Kádár* (Wiebenson and Sisa 1998, between pages 112 and 113, 232). Marosvásárhely has become particularly important in recent times. When the Romanian government created a Magyar Autonomous Region after the Second World War, Marosvásárhely was designated the administrative center. Although the region was eventually abolished, Marosvásárhely is still the cultural and political center for Hungarians in modern Transylvania. When Hungarians in the Hungarian state express concern for the Hungarians of Transylvania, they generally focus on Marosvásárhely.

The other great Hungarian town of Transylvania is Vajdahunyad (now Hunedoara) (Sisa 1990, 55; Wiebenson and Sisa 1998, 43). The castle, one of the most picturesque in Transylvania, is the home of one of Hungary's greatest leaders—János Hunyadi. A replica of the castle was erected in the middle of Budapest for the Millennial Celebration in 1896 (Légrády Brothers 1930, 62–63). This replica serves as a constant reminder to Hungarians just how important Vajdahunyad and Transylvania are in the shaping of Hungarian identity. The significance of Vajdahunyad Castle is underscored by the castle's being one of the first monuments in Hungary to be restored during the modern restoration movement (Dercsényi 1969, 16–17).

Segesvár (now Sighişoara) became an important part of national consciousness with the battle that was fought against the Russians outside the town in July 1849. Of the many battles fought in the war, the one outside of Segesvár came to be seen as the most significant because Hungary's greatest poet, Sándor Petöfi, died during the struggle here. The memory of Petöfi's heroic devotion and self-sacrifice for the Hungarian nation was preserved in a monument of him erected in the town (Légrády Brothers 1930, 93).

Brassó (now Braşov; Kronstadt) is also an important cultural center of Transylvania. Interestingly, it was a Saxon settlement, and many of the accomplishments achieved in Brassó were actually those of Saxons. Nevertheless, Brassó cannot be overlooked when discussing the cultural and political achievements of Transylvania. Consequently, the achievements of Brassó's Saxons have been incorporated into Hungarian history (Erdei 1968, 555, 589, 618). In some form or another, any event or deed of significance that takes place in Transylvania is considered to be a Hungarian accomplishment because Transylvania is a Hungarian territory. This type of association illustrates the important role that place plays in shaping a people's identity. Moreover, the need to incorporate the achievements of Brassó's Saxons into Hungarian history illustrates the overall core importance of Transylvania to Hungarian national identity.

The belief that Transylvania is the preserve of Hungarian culture is related to other factors besides the exercise of political independence. When Hungarian Romantics set out to collect folk songs and record folk customs, many of them went to Transylvania. Because Transylvania was relatively isolated and on the periphery of Europe, many cultural practices in Transylvania remained unchanged for centuries. As a result, many Hungarian Romantics considered Transylvania to be representative of true Hungarian culture. However, while many inhabitants of Transylvania accept a Hungarian identity, many of them also think of themselves as Szeklers (Székely). The precise origin of the Szeklers is not known. They are a tribe related to the early Magyars who either traveled to the Carpathian Basin with the Magyars or migrated there not long afterwards. In either case, they became politically integrated into the Hungarian Kingdom from an early period (Palmer 1970, 11–12) and developed a Hungarian identity. Nevertheless, the Szeklers are distinctly different from other Hungarians. Yet through the work of Hungarian Romantics, Szekler culture is heralded as true Hungarian culture. One of the areas where scholars such as Bartók and Kodály collected folk songs is Csik County (Suchoff 1981, 95), a distinctly Szekler area. Outside the Szekler areas,

Torda (now Turda), Zilah[19] (now Zalâu) and the Kalotaszeg (now Calata) region are seen as important areas of Hungarian folk tradition (Erdei 1968, 985). One of the oldest Hungarian folk songs, *The Walled Up Wife*, describes the building of the castle in Déva (Vargyas 1983, 2: 18–57).

The Core: The Tenacity Factor

The last thousand years of history is marked by numerous struggles to defend the Kingdom of Hungary. While Romantic historians view these struggles as national ones, it is not appropriate to depict them as national struggles until the emergence of modern nationalism at the end of eighteenth century; struggles prior to this time took place in another social context. In fact, because territorial sovereignty is a condition of national consciousness, Hungarian national consciousness does not really come into full blossom until the mid-nineteenth century, the time when Hungarian leaders began calling for an independent Hungarian national state.[20] Until that time, most Hungarian leaders only pushed for more autonomous decision making within the Hapsburg monarchy. Their willingness to remain within such a political-territorial structure (i.e., a multi-ethnic state) indicates that their sense of identity was formulated in a social context much different than that of a nation. Therefore, in applying the tenacity factor, we consider only events from the mid-nineteenth century to the present.

Transdanubia, southern Slovakia and southwestern Ruthenia, the Great Alföld, and Transylvania fall within the core territory of Hungarian sense of territory because they are the territories where the struggle for national independence began and continued throughout modern times. When Hungarian leaders began their struggle for an independent Hungary, they were centered in Hungary's capital (Pozsony) in southern Slovakia. When the diplomatic struggle turned into an armed one in 1848, the Hungarian independence movement relocated to Budapest and then to the Great Alföld. During the later struggles of the Revolution of 1848–49, southern Slovakia and Transylvania played key roles as well. In fact, on the eve of the revolution, the Hungarian Diet passed a set of laws, now known as the April Laws, which brought about many social and political reforms. These laws, however, were just as significant for the political organization of territory because they brought together the historic territories of the Hungarian Kingdom into a unitary state (Kann and David 1984, 344). Specifically, they incorporated Transylvania into Hungary, which had been governed directly from Vienna.

After the Hungarian defeat in the Revolution of 1848–49, Hungarians did not find an opportunity to begin another independence movement until the defeat of Austria in a war with Prussia in 1866. By this time, Transdanubia had become the political center of Hungary. With a weakened Austrian government, Hungarian leaders were able to demand enough concessions to bring about the Compromise of 1867. The compromise ensured greater independence by putting the Hungarian government on an almost equal footing with the Austrian government through the establishment of the dual monarchy, more commonly known as the Austro-Hungarian Empire. The Hapsburg Emperor remained the king of Hungary, but a new Hungarian government gained control over Hungary's domestic affairs; such control was of course made possible because the Hungarian government gained greater control over its territory. The importance of Transylvania as a core territory was once again illustrated when Hungarian leaders successfully demanded and secured Transylvania's return to the Hungarian Kingdom. By the 1890s, the Hungarian government began implementing vigorous Magyarization policies in an attempt to integrate the territories of the Hungarian Kingdom. These Magyarization policies were primarily directed at Transylvania.

With the defeat of the Central Powers in the First World War, the Hungarian government finally saw its opportunity to declare its full independence from Austria. Unfortunately, it had lost credibility with the Hungarian people as soon as foreign troops began occupying Hungarian territory.[21] Mihály Károlyi, a count from Transylvania, gained the confidence of many Hungarians by claiming that he could preserve the territorial integrity of Hungary (Burant 1990, 35; Macartney and Palmer 1962, 90). As a staunch advocate of democracy, Károlyi believed that Hungary had to redeem itself to the Western Allies by doing four things: first, denounce the Alliance with Germany; second, dissolve the dual monarchy with Austria; third, recognize the rights of the ethnic minorities; and fourth, orient the country to Wilson's Fourteen Points as soon as possible.

Unfortunately for Károlyi, Allied troops moved into Hungary from the southeast despite the signing of the Belgrade Armistice on November 13, 1918. The Allies approved of Károlyi but did little to stop the Serbian, Czechoslovak, and Romanian military units from claiming and occupying Hungarian territory, looting Hungary, and blockading food and medical shipments destined for Hungary. After several months of chaos, it became clear to many Hungarians that Károlyi's western orientation would not preserve the Hungarian Kingdom. In fact, Károlyi could not free southern Slovakia, southwestern Ruthenia, portions of the Great Alföld, and Transylvania from foreign occupation. He had no choice but to resign.

By March 1919, the old monarchy and the believers in democracy had failed to preserve the Hungarian Kingdom. As the Hungarians looked elsewhere for leadership, only the Communists under the leadership of

Béla Kun seemed able to protect Hungary. Part of the Communist movement, Béla Kun believed that he could protect Hungary through an
alliance with the Russian Bolsheviks. The Hungarians had little affinity
for the Russians, but they also believed that the Western Allies had little
concern for the welfare of Hungary. One Hungarian leader even
remarked, "We must take a new direction and obtain from the East what
has been refused to us by the West" (Polonsky 1975, 47).

Because the Western Allies would not negotiate with a Communist, Kun
decided that he needed a military strategy. He believed that he would
have to break through Czechoslovak lines on the northeast, establish a
Slovak Soviet Republic, and secure Ruthenia so that the Russian Red
Army would have a passageway to enter and protect Hungary. Kun then
planned to attack the position that the Romanian army had established
on the Tisza River and then drive it completely out of the core territories of the Great Alföld and Transylvania. At first, Kun's plan met with
some success when he established a Soviet Republic of Slovakia. However,
Kun's successes were short-lived; the Russian Red Army never came to
aid, and then the Hungarian Red Army began to fall apart. The Czech
government abolished the Soviet Republic of Slovakia and moved south
again to Miskolc. The Romanian army went on the attack and insisted
upon advancing all the way to Budapest despite Allied objections. On
August 1, 1919, Kun resigned; the short-lived revolutionary Red Republic
disintegrated. Kun's government and military operations proved only to
exacerbate relations with the neighboring states. On August 6, 1919, the
Romanian Army occupied Budapest (Palmer 1970, 161). Kun's
Communist revolution had ended, and the Hungarians lost control over
even more of their territory than before. Noteworthy was the decision
of the Allies during the Communist reign in Hungary to award Western
Hungary (Burgenland) to Austria.

Following Kun's resignation, a period of chaos ruled before Miklós
Horthy, the admiral of the Hungarian navy, rode into Budapest with his
"National Army" and established control. Horthy was an ultra-conservative who believed in the preservation of the Hungarian Kingdom and
its ruling nobility. Just prior to the national elections in January 1920, the
Allies had the Treaty of Trianon presented to the Hungarian public. The
treaty demanded that two-thirds of the territory of the Hungarian
Kingdom be stripped away and awarded to other countries. The core territories of Transylvania, southern Slovakia, southern Ruthenia, and sec-
tions of Transdanubia and the Great Alföld were included in those
territories to be taken away from the Hungarians. Although all political
parties denounced the treaty, most Hungarians lacked confidence in the
liberals and Communists who had already proved themselves unable to
protect and preserve the Hungarian Kingdom. On the other hand, the

rhetoric of the conservatives seemed most convincing; hence, they were victorious in the elections. Horthy established himself as leader of Hungary, and his government resisted signing the Treaty of Trianon for as long as possible. Nevertheless, with great Allied pressure and having no other alternative, the Hungarian Parliament ratified the treaty on November 13, 1920.

Although the Hungarian Parliament was forced to ratify the Treaty of Trianon, the government did not fall. In fact, Admiral Horthy remained in power until 1944. Despite the ratification of the treaty, Hungarian leaders continued to pursue a foreign policy directed at recovering lost territories. Even domestically the Hungarian government began expanding the university system so that administrators could be produced to carry out the Magyarization of Hungary's lost territories once they were regained (Polonsky 1975, 54). Moreover, despite practical needs, the Hungarian government refused to reorganize its internal political-administrative structure. Of the original sixty-three counties in Historic Hungary, only ten were left intact, twenty-four were divided into two or more parts, and twenty-eight were lost completely. Of the twenty-four that were still partially remaining, some had no county seats, whereas others were county seats without territory (Kovács 1989, 82–83).

In the years that followed, the Hungarian government was unable to recover any lost territories to any large degree. The minor exception was the city of Sopron and its hinterland in Western Hungary, formerly the western part of the core territory of Transdanubia and now known more explicitly as Burgenland. This territory had been awarded to Austria, but the Hungarian government refused to withdraw its military from the region. While the Western powers had armed the Slovaks, Romanians, and Serbs, so that these peoples could drive the Hungarian army out of territories that they claimed, the Western powers were unwilling to arm the Austrians, whom they viewed as Germans, to do the same in Burgenland. The Hungarian government expressed a willingness to vacate Burgenland if the Allies were willing to hold a plebiscite in the city of Sopron and its hinterland. The Allies agreed, and the plebiscite, held December 14–16, 1921, showed that the people of Sopron wanted overwhelmingly to be a part of Hungary. Therefore, on January 1, 1922, the Allies awarded Sopron to Hungary (Spira 1982, 321–22). The determination of Hungarians to hold onto Sopron illustrates that the city and its hinterland fall within the core territories of Hungarian national identity. The regaining of Sopron also was the first success of any Hungarian leader to rebuild Historic Hungary since the end of the war. As a result, the Sopron plebiscite helped to solidify Horthy's power.

Although the reacquisition of Sopron restored some pride to the Hungarian nation, Hungarian nationalists had to wait until the eve of the

Second World War before they could continue to rebuild their self-esteem by reasserting their control over more of the lost territories of Historic Hungary. What became significant in the interwar years was the migration of Hungarian nationals from the lost territories to Trianon Hungary, the country that we know today. Significantly, of the 2.5 million Hungarians who found themselves suddenly outside of post-war Hungary, only about 350,000 (about 14 percent) relocated to the reduced Hungarian state (Dávid 1988, 336 and 345). This small number of migrants contradicts the underlying assumption of many international political leaders who treat territory generically, frequently as a mere economic commodity. If it were true that the Hungarian nation, like any nation, simply required some territory, any territory, and only to facilitate self-determination through self-government, then the entire 2.5 million Hungarians who were in foreign states would have migrated to the newly created Hungarian state. However, the low number of migrants indicates that the Hungarians from the core territories of southern Slovakia, southwestern Ruthenia, and Transylvania had strong emotional attachments to the places they inhabited. Despite any agreements made by world leaders on boundaries, these people saw themselves as Hungarians and their places of habitation as Hungary. When the amount of discrimination that these Hungarians endured is taken into account,[22] the significance of place becomes even more poignant. Those who did migrate to the shrunken Hungarian state did not forget about their lives in southern Slovakia, southwestern Ruthenia, or Transylvania, or stop believing that these homelands of theirs were truly Hungarian. On the contrary, they are even partially responsible for the irredentist policies of the Hungarian government following the First World War.

By the early 1930s, Horthy's credibility began to erode in Hungary. The world economic crisis certainly played a role, but it had also been ten years since any of Historic Hungary had been reclaimed. This second factor is underscored by the right-wing extremists' becoming very popular in Hungary by overtly advocating the belief that more aggressive policies were needed to regain Hungary's lost territories. As a means of preserving his authority, Horthy decided that he had to allow some of the right-wing extremists into his government. The main figure was Gyula Gömbös, who became prime minister. Portraying himself as the Hungarian Mussolini (Carsten 1980, 173), Gömbös forged such strong alliances with Italy and Germany that not even his successors could break them (Polonsky 1975, 58). With each one of Hitler's successes in violation of the Treaty of Versailles, the right-wing extremists became increasingly popular in Hungary. Hungarians soon realized that Germany was becoming the dominant power in Central and Eastern Europe while France was losing control. Moreover, France's policies ran counter to Hungary's aims, while Hitler's Germany showed sympathy for Hungary. As early as 1921, a Hungarian, Count Csáky, wrote the following:

> And if public opinion in Hungary nevertheless did not seriously oppose the German Alliance [in World War I], it was because Germany was the only European Power which had no aspirations towards Hungarian territory; which left the 2 million Germans living in Hungary to themselves, and avoided by external pressure the inner politics of the country.
>
> The Hungarian people, standing alone in Europe, are ready to join hands with whomever will honestly help them. (Csáky 1921, 22)

Adolf Hitler understood the desire of the Hungarians to regain their lost territories. By 1938, he was able to manipulate the Hungarians into supporting his war effort by rewarding them with territory for every contribution that they would make (see Figure 4.7). In Hitler's "First Vienna Award" (November 2, 1938), he returned the core territories of southern Slovakia and southern Ruthenia to the Hungarians in return for passing anti-Semitic legislation (Macartney and Palmer 1962, 389; Seton-Watson 1956, 302). Later, in 1939, after more anti-Semitic laws were passed, Hitler awarded the Hungarians part of the core territory of Transylvania—the northern part—in the "Second Vienna Award" (August 30, 1940) (see Figure 4.7) (Macartney and Palmer 1962, 427).

Following the German military invasion of the Soviet Union, the Hungarian government declared war on the Soviet Union. Lacking the desire to send troops deep inside the Soviet Union, Hungary's government convinced Hitler to let the Hungarian army protect the Carpathians against a possible Russian counter-offensive. When the Russian campaign began to stall, Hitler put more pressure on his allies (e.g., Hungary, Romania, Bulgaria) to contribute to the war effort. When his allies balked, especially Hungary's government, Hitler announced that he would grant territorial rewards to those countries that gave him support. He even intimated that he would give northern Transylvania back to Romania if the Romanian government gave more support than the Hungarian government. In fact, Hitler even suggested that he would rescind the First Vienna award as well if the Hungarians did not cooperate. When Romanian leaders accepted the challenge, Hungarian leaders grudgingly continued their support of Hitler's war effort in fear that they would lose the core territory of northern Transylvania, and even southern Slovakia and southwestern Ruthenia. The willingness of many Hungarians to continue contributing to a war they no longer believed in illustrates just how significant these core territories are to Hungarian sense of identity.

By 1942, Horthy became uneasy about Hungarian support of the Nazi war effort. Even though the alliance had allowed the Hungarians to regain control over much of their national territory as they defined it, it was now

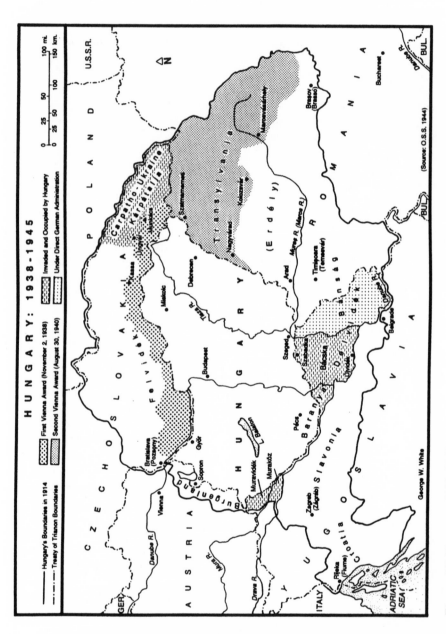

Figure 4.7 Hungary: 1938–1945.

becoming clear that a continued alliance with the Nazis might, in fact, hinder Hungarian efforts to control their national territory. Because the Western Allies would likely win the war, the Hungarians would have to be in their good graces if they wanted Allied support in reestablishing control over Historic Hungary. Therefore, Horthy decided to replace the pro-German prime minister, László Bárdossy, with Miklós Kállay, who was pro-Western. Kállay began secretly negotiating with the West. He had wanted American and British troops to parachute into Hungary while Hungarian troops would withdraw from the Russian campaign to the Carpathians. Although the plan was never initiated, Hitler became incensed and decided to have German troops occupy Hungary in mid-March 1944. By the end of the month, Hitler stated that the "Second Vienna Award" no longer existed, thus giving Transylvania back to Romania (Palmer 1970, 278–280). He allowed Horthy to stay in power, but when Horthy announced an armistice with the Russians in late 1944 as the last hope for preserving Hungarian territory, Hitler forced Horthy to resign and announced that he was turning the reins of government over to Ferenc Szálasi (fascist leader of the Arrow Cross). Szálasi tried to stop the Russian advance, but it was too late. By early April 1945, the last German troops pulled out of Hungary, ending the twenty-five year period of ultra-conservative, right-wing extremist rule and their attempt to regain control over Historic Hungary.

With the defeat of the Axis powers in the Second World War, Hungarians not only lost control of the territories they acquired during the war, they even lost control of Transdanubia and the Great Alföld as the Soviet army entered the country and a pro-Soviet government was installed by 1948. Stalin decided that Hungary would have the same borders stipulated in the Treaty of Trianon with one minor exception. The Hungarians had to cede a small piece of territory across the Danube from Bratislava (Pozsony) (in Transdanubia) to Czechoslovakia (Palmer 1970, 293).[23] With firm control of Hungary and surrounding countries, Austria the only exception, Stalin expressed little patience for the territorial claims of the Hungarians or those of any other nation. Furthermore, the stationing of Soviet troops in East European countries kept these countries from entering into military conflicts, especially any conflicts directed at regaining "lost" territories.

Because the Hungarian government cooperated with Hitler and was awarded numerous territories, which included southern Slovakia, Ruthenia, and northern Transylvania, Hungarians living in these territories found themselves in an even more precarious position than they had during the interwar years. Both the Czechoslovak and Romanian governments tried to remove the Hungarians from their state territories, with the Czechoslovak government acting most vigorously.[24] However, once again, most Hungarians refused to leave their homelands.

Many Hungarians within the Hungarian state continued to be concerned about the "lost" territories of Historic Hungary though the Soviets did not allow them to pursue an overt foreign policy to regain these territories. The Hungarians, of course, faced an even greater problem—the core territories of Transdanubia and the Great Alföld were not fully under their control anymore either. By 1956, they, like many other East Europeans, found Soviet domination intolerable. A revolution began in Hungary on October 23 and was led by students who had four demands: (1) the withdrawal of Soviet troops from Hungary; (2) the restoration of basic freedoms; (3) replacement of the alien insignia by "the old Hungarian arms of Kossuth"; and (4) the recognition of March 15 as a national holiday in memory of the struggle for Hungarian independence in 1848–49 led by Kossuth (Palmer 1970, 330). It should be noted that the struggle for independence in 1848–49 was a struggle to free the territory of the Kingdom of Hungary, not the territory conterminous with the Hungarian state of 1956. The Soviets were alarmed by the wave of nationalism in Hungary and sent troops into the area to crush the revolution.

In the face of a failed revolution and the inability to pursue an overt foreign policy aimed at regaining their "lost" territories, Hungarians had to find more subtle ways of restoring Historic Hungary in the future. In the meantime, however, the concept of Historic Hungary needed to be preserved, if not by the Hungarian government then by individual Hungarians both inside and outside of Hungary. This preservation has been nurtured through writings on geography, history, and literature. For example, Leslie Konnyu wrote a book, titled *A Condensed Geography of Hungary* (1971) with regional descriptions of Hungary. Chapter 1 is a description of the Carpathian Basin (Historic Hungary) as a natural, integrated, political-physiographic unit. Chapter 2, titled "Political Division of 1920," describes the territories of Historic Hungary that no longer belong to Hungary. Chapter 3 is titled "Present-Day Mutilated Hungary." A few years later, Yves De Daruvar wrote a book titled *The Tragic Fate of Hungary: A Country Carved up Alive at Trianon* (1974). He also refers to Historic Hungary as a natural physiographic unit and uses the term "mutilated Hungary" to describe present-day Hungary. Such views continue to be expressed in the 1990s. For example, Sandor A. Kostya focuses specifically on Slovakia in his book but the very title, *Northern Hungary* (1992), poignantly illustrates the continued significance of Historic Hungary to Hungarian nationalists.

Many Hungarians have changed their rhetoric in the last couple of decades. Although many continued to write about Historic Hungary, they also denied any irredentist aspirations; even Konnyu's and De Duruvar's books did not advocate irredentism. Instead, Hungarians began to focus their arguments on the protection of Hungarian minorities outside of

Hungary. Even though most Hungarians may have rejected irredentism, their concern for minority rights is deeply rooted and argued from a particular historical-spatial perspective. The arguments continue to be premised in the belief that Hungarian minorities in the lost territories have rights because they live on territory that is really Hungarian, although no longer claimed by Hungary.

With the relaxation of Soviet control in the mid to late 1980s, the Hungarian government was able to allow Hungarians to express their sense of identity more openly. In fact, the Hungarian government allowed the publication of a three-volume history of Transylvania by the Hungarian Academy of Sciences (Chazanoy 1987, 10). In it, the Hungarian academics reiterate the Hungarian claim to Transylvania—all of it, not just the Hungarian-inhabited areas. In 1988, the Hungarian government allowed the publication of *One Thousand Years: A Concise History of Hungary* (Hanák 1988). In many subtle ways, this book also reiterates the legitimacy of Historic Hungary. Notably, the book was published in English, making it available to a larger audience.

Although the Soviets have relinquished control in Central and Eastern Europe, the Hungarian government has not returned to its irredentist policies of the past, despite such claims by Hungary's neighbors. Certainly some Hungarians advocate such policies. In fact, the Hungarian government has been supporting, even promoting, "ethnic autonomy" for Hungarians living in the former territories of the Hungarian Kingdom[25] (Engelberg and Ingram 1993). For example, it sponsored a Hungarian Minority Summit in 1996 which concluded with a call for "ethnic autonomy" for Hungarians living in the former territories of the Hungarian Kingdom. In another context, books and maps of Historic Hungary, especially on Transylvania, are as popular as ever in Hungary.[26]

For now the future is uncertain in many of Hungary's former territories, and it is still difficult to know if recent events will swell the ranks of Hungarians who advocate irredentist policies. Most Hungarians celebrated the fall of Nicolae Ceaușescu, but relations with Romania remained poor for some time. The signing of a basic treaty between Hungary and Romania was delayed because the Hungarian government wanted to obtain more rights for the Hungarians of Transylvania (*New York Times* 1996). Relations between the Hungarian and Slovak governments have been just as poor over similar issues in southern Slovakia.

The Semi-Core: Site Identification and Landscape Description

The semi-core of modern Hungarian national identity encompasses Burgenland, Muravidék, and Muraköz, northern Slovakia, northeastern Ruthenia, and Bácska and Bánság. These territories contain fewer places

of importance than the core territories; they derive much of their significance from the broader perception that the natural territorial extent of
Hungary is synonymous with the Carpathian Basin.

Burgenland, Muravidék, and Muraköz

Before the First World War, Burgenland, Muravidék (Prekomurje), and
Muraköz (Medjumurje) were part of Transdanubia and not thought of as
distinct areas (see Figures 4.2 and 4.8). Within the thin strip of these territories, only two notable places stand out: Doborján (now Raiding) and
Kismarton (now Eisenstadt). Doborján is the birthplace of Ferenc Liszt,
one of Europe's great composers (Dobszay 1993, 147; Konnyu 1971, 31).
Kismarton is associated with one of Hungary's great families, the
Esterházys. The Esterházys built many palaces in western Hungary. One
of their more splendid palaces is in Kismarton (Gates-Coon 1994, 146).
Joseph Haydn spent thirty years in this palace and composed many of his
great works there (Légrády Brothers 1930, 125). Both of these places help
to establish the close cultural connections that Hungarians feel with
Western Europe.

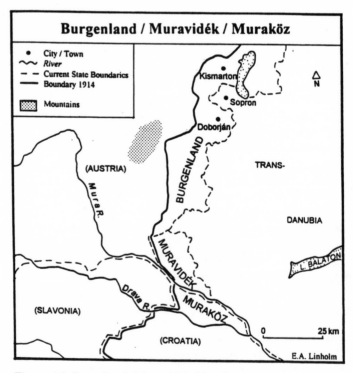

Figure 4.8 Bugenland, Muravidék, Muraköz.

Northern Slovakia and Northeastern Ruthenia (Felvidék and Kárpátalja)

Both northern Slovakia and northeastern Ruthenia are important because they fall within the physiographic limits of the Carpathian Basin (see Figures 4.2 and 4.9). In a similar context, these territories are important because they are seen as the economic counterparts of the core territories. Specifically, they provide a significant proportion of Hungary's timber and mineral resources while the core produces most of its agricultural products. In addition, these territories, like those of southern Slovakia and Transylvania, are viewed as the refuge of the Hungarian nation. A number of specific places illustrate these roles that northern Slovakia and northeastern Ruthenia play in Hungarian sense of territory. For example, Besztercebánya (now Banská Bystrica), Körmöcbánya (now Kremnica), Lőcse (now Levoča), and Selmecbánya (now Banská Štiavnica) are important timber and mining towns. The latter even had a College of Mining and Forestry (Erdei 1968, 569; Légrády Brothers 1930, 120). Bártfa (now Bardejov) once was one of the centers of Hungary's linen and bleaching industry (Erdei 1968, 193). Eperjes (now Prešov) is one of the large trading towns of the territory and is associated with a great Hungarian family, the Rákóczis. The castle of Rákóczi family is in Nagysáros (now Šariš). Árva (now Oravský Podzámok), and Trencsén (now Trečin) also have fortresses that played important roles in Hungarian history. Árva, the largest fortress in central Europe, is closely associated with the Thökölys. The places in these territories are not just significant for their economic and political roles. Körmöcbánya, Eperjes, Bártfa, and Lőcse are also known as centers of Hungarian music (Dobszay 1993, 71, 77).

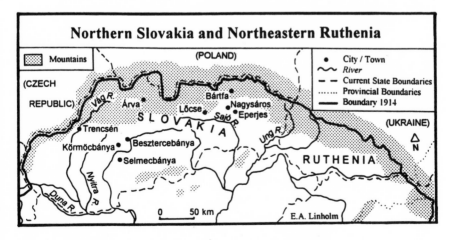

Figure 4.9 Northern Slovakia and Northeastern Ruthenia.

Bácska and Bánság

Bácska, Bánság (the Banat) (often collectively referred to as the Vojvodina [Délvidék]), and even the southern tip of Baranya are important because they are the southern areas of the Great Alföld (see Figures 4.2 and 4.10). They represent the southern extent of the "natural" physiographic limit of Hungary as defined by the Drava and Danube Rivers. The most important towns of this region are Orsova, Szabadka (Subotica), Temesvár (Timişoara), Úvidék (Novi Sad), and Zenta (Senta). Temesvár is one of the most noteworthy of these places. It was the capital of Hungary in the early part of the fourteenth century and was later associated with János Hunyadi, major figure in Hungarian history (see Transylvania). Temesvár was also the last major battle for the Hungarians in the Revolution of 1848–49. The significance of this national event is captured in a painting (Deák 1979, between pages 168 and 169). After the revolution failed, the Hungarian crown and the insignia of the revolution's leader, Lajos Kossuth, were buried in Orsova. A few years afterwards, the king of Hungary had the Crown Chapel built on the site (The Eighty Club 1907, 322). A monument to Stephen Széchenyi, one of Hungary's great statesmen, was erected nearby at the Iron Gate to commemorate his efforts to modernize Hungary's transportation system (Alden 1909, 68–69).

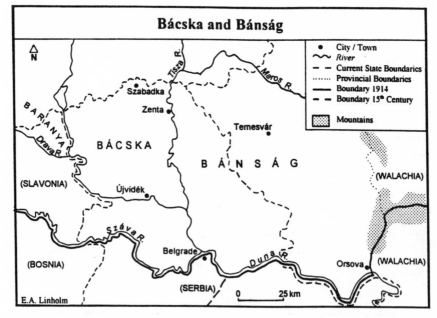

Figure 4.10 Bácska and Bánság.

The Semi-Core: The Tenacity Factor

Burgenland, Muravidék, and Muraköz, northern Slovakia and north-eastern Ruthenia, and Bácska and Bánság are classified in part for the degree of effort that Hungarians have invested in holding on to or reacquiring these territories. The importance of these semi-core territories in the nineteenth century is illustrated by the overall struggle of the Hungarians to regain control of the Kingdom of Hungary.

The importance of Burgenland was illustrated after the First World War when the Hungarian government initially refused to withdraw its military from the territory. However, the Hungarian government was willing to relinquish control of the territory without bloodshed after negotiations, demonstrating that the territory was not significant enough to be considered a core territory.

The significance of northwestern Ruthenia was shown in 1939 when the Hungarian army marched into the territory and then the Hungarian government annexed it to Hungary (Macartney and Palmer 1962, 389; Palmer 1970, 241; Seton-Watson 1956, 302) (see Figure 4.7). The Hungarian army then began an advance into northern Slovakia from Ruthenia to acquire additional territory (Macartney and Palmer 1962, 401).

The importance of Bácska and Bánság was first illustrated in the mid-nineteenth century. At that time, the southern fringes of these territories were part of a zone called the Military Frontier, directly governed from Vienna. The Hungarian government successfully negotiated their return to the Hungarian Kingdom in the Compromise of 1867.

The actions taken during the Second World War in regard to Muravidék, Muraköz, Baranya, Bácska, and Bánság illustrate the semi-core status of these territories; many Hungarians clearly wanted these territories but were unwilling to make great sacrifices for them. In April 1941, the Hungarian government allowed German troops to cross Hungary to attack Yugoslavia. Hitler encouraged Hungary's leaders and his other allies (i.e., Bulgaria's, Italy's, and Romania's leaders) to participate in the invasion and "satisfy their territorial ambitions" (Palmer 1970, 253). The Hungarian government had no great desire to go to war with Yugoslavia and, therefore, did not join in on the early stages of the invasion. The Hungarian army waited until the latter part of the two-week campaign to join in, just in time to occupy the semi-core territories of Muravidék, Muraköz, Baranya, Bácska, and Bánság. The Hungarian government then attempted to immediately annex these territories (Macartney and Palmer 1962, 446) (see Figure 4.7). A dispute quickly emerged between the Hungarians and the Romanians over the control of Bánság (the Banat). Hitler was incensed that his allies were fighting over this small territory. He had wanted them to invade, conquer, and even take control over Serbia proper. However, the Hungarians and Romanians did not want any territory that they did not perceive to be theirs. In response to the dispute over Bánság, Hitler decided to administer the territory directly from Germany (Palmer 1970, 254), depriving the Hungarians (and the Romanians as well) of one of their semi-core territories. With the defeat of Nazi Germany in 1945, all the territories gained during the war were lost once again. Since the war, no attempts have been made to regain any of the semi-core territories; however, many Hungarians still express an interest in these places.[27]

The Periphery: Site Identification, Landscape Description, and the Tenacity Factor

The periphery of Hungarian national identity is quite extensive and includes such places as Vienna and Wiener Neustadt, and the territories of Croatia, Bosnia, Dalmatia, Serbia, Walachia, Moldavia, and Bukovina (see Figure 4.4 and 4.11). These places and territories have some significance, but Hungarian national identity is only marginally derived from the periphery, and Hungarian claims to these territories have seldom been advanced. Yet the periphery is significant for a variety of reasons. In general, Hungarian control of the periphery during various periods of history illustrates for many the greatness of the Hungarian nation. The periphery places the Hungarians on an equal footing with the other great nations of Europe by demonstrating that the Hungarians, by being involved in international affairs, have shaped the course of history; in other words, Hungarians are not just an introverted people trying to desperately preserve some control over their territory and their lives.

Croatia, the peripheral territory over which Hungarians have exercised the greatest control through history, is the best example. The Hungarians have made only modest efforts in gaining control of Croatia since the rise of nationalism. For example, following Hitler's invasion of Yugoslavia in 1941, the Hungarian government hoped for an autonomous Croatia and a strip of the Dalmatian coast (Palmer 1970, 254) but did little to bring it about. Again in 1991, the year Slovenia's and Croatia's governments declared their independence from Yugoslavia, the Hungarian government secretly shipped weapons to the Croatians. When the Hungarian government was forced to admit to its actions, it declared a ban on all arms sales to Yugoslavia to prevent hositilies with the Serbian dominated government of Yugoslavia (Bohlen 1991).

Bohemia, Poland, Bosnia, Serbia, Walachia, and Moldavia are all peripheral territories that demonstrate the greatness of the Hungarian nation. The kings of Hungary demonstrated their immense power when they also became the kings of Bohemia and Poland. They also demonstrated the greatness of the Hungarian nation when they turned Bosnia, Serbia, Walachia, and Moldavia into vassal states at one time. During the First

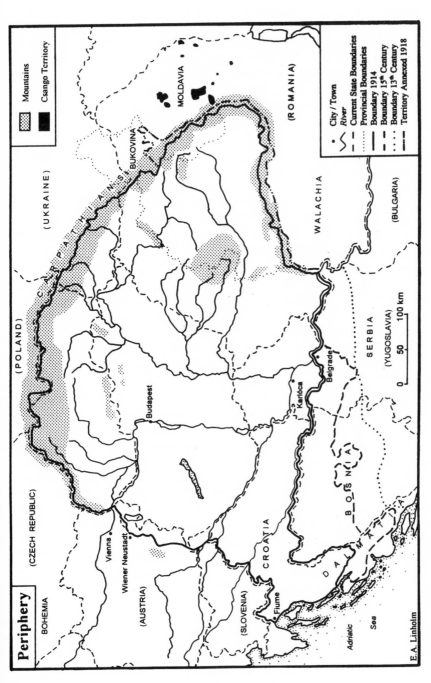

Periphery

		Mountains
		Csango Territory

BOHEMIA

(CZECH REPUBLIC)

(AUSTRIA)

(SLOVENIA)

(POLAND)

(UKRAINE)

C A R P A T H I A N S BUKOVINA

MOLDAVIA

(ROMANIA)

WALACHIA

(BULGARIA)

SERBIA

(YUGOSLAVIA)

BOSNIA

CROATIA

D A L M A T I A

Adriatic

Sea

Vienna

Wiener Neustadt

Budapest

Belgrade

Karloca

Fiume

City / Town
River
Current State Boundaries
Provincial Boundaries
Boundary 1914
Boundary 15th Century
Boundary 13th Century
Territory Annexed 1918

0   50   100 km

E. A. Linholm

Figure 4.11 The Periphery.

World War, the Hungarian government exercised its power by annexing a strip of Romanian territory along the Hungarian-Romanian boundary. No claim had been advanced to the territory before the war. Yet, with the fortunes of the war, the territory was taken primarily to create a buffer for the protection of the core territory of Transylvania.

In addition to the issue of control, the peripheral territories played other roles in shaping Hungarian national identity. For example, many of the Romantics who collected Hungarian folklore went to Bukovina (Dobszay 1993, 176) and Moldavia, to the Csángó communities (Suchoff 1981, 95); the Csángós are a people closely related to the early Magyars and Szeklers (Tatrosi 1920, 1–2). By going to these regions, Hungarian Romantics helped to create a sense of modern Hungarian national identity that has many components of Csángó culture. The geographical location of the Csángós is significant as well. Living between the Carpathian Basin and the steppes of Eurasia, the Csángós represent a physical link that legitimizes the spiritual link that the Hungarians of the Carpathian Basin have with their ancestral homeland in the steppes of Eurasia.

Specific cities such as Vienna (Bécs) and Wiener Neustadt (Bécsújhely) are noteworthy as a result of the close political connection between Hungary and the Austrian Empire. Hungary not only was controlled for long periods from Vienna, but Hungarians traveled and resided in Vienna and Wiener Neustadt for a number of reasons, even to receive an education.

Belgrade (Nándorfehérvár) was once a key fortress in the southern defense of the Hungarian Kingdom. It is also associated with one of Hungary's greatest heroes, János Hunyadi (Sisa 1990, 51, 53). In a similar context, Karlóca (Sremski Karlovci; Karlowitz) is associated with the Treaty of Karlowitz, which freed Hungary from Ottoman rule in 1699 (Hanák 1988, 72). Fiume (Rijeka) is important because it was Hungary's only seaport. With the long-held belief of many Europeans that a nation could achieve greatness only by becoming a sea power, Fiume became one of the symbols of the greatness of the Hungarian nation. The significance of Fiume is underscored by its direct control by the Hungarian crown following the creation of the dual monarchy, not allowed to be governed by the autonomous government of Croatia.

Notes

1. Even István Szécheny wrote many of his diaries in German, and when not in German, then in Italian, French, or English (Barany 1968, 5). Szécheny's language practices are noteworthy because he was dubbed "the Greatest among Magyars," and even the father of modern Magyar nationalism (Barany 1968, 3, 295). His fame partially derives from his being the first person to have had enough gall to address members of the upper chamber of the Hungarian Diet in Hungarian, instead of Latin as expected. It should be noted, however, that this

action shocked his Hungarian colleagues (Ignotus 1972, 51). After Szécheny began to use Magyar more frequently, he claimed that the Hungarian nation had degenerated because so few Hungarians still spoke Magyar. He laid the blame on Hungarians themselves, specifically their poor attitude toward Magyar, not foreigners (Barany 1968, 297), whom Romantic nationalists would tend to blame. Magyar then had obviously been in the process of dying out until the advent of nationalism because most Hungarians did not see Magyar as a fundamental component of their identity.

2. The new language law immediately caused some practical problems because there was no textbook in existence at the time in Hungary to teach the Magyar language. Latin had always been the language of education (Barany 1968, 409–10).

3. Certainly Hungarians did not fear the German language or German culture because they had so thoroughly embraced both over the preceding centuries, even to the extent that the major urban centers of Hungary had become culturally German by the early nineteenth century (Barany 1968, 224). Budapest was no exception. A majority of its inhabitants were German-speaking up to the middle of the nineteenth century (Dávid 1988, 334).

4. This desire, however, did not develop until the latter half of the nineteenth century. During the first half of the century, most Hungarian leaders remained loyal to the Hapsburg monarchy, even those who agitated for the linguistic rights of the Hungarian language. Even István Szécheny, the father of Hungarian nationalism and first promoter of the Hungarian language, remained loyal to the monarchy (Barany 1968, 117, 297). Such loyalty to a non-national government does not conform to modern understandings of nationalism.

5. Paul Ignotus points out that the terms *Hungarian* and *Magyar* were synonymous until the end of the eighteenth century because "nobody thought that the mother-tongue should be made the main criterion of nationhood" (1972, 12). With the new emphasis placed on language, *Magyar* developed a more restricted meaning for those who spoke a particular language, while *Hungarian* maintained the broader meaning of those who lived in the Hungarian Kingdom. To put it very bluntly, the term *Hungarian* referred to a form of human identity based on where people lived, not what language they spoke. With the rise of nationalism, however, Magyars began to feel themselves to be the true Hungarians because they thought that they spoke the true language of Hungary. They, nevertheless, continued to identify with the Hungarian Kingdom, not just the Magyar-speaking areas. In fact, the Magyars came to believe that their language made them the rightful inheritors of the Hungarian Kingdom (Barany 1968, 410).

6. Government representatives from neighboring countries expressed their dismay to the Hungarian government in regard to its sponsorship of the celebrations. They stated that the celebrations were irredentist because the Hungarian Kingdom included territories that are now part of other countries.

7. It is not uncommon for differing peoples to blend together to form one genealogy. Often the common denominator is common territory. Differing peoples will see themselves or behave as a single people if they occupy the same locations, and not necessarily at the same time. Americans of European descent, for example, will celebrate the histories and cultures of Native Americans as if they were their own. American immigrants also are expected to accept the history of their new land as their own.

8. In 1892, the Hungarian government issued a statute declaring that the year 895 was the founding date and began making preparations for the millennial anniversary. When the government realized that it could not prepare for the celebrations in time, it postponed the founding date until 896 (Gerő 1990, 6).

9. Hungary, nevertheless, was stripped of two-thirds of its territory following the Paris Peace Conference; the Hungarians lost more of their territory than any other defeated powers. The approach that the Hungarian representatives took at the Paris Peace Conference did little to prevent the loss of territory. The Hungarian representatives made the fatal mistake of basing their defense of their country's boundaries on the natural unity of the Hungarian Kingdom. In retrospect, they should have focused on the distribution of peoples (Deák 1972, 209–10). They, however, were oblivious that the world's political leaders had recently come to the conclusion that the distributions of peoples were relevant to boundary delineation. In their defense, the Hungarian representatives were not aware of this shift in attitudes because they were not summoned to the conference until its end, and then they were not allowed much contact with the other participants before presenting their arguments (Deák 1972, 176–203).

10. The Treaty of Trianon was written at the Paris Peace Conference and then imposed on the Hungarian people. It is most known for having stripped away two-thirds of the Kingdom of Hungary.

11. Of course, sense of identity changes over time. Subsequently, the cultural landscapes have to be altered to reflect changing senses of identity. András Gerő recently wrote about the Millennium Monument and how its individual elements have been altered to reflect the changing identity of the Hungarian nation (1990).

12. The university was forced to move to Pécs after the First World War.

13. Although Hungarian national identity has a strong anti-Hapsburg component, it is interesting to note that the statue of Austrian Empress Maria Theresa in Pozsony became a symbol for many Hungarians after it was torn down by Czechs after the First World War (Légrády Brothers 1930, 87; Konnyu 1971, 23).

14. One of Hungary's greatest composers, Ferenc Erkel, came from Pozsony (Dobszay 1993, 141).

15. Note that the Carpathians, which served as the boundaries of the Hungarian Kingdom, are still embodied in Hungarian poetry even though they are not in the modern state of Hungary.

16. Even though few Hungarians actually live out on the Alföld or descend from people who lived there, the Alföld is seen as the heartland of Hungary; as such, Hungarian national identity is intimately tied to it. This situation is by no means unique. Few Americans, for example, live or even desire to live in America's agricultural heartland or in the rugged West—domain of the cowboy, an independent, free-thinking man. Nevertheless, the traditional American way of life is associated with the farms of the agricultural heartland, and freedom, independence, and the belief that life is filled with unlimited possibilities is tied to the rugged landscapes of the West. The American nation would not be what it is without these places. Though many Americans have not been to these places, American national identity would not be what is without them. Not surprisingly then, the farmer's billed cap and the cowboy hat—clothing items developed in the natural environments of the mid-West and West—are popularly worn by many Americans no matter where they live.

17. *Paprika* is one the traditional foods of the Hungarians. It plays such a role that it is difficult to imagine Hungarian culture without it. The paprika, however, is grown primarily in the Great Alföld. It is possible to grow it in some other areas of the world, but Hungarians have a particular fondness for paprika from the Great Alföld. From the perspective of national cuisine, Hungarian culture simply would not be what it is without the Great Alföld.

18. Transylvania was even recognized as a sovereign state in the Treaty of Westphalia (1648) (Burant 1989, 17).

19. A statue of a Hungarian leader named Miklós Wesselényi also gives Zilah political significance.

20. Other elements of modern Hungarian national identity began as early as the 1780s, but not the desire for self-rule, which requires territorial sovereignty. Because the desire for self-rule initiates the struggle for territorial sovereignty, the absence of an independence struggle likewise indicates a lack of desire for self-rule, in turn indicating an incompletely formed sense of national identity.

21. The Serbian army had moved in the south, the Romanian army from the southeast, and a new Czechoslovak army from the north.

22. For detailed information on the discrimination policies enacted by governments to drive Hungarians out of the former territories of the Hungarian Kingdom and into the modern Hungarian state, see *The Hungarians: A Divided Nation* (Borsody 1988) and *Transylvania: The Roots of Ethnic Conflict* (Cadzow, Ludanyi, and Elteto, 1983).

23. The reasons for this cession of land were never clearly explained. Czech leaders had claimed this land after the First World War but did not receive it. Perhaps, as a means of compensating Czechoslovakia for the loss of Ruthenia (which became part of the Soviet Union, specifically the Ukrainian Republic), Stalin decided to allow the Czechoslovak government to annex this small piece of territory. Although Hungary lost Ruthenia once again, this time it was to the Soviet Union and not to Czechoslovakia as it had been in 1920. Hungary then found itself bordering the Soviet Union, which it had never done before. Historic Hungary was now divided among seven countries (modern Hungary, Austria, Czechoslovakia, Romania, Yugoslavia, Poland, and the Soviet Union).

24. For detailed information on the policies of the Czechoslovak government on this issue, see Czechoslovak policy and the Hungarian Minority, 1945–1948 (Janics 1982). Additional information can also be found in *The Hungarians: A Divided Nation* (Borsody 1988). For information on the Hungarians of Transylvania, see *Transylvania: The Roots of Ethnic Conflict* (Cadzow, Ludanyi, and Elteto 1983) and *The Hungarian Minority's Situation in Ceauşescu's Romania* (Joó 1994).

25. The meaning of "ethnic autonomy" has not clarified, but certainly it, like any other form of autonomy, requires some degree of control over territory.

26. The Hungarian Academy produced a new volume on the history of Transylvania in 1994 (Köpeczi); a three volume set of picture books with text explaining the Hungarian character of the territory was published in 1993 (Szacsvay and Írta); a work of poetry with landscape photography appeared in 1995 (Váradi and Lilla). Over the last few years, the most accurate and detailed maps of Transylvania have been designed and produced in Hungary, not Romania. Probably the best one is published by DIMAP (1995); the quality is so

good that it is commonly found in Romanian bookstores as well. These are only a few examples; many more exist.

27. In fact, a series of picture books have been published on these semi-core territories. Two of the most notable are *Bácska és Bánság* (Legeza and Szacsvay 1992) and *Kárpátalja* (Szacsvay, Szacsvay, and Legeza, 1990). These books, of course, emphasize the Hungarian character of these territories.

5

Romania and the Romanians

One look at the language map of Europe quickly shows that Romanian stands out as a Latinic language in a sea of Slavic languages. The Hungarian language region lies on the western flank of the Romanian language region, but Hungarian is more alien to Romanian than to the Slavic languages. Despite the geographic uniqueness of the Romanian language, we should not fall into the trap that many Romantics have fallen into and conclude that the uniqueness of the Romanian language gave birth to the Romanian nation. Although Romanian is a distinct Latinic language today, we should not project this current distinctiveness into the past and thereby create the assumption that it has always existed. On the contrary, it is not the Romanian language that created the Romanians but the Romanians who created the Romanian language. Prior to the rise of modern nationalism, the so-called Romanian language had many Slavic, German, Magyar, Greek, and even Turkish words, concepts, and grammatical constructs in it, making it not always so distinct from its neighboring languages as it is today. Over the course of the era of nationalism, Romanian Romantic nationalists have worked to make the Romanian language separate and distinct because they *imagined* themselves to be separate and distinct from the peoples around them. Thus if language does spawn nationhood as Romantic nationalists argue, it does not mean that it is an inevitability but rather a self-fulfilling prophecy brought about by much contrived hard work.

Romanian Romantic nationalists, of course, did not fabricate the "Latinness" of the Romanian language out of nothing. What their ancestors spoke had a number of Latin elements in it, but whatever degree of "Latinness" the language had was meaningless to the people who spoke it. Indeed, what was spoken was not even referred to as Romanian, and the people who spoke it did not even call themselves Romanian. The three provinces of Walachia, Moldavia, and Transylvania are primarily what now comprises modern Romania.[1] Until the rise of modern nationalism a little over two hundred years ago, the term *Romanian* was not in general application but rather the terms Walachians, Moldavians, and Transylvanians. Because these peoples shared similar cultural characteristics and because Walachia tended to be the territory that exerted greatest political autonomy through the Middle Ages and into the modern era, Central Europeans were inclined to refer to all of these peoples as Walachians. The Saxon, Magyar, and Szekler populations of Transylvania reserved the term *Transylvanian* for themselves and would not share the term with their fellow inhabitants who shared so many characteristics with the Walachians, whom they also looked down upon. Thus they employed the term *Walachian* to these people to separate themselves.

The Saxons, Magyars, and Szeklers did not distinguish themselves from the Walachians in language but by way of life. For the Saxons, Magyars, and Szeklers, the term *Walachian* (or *Walach, Vlach*) was not synonymous with Latin speaker but with shepherd, or simply peasant. In short, these peoples looked down on the Walachians and were thus unwilling to refer to them as fellow Transylvanians. Being at the lower end of the social scale, the Walachians tended to communicate with the Saxons in German, with the Magyars and Szeklers in Hungarian, or in Latin during those periods when Transylvania was a part of Hungary; Latin was the official language of Hungary until 1840 (Hobsbawn 1962, 167). Evidence demonstrates that Walachian was also a term of self-designation. For example, in 1791 the Walachians of Transylvania sent a petition to the imperial crown of Austria calling for the Walachians to be recognized as the fourth nation of Transylvania. We know that Walachians called themselves Walachians and not Romanians because the document was titled *Supplex libelus Valachorum* ("Humble petition of the Walachians") (Verdery 1983, 119).

Evidence also shows that Walachians did not consider their own language to be particularly meaningful. The Protestants of Transylvania, for example, had translated a number of religious works into Romanian in the 16th century and then the Bible itself in 1648 (Elteto 1983, 69–70), but most Walachians did not embrace such works. Because most were Orthodox Christians, they did not share in the Protestant belief that one should practice one's faith in one's own language. Instead, most Walachians used Church Slavonic in their churches. In short, the evidence suggests that the characteristics of group distinctiveness derived more from socio-economics than from language.

Because Romantic nationalists believe that religion is just as much a national determinant as language, religious belief and practice should be examined to see if it is truly a parent of the Romanian nation. A close examination of religion, however, shows that Romanian national identity grew even less out of religious distinctiveness than it did out of linguistic distinctiveness. Through history, the ancestors of the Romanians were mostly Eastern Orthodox Christians. Prior to the rise of nationalism in the nineteenth century, nothing existed within the general Eastern Orthodox Church that cultivated a distinct Romanian national identity. The language of the church, including worship service, was Church Slavonic. Administratively, Romanian Orthodox churches were controlled by Serbs from Sremski Karlovci.[2] At the same time, the Orthodox Church in Eastern Europe had been administered from the highest level by the Patriarchate of Constantinople, the so-called Great Church. That the pinnacle of the church had been in a Greek city, or at least the Greek part of Constantinople, meant that the ecumenical patriarch was usually Greek. Not surprisingly, Greek language and culture were the foundation of Europe's Eastern Orthodox world (Hobsbawn 1962, 173), but not for nationalistic reasons.

With the rise of nationalism in the nineteenth century, Greeks in the higher echelons of the Orthodox Church began to see the Orthodox Church as the Greek national church. As a result, Greeks imbued with the new nationalist ideology tried to Hellenize the Orthodox world. A concurrent growth of national awareness among other Orthodox Christians led to the resentment of Hellenizing policies and practices. Indeed, the growth in national awareness among other groups led these other groups to try to nationalize their Orthodox churches. Because Romanians were administered by Serbs from Sremski Karlovci, they had to endure Serbianizing as well as Hellenizing policies and practices. In many ways, Serbianizing and Hellenizing contributed to the rise of Romanian nationalism and subsequently led the Romanians to desire their own national church. In 1864 the Romanians of Transylvania obtained permission from the Austrian Empire to establish a separate autonomous Romanian Orthodox Church with its metropolitan seat in Sibiu. Similarly, in 1873 the Romanians of Bukovina obtained the consent of the Austrian Empire to establish a metropolitan for Bukovina in Rădăuți (Magocsi 1993, 116–117). In 1859 Walachia and Moldavia were united into a single autonomous province within the Ottoman Empire; in 1864 the new government of the united principalities organized the Romanian Orthodox Church[3] (Ware 1964, 100). However, no semblance of a Romanian national church emerged until after the appearance of a Romanian national consciousness, not before. Moreover, the Romanian state created the Romanian Orthodox Church, not the other way around. More important, because no separate strain of Romanian Orthodoxy or even anything uniquely Romanian existed within the Orthodox Church prior to the rise of nationalism in the nineteenth century, Eastern Orthodoxy could not have given birth to the Romanian nation.

While Eastern Orthodoxy was not the birth mother of the Romanian nation, another religion was instrumental in the creation of the modern Romanian nation: the Uniate Church.[4] Although the Uniate belief was unique, it is not a national identifier in the sense that its believers stood apart from the people around them and thus came to see themselves as a separate nation. Only a minority of Walachians believed in the Uniate faith; they were geographically limited in their distribution among the eventual population of the Romanian nation,[5] and many of the Uniate faith would subscribe to other national identities than a Romanian one. The Uniate Church is significant because the idea of the modern Romanian nation traces its roots to Uniate clerics who first *imagined* the Romanian nation and then propagated and cultivated it into its mature being.

The Uniate Church is a unique blend of Roman Catholicism and Eastern Orthodoxy: liturgy and traditions are primarily Eastern Orthodoxy but Uniates are loyal to the pope in Rome (Magocsi 1993, 53). Interestingly, the Uniate Church developed in the contact zone between Roman Catholicism, Eastern Orthodoxy, and Protestantism. These three branches of Christianity competed vigorously for converts in east Central Europe. This competition paradoxically stimulated the desire of many Christians within this zone of competition to unify the Christian churches. Thus the Uniate Church came into being.

Although Austria's political leaders did not have a direct hand in creating the Uniate Church, Austrian leaders quickly realized that the Uniate Church could serve their political aims, especially their territorial ambitions. As Roman Catholics, Austrian leaders always had difficulty expanding their empire into territories inhabited by Eastern Orthodox Christians because Eastern Orthodox Christians could not accept the political leadership of those who were not their spiritual leaders; church and state were not separate throughout most of European history. Conversion was the logical means of convincing a conquered population to accept the imposition of a new imperial order. Certainly, as good Catholics, Austrian leaders tried to convert the populations under their rule to Roman Catholicism. People, however, do not readily and easily change their religious convictions, especially not in a region of the world where the control of territory by any one empire and its affiliated religion is ephemeral. The Uniate Church, however, provided a solution for many of the difficulties that the Austrian Empire had been fighting to overcome. No longer would Austria's leaders have to invest large amounts of energy to change the practices and beliefs of Orthodox Christians while they simultaneously subdued them until the conversion to Roman Catholicism was complete. The Uniate faith was much easier to spread among Orthodox populations because it did not require Orthodox Christians to change their behavior, only recognize the pope as their spiritual leader. Once Orthodox Christians converted to the Uniate faith by making the more modest step of recognizing the pope, Austrian emperors could legitimately extend their control over Uniates because, as Roman Catholics, they were political agents of the pope. Indeed, Uniate converts would naturally desire to have their territories incorporated into the Austrian Empire and be out of the jurisdictions of Orthodox political leaders such as the Russian czar, who became the enemy upon the moment of conversion.

Because the Austrian emperors saw the Uniate Church as an instrument that could advance their ambitions, they promoted the Uniate Church on their empire's frontier whenever they had the opportunity. In 1699, not long after the Austrian imperial armies drove the Ottomans out of the Carpathian Basin, Austrian emperor Leopold I issued an imperial diploma which created a union between the Roman Catholic and Uniate churches. The union elevated the status of the Uniate Church within Transylvania (Hitchins 1977, 2–3; Seton-Watson 1963, 124–25). Soon after the union, the court in Vienna began financing the construction of Uniate educational institutions and opened the Roman Catholic schools and the University of Vienna to Walachians wanting to join the priesthood (Hitchins 1977, 3). Just as important, the imperial court even financed travel to Rome.

The incorporation of Transylvania into the Austrian Empire and the subsequent actions of the Viennese court were significant because they brought Walachians into more intimate contact with Central and Western European civilization (Verdery 1983, 119). As a result, many Walachians began to see themselves in terms of Central and Western European civilization. Soon Uniate clerics residing in Rome began to see the connections between their own culture and that of the Latin world. They gazed almost daily upon emperor Trajan's column (Campbell 1971, 23) and then learned how Trajan conquered the territories which they identified as their very own homeland. Also finding traces of the Latin language in their own language, they began to make the most of these connections. Within a few decades, they began to see themselves not as mere Walachians but as Romanians, the descendants of Romans, builders of one of the greatest civilizations in human history.

Over the decades that followed, the number of Uniate clerics who built on the belief that Walachians were really Romanians began to grow. By the end of the eighteenth century, they became collectively known as the "Transylvanian School" (*Şcoala ardeleană*) (Deletant 1991, 65–66; Jelavich and Jelavich 1977, 239). The key figures were Samuil Micu-Clain, Gheorghe Şincai, and Peter Maior, but many more figures were involved as well (Hitchins 1969). These figures fully developed the idea of the *Romanian nation*[6] and argued that its ethnogenesis was brought about by the genetic and cultural mixing of Roman soldiers and native Dacians, the peoples who occupied the territories of what we now know as Romania. They began writing histories to illustrate and prove their belief and were very prolific.

Just as significantly, members of the Transylvanian School, as well as others in Walachia and Moldavia who were influenced by the Transylvanian School, began to work on the *Romanian language*. At the time, their language, with its varied dialects, was distantly related to the other Latinic languages, but with many elements of Magyar, German, Turkish, Greek,[7] and the various Slavic languages.[8] Instead of accepting their language for what it was, they concluded that their language had been degraded by many centuries of foreign domination and it would, therefore, have to be *purified*. So they published dictionaries and grammars which, over the course of time, systematically purged non-Latin based words and replaced them with Latinic words (Berend 1987, 31; Campbell 1971, 25; Comrie 1987, 305; Gallagher 1995, 13; Hitchins 1969, 108, 159).[9] Even if they did not see the need to cleanse the language, other ideas that were developing under the new ideology of nationalism required the language to be altered. Namely, nationalism called for each nation to create literary works and write down scientific accomplishments in its own language. As it was, the language of the emerging Romanian nation was too oriented to a peasant's way of life to be used as either a literary or scientific language (Close 1974, 2, 6, 9–10; Hitchins 1969, 83, 149–50). Thus, Romanian nationalists tapped Latin, Italian, and French[10] for the necessary neologisms. The new ideas of nationalism also led to the desire to alter the alphabet. Walachians had used the Cyrillic alphabet in their writing because most of them were Eastern Orthodox Christians. Continued use of the Cyrillic alphabet for the newly developing Latinized Romanian language, however, blatantly contradicted the belief that the Romanian nation was the child of Roman culture. To demonstrate the close ties, Romanian nationalists began insisting that the Latin alphabet be adopted.[11]

Although the term *Romanian* came into heavy use during the rise of nationalism in the nineteenth century, it had origins that predated the Transylvanian School and the general period of Romantic nationalism. However, it was spelled *Rumanian*, with a *u* instead of an *o*. *Rumanian* spelled with a *u* derived from the Turkish word *rumlar* (Elteto 1983, 68–69), which meant Roman but referred to the Byzantine inheritors of the Roman Empire whom the Ottomans conquered. The Ottomans applied this term not just to the people who would become modern-day Romanians but to all Eastern Orthodox Christians. The Ottomans never referred to a place called Rumania; nevertheless, it became one of the modern ways of spelling the name of the current nation-state of Romania. Romania spelled with an *o* means *land of the Romans*. The term emerged in the fifth century to refer to those former regions of the Roman Empire (Pei 1965, 325) but was quickly expropriated by Romanian nationalists for their country in the nineteenth century.

A modern Romanian national identity derived from Roman civilization appealed to many Walachians (Verdery 1991, 32). As a peasant people, Walachians were always scorned and looked down upon by the various peoples who ruled them. On the other hand, the new Romanian national identity, so intimately tied to Roman civilization, instantly brought Walachians a list of great accomplishments that catapulted them to the top of the list of great nations. Their Roman ancestry provided them with accomplishments that overshadowed any of those made by the Magyars, Austrians, Ottomans, or Russians. Indeed, as Romanians, they could feel a great sense of national pride.

Despite this great sense of national pride, mapping Romanian national identity to determine the appropriate boundaries for a Romanian nation-state was extremely problematic. Romanian national identity, like many other national identities, was, as Eric Hobsbawn would say, invented. Although Romantic nationalists believe that nationhood is born of language and religion, it has just been shown that Romanian nationhood grew out of neither. Therefore, language and religion could not, and cannot, be mapped out and thus be used to identify the appropriate boundaries of the Romanian nation-state. What then was the appropriate territory for the Romanian nation-state? Unfortunately for the Romanians, the answer was not as simple as that for the Hungarians, who had a kingdom with a well-defined territory that had existed for almost a thousand years. The territoriality of Romanian nationhood had a more complex evolution than that of Hungarian nationhood. Those who adopted Romanian nationhood found themselves to be spread over at least three different politically organized territories: Walachia, Moldavia, and Transylvania. These territories had meaning and corresponding scales of human identity attached to them. Unfortunately, the nation-state ideal conceptualized one nation-one state (and vice versa), not one nation-three states. Even though unification could certainly be argued for, a single state had to be identified sometime in history that gave birth to the Romanian nation, a state with which Walachians, Moldavians, and Transylvanians could all identify. The identification of an early state was required not only to prove the legitimacy of the Romanian nation but also to delimit spatially the Romanian nation-state, which in turn provided a means for identifying who should and should not be a Romanian. Indeed, boundaries determine identity as much as identity determines boundaries.

The search for a single state that included within it Walachia, Moldavia, and Transylvania finds only one example in the last thousand years: that of Michael the Brave, who unified the three principalities in 1600 and declared himself to be the "Prince of Ungro-Walachia, of Transylvania, and of Moldavia"[12] (Seton-Watson 1963, 69). Michael the Brave's state, however, lasted less than a year. It would be impossible to argue that such a short-lived state was able to set up a field of spatial interaction intense enough to mold its inhabitants into a single people. Even if the state was able to do so, it had a major weakness which it could not overcome. Namely, it postdated Transylvania's incorporation into the Hungarian Kingdom. In the reasoning of Romantic nationalism, not only were language and religion paramount to national identity, but also history. It was, and continues to be, blindly accepted by Romantics that those who could claim that they occupied a territory first had the legitimate right to it. Because Michael the Brave ruled over Transylvania after the Magyars had control over it, Romanian Romantic nationalists felt compelled to search for a state that legitimized the unification of Transylvania, Walachia, and Moldavia *and* predated Magyar occupation of Transylvania.

The search for the progenitor state of the Romanian nation was not difficult even though it had to be found in the dark obscurity of the ancient past. The interest that Romanian Romantic nationalists had in the Roman past brought with it an answer to their territorial question. Because it was the Romans who provided the Romanians with their language (though as the result of modern contrivance), the Romans must have given them their state territory as well. It would be absurd to think of themselves in terms of the entire Roman Empire, especially because the other descendants of the Roman Empire varied to the extent that they did not identify with Romanians and because the Walachians, Moldavians, and Transylvanians did not identify with the entire territory of the Roman Empire. In the study of their territory, Romanian nationalists noted that their territory had been the Roman province of Dacia, named after the state and people that the Romans had conquered. Therefore, their strain of Latinness must have come from the mixing of Romans and the indigenous Dacians. The pre-Roman Dacian state was also attractive, and indeed meaningful, because its territory roughly coincided with that of the modern principalities of Walachia, Moldavia, and Transylvania. It was a territory with which Walachians, Moldavians, and Transylvanians could identify collectively.

The Daco-Roman mix was perfect for Romanian nationalists. The Roman part of the equation provided the Romanian nation with an intense sense of pride and accomplishment while the Dacian state (later Roman province of Dacia) part of the equation provided the Romanians with a progenitor state territory. Recreating the Dacian state and unifying Walachia, Moldavia, and Transylvania were essentially one and the same. Legitimacy for unification of the modern territories was derived from the ancient state territory. Most important, the Dacian state predated Transylvania's membership in the Hungarian Kingdom, thereby delegitimizing Hungarian claims to Transylvania.

The belief that the modern-day Romanian nation is the product of a Roman and Dacian cultural and genetic mixing which took place almost two thousand years ago is not without its problems. Indeed, it is very controversial. Very little evidence exists that can support this belief and thus it is still just a theory, commonly called the Daco-Roman theory. Moreover, Romantic nationalism mandates not only an argument of first-occupation in advancing a territorial claim but also a demonstration of continuous settlement. Thus *continuous* and *continuity* are powerful words in the rhetoric of Romantic nationalists, and Romanian Romantic nationalists employ them frequently in conjunction with their Daco-Roman claims. The continuous settlement of a Daco-Roman people in the territory of what is now Romania is even more difficult to prove than the Daco-Roman origin of modern Romanians. Gaps in the historical record of the last two thousand years still need to be bridged, especially a huge gap of evidence that currently exists between the third and fourteenth centuries.

Romanian nationalists conceived of the Daco-Roman theory to counter and even delegitimize the Hungarian claim to one of the territories that defines the Romanian nation. Unfortunately, the Daco-Roman theory became, by its very creation, a threat to Hungarian national identity, specifically through its legitimization of Romanian control over Transylvania, a fundamental component of Hungarian national identity. But if the Daco-Roman theory is correct, Romantic nationalism sides with the Romanians on the dispute over Transylvania. Therefore, the Hungarians are just as compelled to disprove the Daco-Roman theory as the Romanians are compelled to prove it. Unfortunately, neither side realizes that the other side will not be dissuaded by facts, no matter how irrefutable. Territory and identity are inseparable, and because identity is derived from belief, though a belief in oneself, facts—although potent weapons—will not always alter belief, no matter how compelling. Consequently, bold claims, no matter how fiercely asserted, are countered with equal boldness and ferocity by the opposing side.

So despite the inherent weaknesses of the Daco-Roman theory and all the evidence that Hungarian nationalists have brought forth to disprove it, the Romanian nation holds firmly to the ideas of the Daco-Roman theory because they legitimize Romanian control over the territories that define the Romanian nation. The Daco-Roman theory then is the best vehicle for understanding the territoriality of Romanian nationhood. Indeed, applying site identification and landscape description to the Daco-Roman theory reveals many of the individual places and territories that define the Romanian nation, thus making the mapping process possible. Because numerous places exist, they are presented in regional groupings for the sake of clarity, and even regrouped more broadly into a core, semi-core, and periphery categorization. The depth of their importance is revealed by the application of the tenacity factor. Because modern Romanian national identity is only about two hundred years old, the tenacity factor is applied to only the last two centuries. Even though peoples fought over territory through history, identity existed in a different context prior to the late eighteenth century. Therefore, the meaning of place and territory was likewise much different as well. It would be inappropriate to apply the tenacity factor to prenationalist struggles as if they were nationalist ones, even though Romantic nationalists insist that they were.

Although the tenacity factor cannot be applied much earlier than the end of the eighteenth century, it does not mean that events before this time are irrelevant. On the contrary, in terms of site identification and landscape description, many places highlighted are associated with figures and events of much earlier periods. It always must be remembered, however, that places are brought to light not for the significance of their time but for their importance to the modern Romanian nation. In fact, many of the places identified have become memorialized with monuments, shrines, and the like only since the rise of nationalism, some only in the last few years even though they signify an event that may have taken place two thousand years ago. Therefore, all places and territories are identified in terms of their current significance, even though many represent something much older.

Because Romanian national identity contains many Romantic elements, history cannot be disregarded. On the contrary, the Romanian nation has developed emotional-psychological bonds to a long list of places that it now regards to be historically significant. An understanding of Romanian history facilitates an appreciation of Romanian territoriality. Therefore, while the purpose of this chapter is not to retell Romanian history, it is, nevertheless, necessary to provide an outline of relevant history, no matter how coarse and generalized, in order to set the territorial component of Romanian national identity in its proper context.

Brief Overview of Romanian History

Romanian historians have written a history for their people that extends back more than two thousand years, to a people called the Dacians (in Latin or Getae in Greek), whom Romanians consider to be their forefathers. The Dacians inhabited territories from the Tişa (Tisza) River in the west to the Nistra (Dnestr) and Black Sea Coast in the east as early as 2,000 B.C. (Giurescu 1981, 26) (see Figure 5.1). Like most of the people of the time, the Dacians were a broad association of tribal units sharing similar cultural characteristics. The lumping together of these people is a modern convenience; therefore, we should be careful not to overstate their sense of unity. Nevertheless, Romanian historians treat the Dacians as a unified people with a shared sense of identity, a common purpose, and an unyielding desire to be united. For much of their history, however, the Dacians did not organize into a single political state.

Roman presence in the territory that we know today as Romania began in the first century B.C. when the Romans conquered their first Dacian territory, Dobrogea (Dobrudja). The Dacians resisted Roman control for some time but by A.D. 106 their territories were incoporated into the Roman Empire as the Roman province of *Dacia Felix* ("Happy Dacia"). *Dacia Felix* served the Roman Empire as a bulwark against hostile tribes that frequently appeared from the steppe region to the east. However, by the third century, it became vulnerable to these tribes as they grew in strength. Thus in A.D. 271, Roman legions began withdrawing to positions south of the Danube (Georgescu 1991, 8), completely abandoning the Dacian province by A.D. 275. In the end, Roman control of Dacia lasted less than 170 years. However, while *Dacia Felix* was an integrated province of the Roman Empire, the interaction of the inhabitants of Dacia and the rest of the Roman Empire increased, with many Roman soldiers settling in Dacia. It is unknown exactly how much native Dacians intermingled with Roman soldiers, but Romanian historians believe that it was so extensive that it produced the ethnogenesis of the Romanian people.

The history of Dacia from Roman abandonment to the Middle Ages is a highly controversial matter. Little remains in the historical record that gives us a clear indication of who lived there, let alone how people lived. Not surprisingly, the time period is popularly known as the Dark Ages, a term applied to all of Europe, not just the Dacian areas. Scholars often refer to it as the Age of Great Migrations. During this time, tribes from Eurasia (e.g., the Visigoths, Ostrogoths, Huns, Gepides, Lombards, Avars, Bulgars, and eventually the Slavs) began to migrate into Europe. Most of the groups were made up of militaristic peoples who seldom settled long in any given place. Because the Carpathian Mountains were a physiographic barrier, most migratory peoples moved southward around them and through Moldavia and Walachia, which were river plains, before penetrating deeper into Europe. In short, Walachia and Moldavia lay on the main invasion route into Europe. Because these marauding tribes from the east completely disrupted the lives of those whom they encountered, it is difficult to imagine how the Walachians and Moldavians would have survived if they chose to stay where they were. The archeological record is scant. The Daco-Romans of Transylvania would have been protected by the mountains, provided that a Daco-Roman people existed. Unfortunately, little archeological evidence exists in Transylvania to prove their existence. But then again, little archeological evidence exists anywhere in Europe to show us who was where and what they were doing during this time period. Because it is important for Romantic nationalists to demonstrate a continuous history of settlement, Romanian

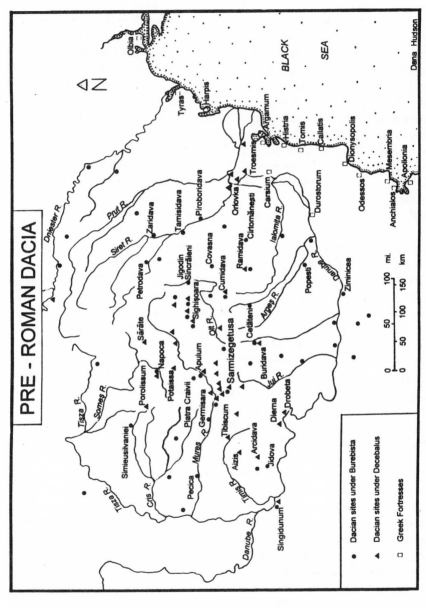

Figure 5.1 Pre-Roman Dacia.

PRE - ROMAN DACIA

BLACK

SEA

Dana Hudson

Olbia

Tyras

Harpis

Argamum

Histria

Tomis

Callatis

Troesmis

Dionysopolis

Carsium

Mesembria

Durostorum

Odessos

Anchialos

Apollonia

Dniester R.

Prut R.

Siret R.

Zaridava

Tamisidava

Piroboridava

Ortovka

Cirtomănești

Ialomița R.

Ramidava

Covasna

Cumidava

Petrodava

Jigodin

Sincrăieni

Sighișoara

Olt R.

Argeș R.

Popești

Ziminicea

Sărăte

Sarmizegetusa

Cetățenie

Napoca

Apulum

Buridava

Danube R.

Potaissa

Piatra Craivii

Germisara

Porolissum

Tibiscum

Acidava

Drobeta

Simieusilvaniei

Jidova

Diema

Mureș R.

Timiș R.

Crîș R.

Aizis

Somes R.

Tisza R.

Pecica

Timiș R.

Singidunum

Danube R.

N

- Dacian sites under Burebista
▲ Dacian sites under Decebalus
□ Greek Fortresses

| 0 | 50 | 100 | mi. |
| 0 | 50 | 100 | 150 | km |

nationalists insist that the Daco-Romans, the early ancestors of the Romanian nation, either stayed in Walachia and Moldavia and simply coped with the situation (Giurescu 1981, 76; Stoicescu 1983) or they moved to Transylvania with their brethren. Indeed, if the Romanians are the descendants of the Daco-Roman people as Romanian nationalists believe, then proving the survival of the Daco-Romans is essential to confirming the legitimacy of modern Roman national identity and its claim to its perceived territory.

Not until the end of the Middle Ages, with the rise of modern states in Europe, is it possible to point to any political-territorial formations that could be considered distinctly Romanian. These early states were Walachia and Moldavia, and they emerged at the end of the thirteenth century.[13] Although it is possible to speak of Walachia and Moldavia as integrated territories in general terms, both territories were often ruled by multiple leaders, acting independently of one another and holding control over their own territorial niches. Because a Romanian national identity did not exist as we understand nationhood today, it was also not unusual for their leaders to be at odds with one another and even see one another as the enemy, especially when they allied themselves to differing geopolitical realms. Depending on the time period, these realms could have been those of the Ottomans, the Russians, or those of the West, such as those of the Poles, Hungarians, or Austrian Hapsburgs. Indeed, it was not unusual for Walachian leaders to prefer an alliance with the Ottomans or Hungarians over an alliance with Moldavian leaders, and the same can be said of Moldavian leaders in regard to Walachian leaders. If Romanian nationhood had existed at the time, the shared sense of Romanian national identity would have led the leaders of both states to ally with one another and even unite the two territories.

The geopolitical realms played a major role in the evolution of the Walachia, Moldavia, and Transylvanian states, the development of a Romanian national consciousness, and the creation of a Romanian nation-state. Indeed, Walachia and Moldavia had just come into existence in the fourteenth century when they came under pressure from the Ottoman Empire. Both Walachian and Moldavian princes fought to preserve their rule but eventually found their causes to be lost. Rather than fight to the end, both Walachian and Moldavian leaders decided to pay annual tribute to the Ottoman Sultan (Hitchins 1996, 5–14). The decision to acquiesce was an unusual one considering that other leaders in southeastern Europe had resisted Ottoman rule to the very end. Consequently, in those cases, indigenous political structures were thoroughly destroyed and supplanted by Ottoman ones. Because Walachia's and Moldavia's leaders acquiesced, the Sultan preserved Walachia and Moldavia as principalities and allowed continued but limited rule of native Walachian and

Moldavian leaders. Thus Walachia's and Moldavia's autonomy was preserved and subsequent Walachian and Moldavian leaders were able to revive the struggle for independence whenever opportunities presented themselves. Transylvania's history was somewhat different. It was absorbed into the Hungarian Kingdom between the eleventh and thirteenth centuries before it was able to develop into its own state. It then came under Ottoman suzerainty just like Walachia and Moldavia in 1541, not long after the Ottomans destroyed the Hungarian army and annexed most of the Hungarian Kingdom. Even though Transylvania's leaders tried to act independently, they were not descendants of Daco-Romans, and they never developed a Romanian national identity.

With one brief but important exception, Walachia, Moldavia, and Transylvania remained firmly under Ottoman control until the end of the seventeenth century. For a short time at the end of the sixteenth century, a leader who became known as Michael Viteazul (the Brave) came to the forefront. Michael's rise to power began when he acquired the Walachian throne in 1593 by paying the appropriate Ottoman overlords. Once in power, Michael turned on the Ottomans by attacking them militarily and defeating them in a number of battles. In 1599, Michael's army crossed the Carpathians, defeated the Transylvanian prince in a single battle, and then assumed control of the Transylvanian state. In 1600, Michael invaded Moldavia and quickly took control. To Romanian Romantic nationalists, Michael was a Romanian national hero who demonstrates the centuries-long desire of Romanians to be politically united into a single territorial state. Michael then is an important pillar in the *continuous* history of the Romanian people. Indeed, although the union lasted for less than a year, it remains the only time from the fall of the Roman Empire until the twentieth century that the three territories were united into a single state. Michael's state also gave Romanian Romantics the opportunity to herald a moment of national triumph. By doing so, Romanian Romantics could put the Romanian people on a parity with the other great nations of Europe (Giurescu 1981, 166).

The treatment of Michael the Brave as a national hero imbued with a sense of Romanian nationalism and willing to make the sacrifices to unite his people is open to serious question. Modern nationalism did not exist in the sixteenth century as it does today. Instead, Michael the Brave was part of the ruling classes of Europe and was primarily concerned with the exercise and enhancement of his own authority (Stavrianos 1958, 344). Thus, when Michael entered Transylvania, he did not free or grant rights to the Romanian inhabitants who were primarily peasants but, nevertheless, constituted more than 60 percent of the population. Instead, he sought the support of the Hungarian, Szekler, and Saxon nobles by reaffirming their rights and privileges. Michael demonstrated his support by upholding the Union of the Three Nations, which recognized only the fundamental rights of the Magyars, Szeklers, and Saxons, not those of the Romanians (Bachman 1991, 16; Seton-Watson 1963, 67–68). Indeed, if Michael had been inspired and supported by a feeling of Romanian nationhood, he would have declared himself prince of the Romanians. Michael's self-declaration of "Prince of all Ungro-Walachia, of Transylvania, and of Moldavia" (Seton-Watson 1963, 69) demonstrates that Romanian national identity did not yet exist, nor did the terms *Romania* or *Romanian*. Nevertheless, Michael serves today as an important component of modern Romanian nationhood, even if Michael himself would not identify with it or even recognize it.

Michael the Brave was overthrown before he was able to rule very long, and the Ottomans quickly reasserted their control over Walachia and Moldavia. Transylvania preserved its independence for some time and was even recognized as a sovereign state at the Peace of Westphalia in 1648. Before long, however, Transylvania once again lost its independence to the Ottomans after Transylvania's leaders undertook a few military campaigns which failed.

Following the defeat of the Ottoman armies outside Vienna in 1683, Ottoman power in Europe declined steadily. In the wake of the slow Ottoman withdrawal from Europe, the Hapsburg and Russian empires competed for control of Walachia, Moldavia, and Transylvania. The Hapsburgs quickly took possession of Transylvania and did not relinquish control of it until the Austro-Hungarian Empire disintegrated at the end of the First World War. Control of Walachia and Moldavia came only after a series of wars, primarily instigated by the Russian Empire, that spanned the eighteenth and nineteenth centuries. The wars brought a number of victories, some of the achievements reversed from one war to the next, but the Russians slowly gained control over the two territories.[14]

After the Russian defeat in the Crimean War of 1854–56, Walachia and Moldavia ceased to be Russian protectorates. Instead, the two principalities came under a joint European guarantee (Tihany 1976, 158). In 1858, an international conference in Paris accepted the name "United Principalities" for the two states. In 1861, the Great Powers accepted the political unity of the principalities. In 1866, the government of the principalities changed the name of the province to "Romania" (Hitchins 1996, 20), marking the first year in history that the term *Romania* was officially applied to a territory. In 1878, the Great Powers recognized Romania's independence in the Treaty of Berlin. In 1881, the Romanian parliament proclaimed Romania a kingdom.

During the First World War, the Romanian government decided to join the Entente effort, which brought the Romanian state great territorial awards at the Paris Peace Conference of 1919 (see Figure 5.2). The

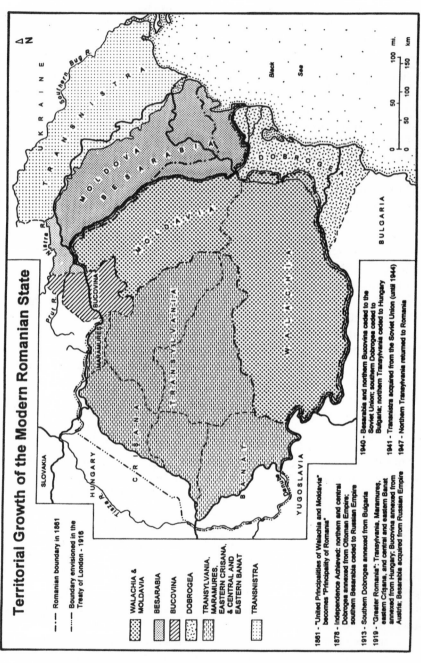

Figure 5.2 Territorial Growth of the Modern Romanian State.

territories added to the Romanian state were Transylvania, Maramureş, eastern Crişana, the central and eastern Banat, Bucovina, and Besarabia. With the world economic crisis in the 1930s, Romania's fragile economy began to collapse. As unemployment consistently rose, more and more Romanians supported the ultranationalists and fascists. By the outbreak of the Second World War, the Romanian nation and state were firmly in the Axis camp and supporting Hitler's war effort. When the Axis began to crumble, the Romanian government found itself in a difficult situation. In an attempt to preserve the territorial integrity of the Romanian state, the Romanian government decided that it had to appease the Allies by declaring war on Germany. The last-minute effort, however, did not prevent the Red Army from entering and occupying Romania. The Romanian nation-state, nevertheless, remained intact; however, some territories were lost—namely Besarabia. From then until the late 1980s, Romania was dominated by the Soviet Union. With relaxation of Soviet control over Eastern Europe in the late 1980s, Romanians, discontented with their leader Nicholae Ceauşescu and his repressive governing style, overthrew the government and executed Ceauşescu in 1989. Since then, and facilitated by the dissolution of the Soviet Union, the Romanian government has become more democratically and Western oriented. Besarabia, now named Moldova, has not rejoined the Romania state but many Romanians believe that the union is inevitable.

Places Significant to Romanian National Identity

The three indicators of a nation's sense of territory show that Romanian national identity is tied to a number of places (see Figure 5.3). The location of highly significant places within different regions has facilitated the perception that certain regions naturally fit together into an integrated Romanian territory. Before discussing any of the individual regions and the specific places within them, one must understand the nature of this Greater Romanian territory. Once Greater Romania is depicted, it is then possible to examine its component parts which are divided into a core, semi-core, and periphery. The core includes Walachia, Moldavia, Bucovina, and Transylvania; the semi-core encompasses the central and eastern Banat, central and northern Dobrogea, Besarabia, northern Bucovina, Maramureş, and eastern Crişana; the periphery consists of southern Dobrogea, Transnistria, western Crişana, and various sites within the Balkan peninsula, particularly in northern Bulgaria and Macedonia.

Treating Romania as a series of discrete regions that neatly fit into a core, semi-core, and periphery is a difficult proposition. Over time, some regions have been divided politically, and consequently the divided parts

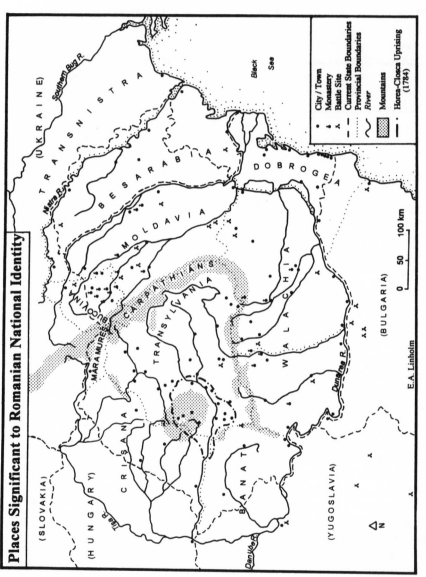

Figure 5.3 Places Significant to Romanian National Identity.

have taken on different degrees of significance. For example, Besarabia and Bucovina were once integral parts of Moldavia and not thought of as distinct entities, not even distinct regional entities within Moldavia. Long periods of separation have resulted in differing perceptions and degrees of emotional attachment to these regions over time. Moreover, Besarabia and Bucovina were themselves later divided when the southeastern portion of Besarabia and the northern portion of Bucovina were attached to the Ukraine and not to the Moldavian Soviet Republic. Political separation has also had its effect on southern Dobrogea, the western Banat, and western Crişana.

With the historical overview of Romanian history in mind, the core, semi-core, and periphery now can be analyzed in detail. Poetry and music have played their role in the development of Romanian sense of territory; however, Romanian Romantic nationalists have placed more emphasis on archeology and art to write a common history for the Romanians and cultivate a Romanian sense of territory. Therefore, archeology and art as well as poetry and music are used to identify sites and measure their significance in the Romanian case study.

The Romanian Land (Tara Româneasca)

O, forest with thy broad leaves,
What a good a father thou wert for me,
When hatred was all around.
O, forest with thy long leaves,
Once thou wert my shelter,
And mother dear alike,
When hatred was all around.
O, forest with thy princely leaves
May frost not wither thee
Since thou art Romanian home.
  (Giurescu 1981, 11)

And when the Reaper comes to show me out,
With dying lips I'll leave a testament
. . .
To take my ashes, scatter them about
My native countryside magnificent.

Then I'll be home again among my hills,
Blossoming every spring in daffodils;
And you, Romania, glorified will be
As the plowman every furrow blends with me.
  (Excerpt of *Testament* by Nicolae Novac; Popa 1966, 133)

Because environmental determinism greatly influenced thought in the nineteenth and early twentieth centuries, it is no surprise that Romania was not only delimited by physiographic features but also conceived of as a natural, integrated physical-political unit (Giurescu 1981, 7–8). In the center of Romania stand the Carpathian Mountains, seen as a fortress that protects the Romanian people. The mountains create a radial drainage pattern that feeds into a series of rivers serving as a moat, Romania's "natural" boundaries. Romania is seen to be bounded on the south by the Danube River (Dunerea), on the east by the Tişa River (Tisza; Theiss), on the southeast by the Black Sea, and on the northeast by the Nistra (Dnestr) (Academia Română: Institutul de Geografie 1996, 87). The north is somewhat problematic, but a somewhat short and relatively direct line can be drawn that connects the headwaters of the Tişa, Siret, Prut, and Nistra Rivers to complete an almost circular boundary for Romania (Ceauşescu 1983, between pages 18 and 19; Stoicescu 1986, 9–13).

Romania's diverse regions are seen to be the basis of a strong and self-sufficient nation. Likewise, the Magyar conquering of Transylvania, the very "heart" of Romania, is viewed as the cause of the arrested development of the Romanian nation and subsequent development of Walachia and Moldavia into separate political states (Stoicescu 1986, 9–10). Despite the "natural" unity of Romania, political unity of Romania's territories was achieved only in the twentieth century, after the First World War. In order to find some historical precedent for political unity, history has to be traced back to the Roman Empire and the Dacian state before that; the eight-month reign of Michael the Brave in 1600 is not sufficient to establish legitimacy. It is no surprise then that Romanian identity is founded on a Daco-Romanian theory. The greatness of the Romans is unquestioned by other Europeans, and no other nation in southeastern Europe can claim that their ancestors inhabited Romanian land before the Romanians. Not surprisingly then, the Roman component of Romanian identity is reflected in the landscape all over Romania with the statue of the "She-Wolf" (with Romulus and Remus), a replica of the original in Rome. Not only do these statues inform outsiders of an aspect of Romanian national identity, they inculcate a particular sense of identity in the Romanians who see it. That the Dacian and Roman province of Dacia tended to be politically and economically centered in Transylvania and the Banat is important.

The Core: Site Identification and Landscape Description

The core area of modern Romanian national identity is centered on three regions: Walachia, Moldavia, and Transylvania. Modern Romanian identity has come about as a result of the interrelationships of these three territories. Walachia and Moldavia, particularly Walachia, are the two centers around which the modern political state developed. Transylvania is the cultural-intellectual center where modern Romanian national identity emerged in the eighteenth and nineteenth centuries.

Walachia

I need caressing from afar—
The dew soaked glory,
the thick wide fresh groves
of Wallachia
  (Quoted from Ciopraga 1981, 117)

Walachia is important as a political center of Romania not just because Romania's capital, Bucharest, is located there but also because it exerted its political independence earlier than any of the other Romanian territories. Walachia's role in shaping Romanian identity is shown through history by all Romanians usually being called Walachians, regardless of where they lived. Even Moldavia was referred to in some form or another as the other Walachian state (Stoicescu 1986, 165–73). Furthermore, the term *Tara Româneasca* (The Romanian Land) was initially applied to Walachia.

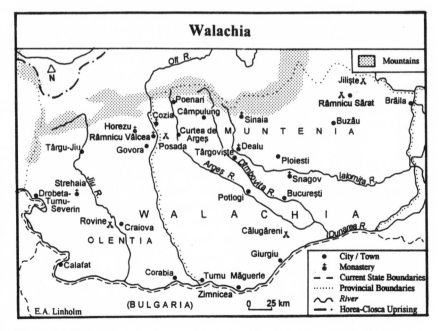

Figure 5.4 Walachia.

As the first politically independent Romanian territory in post-Roman times, Walachia has a number of specific places that testify to the early political power of the Romanian people as well as to great Romanian cultural achievements. The most notable of these places are Walachia's early capitals: Câmpulung, Argeş (now Curtea de Argeş), and Târgovişte (formerly Tîrgovişte). All of these places lie in the major subregion of Walachia known as Muntenia—the area east of the Olt River.

Little remains in Câmpulung, but Curtea de Argeş still has some noteworthy features in its landscape that provide a physical link to the glorious past of the Romanians (Musicescu and Ionesco 1976). The most notable of features are the church of Saint Nichulae and the Episcopal church (Treptow 1996, 68, 94); a fresco of Mircea the Old, prince of Walachia (1386–1418), is also found in Curtea de Argeş (Georgescu 1984, 60). The church of Saint Nichulae was founded by Besarab I; it is one of the best preserved buildings in southeastern Europe that dates back to the fourteenth century (Georgescu 1984, 33–34; Giurescu 1981, 117). The Episcopal church, built in the early sixteenth century, is an even more remarkable piece of architecture and proof of early Romanian accomplishments (Giurescu 1981, 151). Because the Metropolitan of Argeş received the recognition of the Patriarch in Constantinople in the fourteenth century, Argeş serves as an early example of Romanian prestige in southeastern Europe.

Târgovişte, the town that succeeded Argeş as capital, is also a symbol of Romanian authority and accomplishment in the Middle Ages. As the location of one of the first printing presses in southeastern Europe, Târgovişte was an important center for the dissemination of information (Giurescu 1981, 314). Târgovişte also is immortalized in a painting that depicts its liberation from the Turks in 1595 (Giurescu 1981, 163). Near Târgovişte is the Dealu Monastery church (Treptow 1996, 148), the burial place of Michael the Brave, one of Romania's greatest heroes.

The importance of Bucharest (Bucureşti) as a political-cultural center in modern history is a key factor in Walachia's role as a core territory. First as capital of Walachia, then of Romania, Bucharest has become the location of many of the nation's major political and cultural institutions. Bucharest has many features in its landscape that remind Romanians of their great accomplishments. Of the great monuments, a few are particularly noteworthy. The Arch of Triumph (1936), honoring the Romanian heroes of the First World War, confirms the nation's great sacrifices. Moreover, modeled after the Arch of Triumph in Paris, the Arch reinforces the belief that the Romanians and the French, sharing a similar Latin heritage, are culturally akin. By emphasizing the common heritage and memorializing the common struggle in the war, Romanians are placed on equal footing with one of the great nations of Europe. In the same context, Trajan's column, a replica of the original in Rome, creates a similar physical link between Romanian and Italian culture. In addition to many of the buildings in Bucharest, the palaces of Mogoşoaia and Potlogi, just outside the city (Clark 1971, 258–59; Giurescu 1981, 286–87), are architectural examples of what the Romanians have accomplished. Bucharest also has a Village Museum that contains peasant houses from the various regions of the country. Such a museum familiarizes Romanians with the diverse architectural styles of Romania's various regions. By becoming familiar with such differing styles, Romanians begin to see these styles as part of a greater Romanian heritage.

In addition to the historic capitals of Walachia, Craiova is significant because it served historically as a political center and is now an important regional center. Craiova lies in the western subregion of Walachia, known as Olentia—the area west of the Olt River. Târgu-Jiu (formerly Tîrgu-Jiu), Olentia's secondary city, is more noteworthy because it is closely associated with one of Romania's famous sculptors, Constantin Brâncuşi (1876–1957). Brâncuşi's works, such as *Poarta Sarutului* (Kissing Gate) and the *Masa Tecerii* (Table of Silence), not only shape the city's landscape but also stand as great Romanian artistic achievements (Giurescu 1981, 540, 542; Treptow 1996, 391, 447). A World War I monument testifies to the great sacrifices of the Romanians; the Jiu River Valley was an area of particularly intense fighting. In Olentia are the monasteries of Horezu and Cozia (Clark 1971, 258–59; Giurescu 1981, 177; Treptow 1996, 93, 203). Mircea the Old is buried in the cemetery at Cozia, and a fresco of him is in the monastery (Giurescu 1981, 122, 275; Seton-Watson 1963, between pages 32 and 33).

A number of other places in Walachia illustrate the cultural history of the Romanians, reaffirm the nation's sense of a long and continuous history, and testify to the great cultural achievements of the nation. Buzău, Govora, Râmnicu Vâlcea (formerly Rîmnicu Vîlcea), Snagov, Sinaia (named after Mt. Sinai), and Strehaia are the most important of these places. All of these places were among the first in Walachia to establish printing presses (Giurescu 1981, 314) and hence became centers for the dissemination of information. At the time, which predated the period of modern nationalism, material was printed in Church Slavonic using the Cyrillic alphabet. Nevertheless, this fact is overlooked as the accomplishments of these places are heralded. Govora is the location of the press that printed the first book in the Principalities (Seton-Watson 1963, 80), whereas Buzău is the location where the first complete Romanian Bible was printed (Fischer-Galati 1957, 165). Snagov Monastery, just outside Bucharest, is also the place where Vlad the Impaler is buried. Vlad the Impaler (popularly known as Dracula in the West) is now a great national hero, primarily because he fought the Ottomans. In addition to the monastery, Sinaia is known for Peleş Castle (Treptow 1996, 358), the summer residence of King Carol I, first king of Romania. Vlad the Impaler is given credit for the founding or fortification of many places, including Bucharest. His original castle, known as Poenari (formerly Poienari) Fortress, is along the border of Transylvania and is now being restored by the Romanian government (McNally and Florescu 1994, 75–76).

A number of places in Walachia are significant because they are associated with the defense of the territory and, likewise, with Romanian independence. When Romanians had control of these places, they were able to exercise their independence. Most of these places lie along the Danube River, seen as the natural boundary of Romania. Most noteworthy are Drobeta-Turnu-Severin, Calafat, Corabia, Turnu-Măgurele (formerly just Turnu), Zimnicea, Giurgiu, and Brăila. Romanian history is replete with struggles for the control of these important places; as a result, these places are firmly rooted in the national consciousness of many Romanians.

Drobeta-Turnu-Severin is also important in another context. The Roman Emperor Trajan had a bridge built here to connect Roman Dacia with the rest of the Roman Empire. The ruins of the bridge (Treptow 1996, 28) stand as the physical evidence legitimizing the modern Romanian national belief that Romanians are the product of a Daco-Roman racial intermingling. The significance of this place was emphasized when the old Dacian name Drobeta was added to the modern, Latin-derived name of Turnu-Severin in the 1970s. Thus the belief in the Daco-Roman ethnogenesis is reinforced in the national consciousness by the renaming of one of Romania's important cities.

The role that Walachia plays as a core territory is underscored by a number of historical battles that have been used to celebrate the centuries-long struggle for Romanian independence. The battles also testify to the Romanian ability to overcome great forces that have threatened them. For each of the foreign peoples that threatened the Romanians in the past, at least one battle site exists to commemorate a victory against these foreign threats. The Battle of Posada, fought just outside Argeş, commemorates a victory over the Hungarians in 1330. A painting of the battle depicts Walachians throwing stones down upon the Hungarian army, trapped in a river gorge (Berindei 1976, between pages 95 and 96; Giurescu 1981, 115–18; Treptow 1996, 66). The Battle of Rovine, fought just outside Craiova in 1394, is celebrated as a great victory over the Ottomans. In the fifteenth century, after Walachian leaders submitted to the Ottomans, Stephen the Great of Moldavia successfully defeated Ottoman forces at Râmnicu Sărat (formerly Rîmnicu Sărat) in eastern Walachia in an attempt to prevent the Ottoman conquest of Moldavia (Giurescu 1981, 143). In 1574, the Moldavian army defeated Ottoman forces at the Battle of Jiliște, just south of Focșani. One of the most noteworthy victories scored by the Walachians against the Ottomans was the Battle of Călugăreni in 1595 (Giurescu 1981, 164). Led by Michael the Brave, the victory precluded greater Ottoman control of Walachia and made possible the establishment of a large dynastic state that could be heralded as the precursor of a modern Romanian state. The battle is immortalized in a painting that depicts Michael the Brave and his forces overrunning Turkish lines (Berindei 1976, between pages 96 and 97).

Ploești (formerly Ploiești) is also an important place in Walachia. As a relatively new city, Ploești is obviously not historically significant. However, as the center of petroleum production for Romania, Ploești contributes greatly to Romania's economic well-being. A nation's ability to exert its independence is often dependent on its economic well-being. Overall, the Romanian state has generally been economically very weak. Yet the oil produced in Ploești has given the Romanian government some means of providing some wealth for the Romanian people. The Oil Museum in the city is in many ways a testament to Ploești's importance. One of the most intense military clashes between German and Romanian troops at the end of the Second World War occurred around Ploești (Giurescu 1981, 569).

Bucovina and Moldavia

Sweet Bucovina
Blithe garden
With fruitful trees
. . .
Sweet Bucovina!
The wind that bends
With its wing
The grass of the field
Rouses by its whisper
The dear memory of a beautiful past
Great, glorious.
Be ever happy
As thou art beautiful!
. . .
Ah! he who sees thee
Actually believes
Himself in Paradise
. . .

     (Quoted from Clark 1971, 80)

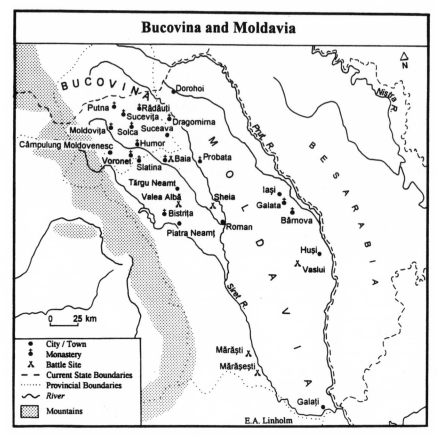

Figure 5.5 Bucovina and Moldavia.

Moldavia is a core territory of Romanian national identity because it, like Walachia, exerted its political independence early. In fact, Moldavia's history parallels that of Walachia, with events taking place in Moldavia only a matter of a few years after they took place in Walachia. Consequently, Walachia became the center of the modern Romanian state. Nevertheless, Moldavia has acted as a twin territory to Walachia. Likewise, many places in Moldavia play roles of similar importance to those in Walachia.

Bucovina is included with Moldavia because Bucovina was historically an integral part of Moldavia. Bucovina was not thought of as a separate region until the Hapsburg Empire carved it out of Moldavia in 1774 and gave it the name *Buchenland* ("Land of the Beech Trees") (Roucek 1932, 9). In fact, Bucovina was the original core of Moldavia (Livezeanu 1995, 52), much in the same way that the area around Câmpulung, Argeş, and Târgovişte was the early core area of Walachia. Likewise, Bucovina has many elements in its landscape that testify to a long and continuous history of the Romanian people. For example, Suceava, now located in Bucovina, was the early political center of Moldavia. Suceava served as capital of Moldavia from 1388 to 1565; the Metropolitan was recognized by the Patriarch of Constantinople in 1401 (Giurescu 1981, 256). During this period, Stephen the Great (1457–1504) ruled Moldavia from Suceava, and an equestrian statue in the city commemorates his reign. Also in Suceava is the Mirauti Church—the original coronation church of Moldavian princes, and Cetatea de Scaun—the fortress that fended off a Turkish assault in 1476 (Treptow 1996, 118).

The presence of many old and famous monasteries shows that Bucovina is a core territory. Often referred to as the painted monasteries, most of them are in the vicinity of Suceava. Of the twenty-five or thirty that exist, the following are the best-known: Suceviţa (1586), Rădăuţi, Moldoviţa (1531), Humor (1530), Putna (1466–69), Dragomirna (1602), Solca, and Voronet (1470) (Drăguţ 1973; Ionesco 1972; Musicescu and Ulea 1971; Treptow 1996, 122, 129, 201). Probota and Slatina Monasteries are just south of Bucovina in northern Moldavia; of course, at the time the two territories were conceptually thought of as one. Putna Monastery is well-known, for example, because it was founded by Stephen the Great in 1466 to commemorate his victory over the Tartars; Putna is also Stephen's burial place. Some of the earliest histories of Romania were written in Putna Monastery (Clark 1971, 289). Rădăuţi became an important center when it became a diocese in the fifteenth century. Humor and Voronet Monasteries are associated with their founder, Stephen the Great. The other early important centers of Bucovina were Câmpulung Moldovenesc and Siret.

In more recent history, the political center of Moldavia has been in Iaşi (also Jassy). Iaşi became the capital of Moldavia in 1565. Until the principalities were united, and even long after, the political, economic, and religious importance of Iaşi rivaled that of Bucharest. Iaşi also became an important center for book printing and subsequently a center of agitation for the Romanian national movement in the nineteenth century. When the Central Powers overran and occupied Bucharest in the First World War, Iaşi functioned as the capital of Romania. With the growth of Iaşi as a political center, two nearby monasteries became influential as well: Galata and Bârnova (formerly Bîrnova) (Iorga 1925, 143). The other towns of significance in eastern Moldavia are Dorohoi and Huşi. Dorohoi is associated with Stephen the Great, who built one of his forty churches there. Huşi functioned as an important religious center after it became a diocese at the end of the sixteenth century (Giurescu 1981, 256; Seton-Watson 1963, 47).

The Prut River, once flowing through the middle of Moldavia and now serving as the eastern border of the current Romanian state, is seen as the protector of the people:

O Pruth, accursed stream
You must make yourself deep and wide
Like a muddy flood!
Let one bank not be seen from the other
Let one voice not carry to the other
Let eyes not reach one another
Over thy waters so broad.
Whenever the locust pass
In the middle may they drown!
Whenever the plagues pass
In the middle may they drown!
Enemies of our country if they pass
At this bank may they drown.
While you in your waves
May you carry them all down-stream
Down to the Danube, that great river,
Down into the Danube and the sea!
        (Quoted from Clark 1922, 9)

Though Iaşi lies in the eastern part of Moldavia, most of Moldavia's important places that testify to the many accomplishments of the Romanians lie along the Siret River or within the Siret River valley. On a tributary of the Siret, the Neamţ, is Târgu Neamţ (formerly only Neamţ). In the Middle Ages, the fortress in Neamţ protected the area and is now a historical monument (Treptow 1996, 120). West of the town is Neamţ Monastery, founded by Stephen the Great in 1497. Neamţ is a source of national pride in the monks who produced art and made books (Iorga 1925, 144, 198). Farther south on the Siret is the town of Roman. In the Middle Ages, Roman was a key trading town with a fortress. An Episcopate was founded in Roman in the fifteenth century, and one of the first books translated into Romanian was the Psalter in 1673. Piatra Neamţ (formerly only Piatra), on the Bistra River, was also an important trading center with a fortress in the Middle Ages. Stephen the Great built a church in the town between 1497 and 1498. Bistriţa Monastery, just to the west of the town is where some of the earliest histories of Romania were written (Clark 1971, 289). The southernmost city in Moldavia is Galaţi, located on the confluence of the Siret and Danube Rivers. Galaţi is Moldavia's largest port and historically served in a defensive line along with the Walachian cities along the Danube.

Similar to Walachia, Moldavia has many great battle sites that are used to emphasize the successful struggles of the Romanian people through history. These battle sites commemorate the Romanian victories over not only the Hungarians and Turks but over the Poles and Tartars as well. The bell tower in Baia, erected by Stephen the Great, commemorates a decisive defeat of the army of King Matthias Corvinus outside the town and marks the end of the Hungarian threat to Moldavia (Castellan 1989, 41; Seton-Watson 1963, 44, 47). Baia was also the residence of Dragoş, the first leader of Moldavia (1352–53). Vaslui (in Racova), the site of Stephen the Great's victory over the Turks in 1475, is heralded as one of the greatest Romanian victories in history. Because this victory prompted Pope Sixtus IV to name Stephen the "Athlete of Christ" (Seton-Watson 1963, 45; Treptow 1996, 116), Romanian historians have been able to use this event and place to put the Romanian people on a parity with the other great nations of Europe by defining the battle as a great European struggle shouldered by the Romanians. Other battles fought by Stephen the Great and heralded as great moments in Romanian history are Valea Albă (also known as Răsboieni) in 1476 and Scheia in 1486 (Giurescu 1981, 143).

Modern battles also testify to the bravery of the Romanian people and to the sacrifices that Romanians have made in the defense of European culture and civilization. In the First World War, the Central Powers occupied Romania up to the Siret River, where the Romanian army had a strong defensive line. Difficult but victorious battles were fought at Mărăşti and Mărăşeşti in 1917.

Transylvania (Transilvania)[15]

Look upon those high and verdant hills,
On those broad glades, covered with flowers,
Look at those Romanian shepherds, strangers to the world,
Beside their flocks guarded by their dogs,
Leading a gentle life in mysterious nature,
With horn in hand, flute at their lips,
Heavenly clearness, as within a spring,
Mirrors itself calm in their spirits.
 (Quoted from Clark 1922, 41)

Transylvania, meaning "across the forests,"[16] has been called the very heart of Romania—the "natural" fortress that has protected and nourished the Romanian people (Stoicescu 1986, 9–13). Transylvania is very much a part of the core area of Romanian national identity. In part, Transylvania is seen as the mountainous refuge and hence the cultural and physical preserve of the ancestors of the Romanians. Without Transylvania, the Daco-Romans would have hardly survived to spawn the modern Romanian nation.

In fact, the very notion of a Daco-Roman past actually originated among the Romanians of Transylvania (Deletant 1991, 65; Hitchins 1969, 61–62; Seton-Watson 1963, 271–73). Because Transylvanian Romanians were assigned a low status in Transylvania in modern times, they could have

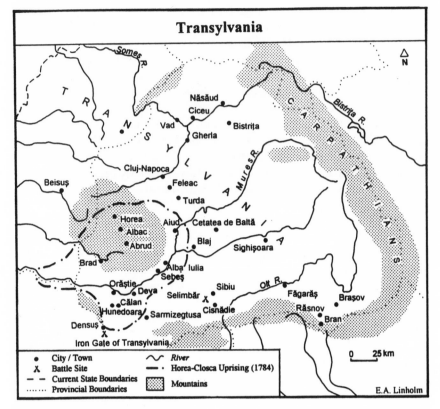

Figure 5.6 Transylvania.

migrated into Walachia and Moldavia. However, on regional and local levels, these people were very attached to Transylvania. It had been their home for generations. Upon developing a Romanian national identity, they naturally considered their home, Transylvania, to be part of the greater territory known as Romania. However, the other groups that ruled Transylvania (e.g., Austrians, Saxons, and Hungarians) tried to sever the contact that Transylvanian Romanians had developed with Walachians and Moldavians, and attempted to keep Transylvania's Romanians oriented and thus loyal to the West European powers. Indeed, the rulers of Transylvania succeeded in cultivating a western-oriented identity among Transylvania's Romanians. On the other hand, the rulers of Transylvania failed to sever the bond that was growing between Transylvania's Romanians and Walachians and Moldavians. Subsequently, Transylvania's Romanians used their western education to construct an identity for all Romanians that is oriented to the west. In short, Transylvania developed into the intellectual-cultural center of Romania.

The belief that the Romanians are the descendants of a Daco-Romanian racial mix is highly controversial. In particular, many Hungarians have been determined to disprove the Daco-Roman theory because it legitimizes Romanian control of Transylvania. Therefore, in order to provide tangible proof that the theory is correct, concrete evidence has to be found to turn the theory into historical truth. The identification of Daco-Roman places serves as some of the best evidence that supports the Daco-Roman belief. Transylvania was, in fact, the very heart of pre-Romanian Dacia; it is, therefore, no surprise that Transylvania's Romanians were so intrigued with Dacia and the Roman province of Dacia. Transylvania's central role in these earlier territorial configurations is another reason why Transylvania is a core territory for modern Romanian ethnonational identity.

As the core territory of Dacia and the Roman province of Dacia, Transylvania contains many of the great cities of these periods of early "Romanian" history. Sarmizegetusa (full name: Ulpa Traiana Augusta Dacica Sarmizegetusa) was the capital of Dacia. In Roman times, Sarmizegetusa remained important as one of the province's eight *colonia*. In addition to Sarmizegetusa, four other *colonia* were also in Transylvania: Apulum (now Alba Iulia), Aquae (now Călan), Napoca (now Cluj-Napoca), and Potaissa (now Turda) (Giurescu 1981, 64). All of these places testify to the legitimacy of the Daco-Roman belief. In fact, the connection was reinforced in the 1970s when the Roman name Napoca was added to the Romanian name Cluj, thus making the city's name Cluj-Napoca. The name Cluj-Napoca is a constant reminder of the connection that modern Romanians have with their Daco-Roman past. The implication, of course, is that the double name existed long before. Moreover, it is perhaps no surprise that Romania's leaders decided to Romanize the name of a city that has been historically Hungarian in character—particularly because Cluj is the largest city in Transylvania.

Cluj is currently one of the best examples in all of Europe to illustrate the meaning of place and how identity is expressed in the landscape. In fact, it can be said that the city is experiencing a battle of monuments (Von Reiner Luyken 1994). It began a few years ago when the city's nationalist mayor began altering the city's landscape to emphasize the Romanian character of Transylvania. In the process, the mayor has offended the local minorities, especially the Hungarians. For example, in front of the main Romanian Orthodox Church now stands a statue of Avram Iancu, a revolutionary leader who fought against Hungarian rule. On the corner of the main city square, which has historically been dominated by Hungarians and Hungarian monuments, now stands the Memorandum Monument, which commemorates the petition put forth in 1848 by Transylvania's Romanians asking for equal status with the other national groups of Transylvania (Treptow 1996, 272). Most contentious have been activities on the main square. Roman ruins have been found underneath the square. Because Romanian nationalists believe that Roman ruins are concrete evidence of their Daco-Roman identity, which, therefore, legitimizes the Romanian claim to Transylvania, Romanian nationalists believe that it is imperative that any such ruins be excavated and exhibited. Unfortunately, the ground above these ruins is a landscape of monuments important to the Hungarian nation and Hungarian sense of national identity (see Cluj in Chapter 4). Excavations of the Roman ruins simultaneously threaten to destroy the Hungarian landscape. Thus the issue is very contentious with ethnic and national conflict centering on the meaning and control of place and landscape.

Other places are important because they show that the Romanians continued to live in Transylvania after the fall of the Roman Empire and into the Middle Ages. Some of these places are churches: Călan, Cisnădie, and Densuş (Giurescu 1981, 110, 117, between pages 320 and 321; Treptow 1996, 90); many of these churches are also among the oldest in Romania. Făgăraş is one of the earliest places of importance in medieval times. It is the supposed origin of Negu-Vodă, who migrated to Câmpulung in 1290 and founded the Walachian state (Seton-Watson 1963, 24–25). Sighişoara is the birthplace of Vlad Ţepeş (the Impaler), prince of Walachia (McNally and Florescu 1994, 15–16); he and members of his family resided for periods of time in Făgăraş and often stayed at the castles of Bran and Râşnov (fomerly Rîşnov). Histories of Negu-Vodă and Vlad Ţepeş, and many of the others like them, establish a close connection between Transylvania and either Walachia or Moldavia. For example, the name of the major subregion Muntenia in Walachia confirms the connection. Muntenia means "land of the mountains," yet the modern territory of Muntenia is primarily a river plain. The term, however, supports the Romanian belief that their ancestors took refuge in Transylvania after the fall of the Roman Empire, during the dangerous period of great migrations in the early Middle Ages. Transylvania then is also a core territory of Romanian national identity because it served as the refuge of Romanians and early home of Walachian and Moldavian leaders.

Hunedoara, a medieval Hungarian town, contains one of the most picturesque castles in all of Romania (Giurescu 1981, 272), built by a figure that the Hungarians call János Hunyadi and the Romanians call Iancu Hunedoara. Romanian historians have depicted Hunedoara as one of Romania's great national heroes. Indeed, Hunedoara is an important historical figure, but he lived at a time that predated understandings of modern national identity. Therefore, it is not really appropriate to classify him as either a Hungarian or a Romanian. Nevertheless, claiming this figure as a national hero can do much for the national prestige, primarily because he led many victories against the Ottomans. However, because

Hunedoara was from Transylvania, Romanian historians have had almost no choice but to depict him as a great national hero. Another of the Hungarian castles now considered to be a Romanian landmark is the Bethlen-Haller Castle in Cetatea de Baltă (Giurescu 1981, 281), located in modern-day Romania. Romanian historians emphasize that King Matthias Corvinus of Hungary awarded the castle to Stephen the Great of Moldavia at the end of the fifteenth century. King Matthias also awarded Stephen the Ciceu Castle on the Someş River in northern Transylvania (Castellan 1989, 42).

As a further means of emphasizing the Romanian character of Transylvania and of demonstrating the centuries-long desire of the Romanians of Transylvania to free themselves and their territory from the Hungarian Kingdom, Romanian historians have depicted the Horea-Cloşca uprising in 1784 as a national uprising. The uprising began in the Apuseni Mountains in the vicinity of Brad and spread in all directions, even encompassing the large towns of Hunedoara and Alba Iulia. Subsequently, these towns and the Apuseni Mountains—where the rebels also found final refuge—have become very important to Romanian sense of territory, illustrated by a number of monuments in the area. For example, an obelisk stands in Alba Iulia, dedicated to the three leaders of the uprising, Horea, Cloşca, and Crişan; a bust of Horea was erected in his hometown of Albac (Edroiu 1978, 74, 77). In addition, a small town in the area is now called Horea.

The large towns of Alba Iulia, Braşov, and Sibiu are also very important to Romanian sense of ethnonational identity because crucial historical events for the Romanians occurred in these places. For example, Michael the Brave had himself crowned in Alba Iulia, where he had a coronation church built. Alba Iulia and Michael the Brave are immortalized in a popular painting (Pascu 1982, 109). In 1918, "The National Assembly of the Romanian Nation" gathered in Alba Iulia and proclaimed the unification of all the Romanian territories (Giurescu 1981, 396–97). King Ferdinand was crowned the first king of a united Romania in 1922 in the same city. In many ways, the last two events were legitimized by the act of going to the place of the first event. A church built specifically for Ferdinand's coronation stands as a visual reminder of that event, thus making Alba Iulia the focus of Romanian unity. In fact, Romania's parliament discussed the possibility of moving Romania's capital to Alba Iulia in 1996; however, the bureaucracy in Bucharest, which is quite sizeable, resisted such a move. All three towns, Alba Iulia, Braşov, and Sibiu, also had active printing presses and were, therefore, important centers for the dissemination of information. Braşov was the first town in Transylvania to have a printing press (1535). The first printing press using Latin script for Romanian was in Sibiu. The New Testament was translated from Greek into Romanian in Alba Iulia in 1648 (Giurescu 1981, 312–14).

Transylvania is also a core territory of Romanian sense of national identity because it is seen as the center of the modern struggle to attain national "self-determination." The modern Romanian national movement began in a number of Transylvania's religious and educational centers: Aiud, Alba Iulia, Beiuş, Blaj, Braşov, Cluj, Feleac, Gherla, Năsăud, Ohaba, Orăştie, Sas-Sebeş (now just Sebeş), Sibiu, and Vad. Blaj is the most significant of the places. This small town, which began as the headquarters of the Romanian Uniate Church in 1738 (Seton-Watson 1963, 178), developed into the very center of the modern Romanian national movement. The significance of Blaj is illustrated in a painting titled "The Field of Liberty," which depicts the largest gathering of Romanians in the Revolution of 1848 (Bodea and Cândea 1982, between pages 98 and 99; Pascu 1982, 195; Treptow 1996, 269). A large monument now stands at the site as well (Treptow 1996, 269). Both the painting and the monument testify to the importance of Blaj and the important role that Blaj played in shaping modern Romanian national identity. They also educate Romanians as to who they are. Many events happened in Blaj, but the choice to depict the gathering of 1848 in a painting has made Blaj into an important national gathering place.

Many significant events for the Romanians happened in a number of Saxon and Hungarian towns. Subsequently, important Romanian events and accomplishments have been emphasized by Romanian historians to establish the Romanian character of these places; similarly, the Hungarian and Saxon character of these towns has been downplayed or re-altered to fit into Romanian history. In other Saxon and Hungarian towns, very little happened that is significant to Romanian sense of national identity. With the rise of modern nationalism, however, it became important to demonstrate that Transylvania was thoroughly Romanian. For example, in the Hungarian town of Deva, a statue of the Dacian king Decebalus was erected, as a well as statues of "She-Wolf" (with Romulus and Remus) and statues of Horea, Cloşca, and Crişan. In fact, statues with these themes are common in towns that have a distinct Hungarian or Saxon character. Another solution has been to build ethnographic museums that depict the Romanian character of life in Transylvania throughout time. Thus ethnographic museums were built in towns such as Cluj-Napoca, Sibiu, and Bran, the latter being near Braşov. Ethnographic museums also make regions with different characteristics seem familiar to all members of the dominant nation, in this case the Romanian nation. Another method of regional integration is simply to reclassify all the elements in the landscape; in other words, classify anything that exists in Romania as Romanian, even if elements in the landscape were created by other ethnic and national groups. For example, all the buildings built by Saxons, Hungarians, or the Austrian imperial government have simply been heralded as great Romanian accomplishments. That many of these buildings have distinct Central and Western European architectural styles only reinforces the notion that Romanians are the products of a Latin culture and that Romania is the eastern outpost of Western Europe.

Although Transylvania has been a place of great activity and intense social upheaval through much of history, few large-scale battles have taken place in the territory that have shaped Romanian sense of national identity. Of these, a battle outside Sibiu, a battle at the Iron Gate of Transylvania (Poarto de Fier a Transilvaniei, not to be confused with the famous Iron Gates on the Danube, next to Drobeta-Turnu-Severin), and the Battle of Selimbăr highlight the Romanian struggle to protect or obtain Transylvania. The site outside Sibiu marks a victory of Iancu of Hunedoara over the Turks in 1442. The Iron Gate of Transylvania testifies to Hunedoara's victory over the Turks in the same year (Giurescu 1981, 136). The Battle of Selimbăr outside Sibiu in 1599 signifies the beginning of Michael the Brave's rule of Transylvania.

The Core: The Tenacity Factor

During the last thousand years, Walachian and Moldavian leaders have fought to obtain or achieve political independence. Romantic historians even depict these events as national movements. However, even before the rise of modern nationalism, various peoples and their leaders struggled for control of their own lives. That Walachians and Moldavians often allied and fought against each other illustrates that Walachians and Moldavians did not share a strong sense of common Romanian identity. Only in the nineteenth century, with the rise of modern nationalism, did Walachian and Moldavian leaders begin to develop a common Romanian identity and begin working together for a common Romanian cause.

In terms of the tenacity factor, Walachia, Moldavia, and Transylvania fall within the core area of Romanian sense of territory because they are the territories where the struggle for national independence began and continued through modern times. The struggle began first in Walachia and Moldavia, partly in response to the Phanoriot princes who had ruled in both principalities since 1711. The Phanoriot princes were Greeks from the Phanar district in Constantinople, and had obtained their positions by paying the Sultan the proper tribute. They had no concern for their Walachian and Moldavian subjects and sought only to enhance their personal prestige and power. Consequently, Walachia and Moldavia went into a period of economic decline. With the rise of Romanian nationalism in the nineteenth century, Walachians and Moldavians became increasingly hostile to their Greek leaders. The revolutionary leader Tudor Vladimirescu seized power in Walachia in 1821 after overthrowing the Phanoriot prince (Bachman 1991, 24; Castellan 1989, 117–20). It should be remembered, however, that Romanian national identity was still in its infant state, for Vladimirescu did not attempt to claim full independence for Walachia but instead proposed a government under Ottoman suzerainty. At the same time, a revolution took place in Moldavia when Alexander Ypsilanti took control of the government. Unlike Vladimirescu, Ypsilanti was a son of a Greek Phanariot prince and general in the Russian army. Ypsilanti had the support of many Romanian *boyars* but even greater support of Greek nationalists (particularly in Odessa), who wanted to make Moldavia and Walachia the first independent Greek nation-state of modern times (Seton-Watson 1963, 192–93). So the Moldavian revolution was just as much Greek as it was Romanian. The revolutions, however, were short-lived. After Vladimirescu and Ypsilanti argued in Bucharest, Greek officers shot and killed Vladimirescu (Bachman 1991, 24). Ypsilanti had to flee to Transylvania after Ottoman troops, with approval from the Russian government, entered Walachia and Moldavia to crush the rebellion. The Phanariot period ended, but Walachia and Moldavia were not yet independent Romanian states but still within the Ottoman empire with the Sultan continuing the practice of choosing the princes of the two territories.

Despite the brevity of the revolution, Romanian national identity continued to grow, and with it the desire for an independent Romanian nation-state. With the wave of nationalism that swept across Europe in the late 1840s, Transylvania also became a key territory of national agitation. Inspired by the ideas of nationalism, the Magyars in Transylvania made Magyar the official governmental language in Transylvania in 1847. During the revolution of 1848, the Hungarian Diet declared a union of Hungary and Transylvania; Romanian peasants rallied in Blaj in opposition. The Hapsburg emperor sent imperial troops to suppress the Hungarian revolution. Many Romanians supported the imperial actions, believing that the emperor was more sympathetic to the Romanian cause than that of the Hungarians. By 1849, the Russian army crushed the Hungarian revolution upon the request of Emperor Franz Joseph (1848–1916). Transylvania came under direct control of the imperial government, and German was made the official language. The Emperor, however, abolished the Union of Three Nations, which only recognized the rights of Hungarians, Szeklers, and Saxons, and granted citizenship to the Romanians of Transylvania.

The revolution spread from Transylvania to Moldavia and Walachia in 1848, but it was short-lived. In Moldavia, Prince Mihai Sturdza (1834–49) squelched the revolution almost overnight (Jelavich and Jelavich 1977, 95). The revolution lasted somewhat longer in Walachia, where there were calls for universal suffrage and the unification of the two principalities. The Russian czar was alarmed by the activity and dispatched Russian troops to the principalities to restore order. The Russian army did not leave until 1851.

Romanians in Walachia and Moldavia did not find an opportunity to create an independent Romanian nation-state until the Russian defeat in the Crimean War of 1854–56. At that time, Walachia and Moldavia ceased to be Russian protectorates but came under a joint European guarantee (Tihany 1976, 158). By this time, the wave of nationalism had spread across Europe, resulting in the development of a common sense of Romanian nationhood among Walachians, Moldavians, and Transylvanians. The first result was a movement to unite Walachia and Moldavia. Delegates assembled and voted for unification, autonomy, and a constitutional government. In 1858, an international conference in Paris rejected unification and autonomy, but allowed the drafting of common laws and titled the two states the "United Principalities." In response to the rejection of unification, separate assemblies in Iași and Bucharest elected a single man, Ioan Cuza, as governor of each state in 1859 (Jelavich and Jelavich 1977, 116; Jelavich 1984, 71–98). Although leaders of the Great Powers objected to the reign of Cuza in both states, other foreign matters prevented them from taking action. After Cuza worked to unite the administrations of the two principalities, the Great Powers finally recognized their unity in 1861 (see Figure 5.2).[17] The new government took up the task of writing a constitution, which was completed in 1866. The constitution addressed numerous issues, significantly changing the name of the province from "United Principalities" to "Romania" (Hitchins 1996, 20). Thus 1866 marked the first year in history that the term *Romania* was officially applied to a territory.

The next opportunity to free the unified core territories of Walachia and Moldavia came during the Russo-Turkish War of 1877–78. Although wanting to be free of the Ottoman Empire, the Romanian government cautiously cooperated with the Russian government out of fear that the principalities would come to be dominated by the Russian Empire. In exchange for the recognition of Romania's territorial integrity, the Romanian government agreed to allow Russian troops to pass through Romania. Following the Russian victory, the Russian government drafted the Treaty of Stefano, which prescribed a new political geography for the Balkans. The other Great Powers rejected the treaty and instead held a conference in Berlin to draft a new treaty. Although different in detail, the Treaty of Berlin (1878) also outlined a new political geography for the Balkans. Most noteworthy, the treaty recognized Romania's independence, thus bringing to fruition the Romanian nationalists' desire and goal of creating a true nation-state.

The Romanian nationalists had succeeded in turning the core territories of Walachia and Moldavia into a Romanian nation-state; however, the new Romanian state did not yet include all territories that Romanian national identity was linked to. A number of territories were missing, most consciously the core territory of Transylvania. Thus Transylvania became the focus of Romanian nationalists as they made the unification of Transylvania with the two other core territories a priority. The union with Transylvania became so important that it, more than any other issue, dictated the foreign policy of the Romanian government during the First World War (Georgescu 1991, 167; Giurescu 1981, 390; Stavrianos 1958, 564).

For example, when King Carol I advocated an alliance with the Central Powers, he fell out of favor with both the Romanian people and the Romanian government because such an alliance would have prevented a union with Transylvania. On the positive side, Carol's desire for an alliance with the Central Powers would have led to the annexation of Besarabia if the Central Powers were successful in their war effort; however, because Transylvania was an integral part of the Central Power of Austria-Hungary, a Central Power victory would have precluded Romania from annexing Transylvania. Because the core territory of Transylvania was more important to the Romanian sense of national identity than the semi-core territory of Besarabia,[18] the Romanian government favored an alliance with the Entente. Thus the desire to gain the core territory of Transylvania dictated the Romanian government's foreign policy during the war. The Romanian government initially stayed neutral, however, before it actually joined the Entente powers.[19] The decision to remain initially neutral actually strengthened the Romanian government's claim to Transylvania. As the Entente powers became desperate for allies in the war, they courted the Romanians, and thus the Romanian government was able to secure the promise of Transylvania—before ever entering the war. Upon entering the war, the Romanian military began its contribution to the war effort by invading Transylvania. The military campaign was such a disaster that Romania was overrun and conquered. The strong desire to obtain Transylvania had, indeed, led to the temporary loss of Walachia and half of Moldavia. Nevertheless, when the Central Powers later began losing the war, the Romanian army initiated another campaign that succeeded in recapturing Walachia and the lost portions of Moldavia. The Romanian army then invaded Transylvania again, this time taking control.

With the end of the First World War and the Paris Peace Conference of 1919, the desire of many Romanians to unite the core territories of Walachia, Moldavia, and Transylvania into a single Romanian nation-state had come to fruition (see Figure 5.2). However, the attainment of a Greater Romania had its consequences. First, many minorities were present within Greater Romania, and the Allied powers wanted to impose a Minorities Treaty at the Paris Peace Conference that ensured the rights of all ethnic minorities (Temperely 1921, 5: 112–49, 454–60). The Minorities Treaty became an issue that evoked passionate nationalist feelings as strong as those related to the issue of boundary delineation. Efforts of a nation to gain or maintain control of given territories often are undermined by the imposition of a treaty that limits a nation's sovereignty over a territory. Because the Minorities Treaty drafted at the Paris Peace Conference prevented the Romanian government from assimilating or persecuting ethnic minorities, the Romanian government was unable to develop and pursue policies that would make the territory of the Romanian state an ethnically pure Romanian land. The hostile reaction of Romanian diplomats to the Minorities Treaty at the Paris Peace Conference led to great difficulties in establishing peace in Europe. Ion Bratinau, prime minister of Romania, was so outraged at the Minorities Treaty that he resigned from the government in protest, leaving no one in the Romanian government with whom the Western Allies could negotiate a peace treaty (Temperley 1921, 4: 230–36). Eventually a new government formed and realized that it had no choice but to accept the Minorities Treaty.

A Greater Romanian national state with many ethnic minorities was only one problem. The new Greater Romania also faced many problems with its neighboring nation-states. Specifically, every country bordering Romania lost territory to Greater Romania. Romania, therefore, found itself surrounded by governments seeking to rectify national boundaries, particularly the Hungarian government, which wanted Transylvania to be returned. Consequently, in order to hold on to the newly acquired core territory of Transylvania, the Romanian government became preoccupied with obtaining international recognition of Romania's territorial integrity. Most noteworthy was the forging of numerous alliance systems to protect the country's borders (Macartney 1962, 252–54). The most notable of these was the Little Entente, an alliance of Romania, Czechoslovakia, and Yugoslavia. All three of these countries had obtained territories from Hungary. Thus, with a potential mutual enemy, the Little Entente ensured the military cooperation of all three states in the event that the Hungarian military attempted to reclaim any of Hungary's lost territories, which included Transylvania (Temperley 1921, 4: 519).

The issue of Transylvania once again determined the actions of the Romanian government in the Second World War. After Hitler awarded northern Transylvania to Hungary in the Second Vienna Award in 1940 (see Figures 4.7 and 5.3), many Romanian leaders fell into disfavor for not having prevented the loss; their policy of neutrality clearly failed in preserving Romania's territorial integrity. The Romanian public soon supported leaders who believed that the lost territories could be regained by collaborating with Hitler. Romanian troops aided Hitler's war effort for a number of years in the hope that Hitler would return northern Transylvania to Romania. In return for Romanian cooperation, Hitler offered the Romanian government the opportunity to annex the Transnistria region in the Ukraine (which was larger and more agriculturally productive than Transylvania) but the Romanian government declined the offer in fear that Hitler would decide that Transnistria was just compensation for the loss of northern Transylvania (Hitchins 1996, 473). Despite the Romanian contribution to Hitler's war effort and the Romanian declining of Transnistria, Hitler never returned northern Transylvania to Romania.

When the Axis began to crumble, the Romanian government found itself in a difficult situation. The Romanian government knew that its sizable contribution to Hitler's war effort would not sit well with the Soviet government. Not only was the core territory of northern Transylvania in danger of permanent loss, so were the core territories of Walachia, Moldavia, and what it still held of Transylvania—the southern portion. Attempts were made to negotiate a surrender with the Western Allies in the hopes of precluding a Soviet invasion of Romania, but to no avail. In a further attempt to appease the Allies, King Michael dismissed Romania's ultra-conservative leader—Antonescu—from the government on August 23, 1944, and set up a government that included a number of socialists (Jelavich 1983, 2: 254). The next day, with Allied insistence, the Romanian government declared war on Germany and began its contribution to the Allied war effort by initiating a drive to push German troops out of Moldavia, Walachia, and all of Transylvania. Nevertheless, within a week, the Red Army occupied Bucharest; on September 12, the Romanian and Soviet governments signed an armistice. The core territories of Walachia, Moldavia, and Transylvania were then in the hands of the Soviets. In the hopes of gaining the favor of the Soviets, the Romanian army aided the Red Army in military operations in Hungary and Czechoslovakia. In 1947, following the post-war peace negotiations, the Allies signed the final peace treaty with the Romanian government; the treaty allowed the Romanian reannexation of northern Transylvania. However, Romania was soon brought into the Soviet geopolitical sphere and the Romanian nation forced to act against its will and violate its sense of national identity.[20]

The Soviets acted in two ways that violated Romanian sense of national identity and sense of territory: in regard to the Hungarians of Transylvania and to language and history. On the first issue, Stalin sought to alleviate tensions between Romanians and Hungarians by insisting that the Romanian government establish an autonomous region for the Hungarians in Transylvania; a Magyar Autonomous Region was established in 1952 (Ludanyi 1983, 234) (see Figure 5.7). Because Romanians believed that Transylvania was a Romanian territory and of course because Transylvania was a core territory to Romanian national identity, the Romanian nation was offended by the act. Nationalist ideology requires total control of the national territory. Hungarian autonomy within the Romanian national territory clearly violated this principle as well as Romanian sense of national identity. Not surprisingly, Romanians looked for opportunities to undermine and destroy the Magyar Autonomous Region. In 1960, the Romanian government undertook an administrative reorganization of the entire country, which not coincidentally also redrew the boundaries of the Magyar Autonomous Region to exclude many Hungarian-inhabited areas while adding Romanian-inhabited areas. As a result, Hungarians became a smaller proportion of the population within the region. The region was then renamed the Mureş-Maghiar Autonomous Region to reflect its reduced size (see Figure 5.7). In 1968, after another administrative reorganization, the Mureş-Maghiar Autonomous Region was abolished when the Bucharest government redrew the county boundaries of the country, leaving no special ethnic regions (Cadzow, Lundanyi, and Elteto 1983, 32–34). The government used the opportunity to reintroduce Romanian words for its territorial-administrative terms in place of the Slavic terms that were introduced in the 1950s (Graham 1982, 42–44, 62).[21] The government also removed many Russian names from businesses, streets, and other public places and replaced them with Romanian names (Floyd 1965, 95–97), thus recreating more of a Romanian landscape that the Romanian nation could identity with.

In addition, the Soviets also had manipulated Romanian language and history to reorient Romanians to the Soviet Union. For example, a Russian colonel, Nicholae Pleşoianu, was heralded as an important figure in the Romanian revolutionary movements of 1848 (Pleshoyano 1991). The Slavic elements of Romanian culture, especially language, were emphasized as well (Schöpflin 1974, 84). However, despite such emphasis, the Romanians still saw themselves as a Daco-Roman people. Because this form of identity represented an intimate tie to Western Europe—most particularly the *Roman* part of Daco-Roman, Soviet authorities felt threatened and subsequently the need to take further steps in reorienting the Romanians to the Slavic world. Since the early eighteenth century, Russian policy makers had insisted that *Romania* be spelled *Rumania*, the *rum* root being a reference to all Eastern Orthodox Christians, an identity which both Romanians and Russians shared. The Soviets insisted on such a spelling after the Second World War (Graham 1982, 62); however, in 1953, they went a step further and insisted that the letter *a* be replaced with the letter *î* (Deletant 1991, 67; Schöpflin 1974, 85). Consequently, *Rumânia* was then written *Rumînia*, and those who persisted with *România* had now to write *Romînia*, neither of which implies Roman ancestry like the term *Romania*. Because the Dacians were not part of the Western European cultural realm, Dacian cultural characteristics were not a threat to the Soviets. On the contrary, to further water down the connection to the Romans, additional emphasis was placed on Dacian origins.

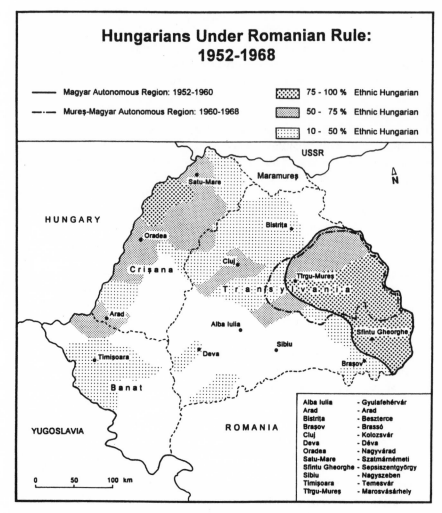

Figure 5.7 Hungarians Under Romanian Rule: 1952–1968.

The Soviet attempt to alter Romanian national identity had very limited results. Many Romanians from Walachia and Moldavia had placed greater emphasis on the Dacian factor in the Daco-Roman equation long before Soviet domination. Primarily the Romanians living under Hapsburg rule, educated in the West, had placed so much emphasis on the Roman part of the equation. The attempt to highlight Russian contributions in Romanian history did little to create a sense of cultural affinity with the Russians among Romanians. If anything, under Gheorghiu-Dej and even more so under Nicholae Ceaușescu, Romanian nationalism continued to grow during the period of Soviet domination, and the Romanian government grew more defiant of Soviet authority. In 1965, not only was the letter *â* readopted in place of *î*, the letter *o* replaced *u* so that the term *Romania* was reintroduced (Deletant 1991, 71; Graham 1982, 62).

In the post-Soviet era of political instability and economic uncertainty, many Romanians are expressing intense feelings of nationalism. The growing strength of such ultra-nationalist political parties as *Unitunea Vatra Româneasca* (Romanian Hearth Union) (Gallagher 1992) is indicative of such feelings. Consequently, many ethnic minorities are being blamed for the country's economic and social problems. In terms of territoriality, Romanian nationalists and ultra-nationalists see ethnic minorities as unwanted infestations that threaten the intimate bond that the Romanian nation has with its core territories of Walachia, Moldavia, and Transylvania.

The Semi-Core: Site Identification and Landscape Description

The semi-core territories of Romanian sense of national territory consist of central and northern Dobrogea, the central and eastern Banat, Maramureş, eastern Crişana, northern Bucovina, and Besarabia. While these regions contain fewer places of great importance than the core territories, the semi-core territories, nonetheless, are very important to Romanian national identity. Significant aspects of Romanian national identity are shaped by the semi-core, and many Romanians have a strong emotional bond to the semi-core territories. The semi-core territories, however, are inhabited by many peoples who do not consider themselves Romanians. Consequently, the issue of control over the semi-core territories has resulted in much conflict between Romanians and these other peoples or between the Romanian government and other governments. The efforts of many Romanians to gain or maintain control of the semi-core territories are in many ways a testament to just how important these territories are to Romanian national identity.

One of the most important aspects of central and northern Dobrogea is that the Romans built a column in Dobrogea to commemorate their victory over a Dacian coalition of forces in A.D. 101–102. In fact, Dobrogea was the first Dacian territory conquered by the Romans. The column, known as the *Tropaeum Traiani*, resembles the Column of Trajan in Rome and is now situated in the small town of Adamclisi (Rădulescu 1977, 3; Treptow 1996, 33). This column, like the replica in Bucharest, serves as a physical link to the Romanian past and legitimizes the Daco-Roman basis of Romanian national identity.

Dobrogea's location is another reason for the region's importance. Situated in the lower Danube valley, between the Danube and the Black Sea, many of the cities of Dobrogea became important centers for the

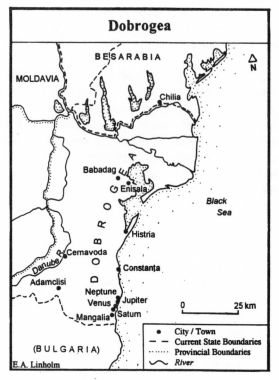

Figure 5.8 Dobrogea.

import and export of Romanian goods. In 1894, a large bridge was opened at Cernavodă at great expense in order to facilitate the flow of goods to and from the port in Constanța (Seton-Watson 1963, 381). Many of Dobrogea's trading centers, and the fortresses that protected them, have been important since early times. For example, Constanța, Mangalia, and Histria[22] were the three Greco-Roman cities of Tomis, Callatis, and Cetatea Histria. All three cities have museums that celebrate their heritage and also emphasize the early and long-standing connection that Romanians have had with Dobrogea. The fortresses at Chilia and Enisala played leading roles in the struggle against the Ottomans. Babadag was originally an Ottoman fortress, but its possession became necessary for control of the region. The Romanian connection to Dobrogea is also emphasized because various Walachian leaders, such as Mircea the Old and Basarab, controlled much of Dobrogea and considered it to be part of the Walachian state (Giurescu 1981, 125–26). In recent decades, many beach resorts have been established in Dobrogea along the Black Sea coast. The belief that Dobrogea is truly a Romanian land has been reinforced by giving these places Roman names such as Neptune-Olimp, Jupiter, Venus-Aurora, and Saturn.

The Banat, eastern Crişana, and Maramureş are important because they fall within the Tişa, Danube, Nistra watershed basin—part of the broader territory that is considered to be innately and organically Romanian (Stoicescu 1986, 9–13). These territories were also part of the Dacian state and the Roman province of Dacia. The Banat was the most important of these territories because it served as the physical link, or bridge, between Dacia and the rest of the Roman Empire. Dierna on the Danube was one of the eight Roman *colonia* in the Dacian province. When the Roman Province of Dacia was divided into different administrative districts,

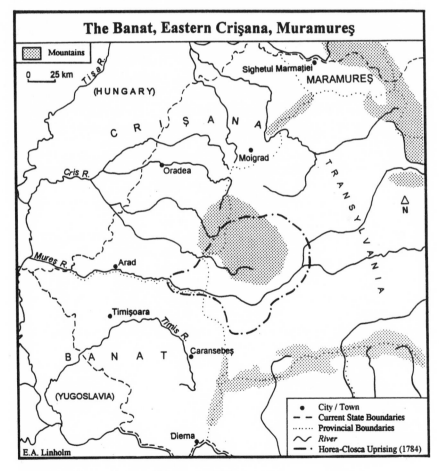

Figure 5.9 Banat, Eastern Crişana, and Maramureş.

Porolissum (now Moigrad) in eastern Crişana, served as the Roman capital of Dacia Porolissenis (Giurescu 1981, 61). All of these places serve as physical proof of the Roman component of Romanian national identity. The historical significance of Maramureş stems mostly from the Middle Ages. Dragoş and Bogdan, the founders of Moldavia, initially came from Maramureş (Giurescu 1981, 119). These two places, therefore, show the close connection between Maramureş and Moldavia.

The Banat and eastern Crişana have played important roles for Romanian national identity in recent times as well. Being in the Hapsburg Empire, the Banat and eastern Crişana played a role similar to Transylvania in the intellectual and cultural development of modern Romanian national identity. Cities such as Arad, Caransebeş, Oradea, and Timişoara were important educational and religious centers in the nineteenth century; many of them had printing presses as well. Much of the Banat, eastern Crişana, and Maramureş is more Hungarian than Romanian. To demonstrate the Romanian character of these territories, museums have been constructed and folk festivals organized. For example, Sighet, the major town of Maramureş, has an ethnographic museum (Mihnea 1973, 140).

Much in the same way that Bucovina was an integral part of Moldavia, northern Bucovina was an integral part of Bucovina until it was severed from Romania in 1940 and again in 1945. A few noteworthy places in

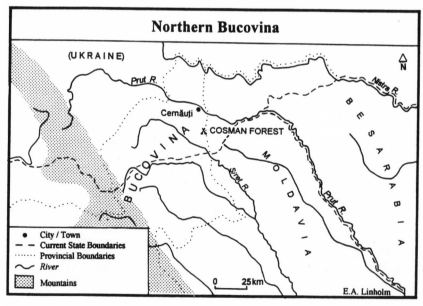

Figure 5.10 Northern Bucovina.

the territory are important to the Romanian nation. For example, while Cernăuţi (now Chernivtsi, Ukraine) was the capital of Austrian Bucovina, a number of important institutions were founded in the town—a university in 1875, a Metropolitan See, Orthodox schools, and a seminary (Seton-Watson 1963, 556). In other words, Cernăuţi was a cultural center that contributed to the shaping of modern Romanian national identity. Northern Bucovina also contains Cosman Forest (Codrii Cosminului), the place of a great military victory where Stephen the Great ended the Polish threat to Moldavia when he defeated the Polish army (Castellan 1989, 42–43).

Besarabia likewise had been an integral part of Moldavia until it was annexed by the Russian Empire in 1812. Chişinău (also Kishinev) was, and in many ways still is, the only significant city of Besarabia. Chişinău played a role as a cultural center with its Romanian schools and printing presses. The town is also associated with one of Romania's great leaders, Stephen the Great; a statue of him stood in the city center (Popovici 1931, 48–A) before Soviet authorities had it removed. Besarabia also has many of Romania's great fortresses and battle sites that testify to a glorious past. Along the Nistra River are the fortresses of Hotin (now Khotyn, Ukraine), Soroca (Clark 1927, 34, 84), Tighina, and Cetatea Albă (also known as Akkerman, now Bilhorod-Dnistovs'kyy, Ukraine); on a tributary of the Nistra, but in the same line of defense, is Orhei. The battle sites of Lipniţi and Cătlăbuga mark two great Romanian victories over two of the peoples that menaced Europe; Lipniţi was fought against the Tartars in 1469 (Castellan 1989, 41), and Cătlăbuga was fought against the Ottomans in 1485 (Seton-Watson 1963, 46); both victories were led by Stephen the Great, now a hero to the Romanian nation.

The Semi-Core: The Tenacity Factor

Although most Romanians have been primarily concerned with the core territories in the nineteenth and twentieth centuries, semi-core territories have not been ignored. Indeed, events have made it possible for the Romanian government to annex semi-core territories at various times. However, some semi-core territories were lost, with some still not part of the modern Romanian state.

Of the semi-core territories, Besarabia figures first in the struggle to create a Romanian nation-state. The territory was created when the Russian government carved it out of Moldavia in 1812. Initially an integral part of the core territory of Moldavia, Besarabia was very important to the Romanian nation. However, with a few exceptions, the territory that became Besarabia had few places of significance even though it was not thought of as a territory separate from Moldavia. Consequently, although

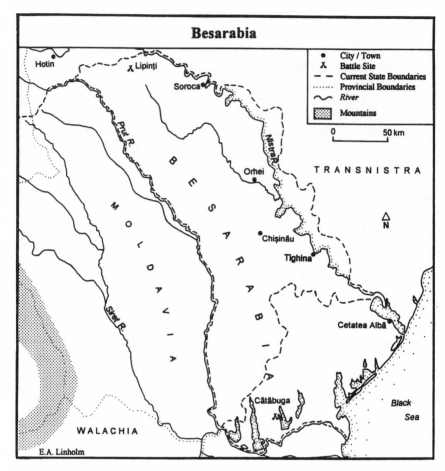

Figure 5.11 Besarabia.

the Romanian nation—still in its infancy—was outraged by the Russian annexation of Besarabia, it was unable to prevent it. Indeed, no Romanian state existed as yet, meaning that the core territories of Walachia, Moldavia, and Transylvania had not been freed. Thus no Romanian was in a position to stop the Russians. Nevertheless, when the Russian army lost the Crimean War to the Ottomans in 1856, Romanian leaders were able to convince the Great Powers to return the three southern districts of Besarabia to Moldavia, even though Moldavia was still a principality within the Ottoman Empire. The Romanians, however, were outraged once again when the Russian government was allowed to retake these three southern districts in the Treaty of Berlin (1878), following the victory of the Russian army in the Russo-Turkish War of 1877–78. The protest from the Romanian government was so strong that the Russian government decided that it was prudent to offer the Romanians the semi-core territories of central and northern Dobrogea (see Figure 5.2) as compensation. The Romanian government accepted these areas of Dobrogea as temporary compensation while it waited for an opportunity to reclaim Besarabia.

While the Romanian nation waited for an opportunity to reclaim Besarabia, opportunities presented themselves for annexing other semi-core territories. During the First World War, the Romanian government saw an opportunity to obtain Crişana, Maramureş, and the Banat. The neutral stance initially taken by the Romanian government prompted the warring governments to offer the Romanians territorial rewards in return for military support. Indeed, many Romanian officials solicited offers. The Romanian government was primarily concerned with obtaining the core territory of Transylvania, but as the war went badly for the Entente powers in the early years, the Romanian government was also able to obtain the promise of eastern Crişana, Maramureş, and the Banat (see Figure 5.2)—all in addition to the core territory of Transylvania. When the Austro-Hungarian imperial government surrendered at the end or the war, the Allies established an armistice line that left western Transylvania, Crişana, and Maramureş under Hungarian control, pending a peace settlement. The Romanian government, however, did not agree with these decisions, and soon the Romanian army pushed past the armistice lines and continued to do so despite reprimands of the Western Powers. Even after the Allies continued to move the armistice lines westwards to accommodate the Romanian demands, the Romanian government continued its operation to secure these semi-core territories. Because the Hungarian government and army had disintegrated by the end of the war, neither the Western Powers nor the Hungarian government was able to resist the advance of the Romanian army.

The First World War also presented a new opportunity to acquire Besarabia. The war facilitated the Bolshevik Revolution in 1917, which in turn led to the disintegration of the Russian Empire. The Romanian government was then able to take Besarabia (Stavrianos 1958, 565) (see Figure 5.2). By 1940, however, the Soviet government was strong enough politically to force the reannexation of Besarabia; for the first time, the Soviets also took northern Bucovina. While many Romanians thought that they could reclaim northern Transylvania by allying themselves with Hitler, the opportunity to reclaim northern Bucovina and Besarabia also played a role in the decision to aid Hitler in his war effort. Indeed, the first Romanian military operation in the war involved the reannexation of Besarabia and northern Bucovina. Despite such action, northern Bucovina and Besarabia were lost again after the war.

As the Soviet Union began to weaken in the late 1980s, Romanian nationalism began to express itself in Besarabia, which the Soviets named *The Soviet Socialist Republic of Moldavia*.[23] Some of the first acts came when the government of the republic voted to make Romanian the official language instead of Russian (*Economist* 1989, 48); in addition, the government rejected the Cyrillic script and adopted the Latin one (King 1993, 283). This was done in 1989, before the disintegration of the Soviet Union and the republic's declaration of independence! Next, the government decided to replace the Russian name *Moldavia* with the Romanian name *Moldova* in the republic's name.[24] Not all Moldovans, however, subscribed to Romanian national identity, or even a Moldovan one. In fact, the wave of Romanian nationalism alarmed the other ethnic groups in the Republic, particularly because it foreshadowed a union of Moldova with Romania. In reaction to Romanian nationalism, and in anticipation of such a union, the ethnic minorities of Moldova turned their fear into calls for independent states to be carved out of Moldova. One was for a *Moldovan Transnistrian Republic (PMR)*—east of the Nistra (Dnestr) River—and the other was for a *Gagauz Republic*—in the south (King 1993, 283). Because Russians and other Slavs reside in the Transnistrian state, not to mention other areas of Moldova, and because many Russians in Russia still value their former territories of the Soviet Union, the former Soviet 14th army has stayed in Moldova to support the movement (King 1994–95, 114–15). So, despite the desire of many Romanians to reacquire as much of Besarabia as possible, their fear of the Russian army has made them cautious and unwilling to ignite a military conflict.

The unification of Romania and Moldova has encountered another problem even though the government of Moldova dropped the words *Soviet* and *Socialist* from the territory's name (making the official name *Republic of Moldova*) in 1991 and then declared independence. Despite the early wave of Romanian nationalism in Moldova, many Moldovans, although culturally akin to Romanians, are now expressing the belief that Moldovans are a separate nation from the Romanians, and thus want to preserve the independence of Moldova as a nation-state (Hamm 1998, 172–73). It appears that Soviet denationalization policies, not to mention Russification policies in the nineteenth century, have caused the Moldovans to reject a broader Romanian identity and to see themselves as a nation unto themselves.[25] Certainly, Romanian nationalists in Romania believe that this is what has happened (King 1994–95, 118). Noteworthy, many Romanians have lost interest in annexing Moldova as well (Hamm 1998, 172), perhaps indicating that Soviet policies have had their effect on Romanian national identity as well. Nevertheless, Romanian national identity is still tied to Besarabia, as shown by all Romanian political parties, regardless of ideology, having to speak of reannexing the lost territories of 1940—Besarabia and northern Bucovina—if they want any support from the Romanian public (King 1994–95). At this time, the annexation of northern Bucovina, the Republic of Moldova, and the southern districts of Besarabia cannot be brought about by the political process. The Ukrainian government has made it clear that it will not give up northern Bucovina or the southern districts of Besarabia, and the government of Moldova is not showing any interest in unification; the presence of the former Soviet 14th army is also a hindrance. Military action seems to be the only alternative currently, but it is unwise because some of the opponents are much stronger than the Romanian army, not to mention the international sanctions that would come about. Moreover, a failed military campaign could threaten the more important core territories of Romanian national identity. The attitude and actions that Romanian leaders have recently taken in regard to northern Bucovina and Besarabia demonstrate that these territories are still important to Romanian national identity. However, the lack of willingness on the part of the Romanian nation to forcefully assert its control also demonstrates that these territories currently rank as only semi-core territories, even if they could have previously been regarded as core territories.

The Periphery: Site Identification and Landscape Description

The periphery of Romanian sense of territory consists of southern Dobrogea, Transnistria, western Crişana, and various sites within the Balkan peninsula, particularly northern Bulgaria and Macedonia. Romanian identity is only marginally derived from the periphery, and rarely has the Romanian government made great and daring attempts to gain control of peripheral territories. Yet the peripheral territories underscore the greatness of the Romanian nation by illustrating how involved the Romanians have been in great events and how they have shaped the course of international history. The expansive areas of the peripheral territories also reinforce the claims that Romanians have to their core and semi-core territories; the peripheral territories show that Romanian claims to core and semi-core territories are not unreasonable because they have the right to claim many more territories if they desired.

The delimitation of Dobrogea has been problematic. Romanian territory has been defined in terms of natural physiographic features—the territory that falls within the Tişa (Tisza), Danube, and Nistra (Dnestr) Rivers. Dobrogea, of course, falls outside of such a territorial conception (see Figure 5.3). Nevertheless, Dobrogea is significant to the Romanian nation's sense of territory for the role that it has played in history and for the elements in its landscape that support Romanian sense of national identity. As a result, it is seen by many Romanians as a Romanian territory. As

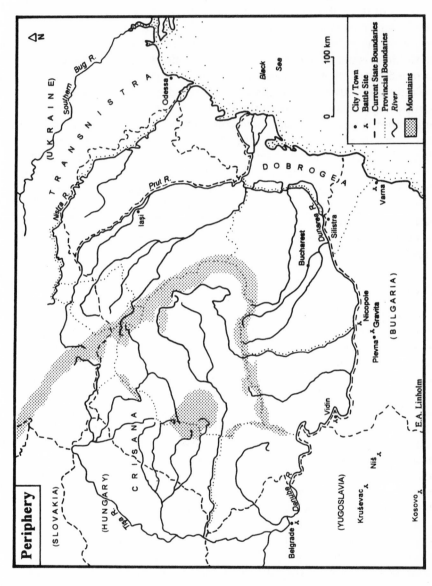

Figure 5.12 The Periphery.

the other Romanian territories are defined physiographically, Dobrogea is likewise defined. Dobrogea is bounded by the Danube River on the west and north and by the Black Sea on the east. However, no physiographic feature defines Dobrogea's southern border. Dobrogea, particularly southern Dobrogea, is important to the Romanian nation's sense of territory because it serves as a buffer against any Bulgarian military initiatives directed at Romania's core territories. In many ways, the Romanian nation feels threatened by the Bulgarian nation because many Bulgarians covet Dobrogea (Dobrudjža). Indeed, Dobrogea falls firmly into the dominant Bulgarian nation's sense of territory (Markoff 1918). Within southern Dobrogea, the most important place to the Romanian nation is the fortress town of Silistra, which historically has played a key strategic role in the region. As a result, many Romanian leaders have seen the possession of Silistra as crucial to the defense of Walachia and the rest of Dobrogea.

Just south of the Danube in northern Bulgaria are a number of battle sites that serve as a testament to Romanian valor. Although the Battle of Nicopole in 1396 was a defeat for the Christian forces of Europe, Mircea the Old and his troops took part in this well-known historical event (Giurescu 1981, 134). Iancu of Hunedoara's heroic action in many great historic battles also bolsters the prestige of Romanian national identity. Hunedoara defeated the Ottomans outside Belgrade in 1441 and outside Niș in 1443. He survived the major Christian defeat at the Battle of Varna in 1444, and even survived the Battle of Kosovo in 1448, which he organized himself. He was victorious again at Kruševac in 1453. His most famous victory was the defense of Belgrade in 1456—a victory that seemed highly improbable at the time (Seton-Watson 1963, 36–39). In more recent times, the battles of the Russo-Turkish War of 1877–78 stand out. In the early days of the war, the Romanian military laid siege to the Turkish stronghold in Vidin and bombarded it. The most glorious moment for the Romanians came at the Battle of Plevna in 1877. The Russian army had become bogged down and found itself in a perilous situation. After the Russian czar offered command to Prince Charles, the Romanian army went to the rescue of the Russians. A great sacrifice made outside Plevna at Gravița turned the war into a victory for the Russian Empire. The heroic struggles of the Romanians in the battles around Plevna have been immortalized in a number of paintings (Berindei 1976, between pages 96 and 97; Treptow 1996, 328).

Ethnic groups in the Balkans which are related to the Romanians also play a role in the Romanian nation's sense of territory. They are generally known as Vlachs (also Kutzo-Vlachs or Aromâni) but subgroups exist, known as Istro-, Megleno-, and Macedo-Romanians (see Figure 5.13). They are offshoots of the same Thraco-Illyrian racial branch as the Romanians, who themselves are classified as Daco-Romanians in the

Thraco-Illyrian racial branch. The idea that modern Romanians are the descendants of a mixture of Dacians (who are Illyrian) and Romans is a highly controversial matter. That other ethnic groups have similar origins supports the Romanian claim to Daco-Roman identity. All three groups of Kutzo-Vlachs have such origins even though the Macedo-Vlachs are the only group that still exists, although in small numbers. The Kutzo-Vlachs also give the Romanians the ability to look beyond their immediate territory and even claim to be the protectors of a people with a broader sense of identity.

Western Crişana, which lies between the current Romanian border and Tisza River, is important because it falls within the boundaries of the Tişa (Tisza), Danube, and Nistra (Dnestr) Rivers. The region was also within the Dacian state and the province of Roman Dacia. Nevertheless, other than some ancient archeological sites, the region lacks places of specific importance.

Transnistria, the territory that lies between the Nistra (Dnestr) and Southern Bug Rivers, has had some importance to Romanian sense of territory. The region conceptually falls within the radial watershed that emanates from the Carpathians. Other than having a similar physical environment to Besarabia, the only important place within Transnistria is Odessa. While Odessa obviously is not innately Romanian, it has served as an important city in northeastern Romania. Interaction was facilitated by a major road, then a rail line, that ran from Iaşi through Chişinău and on to Odessa.

The Periphery: Tenacity Factor

Attempts to annex southern Dobrogea came with the Balkan wars in 1912 and 1913. With the outbreak of the First Balkan War in 1912, the Romanian army did not engage in military operations; however, the Romanian government insisted that the Bulgarian government cede a narrow strip of land along the border in Dobrogea, including the important fortress city of Silistra (Bachman 1991, 31). When the Bulgarian government refused Romanian demands, the Romanian government threatened military action. After British arbitration, Romania received Silistra but little of the other territory that the government demanded. When the Second Balkan War broke out in 1913, the Romanian government joined the Serbian and Greek war effort against the Bulgarian government. With the Bulgarian defeat, the Romanian government annexed southern Dobrogea (Giurescu 1981, 383). Southern Dobrogea was lost to Bulgaria in the First and Second World Wars. The Soviet government allowed the Bulgarian government to maintain control of the territory after the Second World War. Few Romanians have expressed the desire to obtain southern Dobrogea again.

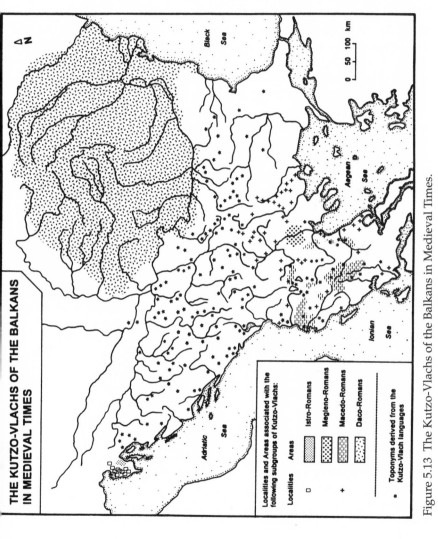

THE KUTZO-VLACHS OF THE BALKANS IN MEDIEVAL TIMES

Localities and Areas associated with the following subgroups of Kutzo-Vlachs:

Localities	Areas	
▫		Istro-Romans
		Megleno-Romans
		Macedo-Romans
+		Daco-Romans

★ Toponyms derived from the Kutzo-Vlach languages

Black Sea

Aegean Sea

Ionian Sea

Adriatic Sea

0 50 100 km

N

Figure 5.13 The Kutzo-Vlachs of the Balkans in Medieval Times.

Romanian involvement with the Kutzo-Vlachs was most intense at the end of the nineteenth century through the beginning of the twentieth century. At the same time that Serbian, Bulgarian, and Greek nationalists were trying to inculcate the people of Macedonia with their national identities, so were Romanian nationalists. A Romanian school was opened in Tirnova in 1864 and later a larger school opened in Bitola (Monastir). By 1905, Romanian diplomats were able to convince the sultan to grant the Vlachs their own *millet*, separating them from the Greek patriarchate (Seton-Watson 1963, 383–84). By 1910, a commercial college, a girls' normal school, three *gymnasia*, and 120 primary schools were functioning (Clark 1922, 82). Although the Romanian government spent large sums of money on the Kutzo-Vlachs, it never advanced a territorial claim to any of their lands. The Romanian government did, however, use the Kutzo-Vlachs to advance territorial claims against the Bulgarians in Dobrogea during and between the Balkan Wars (Jelavich and Jelavich 1977, 210).

The Romanian government saw its opportunity to gain the entire Crişana up to the Tisza River in the First World War. With an initial stance of neutrality, both the Entente and Central Powers were forced to make promises of territorial awards for Romanian cooperation. The Italian government accepted Entente promises of territory in the Treaty of London in 1915. The Entente powers were willing to offer Romanian leaders Transylvania, Maramureş, much of Crişana, and most of the Banat in the same treaty. However, with the war going badly for the Entente powers, Romanian leaders were sure that they could secure the promise of the entire territory up to the Tisza River in exchange for Romanian aid, which seemed to be desperately needed. Although the war went badly for the Entente in the early years, the Russian army broke through the Austrian lines in Galicia by the middle of 1916. When it seemed that the Austro-Hungarian Empire might collapse, Romanian leaders feared that their neutrality would prevent even the annexation of Transylvania. In a moment of haste, the Romanian government accepted the Entente promise of the entire Banat but not western Crişana. Romanian leaders accepted the offer for a new border that was to run northeast from Szeged, paralleling the current Hungarian-Romanian boundary.

After the war, the Romanian army advanced past the armistice lines despite the objections of the Western Powers. Later, the Romanian government refused to accept the modified border (which is essentially the current boundary) agreed upon by the Western Powers. When the Hungarian Red army tried to reclaim some of Hungary's territory in 1919, the Romanian army used the Hungarian action as an excuse to advance all the way to the Tisza, and then on to Budapest, breaking off communications with the Western Powers in the process. When the leader of the Romanian government, Brătianu, refused to respond to demands of the

Western Powers to withdraw, an envoy was dispatched to Bucharest. When the envoy arrived, Brătianu resigned from the government in protest of Western Power demands, making it even more difficult for the Western Powers to hold anyone responsible for the actions of the Romanian army in Hungary. By 1920, a new government was elected in Romania, and it decided to accept Allied demands and withdraw the Romanian army to the new boundary line. No other attempts have been made since then to annex western Crişana.

The only attempt made at annexing the Transnistria was during the Second World War when the Romanian government was allied with Nazi Germany. In return for the Romanian contribution to the Axis war effort, Hitler simply offered the Romanian government Transnistria. The leader of Romania, Antonescu, accepted Hitler's offer and changed the name of the city of Odessa to Antonescu (Stavrianos 1958, 766). Many Romanians felt obligated to justify Romania's acquisition of Transnistria (Jelavich 1983b, 251); for example, maps were distributed that showed that much of the Ukraine had been inhabited by Dacians (Bachman 1991, 41). Despite such rationalizations, many Romanians, including many leaders, began withdrawing their support for the Romanian war effort as the Romanian army crossed over the Nistra River and advanced towards Stalingrad. As the Axis armies were driven out of the Soviet Union during the latter part of the war, the Red Army reoccupied Transnistria. No Romanians protested the actions of the Soviets, and no claim has been advanced to the territory since the end of the war.

Notes

1. In addition to these three major territories, the modern Romanian state is also composed of smaller territories known as the Banat, Crişana, Maramureş, Bucovina, and Dobrogea.

2. Romanian Orthodox churches first came under the jurisdiction of the Serbs in Sremski Karlovci when the Austrian Empire established the Serbian metropolitan province in 1737. In 1766, the province became an independent body and was renamed the Serbian Slav Oriental Church (Magocsi 1993, 116). Prior to 1737, the administrative boundaries of the Orthodox Church in southeastern Europe had nothing to do with the spatial distributions of nations. Indeed, modern nations did not exist prior to 1737.

3. The ecumenical patriarch finally recognized the Romanian Orthodox Church in 1885 (Magocsi 1993, 117).

4. Known officially as the Greek Catholic Church since 1774 (Magocsi 1993, 113).

5. Uniates were primarily found in Transylvania and Bucovina, territories which had usually been in the Hungarian Kingdom, the Austrian Empire, or the Austro-Hungarian Empire over the last thousand years.

6. The term *Romanian nation* had been employed as early as 1739 by the Uniate bishop Ioan Inocentiu Micu-Clain (Hitchins 1977, 4), considered to be the fore-

father of the Transylvanian School. Micu-Clain, however, was not nearly so concerned with the genealogy of the Romanian nation as those who came after him. Instead, he accepted and pushed for new ideas concerning the concept of nationhood, which were more akin to what the concept means today, an ethnically based people comprising all social classes. His ideas conflicted with the prevailing belief that the nation was composed exclusively of the aristocracy. Micu-Clain's radical ideas led him to fight for inclusion of the poorer classes in the political process. Because most Walachians were confined to the peasant classes, modern Romanians look back on Micu-Clain as a national hero.

7. Greek was even the language of government, education, and science throughout much of the Phanariot period (1711–1859), the time when Ottoman authorities had Greeks run the governments of the principalities of Walachia and Moldavia (Close 1974, 14).

8. For a more detailed study on the word origins of the early Romanian language, see André Du Nay's *The Early History of the Rumanian Language* (1977).

9. John Campbell argues that some Romanian nationalists Latinized the Romanian language to such a degree that it was completely divorced from the vernacular language of Romanians (1971, 27).

10. Although Romanians embraced French culture willingly, the influence of the French language also came from places other than France. One of the most notable examples comes from Russian soldiers who occupied Walachia and Moldavia from 1806 to 1812 and again from 1829 to 1834. At that time, Russian officers, not to mention Russian nobility and gentry in general, preferred to speak French, not Russian, even with one another (Close 1974, 20–21).

11. Interestingly, despite the ideological argument for using the Latin alphabet, it did not convey all the sounds of the Romanian language (Fishman 1972, 143; see also Kolarz 1946, p. 22).

12. Notice that Michael did not use the term *Romania*. In addition, although the modern Romanian nation sees Michael the Brave as a national hero, Michael the Brave predated nationalism. He lived during the age of dynastic imperialism and behaved accordingly. For example, he did not liberate the Walachians of Transylvania but instead courted the Magyar and Saxon nobility (Seton-Watson 1963, 67–70). In fact, his conquering army was composed of large contingents of Serbs, Albanians, Cossacks, and Magyars (Seton-Watson 1963, 67).

13. Transylvania, although a core territory of the modern Romanian state, did not function as anything that could be described as a Romanian state until it was incorporated into the Romanian nation-state after the First World War.

14. Also noteworthy was the Hapsburgs' gain of Bucovina in 1774 and the Russian annexation of Besarabia in 1812. Both territories were created when carved out of Moldavia. Both empires also held onto these territories until they disintegrated at the end of the First World War.

15. The Romanian term *Ardeal* is often used as a translation for the English word *Transylvania*, however, this is inaccurate. Ardeal derives from the Hungarian *Erdély*, which was coined to refer to the territories that Hungary lost to Romania after the First World War. Transylvania was the most significant of these territories lost; however, Maramureş, Crişana, and the Banat were also lost and, therefore, included in the term *Erdély/Ardeal*.

16. Because forests and mountains are closely associated with each other in much of Europe, Transylvania is frequently thought of as meaning "across the forested mountains."

17. Significantly, the Great Powers resisted the use of the term *Romania*. In addition, most Europeans continued to use the term *Walachian* even though many Walachians had begun to think of themselves as Romanians over the preceding few decades. In fact, Ottoman authorities only went as far as to recognize the *Moldo-Walachians* (Hitchins 1994, 15).

18. The importance of Transylvania is poignantly stated in Kurt Treptow's book *A History of Romania*, where he quotes the Romanian leader Nicolae Titulescu. Titulescu argued for Romania's alliance with the Entente because such an alliance provided the opportunity to gain Transylvania. At a meeting in 1915 where he tried to whip up support for an Entente alliance, Titulescu said, "Romania cannot be whole without Transylvania. Transylvania is its cradle, the school of its people, the magic that preserved its being. Transylvania is not only the heart of political Romania; look at a map. Transylvania is the heart of our political geography" (1996, 373–74).

19. Pragmatism prevented the Romanian government from immediately joining with the Entente powers even though Romanians valued Transylvania more than Besarabia. On the eve of the war, it was uncertain which side would be victorious. If the Central Powers had overwhelmed the Entente, an alliance with the Entente would not have brought Transylvania to Romania any more than neutrality. Indeed, cooperation with the Entente may have resulted in the loss of the core territories of Walachia and Moldavia. However, initial neutrality allowed the Romanian government to still join the Central Powers in the latter part of their possible and unpreventable victory, bringing the opportunity to gain semi-core territories such as Besarabia. Initial neutrality also did not preclude the possibility of gaining Transylvania because it allowed Romania to join the Entente powers if they were headed down the road to victory.

20. Interestingly, the Soviets had great difficulty in helping the Communists come to power in Romania because the Communists were very unpopular. Romanians disliked the Communists primarily because the Communists believed that Transylvania did not belong to Romania.

21. In 1946 and 1947, Sovietization, or Slavicization, led to the replacement of the historic terms of *județe* and *consiliile populare* with the Slavic words *reiune, raione,* and *sfaturile populare.*

22. For more information on Histria, see Radu Florescu's and Ion Michlea's book *The City of Histria* (1989).

23. The territory of the Republic of Moldova is not coterminous with that of Besarabia. After the war, the Soviets redrew the boundaries to exclude the southern portion of Besarabia, however redrawing the boundaries to include a narrow strip of land on the eastern side of the Nistra (Dnestr) River.

24. Although spellings closest to Romanian were chosen for the names of places and territories in this book, the choice was made to employ the English *Moldavia* in place of the Romanian *Moldova* to differentiate the territory between the Carpathians and the Prut River from the Soviet Republic to the east of the Prut. Unfortunately, such a choice is awkward at this moment because it makes it

appear that the change from Moldavia to Moldova is a move away from Romanian nationalism when in fact it was an expression of it.

25. Interestingly, this new form of national identity is still tied, framed, and defined in large degree by territory.

6

Serbia and the Serbs

On the surface, the Romantic belief that language and religion determine national identity seems to apply to the South Slavs (Yugoslavs): e.g., Slovenes, Croats, Bosnian Muslims, Serbs, and Bulgarians. The Serbs, for example, differ from the Bulgarians in language, from the Croats and Bosnian Muslims in religion, and from the Slovenes in both language and religion. The linguistic and religious differences appear to be so significant that they lay at the root of the conflict between these groups. Indeed, religious affiliation seems to be the dividing issue in the recent war in the former Yugoslavia and the continuing conflicts.

A closer examination of South Slavic identities, however, shows that language and religion did not determine the South Slavic nations although language and religion can be used today to identify them. In fact, the opposite is true: the various South Slavic nations used language and religion to define their respective national identities and not vice versa, as Romantics believe. What existed throughout the Balkans prior to the rise of nationalism, and indeed well into it, was a complex set of identities that varied among individuals, especially from place to place. With the rise of Romantic nationalism in the late eighteenth century, South Slavs began to redefine themselves as they tried to recategorize themselves according to the conceptions of Romantic nationalism, namely according to language use and religious affiliation. Thus, although the Serbian nation is clearly defined today by the combination of the Serbian language and Eastern Orthodox Christianity, this definition is a modern construct which is still not complete.[1] The further back in history we go, the more difficult it is to speak of Serbian identity as something distinct and unique. It was intimately bound up with, and even inextricable from, other forms of South Slavic identity. Therefore, to write and speak of Serbian history accurately, it is often necessary to write and speak of it in conjunction with a more generalized history of South Slavic and Illyrian[2] peoples. It is misleading to project the present back into the past and falsely write a history of the Serbian people as if it were always separate and distinct.

Language use and religious affiliation had not been insignificant to the forms of identity among the peoples of the Balkans through history, but the new ideology of nationalism meant that they were to be used differently to define identity. For example, prior to the rise of nationalism, the Ottoman authorities categorized people according to religious affiliation and called these groups *millets*. The Ottomans, for example, put all Eastern Orthodox Christians into one group and called it the *Millet-i-Rum*, with *Rum* referring to the Eastern Orthodox Christian faith (Bringa 1995, 236). All Eastern Orthodox Christians were the same to the Ottomans. The Ottomans made no attempts to distinguish one Orthodox Christian from another, whether they were Russian, Bulgarian, Serbian, Greek, or other. Ethnicity was irrelevant, and modern nationhood had no meaning. Because Christianity was a universal religion, Eastern Orthodox Christians accepted a common identity for themselves and even saw the world in terms of a Christian/non-Christian dichotomy. Eastern Orthodox Christians universally applied the term *Pravoslavni*[3] to themselves and also did not put great emphasis on their ethnic differences. In fact, although ethnic terms existed, we should not treat them as though they have the same degree of meaning that they have today. Prior to the rise of nationalism, ethnic terms such as Serb, Russian, Bulgarian, etc., were vague terms that had much less relevance to one's identity than they do currently. The only other forms of identity that were as salient as *Pravoslav* (and the corresponding *Katholik, Protestant*, and *Musliman*) were place-based terms of identity. Being from a particular territory was very relevant to one's identity. Therefore, the notion of being Bosnian, Dalmatian,[4] or Slavonian, for example, was something very concrete, more concrete than ethnic terms. In fact, because language use varied from place to place, individuals identified the language that they spoke by the places that they were from. Bosnians, Dalmatians, and Slavonians, for example, referred to their respective languages as Bosnian, Dalmatian, and Slavonian, not Serbo-Croatian, a term not agreed upon until the end of the nineteenth century and not in common use until well into the twentieth century (Naylor 1980, 66).

Because people at the turn of the nineteenth century identified themselves more as *Pravoslavni* and less as Serbs (and Bulgarians, Russians, etc.), nationalism initially fused with *Pravoslav* identity. Thus one of the earliest forms of nationhood to emerge in the Balkans was a *Pravoslav* one. As a result, the earliest demands for a nation-state were ones that called for the unification of all Eastern Orthodox Christians into a single independent state. *Pravoslav* nationhood, however, was problematic. *Pravoslavni* inhabited territories from the Balkans to the northern forests of Russia. Because

Pravoslavni inhabited many different territories, many regional variations of *Pravoslavni* identity existed. Moreover, they lived in different political states. Those in the north, for example, were together in the Russian Empire. Most of the others were in the Ottoman Empire, and a few were located in the Hapsburg realm. The political organization of territory and its impact on the formation of identity cannot be overemphasized. Thus the call was made to unify all the *Pravoslavni* of the Ottoman Empire and to create an independent nation-state that would be carved out of the Ottoman possessions; not surprisingly, help for such a movement was solicited from the *Pravoslavni* of the Russian Empire (Banac 1984, 82).

The *Pravoslavni* used Church Slavonic in religious practice and their local languages for their day-to-day interactions. Because language was not a basis of identity prior to the rise of Romantic nationalism, the *Pravoslavni* were not aware or concerned about the linguistic relationships and differences in their language use. They dealt with their linguistic differences by identifying what they spoke according to whatever regions they lived in. However, with the rise of Romantic nationalism, language began to take on a new meaning. As linguists studied the languages of southeastern Europe, they began to see commonalities in language practice and began making broader categorizations of language use. The term *Illyrian*,[5] for example, began to take on greater significance because it referred to all the South Slavic language speakers. More significant over the long run, however, these language categorizations related to the political control of territory. Although the peoples of southeastern Europe were the subjects of outside realms—the Hapsburg, Ottoman, and Russian Empires—vestiges of many of their former political states still remained and continued to play some role in the administration of territory, although within the empires just mentioned. Thus modern languages grew and developed with the political organization of space. Eventually, a separate language became associated with each political center. For example, a separate and distinct Bulgarian language was codified and cultivated as the modern Bulgarian state was founded and subsequently grew. The Romanian and Greek languages developed in a similar manner as the Romanian and Greeks states respectively came into being and grew. We have witnessed this process this century with the Macedonian language.[6] The same began to happen with Dalmatian and Bosnian until these two territories were incorporated into other political states. Since then, the absorbing governments worked to destroy the uniqueness of these languages.[7] Consequently, these languages are no longer considered to be separate and distinct even though the people who spoke them once considered them to be so.

As Zagreb and Belgrade began exerting their political influence in the nineteenth century, Croatian and Serbian languages began to take shape.

Because the South Slavic languages are closely related, the language classifications of every linguist in the nineteenth century were unique. When compared with one another, the classification systems did not identify the same languages, with many accepted dialects being classified in differing languages.[8] The lack of consensus concerning what was a language and what was a dialect had profound implications when fused with nationalism. With every differing conception of linguistic relationships came a corresponding conception of nationhood. One of the more relevant conceptions of linguistic relationships, one which had a profound effect on nationalist imaginations, was the one created by Vuk Stefanović Karadžić (1787–1864). Karadžić simply classified everyone who spoke the štokavian dialect as a Serb (Banac 1984, 80–81). Because some štokavian speakers were Roman Catholic, Karadžić labeled them as Roman Catholic Serbs, and because some štokavian speakers were Muslim, Karadžić classified them as Muslim Serbs. Significantly, many of these people whom Karadžić classified as Serbs did not consider themselves to be Serbs. The ideas of there being Roman Catholic Serbs and Muslim Serbs clearly runs contrary to the late twentieth-century conception of nationhood in the former Yugoslavia. According to the definition of the last several decades, Eastern Orthodox Christians are Serbs, Roman Catholics are Croats, and Muslims are Muslims, no exceptions!

Karadžić was a Serbian nationalist, but we should not view him in retrospect as one of those popularly labeled nationalists attributed with the behavior of concocting every flimsy excuse to claim as much territory as possible. On the contrary, when Karadžić classified all štokavian speakers as Serbs, he was simply applying the Romantic conception that nations are defined by language. Rather than treat Karadžić as an early example of an extreme Serbian nationalist, it would be more productive to note that Karadžić's attempt to use štokavian to define Serbian nationhood demonstrates that language does not determine nationhood.[9] Furthermore, Karadžić's efforts—as well of those of his contemporaries—demonstrate that the idea of what it was to be a Serb—not to mention a Croat, Bulgarian, or Macedonian—was not clear. The term *Serb* was a vague ethnic term, and the spatial distribution of Serbs was even vaguer.

Despite every failed attempt to identify nations based on separate and distinct languages, those imbued with Romantic nationalism remained undaunted in their efforts to equate language with nationhood. Noteworthy were the activities of the aforementioned Illyrian movement, which asserted that all South Slav peoples were one nation (Naylor 1980, 77). The Illyrian movement was instrumental in creating the Serbo-Croatian language (Greenberg 1996, 396) and thus in helping to bring together the political centers of Belgrade and Zagreb. Specifically, this movement brought about the "Literary Agreement" *(Književni dogovor),* a document signed by South Slavic intellectuals and writers in Vienna in 1850 (Greenberg 1996, 396; Katičić 1984, 278; Naylor 1980, 78–79). The document represented the beginning of a conscious and cooperative effort to bring about a single unified Serbo-Croatian language for the perceived oneness of the South Slavic nation. Despite the expression of the desire to work together on this single language, many important decisions regarding this new language were not laid down in this agreement. Interestingly, not even the term *Serbo-Croatian* was used. In fact, the term *Serbo-Croatian* did not come into general acceptance for the language until the twentieth century (Naylor 1980, 66). The standard for the new Serbo-Croatian language was based in large degree on the work of Vuk Karadžić, whose standard was derived from the vernacular of eastern Herzegovina and western Serbia (Greenberg 1996, 396; Katičić 1984, 278). Interestingly, the general public, especially those who lived in what was to become Serbia, discounted Karadžić as an eccentric (Katičić 1984, 289).

When the government of autonomous Serbia adopted Karadžić's literary standard in 1868 (Naylor 1980, 80; Katičić 1984, 290), everyone within the Serbian state was expected to use it. Thus the language practice of individuals was manipulated. Later, after the First World War and the creation of the first modern Yugoslav state, the Yugoslav government accepted the literary standard—by now being more commonly referred to as Serbo-Croatian—as the official and dominant language of the new state. Thus all citizens of the new Yugoslav state were expected to use the language. Despite the creation of a single state with a single government, Belgrade and Zagreb continued to represent differing political units and cultural realms, namely Serbia and Croatia respectively. In time, the government in Zagreb declared the independence of Croatia (1991). Subsequently, both the Croatian and Serbian governments declared the end of the Serbo-Croatian language (Greenberg 1996, 393). Now that Serbia and Croatia are two independent political states, Serbian and Croatian are now considered by their speakers to be two separate languages. Moreover, efforts are being made to alter the languages so that they will be separate and distinct languages (Woodward 1996). The history of the language and the recent declaration of independent languages demonstrate that language does not determine nationhood but nationhood determines language.

Language and religion certainly played their roles in identity, but their roles were not unidirectional, defining ones. In religion, all Eastern Orthodox Christians, for example, saw themselves as *Pravoslavni* regardless of ethnicity. In language, South Slavs saw themselves as *Illyrians*, also a single people comprised of many ethnicities. Illyrianism, however, was primarily an intellectual construct that had little meaning to the common people in the Balkans. Most people saw themselves as *Pravoslavni* but they also saw themselves in terms of the territories they inhabited (e.g., as Bosnian, Dalmatians, Slavonians, Montenegrins, etc.). Although many peoples of different territories were ethnic Serbs, they did not see themselves as one people. Indeed, Serbs from Belgrade and the Morava Valley considered the Serbs of the Vojvodina and Srem to be so culturally different from themselves that they called them either *prečani*[10] or *nemačkari*[11] (Petrovich 1976, 1:142). Ethnic terms such as Serb or Croat were not nearly so important to an individual's identity two hundred years ago as they are today. What existed two hundred years ago, and indeed well into the twentieth century in the Balkans, was a complex set of overlapping identities. The ideas of Romantic nationalism, however, had the impact of simplifying identity. The Romantic emphasis on language and religion gave birth to the idea that those who spoke Serbo-Croatian with an Eastern Orthodox faith were Serbs even though many of the people with these cultural traits often did not see themselves as Serbs. Thus even though the characteristics of Serbian nationhood were simply conceived, the complex set of identities that individuals actually held made the identification of Serbs a task that was not nearly so easy. In fact, throughout much of the nineteenth century, it was not precisely clear who was a Serb and who was not. In fact, we still find today Serbian nationalists who are claiming that many Croats and Muslims are really Serbs. This claim stems from the importance of territory as a factor in determining who is a member of the Serbian nation.

Because it is not possible to identify Serbs and their spatial distribution by simply noting the locations of Serbo-Croatian-speaking Orthodox Christians, it is also not possible to delineate an appropriate Serbian nation-state by mapping out Serbo-Croatian speaking Orthodox Christians. Indeed, because territory is a key component of Serbian national identity, the territory that defines Serbian nationhood has to be identified before the spatial distribution of the Serbian nation can be identified. The relationship between people and place is symbiotic, not unidirectional. Therefore, one must ask how certain territories became conceived of as Serbian, and thus their inhabitants in turn defined as Serbs. For early Serbian nationalists, the answer was not an easy one. Unlike the Hungarians and many Western Europeans who had kingdoms that could be redefined as nation-states, the Serbs did not have a kingdom on the eve of nationalism that could be so redefined. Interesting, and very noteworthy, the early Serbian nationalist movement defined Serbia in terms of Ottoman territorial conceptions. Namely, after two insurrections (1804–13 and 1815–17), the Serbs were able to exert enough authority to claim semiautonomy within the Ottoman Paşalik of Belgrade (see Figure 6.1). By 1830, they were able to agitate for full autonomy within this Ottoman administrative district. As the Serbian nation grew in strength, it continued to define itself in terms of Ottoman territorial conceptions. In 1833, Serbian leaders extended the boundaries of their autonomous state, primarily southward, and annexed six Ottoman *nahies*.[12] In both cases, Serbian leaders claimed Ottoman administrative units, not territories inhabited by Serbs even though Serbs certainly lived within these territories.

A blatant contradiction existed in the Serbian nation's desire for political independence from the Ottoman Empire vis-à-vis its delineation of Serbia according to Ottoman territorial understandings. It was not long, however, before Serbian nationalists began to conceive of Serbia in different terms. Not long after the Serbs in the Paşalik of Belgrade exerted their autonomy, Serbs from the Vojvodina and Srem began migrating into the territory. The Vojvodina and Srem were important territories for the creation of ideas relating to Serbian nationalism. They played the same role that Transylvania had for Romanian nationalism. The Vojvodina and Srem had already been the hearth for the idea of creating a *Pravoslav* nation-state, and it was where Vuk Karadžić had completed much of his work. Now it was the source of teachers and bureaucrats for the new Serbian autonomous state (Petrovich 1976, 1: 141–42, 217–22). That many Serbian nationalists came from the Vojvodina and Srem is significant because particular cultural, nationalistic, and geopolitical views were cultivated in these territories. Because the Vojvodina and Srem were in the Hapsburg Empire, namely on its frontier, Hapsburg authorities showed an intense interest in the cultural and political developments in this territory. As mentioned in Chapter 5, the Hapsburgs—like other imperial leaders—sought to expand their empires but always had difficulty doing so where the religion differed from that of the empire; in the time when church and state were one, conquered people would not recognize a ruler of a differing religion. As also mentioned in Chapter 5, the Hapsburgs found it to their advantage to promote the Uniate church to further their aims because the Uniate church continued with Eastern Orthodox practices of the people yet recognized the authority of the pope in Rome, and of course his agents such as the Roman Catholic Hapsburgs. In conjunction with promoting the Uniate faith, the Hapsburgs also found it to their advantage to promote certain ethnic terms as well. Thus the Hapsburgs financed the Uniate church in the northeastern territories of their empire to encourage their subjects and the ones beyond their boundaries to think of themselves as Ukrainians and not lesser Russians; the term "lesser Russian," of course, implied closer connections with the greater Russians—the opponents of the Hapsburgs. As discussed in Chapter 5, the Hapsburgs also promoted the Uniate church in Transylvania and encouraged the Walachians to think of themselves as Romanians; the term *Walachian* was not tied to the cultural realm of any opposing power, how-

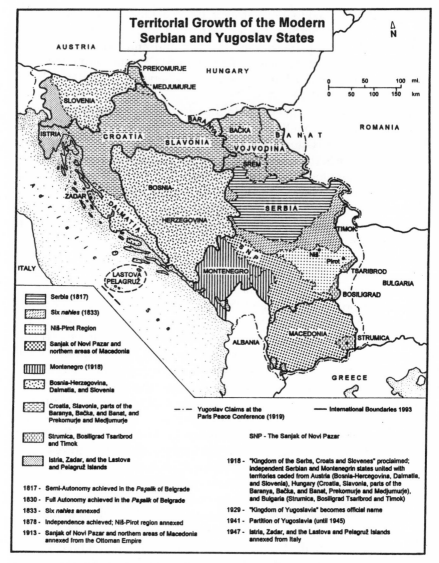

Figure 6.1 Territorial Growth of the Modern Serbian and Yugoslav States.

ever, the term Romanian was preferable because it implied a greater connection to the West than to either the Ottoman or Russian empires. In a similar matter, the Hapsburgs promoted the Uniate church on their southeastern boundary and most likely encouraged the people to call themselves Serbs, if not Illyrians, because the more commonly used term *Pravoslavni* was too intimately tied to the Eastern Orthodox realm of the Russian Empire.

The Uniate church did not prosper in the Vojvodina and Srem as it did in other Hapsburg territories. Nevertheless, the Hapsburgs were successful in building and financing other cultural institutions that successfully oriented the inhabitants of the Vojvodina and Srem to the West. Their success is illustrated in the aforementioned term *nemačkari* (meaning "German"), which the Serbs of the Ottoman Empire called the Serbs of the Vojvodina and Srem because they had adopted so many German characteristics. Eventually, the Hapsburg promotion of Serbian nationalism worked against Hapsburg aims when the Hapsburgs tried to extend the boundaries of their empire farther to the south in the early part of the twentieth century. Nevertheless, up until that point and even to this day, the Hapsburgs succeeded in fostering a form of Serbian nationalism that was, and continues to be, decidedly anti-Turkish.

Integral to those ideas that the Hapsburgs helped spawn in the Vojvodina and Srem were ideas that defined the territory of the modern Serbian nation-state. As Romantics busily collected and codified folk poetry and music, they resurrected stories from the past.[13] The Romantics of the Vojvodina and Srem who worked on the folk tales of the South Slavs heard story after story about a great leader by the name of Stephen Dušan, who had created a vast empire in the fourteenth century that stretched from the Danube and Sava Rivers to the Adriatic and Aegean Seas (see Figure 6.2). Dušan's Empire had great symbolic meaning besides being territorially very expansive. It was a major power in Europe during its time and conceivably might have conquered the Byzantine Empire if Dušan had not died prematurely. The very existence of Dušan's Empire could be a source of great national pride, and it had the potential of placing the Serbian nation on a par with the other great nations of Europe. Thus, much in the same way that the Romanian nation had defined the territorial component of its identity in terms of the Dacian state, and the way that many other nations had done by resurrecting the memories of other defunct imperial states, Serbian nationalists had done for the Serbian nation. Just as important, by redefining Dušan's Empire as the appropriate territory for the modern Serbian nation-state,[14] Serbian nationalists were also able to identify who was and was not a Serb, and those who should leave which territories if they were unwilling to adopt the newly defined Serbian characteristics.

In contrast to many of the other nations of Central and Eastern Europe who framed their national territories and thus identities in terms of historically defunct empires, the Serbian choice of Dušan's Empire was problematic. Namely, it did not incorporate many of the territories where people were developing a Serbian national identity, including the Vojvodina and Srem, where Romantics were busily resurrecting and creating memories of the past. Moreover, Serbian nationalism had grown in

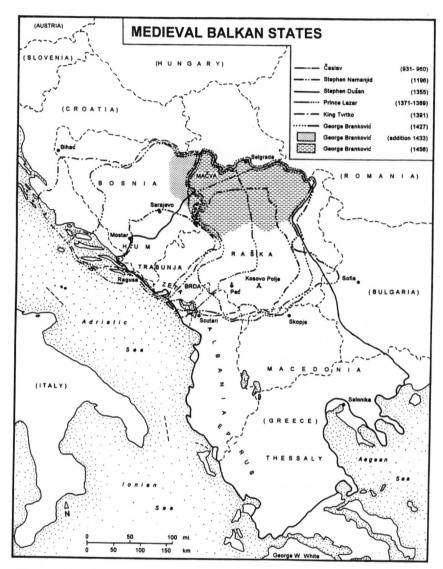

Figure 6.2 Medieval Balkan States.

tandem with other nationalist movements, namely the Illyrian (later Yugoslav) movement. Croatian and Bulgarian national identities also grew concurrently and in overlapping fashion. Related to these forms of identity were also *Pravoslav* identity and strong senses of territorial identities such as the Montenegrin, Slavonian, Bosnian, and Dalmatian identities. Serbian sense of national identity was tangled up in these other forms of identity and was unable to divorce itself completely from them.

It would not be difficult to argue that many Serbian nationalists cannot see the difference between Greater Serbianism and Yugoslavism. It could even be argued that the recent war in the Balkans is a result of the entanglement of these identities and the inability of Serbian nationalists to see the difference between Greater Serbianism and other forms of South Slavic nationalism. The combination of individuals outside the former territory of Dušan's Empire having developed a Serbian national identity and the entanglement of Serbian national identity with neighboring forms of identity meant that the territoriality of Serbian nationhood did not remain confined to the former territory of Dušan's Empire. Other territories were added to it, but they were not simply territories inhabited by Serbs. Instead, other territories of the past were resurrected (see Figures 6.2 and 6.7), namely those of Tomislav's descendants and of Tvrtko. Noteworthy, the state territory of Tomislav's descendants forms the basis of Croatian nationhood and Tvrtko's the basis of Bosnian nationhood.[15] Although the medieval states of the Balkans framed Serbian national identity, the matter of constructing a Serbian nation-state was further complicated by the nationalists' also speaking in terms of the existing territorial-administrative units. Thus Serbian nationalists spoke simultaneously of resurrecting Dušan's Empire (and the other medieval empires) and uniting Serbia, Bosnia-Herzegovina, Dalmatia, Montenegro, etc. Although seemingly convoluted, such talk was not contradictory; the unification of these latter territories would recreate the medieval states.

The significance of Dušan's Empire and the other medieval empires is demonstrated by one figure in particular: Ilija Garašanin (1812–1874). Garašanin was somewhat younger than Karadžić, but he shared the views of Karadžić and the other Romantics of the Vojvodina and Srem. Moreover, he became more directly involved in politics. After Garašanin moved back into the autonomous Serbian state, he entered the civil service and rose to the level of interior minister (1843–52), then to foreign minister (1852–53), and finally to premier and foreign minister (1860–68) (MacKenzie 1985, 2). Garašanin is most known for his geopolitical plan *Načertanije* ("Memorandom" or "Outline"), which he drafted in 1844. *Načertanije* called for the unification of all Serbs into a new Serbian state, but to him the Serbian nation-state was Dušan's Empire (Stavrianos 1941–42, 52) plus other medieval states of the Balkans; thus "all Serbs" were defined as the Slavs, regardless of religious affiliation, that lived within these territories. Because the Serbs were among the first of the South Slavs to assert their independence and were for some time also the strongest militarily, Garašanin and other Serbian nationalists believed that it was the destiny of the Serbs to unite all the South Slav peoples in Dušan's resurrected empire (MacKenzie 1985, 44; Stavrianos 1941–42, 52). Serbia's central location made it the natural "Piedmont of a South Slavic union" (Petrovich 1976, 1: 231–32).

Although Vuk Karadžić and Ilija Garašanin lived in the nineteenth century and summarized the early development of Serbian nationalism, the ideas that they and their contemporaries represented continued to express themselves in Serbian national identity through the twentieth century and are present even today. For example, it can be argued that Yugoslavia failed as a state because too many Serbs saw Yugoslavia as a Greater Serbian state. From its inception, Serbian leaders insisted on making Serbian institutions and symbols those of Yugoslavia.[16] They even insisted that the federal capital be located in Serbia's capital—Belgrade. Even in the recent war, Serbian nationalists fundamentally claimed territories which they perceived to be Serbian. In some cases, these territories were inhabited by Serbs, and in other cases, they were not. Consequently, the Yugoslav army and Serbian paramilitary units spent much of their time and efforts attacking non-Serbian-inhabited territories.[17] The concentration camps and the associated acts of genocide set up by Serbian paramilitary units had nothing to do with claiming Serbian inhabited territories. On the contrary, they were designed to remove non-Serbs from territories perceived to be Serbian with the intent of replacing the non-Serbs with Serbs. A term was coined for the process—*ethnic cleansing*—a concept intimately bound up in the concept of territory, for it is territory which is being cleansed. Therefore, an understanding of Dušan's Empire and other medieval Balkan states is a necessary requirement for understanding the territoriality of modern Serbian national identity. Indeed, applying site identification and landscape description to the medieval states and the historical events subsequent to them, but within their spatial realm, reveals many of the individual places and territories that define the Serbian nation, thus making the mapping process possible. Because numerous places exist, they are presented in regional groupings for the sake of clarity, and even regrouped more broadly into a core, semi-core, and periphery categorization. Their importance is revealed by the application of the tenacity factor, presented as the latter part of each of the broader classifications (i.e., that of the core, semi-core, and periphery). Because modern Serbian national identity is only about two hundred years old, the tenacity factor is applied to only the last two centuries. Even though peoples fought over territory through history, identity existed in a different context prior to the late eighteenth century. Therefore, the importance of place and territory was likewise much different as well. It would be inappropriate, even anachronistic, to apply the tenacity factor to prenationalist struggles as if they were nationalist ones, even though Romantic nationalists believe that they were.

That the tenacity factor cannot be applied much earlier than the end of the eighteenth century does not mean that events before this time are irrelevant. On the contrary, in site identification and landscape description, many places highlighted are associated with figures and events of much earlier periods. It must always be remembered, however, that places are identified not for the significance of their time but for their importance to the modern Serbian nation. In fact, many of the places identified became memorialized with monuments, shrines, and the such only since the rise of nationalism, some only in the last few years even though they signify an event that may have taken place a thousand years ago. Therefore, all places and territories are identified in their current significance, even though many represent something much older.

Because Serbian national identity contains within it many Romantic elements, history cannot be disregarded. On the contrary, the Serbian nation has developed emotional-psychological bonds to a long list of places that it now regards to be historically significant. An understanding of Serbian history facilitates an appreciation of Serbian territoriality. Therefore, while the purpose of this book is not to retell Serbian history, it is, nevertheless, necessary to provide an outline of relevant history, no matter how crudely generalized, in order to set the territorial component of Serbian national identity in its proper context.

Brief Overview of Serbian History

The Romantic view of Serbian history that developed in the early nineteenth century is not unlike the Romantic histories that were created for the other nations of East Central Europe and the Balkans. It begins with the story of a group of tribes living during the Dark Ages; the tribes wandered into the current homeland of the modern nation and eventually founded a great state. In the case of the Serbs, their ancestors migrated into the Balkans sometime in the sixth century (Petrovich 1976, 1: 3; Banac 1984, 33). After a period of adapting to a sedentary life, local chiefs, *župans* in Serbian, began to carve out small territorial states for their individual clans. The župans of the Balkans clashed continually with one another as each sought to enhance his own personal powers. At times unions would form under a grand župan, but internal struggles and the willingness of many župans to solicit aid from other leaders throughout the Balkans and Europe prevented such unions from lasting long (Clissold 1966, 87–89). In fact, the alliances that many župans readily formed with leaders of other cultural groups are in many ways testaments that no concept of a shared identity existed that was analogous to modern Serbian national identity.

Over time larger territorial states emerged, but the alliances that the župans formed with other leaders in Europe complicated the matter of uniting the South Slavs into a larger territorial state. Of greatest consequence to the formation of medium-sized territorial states was that the

Slavic lands of the Balkans lay between the domain of the Western or Latin Christian Church of Rome and the Eastern or Byzantine Christian Church of Constantinople. The competition between the Eastern and Western branches of the Christian Church had profound implications for the development of group identities among the South Slavs because some South Slavs converted to Roman Catholicism and others converted to Eastern Orthodoxy.

While the warring between the župans continued for several centuries, a period of medium-sized territorial state-building eventually began. Some of the first medium-sized states to emerge in the proto-Serbian areas were ones that united the territories of Bosnia, Hum (Herzegovina), Zeta (Old Montenegro), Brda, and northern Albania. However, the competition between the two branches of the Christian Church directed the concerns of the South Slavs in these regions and the rest of the Balkans away from one another despite any physiographic, economic, or familial ties that might have united them. Over time, the people of Raška, Zeta, Brda, and northern Albania became firmly committed to the Orthodox Church, whereas those of the Adriatic coast and farther northwest accepted Roman Catholicism; many of those in between, such as the inhabitants of Bosnia and Hum, developed a mixed faith out of both.

After a period when medium-sized states continued to falter as a result of internal rivalries among leaders, a state was eventually founded that endured for some time. In 1169, Stephen Nemanja, the župan of Raška,[18] founded the Nemanjid Dynasty, that lasted for over two hundred years. In his lifetime, Stephen Nemanja was able to extend his control to the west by uniting Zeta and Hum (Herzegovina), and then to the Adriatic coast, the area that stretched from northwest of Ragusa (Dubrovnik) to southeast of the Bay of Kotor and to Skadar (Shkodër). After Stephen Nemanja's death, his successors were able to keep the state together and even consolidate state power. With the accession to the throne of Stephen Dušan in 1331, this medieval state of the Nemanjids began a period of rapid expansion until it reached its zenith in 1355. After incorporating territories that extended to the Sava and Danube Rivers in the north and the territories of Albania, Macedonia, Epirus, and Thessaly in the southeast, Stephen Dušan created one of the largest and most powerful medieval states of the Balkans (see Figure 6.2). At the height of his power, Stephen Dušan had himself crowned "Emperor and Autocrat of the Serbs and Greeks, the Bulgarians and Albanians" (Clissold 1966, 98). Dušan's self-designation demonstrates that he saw himself and his state in imperialist terms, not nationalist ones.

The establishment of a lasting dynasty meant that disparate groups of people could eventually be molded into a single people with continual, peaceful interaction and the introduction of laws that applied to all uniformly. The Nemanjid Dynasty accepted Orthodox Christianity, made it a state institution, and suppressed Roman Catholicism and the Bogomil heresy within the territory of the state. In 1346, during Dušan's reign, the archbishop of Peć was raised to patriarch (Fine 1987, 309). The patriarchate of Peć, the predecessor of the National Serbian Orthodox Church, contributed greatly to the molding of a group identity which eventually evolved into a Serbian national identity.

Because there was no concept of nation as it exists today, however, there was no notion of creating state territories for nations. With the lack of broad national identities, leaders created state institutions to develop a sense of loyalty among the people they ruled (Hartshorne 1969, 247–48). Because leaders saw the people of other states as just other people who could be ruled by anyone who had the means to do so, nothing ethically prevented leaders from attacking, conquering, or annexing the territories of neighboring states. Consequently, the Middle Ages of Europe were marked by frequent warfare as dynasties sought to increase their power. Nevertheless, a sense of unity often formed among the people who lived in a territory with stable boundaries (Anderson 1986b; Anderson 1988, 20–23).

Despite the growing unity of the people within Dušan's Empire, instability returned after his death in 1355 when various leaders within the empire began personal struggles for power. In a short time, regional leaders began governing independently. The disunity of the empire was brought to light with a great external threat. To the southeast, the Ottoman Empire was growing quickly and beginning to accrete territories in Europe. The princes of Dušan's Empire banded together to meet the Ottoman threat, but they were defeated outside of Adrianople (Edirne, Turkey) at the Battle of Marica (or Cernomen) in 1371. With the continual expansion of the Ottoman Empire into Europe, leaders of southeastern Europe continued to band together to resist the Ottoman armies. With the defeat on Kosovo Polje, "the field of blackbirds" in 1389, however, the remnants of Dušan's Empire were destroyed[19] (Banac 1984, 403).

The defeat at Kosovo in 1389 is seen by modern Serbs as a defeat of Serbian forces and the end of the great Serbian empire of Dušan. As already stated, however, modern national identities as they exist today did not exist at that time. At the time, leaders and their people rallied under a common Christian identity to resist the Islamic faith as it spread with the Ottoman Empire. Many of the forces at Kosovo Polje in 1389 were the ancestors of Hungarians, Albanians, Croatians, and Bulgarians as well as Serbs. Indeed, Dušan proclaimed himself the emperor of Serbs, Greeks, Bulgarians, and Albanians. Although the Battle of Kosovo was really a political struggle between Christian leaders of Europe and Islamic leaders of the Middle East, modern Serbs view the Battle of Kosovo Polje as the struggle to preserve Serbian independence in the face of the menacing Islamic Turks. In reality, however, Serbian Romantic nationalists fail to recognize that some Serbs fought on the side of the Ottomans that day (Judah 1997, 28); later, even more Serbs fought alongside the Ottomans against the Christians forces of Europe at the Battle of Nicopolis (1396) (Temperley 1919, 104).

Although Dušan's Empire came to an end in 1389, not all lands of the ancestors of the Serbs were occupied. Raška and the land to the north, to the Danube and Sava rivers, maintained a degree of independence for an additional seventy years. This principality was ruled first by Stephen Lazarević (1389–1427) and then by Djordje Branković (1427–1456) until the last stronghold, Smederevo, fell in 1459 (Peić 1994, 27). With the exception of many highland communities in Montenegro, the territories of southeastern Europe remained under the control of the Ottoman Empire until the beginning of the nineteenth century.

During the long period of Ottoman rule, the Nemanjid Dynasty died out and no other leadership hierarchy fully emerged. Society became feudal, composed of peasants and landholders. The only social, political, and economic institution that survived and fostered unity among the people was the patriarchate of Peć. It remained the only institution in this region of the Balkans that could serve as the depository of memories and the cultivator of a unique regional identity for the groups of South Slavs who were otherwise reduced to mere peasantry.

By the late seventeenth century, the Ottoman Empire had reached its zenith and begun to wane. The waning of the empire led to continued unrest among the South Slavs. As the borders of the empire were pushed back to the southeast, South Slavs found themselves in the middle of a zone of conflict. In an attempt to shore up their empire, Ottoman authorities began to extract more resources from the South Slavic lands while harshly suppressing any form of dissidence.

During the eighteenth century, the South Slavs found that more and more Ottoman troops were being garrisoned in their lands and many South Slavs were subject to the whims of Ottoman soldiers, particularly of the special units known as *janissaries*. By the turn of the nineteenth century life had become unbearable for many of the South Slavs of the Ottoman Empire, particularly for those in the Paşalik of Belgrade. At the same time, the wave of new nationalist ideology was spreading east across Europe with Napoleon's armies, resulting in the feelings of uniqueness among the Balkan peoples. Within a short time, a sense of national consciousness emerged among the Balkan peoples. Soon the new nations of the Balkans would attempt to establish states (i.e., nation-states) for themselves.

As Ottoman oppression grew worse, Serbs began banding into irregular military bands. By the spring of 1804, widespread rebellion had begun (Jelavich and Jelavich 1977, 29). The rebellion, known as the First Serbian Insurrection, lasted from 1804 until 1813, when it was finally suppressed by Ottoman forces. The main leader of this insurrection was Djordje Petrović, better known as Karadjordje, a pig dealer from the Šumadija region chosen by many of his peers to lead the rebellion. Although the rebels had many successes, the insurrection was finally suppressed in 1813. Ottoman reprisals and the imposition of strict order did not foster a long-lasting peace. By 1815, the Second Insurrection began, led this time by Miloš Obrenović, a rival of Karadjordje. The Second Insurrection was marked by quick military successes and was helped by a Russian government that was in a position to pressure Ottoman authorities into making concessions. Moreover, Obrenović was eager to negotiate a settlement. The Second Serbian Insurrection ended in 1817 when Obrenović secured a number of concessions from the Ottoman government, marking the beginning of semiautonomy. Along with the concessions, Obrenović was recognized as "supreme *knez* and leader of the Serbian people" (Jelavich and Jelavich 1977, 36–37; Petrovich 1976, 1: 101). The resurrections of the early nineteenth century witnessed the birth of a new Serbian dynasty, stemming from the two revolutionary leaders, Petrović (Karadjordje) and Obrenović. Coupled with new rights of governing, the leadership of a growing Serbian nation was able to pursue greater autonomy in a more organized manner.

The pursuit of greater autonomy was facilitated by the evolving relationships between the Great Powers in Europe. As the Austrian and Russian empires pushed the Ottoman Empire out of Europe, the Serbs and other Balkans peoples benefitted. Russian victories in particular allowed Serbian leaders to obtain more concessions from the Ottoman Empire. In 1830, for example, the Sultan recognized the full autonomy of Serbia, and Miloš Obrenović became prince. In 1833, Obrenović saw an opportunity to forcibly add the six *nahies* (districts) to his autonomous district (see Figure 6.1).

The opportunity for independence, however, did not come until the victory of the Russian Empire in the Russo-Turkish War of 1877–78. The Serbian state would have profited by the Russian government's settlement proposal, known as the Treaty of San Stefano, but the Great Powers of Central and Western Europe rejected it. The subsequently proposed and accepted Treaty of Berlin (1878) actually brought even greater benefits (Petrovich 1976, 2: 399–401) (see Figure 6.3). In addition to independence, the Serbian state was allowed to annex a larger tract of territory. Montenegro also gained some territory, but not as much as was called for in the San Stefano Treaty.

By the early part of the twentieth century, the Ottoman Empire had become seriously weak. Balkan leaders conspired to annex the remaining Ottoman possessions in Europe. In 1912, the Montenegrin government declared war on the Ottoman Empire, initiating the First Balkan War. As planned, Serbia, Bulgarian, and Greek armies joined their ally and

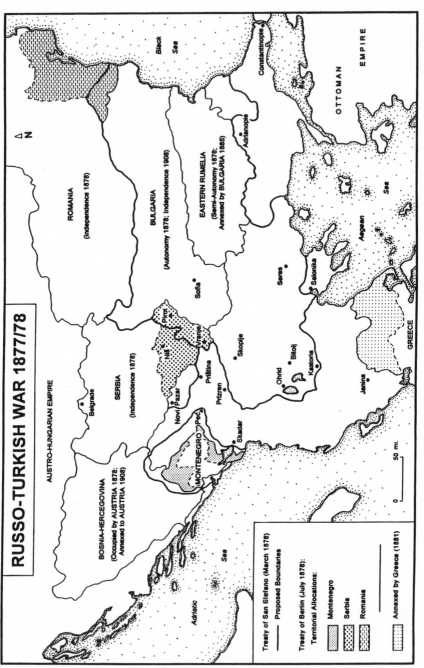

Figure 6.3 Russo-Turkish War of 1877–1878.

scrambled to occupy Ottoman territories. The quick successes of the First Balkan War alarmed the Great Powers, and they quickly blocked further hostilities by imposing the Treaty of London in 1913, barely eight months after hostilities began. Despite the call for peace, the Second Balkan War broke out in 1913 when the Bulgarian army moved to assert the Bulgarian claim to the Ottoman territory of Macedonia, which the Greek and Serbian armies had occupied during the First Balkan War and their respective governments refused to relinquish. The Bulgarian forces, however, were defeated when the Romanian and Ottoman armies came to the aid of the Serbian and Greek armies. The resulting Treaty of Bucharest solidified Serbian and Greek control over Macedonia; at the same time, the Serbian and Montenegrin governments were able to extend their countries' boundaries into the Sanjak of Novi Pazar and create a common border (see Figure 6.4).

The Serbian state was a key player in the events that led to the outbreak of the First World War. While Archduke Ferdinand, heir to the Hapsburg throne, was on a visit in Sarajevo (Jelavich 1983, 2: 112–14) in the summer of 1914, he was assassinated. The Hapsburg government, long displeased with the activities of the Serbian government in Bosnia-Herzegovina, decided to blame the Serbian government for the assassination although the assassination was committed by a Bosnian nationalist. On July 23, 1914, the Austro-Hungarian government delivered an ultimatum. The terms were deliberately harsh, but the Serbian government agreed to meet all the terms but one, which required Hapsburg participation in the investigation of the assassination. The failure to meet the last point of the ultimatum gave the Hapsburg government the excuse to declare war on July 28.

The resources of Serbia were no match against those of the Austro-Hungarian Empire and its Bulgarian ally. Within six weeks the Serbian army had to retreat out of Serbia. At the beginning of October 1918, when the Austria-Hungarian Empire began to disintegrate, the Serbian army began liberating Serbia. At the same time, councils of South Slavs from Hapsburg lands began discussing the political future of their people; the National Council (Narodno vijeće) in Zagreb was the most significant (Lampe 1996, 108–10). As these councils debated internally, they negotiated with representatives from the Serbian government. In the chaos and turmoil that ensued in the aftermath of the war, representatives from these councils agreed to join their former Hapsburg territories with those of the Serbian state. Likewise, a National Council in Podgorica (Titograd) voted to join Montenegro with Serbia. The new political state was called the Kingdom of the Serbs, Croats and Slovenes, officially declared on December 1, 1918 (Petrovich 1976, 2: 680–81).

From its beginning and throughout the 1920s and 1930s, the new

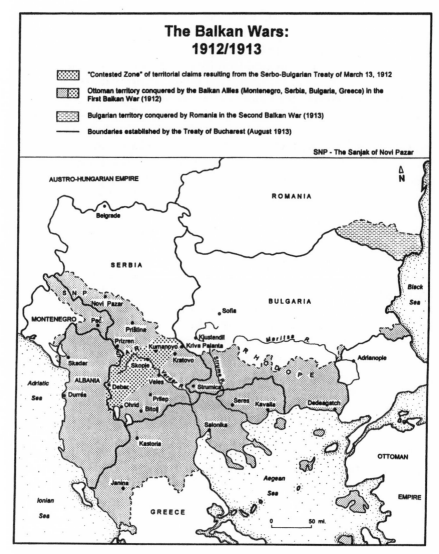

Figure 6.4 The Balkan Wars: 1912–1913.

Kingdom of the Serbs, Croats, and Slovenes had great internal difficulties. The most fundamental conflict was between Serbian leaders who were determined to build a Greater Serbia and leaders of other groups, particularly the Croats, who insisted on preserving a high degree of autonomy for their peoples (Jelavich 1983, 2: 155). Many solutions were tried, but none succeeded. For example, Alexander Karadjordjević, who had been constitutional monarch of the kingdom, tried to remedy the situation in 1929 by abolishing the constitutional regime and introducing his personal dictatorship. Alexander even renamed the country the Kingdom of Yugoslavia and tried to signify the unity of all its people by allowing only the Yugoslav flag to be flown (Dragnich 1992, 69). Both Serbs and non-Serbs were displeased with his policies. Finally, Alexander's personal dictatorship abruptly came to an end with his assassination in October 1934 (Jelavich 1983, 2: 202).

The failure to overcome the tensions between the various national interests within Yugoslavia only exacerbated the collapse of the state in the Second World War. Hitler easily exploited the country's ethnic tensions by focusing his attack on Serbian lands while supporting an independence movement of the Croats. On April 6, 1940, German and Italian forces invaded, and on April 17 an armistice was signed. Yugoslavia was dismantled (see Figure 6.5) as the countries surrounding it annexed territories that had long been claimed. Montenegro, Serbia Proper, and the remainder of the Vojvodina came under direct Axis occupation. An ostensibly independent Croatian state, composed primarily of Croatia and Bosnia-Herzegovina, emerged on April 10 under the leadership of extreme Croatian nationalists (the *Ustaša* Regime).

As the Nazi forces withdrew from Yugoslavia towards the end of the war, resistance fighters, known as Partisans and led by Josip Broz Tito— secretary of the Yugoslav Communist Party—entered Belgrade and began clearing the country of its opponents. The rise of Tito and the Communists changed the nature of conflict between the South Slavs. Tito was the first leader of a government in Belgrade who was not imbued with the idea of creating a Greater Serbia. He averted the immediate reemergence of ethnic tensions, and hence the Greater Serbian-Yugoslav struggle, with several tactics: He defined the war as a great patriotic struggle of Yugoslav citizens against foreign enemies and defined political struggles as Communist versus non-Communist. He focused on the need to rebuild the country. Finally, from a political-geographical perspective, he reorganized Yugoslavia into a federal state with six republics (see Figure 6.6).

Throughout his reign of more than 35 years, Tito was able to prevent the ethnic differences from tearing the Yugoslav state apart. Over time, however, Tito found himself in the position of granting each group more and more rights as he tried not to allow any ethnic group to dominate. Eventually, this practice only led to further divergence within Yugoslav society. To compensate for growing differences, Tito had to exert more and more personal control over the state; however, this practice made the state ever more dependent on Tito's leadership. In the end, all that was left of Yugoslavia was Tito. When Tito died in 1980, the Yugoslav state lost much of its *raison d'être*.

Despite Tito's power and charisma, he was never able to alter fundamentally the basic Serbian belief that Serbia was the Piedmont of the

Figure 6.5 The Dismantling of Yugoslavia: 1941–1945.

Balkans and Serbs were destined to rule the South Slavs. Therefore, to most Serbs, particularly Serbian leaders, Yugoslavia and Greater Serbia were essentially the same. Being the ethnic majority in Yugoslavia and in control of many of the state institutions, particularly the military, Serbian leaders successfully implemented policies of domination. Lacking the political power to resist Serbian leaders in the federal government, many

Figure 6.6 Yugoslavia: 1947–1991.

non-Serbian leaders saw it in the best interests of their peoples to move toward independence.

The desire for independence expressed by many of Yugoslavia's national groups was a severe blow to Serbian identity. The prominent Serbian leader Slobadan Milošević stated that any republics wanting independence had to leave any territories inhabited by Serbs to the Yugoslav state (Sudetic 1991). Despite the threat of having the Serbian-dominated army attacking their republics, the governments of Slovenia and Croatia declared their independence in June 1991. By September 1991, the government in Macedonia declared independence and the government of Bosnia-Herzegovina did the same in 1992. Though few Serbs lived in Slovenia, the Yugoslav army tried to prevent the Slovenians from exerting their independence. The Yugoslav army implemented a number of military operations against Slovenia (Magaš 1993, 313–14) before ceasing in failure. Military action was also taken against Croatia and lasted much longer (Vasić 1996, 128–30). In fact, the Yugoslav army and Serbian paramilitary units were able to hold onto about a third of Croatia's territory for a number of years. The Yugoslav army, however, was not able to cripple the Croatian state. In time, the Croatian army built up to sufficient strength to drive all Serbian forces out of Croatia. In the case of Macedonia, the Serbian-dominated Yugoslav government initially did not recognize this republic's declaration of independence; however, the Serbian-dominated Yugoslav army did not try to prevent Macedonia's independence either.

In response to the declaration of independence by the government of Bosnia-Herzegovina, some Bosnian Serbs formed their own government for Bosnia-Herzegovina and began an armed rebellion. The ethnic diversity of Bosnia-Herzegovina has provided many opportunities for both Bosnian Serbs and other Serbs to exploit and undermine an independent Bosnian state. The drive for Bosnian independence has so far resulted in the most bloodshed of all the independence movements. With aid from the government in Belgrade, nationalist Bosnian Serbs have been able to wreak havoc in Bosnia-Herzegovina. After failing to thwart the entire independence movement of Bosnia-Herzegovina, the Serbs of Bosnia formed their own republic within Bosnia, known as the *Republika Srpska*, which primarily lies in the northern and eastern portions of Bosnia-Herzegovina.

Despite all the independence movements in the former Yugoslavia, most Serbs continue to believe in a Yugoslavia. However, it can be argued that many Serbs still cannot distinguish between Yugoslavia and Greater Serbia. Instead of giving the remaining republics of Serbia and Montenegro a new name, the Serbian government in Belgrade has held onto the name of Yugoslavia and has insisted upon holding on or maintaining everything that once belonged to Yugoslavia, from the military hardware to embassies and diplomatic positions in the international community. The international community, however, did not initially recognize the right of the Serbian government to claim all that which was Yugoslav. In April 1992, in an attempt to legitimate itself as the true heir to Yugoslavia, the Serbian government declared the formation of the Federal Republic of Yugoslavia, which is composed of Montenegro and Serbia with its two autonomous provinces.

Places Significant to Serbian National Identity

In the application of the three indicators of a nation's sense of territory, epic poems and songs figure prominently for the Serbian nation. Serbian sense of national history and identity has developed and been passed on from generation to generation by epic poems and songs, more than by any other medium. The three indicators show that Serbian national identity is tied to a number of places across the Balkans (see Figure 6.7). The range is extensive, but it would be unreasonable to consider all sites to be exclusively Serbian territory. However, a strong concentration of places exists in the center of the range. This concentration can be considered to be the core of the Serbian nation's sense of territory. The core includes the regions known as Serbia Proper, Montenegro *(Crna Gora)*, the Vojvodina and Srem, and Old Serbia (Raška and Kosovo). In the semi-core are the regions of Macedonia, northern Albania, Bosnia-Herzegovina, Dalmatia, the central areas of the Banat, and areas of western Bulgaria. In the peripheral zone, the places of least significance, are southern Bulgaria, northern Greece, central and southern Albania, Croatia-Slavonia, the Pannonian Plain, and the eastern Banat.

With the historical overview of Serbian national history in mind, the core, semi-core, and periphery now can be analyzed in detail. Epic poetry and music are used to identify sites and measure their significance in the Serbian case study because epic poetry and music were used by Serbian Romantic nationalists to write a common history for the Serbian people.

The Core: Site Identification and Landscape Description

The core area of modern Serbian national identity is hardly a homogeneous area. Its component regions—Serbia Proper (centered on the Šumadija and Morava River valley), Montenegro *(Crna Gora)*, the Vojvodina and Srem, and Old Serbia (Raška and Kosovo)—have all contributed differently to the molding of a modern Serbian national identity. Serbia Proper and Montenegro, particularly Serbia Proper, are the two centers around which the modern political state developed. The Vojvodina and Srem are the intellectual-cultural centers where modern Serbian national identity began to emerge in the eighteenth and nineteenth centuries. Old Serbia is the region of greatest historical significance for it is the region that Serbian nationalist thinkers used as a source to create a modern Serbian national identity. Modern Serbian national identity is primarily the product of the interaction of these four core regions.

Serbia Proper

Rise, O Servians, swift arise,
Lift your banners to the skies,
For your country needs her children
Fight to make her free,
Rise, O rise and crush our enemy,

Figure 6.7 Places Significant to Serbian National Identity.

Rise and fight for liberty.
Free the Sav and Duna flow,
Let us too unfetter'd go,
O'er the wild Moravian mountains,
Swift shall flow sweet Freedom's fountains,
Down shall sink the foe.
Rise, O rise, and crush our enemy,
Rise, O rise, and fight for liberty.
      (Bantock 1913, 106–107)

Figure 6.8 Serbia Proper.

Serbia Proper (centered on the Šumadija and the Morava River valley), the location of the First (1804–13) and Second (1815–17) Insurrections, became the center around which a modern independent Serbian state formed. While Serbia Proper had long been important to those people who lived there, the First Insurrection gave new meaning to many of the places within the territory. The titles of many of the epic songs written about the First Insurrection highlight these places:

The Battle of Mišar
The Battle of Deligrad
The Taking of Belgrade
The Taking of Užice
The Battle of Loznica
The Battle of Čačak
The Battle of Salaš
The Battle of Čokešina
The Battle of Čegar

As a consequence of the First Insurrection, a number of the battle sites, many of which were the major fortified towns, became very significant, and the monuments that stand in them illustrate their lasting importance. One of the most noteworthy is the monument that memorializes the battle on Čegar Mountain outside Niš. On Čegar Mountain stands the Ćele-Kula ("Tower of Skulls"), a square tower built with the skulls of Serbian fighters by the Turkish leader of the Pasha of Niš as a symbol of his victory over Serbian forces. Sibnica is known because Karadjordje trapped fleeing Ottoman forces there. Negotin has a monument for Veljko Petrović, who died there defending the town against the Ottomans in 1813. Novo Selo is the place where Serb rebels slaughtered an Ottoman military unit. In fact, the entire Mačva region is associated with battles of the Serbian insurrections.

While the First Insurrection yielded a large number of battle sites that became important to Serbs, the songs of this period also illustrate a close relationship between the Serbs and their physical environment. For example, in "The Battle of Mišar," the Ottoman army from Bosnia was trapped and annihilated in the dense Kitog Forest. The Serbian commander, Jakov Nenadović, was from Valjevo and a monument to him stands in the town. Valjevo is also significant because it is the hometown of other Serbian national heroes and is one of the first places liberated during the First Serbian Insurrection. Physical features also played a role in the battle of Loznica, where Mount Cer is mentioned not only with reverence but as a source of inspiration for the Serbian fighters (Morison 1942, 132). Medvednik Mountain protected Serbs from the Ottomans. Of all physical features, rivers are treated as the greatest allies. The Dunav (Danube), Sava, Drina, Morava, and Timok are mentioned most often. When another group of Turkish soldiers fled from Mišar in a different direction, they were killed and their bodies thrown into the Sava River; a Serbian leader called out, "Sava waters, full of waves, icy cold, swallow, Sava, these Turks, our enemies" (Holton and Mihailovich 1988, 333). Turkish soldiers also were trapped and killed at the Bosut River. The Drina River is one of the rivers mentioned most often. It serves not only as the western boundary of Serbia but also as the protector of Serbia. For example, in the battle of Loznica, Ottoman troops made an unsuccessful attempt to cross the Drina and take the town of Loznica. In the poem about the battle, the Drina River is given much of the credit for the victory of the Serbian defenders:

Few were they that crossed the Drina water,
Many they who in the Drina perished;
For the Drina takes no count of heroes,
She devours them, all unnamed, uncounted.
(Morison 1942, xxiii)

Although Serbian forces had many successes, the First Insurrection failed to free Serbia Proper from Ottoman rule. In fact, Karadjordje, the leader of the First Insurrection, was forced to leave Serbia Proper. The last town he was in, Ravanj, is immortalized in a poem *(Kara-Djordje's Farewell to Serbia)* (Morison 1942, 179). Later some autonomy was achieved, and more gains were made as the struggle continued for several decades. As Serbs were able to assert their independence, more and more institutions were either moved from the Vojvodina and Srem to Serbia proper or simply founded there. Belgrade (Beograd) became the capital of an autonomous Serbia in 1839, and a *gymnasium* was founded there in the same year. In fact, beginning in the early to mid-nineteenth century, universal education became a growing demand throughout Europe and many schools were founded. Because the Serbs in Serbia Proper were exerting their independence at this time, some of the earliest and most important schools were founded in cities such as Čačak, Kragujevac, and Šabac (Petrovich 1976, 1: 220–22).

In Oplenac, just outside of Topola—the birthplace of Karadjordje (leader of the First Serbian Insurrection)—stands a church. It was built by King Peter Karadjordjević during the early part of this century, and it now contains the white marble sarcophagi of Karadjordje and King Peter himself. In the church, historic kings and saints are depicted in "725 mosaic compositions made up of forty million pieces" (Judah 1997, 70–71). The church is a great architectural achievement and source of Serbian national pride. It is also a visual element in the landscape that reminds and teaches people, including Serbs, of the Serbian nation's history and greatness.

Although most of Serbia Proper's significance derives from the nineteenth century, a few places within it derive their importance from earlier times. Some such as the Poreč River valley and Miroč Mountain are associated with Prince Marko but others are tied to the Kosovo epics. The churches/monasteries of Gornjak, Ljubostinja, Ravanica, Manasije, and Rača are perhaps the best examples of places relating to the Kosovo epics. The first three are associated with Prince Lazar (Holton and Mihailovich 1988, 164). Of them, Ravanica monastery (Peić 1994, 199–204) is one of the most honored monasteries in the epics and is closely associated with Kosovo (see Old Serbia section); in fact, it is sometimes referred to as the "Church of Kosovo." The epic poem "The Building of Ravanica" is written about Lazar's decision and plans to build the great monastery (Koljević 1980, 143–46; Pennington and Levi 1984, 104–12). After his death, Lazar's body, his shroud, Jefimija's golden prayer (all three of which are the holiest of Serbian relics) were located in Ravanica until 1683, when they were moved to Nova Ravanica in Srem (Holton and Mihailovich 1988, 23). Manasije is associated with Stephen Lazarević. Rača was a resting place for Arsenije Carnojevic and his followers when they were on their Great Migration from Peć to Sremski Karlovci in 1691 (see section on the Vojvodina and Srem).

Serbia Proper is also significant because it is one of the few territories where modern Serbs can find ancestors that maintained political sovereignty after the defeat at the Battle of Kosovo. Prince Lazar's successors, Stephen Lazarević (1389–1427) and Djordje Branković (1427–1456), maintained an independent state in the north, which extended from the Mačva to Belgrade and Smederevo; both Belgrade and Smederevo served alternately as capitals. Smederevo first fell in 1439, was recovered again, and then fell for the last time in 1459. Thus Belgrade and especially Smederevo are seen as heroic cities. Similarly, the fortress of Stalać is glorified because it too resisted the Ottoman advance; it is heralded in the epic poem "The Death of Duke Prijezda." As in many Serbian poems and songs rivers are spoken of with great reverence. Towards the end of the poem, when Stalać is eventually overrun and burned, the poem focuses on Prince Prijezda and his wife Jelitsa:

> Each of them took the other by the hand,
> they went out high onto the high wall of Stalach,
> and the lady Jelitsa spoke:
> "Prince Prijezda, my dear, my Lord,
> Morava water bred us up,
> let Morava water bury us."
> And they leapt into Morava water.
>   (Pennington and Levi 1984, 28–29)

When Smederevo and Stalać, the last pockets of resistance, fell, many South Slavs, especially their leaders, fled to areas of the Dalmatian Coast, Bosnia-Herzegovina, or north of the Sava-Danube Rivers, to the Vojvodina and Srem. Nevertheless, many stayed behind and their descendants initiated the First and Second Serbian Insurrections in the early nineteenth century.

Serbia Proper is now only a core region of a larger Serbian state. However, in the nineteenth century, those living within the region saw their region as Serbia. Serbia as it was seen by its inhabitants at the time is best illustrated in the song "The Beginning of the Revolt of the Dahijas." In a reference which mentions a prominent Serbian leader, Karadjordje, several lines read,

> When he had power over Serbia,
> when he had signed Serbia with the cross,
> and covered it over under his wing,
> from Vidin as far as Drina water,

from Kosovo even up to Belgrade,
he spoke to Drina water in these words:
"O Drina water, noble boundary,
set between Bosnia and Serbia,
the time also will come, it will come soon
when I shall cross your waters at last
to visit honourable Bosnia!"
    (Pennington and Levi 1984, 166)

Not long after achieving a degree of autonomy, many Serbs began to define for themselves a modern nation-state that would extend far beyond the limits of Serbia Proper. In some cases, a growing acceptance of a Serbian identity among South Slavs living in other regions meant that such people wanted their lands to be included within a Serbian state. In other cases, Serbian nationalists defined other South Slavs as Serbs; subsequently the land of these people was defined as Serbian territory (Jelavich, C. 1988).

Montenegro (Crna Gora)

Take my sword, my hands are tiring;
While my wounds with blood are weeping.
Lift my gun again for firing,
Speed the bullet, Montenegro!
So falls the foes of our country!
Numbered by the warm drops falling,
From my heart each drop is calling,
O avenge me, Montenegro!

Shed no tears upon the furrow
In the mountains where you hide me,
With my long bright sword beside me.
Shed not tears, my Montenegro!
But when tyrant rule is ended,
Bring my sons to kneel around me,
Tell them how you sought and found me,
How I died for Montenegro!

Sweeter than the hidden laughter
Of the Piva and the Tara,
Are the voices of thy daughters,
Loved and lovely Montenegro!
Children of our mighty mountains,
All who know us, all who love us,

Figure 6.9 Montenegro.

Shout to God who reigns above us,
Freedom lives in Montenegro!
  (Botsford 1933, 481)

In the early nineteenth century, the Slavs of Montenegro *(Crna Gora)* began developing a sense of national identity akin to that of the Slavs of Šumadija, and the Vojvodina and Srem. The Serbs living in Šumadija, and the Vojvodina and Srem readily viewed the Slavs of Montenegro as fellow Serbs. Indeed, all of them shared similar cultural characteristics. More important, Montenegro was a very significant territory to Serbian national identity, for it was an integral part of Dušan's Empire, meaning that it was a territory of key historical events and a source of Serbian folklore and poetry. For example, in the poem, "The Marriage [or Wedding] of King Vukašin" (Low 1968, 1–9), an incident arises between King Vukašin and Duke Momcilo. The Duke originally had a stronghold in the Rodopa

Mountains and was killed in a battle against the Turks in 1361 in the town of Peritheorion. Chroniclers began to refer to him as the Duke of Peritheorion. Over time, the name was reduced to Pirlitor and moved to a location in the vicinity of the Durmitor Mountains, now in Montenegro but formerly in Herzegovina (Pennington and Levi 1984, 85). The poem therefore refers to Duke Momcilo of "the white stronghold of Pirlitor." Also figuring prominently in the poem are the Durmitor Mountains and the Tara River.

Montenegro is also meaningful because it is one of the few places in the Balkans not conquered by the Ottomans after the fall of Dušan's Empire. When the Romantic Serbian nationalists set the goal of resurrecting Dušan's Empire, the unification of Montenegro with other Serbian lands became crucial. In addition, the relatively successful struggle of the Montenegrins against the Ottomans was glorified by the fervently anti-Turkish Serbs of the Vojvodina and Srem. The success of the Montenegrins became successes of the Serbian nation. As Montenegro became important to Serbs in the other areas of the Balkans, all of the places within Montenegro that were important to the Montenegrins became important to the entire Serbian nation as well.

The close connection that Montenegro had with the Nemanjid dynasty is illustrated by Podgorica, the birthplace of Stephen Nemanja, founder of the dynasty. A church was consecrated in his name in 1702. Throughout the Middle Ages, when Montenegro was within Dušan's Empire, coastal towns such as Bar, Budva, Kotor, and Ulcinj were important centers of Montenegro. After the fall of Dušan's state, Ottoman forces advanced into the Balkans, causing the South Slavs of Montenegro to retreat from the coast into the mountains. Nevertheless, the South Slavs of Montenegro were the most successful of the Balkan peoples in resisting the Ottomans and were able to maintain a high degree of independence. Cetinje became the capital of the independent state while other towns such as Berane (now Ivangrad, with Djerdjevi Stopovi monastery), Kolašin (with Morača monastery), Nikšić, and Pljevlja became important centers as well.

Although independent, the South Slavs of Montenegro continually had to repel Ottoman advances. Cetinje was even overrun and its monastery burned at one time. The fortress of Spuž was fought over continually. Podgorica is immortalized in an epic poem written about the Piperi (a tribe) who resisted paying tribute to the Ottomans in the eighteenth century. Podgorica is also known because the Ottomans killed 22 Montenegrins there in 1874. The South Slavs of Montenegro were often outnumbered and had to rely on the steep terrain to evade their enemy. They were successful in fighting on and around many mountains such as Mount Ostrog, Mount Gorica (in Podgorica, now Titograd), Mount Lovćen and the Durmitor Mountains.

A number of places in Montenegro are also associated with Serbian struggles in the twentieth century. Of these, Mojkovac and the Durmitor Mountains are noteworthy. A monument stands at Mojkovac where a small Montenegrin force defeated a much larger Austrian force in 1916. The Durmitor Mountains contributed greatly to Tito's struggle against the Nazi occupation forces by providing the Partisans with the shelter of an inaccessible location.

The poem "Mountain Wreath," often heralded as the greatest Serbian poem (Holton and Mihailovich 1988, 150; Njegoš 1986), is about an event that took place on Mount Lovćen in 1702. The poem is about the massacre of South Slavs from Montenegro who converted to Islam. Towards the beginning Prince Danilo of Montenegro laments the centuries of Turkish domination in the Balkans. Later the poem asserts that Montenegro is a Christian land. As in many Serbian poems and songs, Islam is treated as a threat that must be overcome. However, the threat of Islam is not expressed in fundamental opposition to religious tenets but in opposition to its strong influence and expression in the landscape of Serbian lands:

> The high mountain is reeking with heathens.
> In the same fold are both the wolves and the sheep,
> and the Turk is one with Montenegrin now.
> The hodja bellows on Cetijne's plain!
> A stench has caught the lion in the trap,
> the Montenegrin name is now wiped out;
> no one crosses himself with three fingers.
> . . .
> So why does the Crescent mar the Cross?
> . . .
> I see precious offerings piled up high
> at the altar of our Church and nation.
> Wailing echoes I hear in the mountains.
> We must uphold our honor and our name!
> Let the struggle go on without respite.
> Let it be what men thought could never be.
> Let Hell devour, let Satan cut us down!
> Flowers will sprout and grow in our graveyards
> for some distant, future generation.
> (Holton and Mihailovich 1988, 150–55)

When the Ottoman armies were driven out of the Balkans, Montenegrin forces moved back down to the coast. They retrieved not only the coastal areas from Bar to Ulcinj but also the Bay of Kotor. Since the late nineteenth century, Kotor, Herceg-Novi, and other towns along the bay have been an integral part of Montenegro and have served as important trading centers.

The Vojvodina and Srem

While Serbia Proper and Montenegro were the first regions to achieve political independence, the Vojvodina and Srem became the early intellectual-cultural center of modern Serbia (Petrovich 1976, 1: 344–45). The South Slavs of the Vojvodina and Srem founded the national institutions of the modern Serbian state and wrote the history of the Serbian nation. The Serbian identity that developed among the South Slavs of the Vojvodina and Srem was distinctly different from that of either Serbia Proper or Montenegro. Therefore, in order to understand why they wrote the history of the Serbian people as they did, it is important to understand how their regional form of Serbian identity developed.

The Serbs of the Vojvodina and Srem were descendants of South Slavs who, unwilling to live under Ottoman rule, migrated north of the Sava-Danube line. However, they did not escape Ottoman domination for long. The Ottoman advance continued steadily until much of the Hungarian lands were occupied by the middle of the sixteenth century. By that time,

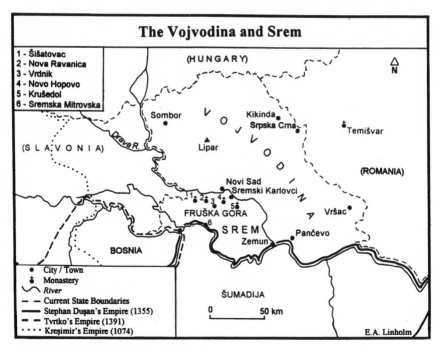

Figure 6.10 The Vojvodina and Srem.

most South Slavs did not flee farther northwest but, instead, remained clustered in colonies. Szentendre was the colony farthest to the north but most migrants settled in the Vojvodina (including Baranja, Bačka, and the Banat), with the highest concentrations of migrants settling between the Sava and Dunav (Danube) Rivers in an area known as Srem. In fact, within Srem, the Fruška Gora became an important refuge. The Fruška Gora is a low mountain range of parallel ridges with heights under two thousand feet; it extends almost fifty miles in an east-west direction and is located just south of the Sava River. Srem was actually the eastern extension of Slavonia but, with the immigration of more and more people from the southern Balkans, it forged a closer association with the regions to the southeast. Eventually, Srem became part of the Vojvodina.

After the Ottoman Empire reached its zenith of territorial expansion in Europe, the Vojvodina and Srem emerged as an important region for Serbian national culture. In the beginning, the Vojvodina and Srem simply served together as a cultural preserve, but, with the waning of the Ottoman empire, it became the first of the Serbian-inhabited areas to become liberated. More and more Serbs migrated into the region from the south, including the early mass migration of a group of South Slavs to Sremski Karlovci, who were led by Arsenije Carnojevic, the patriarch of Peć, in 1691 (Holton and Mihailovich 1988, 37–38; Peić 1994, 224–25). Arsenije and his predecessors had tried to preserve their people's culture in Peć and the monasteries of Old Serbia, but his decision to move illustrates the difficulties he encountered.

Although initially a refuge, the Vojvodina and Srem became home to those South Slavs who occupied the territory for centuries. The poems "On Lipar," a hill between Sombor and Novi Sad, and "In the Srem," with its particular references to the Fruška Gora (Holton and Mihailovich 1988, 165–66, 174–75), illustrate the emotional attachment that the South Slavs of the Vojvodina and Srem developed for the region. Subsequently, when modern Serbian national identity developed, it incorporated the strong emotional attachment that the South Slavs had formed with the region. Many Serbian intellectuals and leaders were born and grew up in the numerous small towns of the territory (e.g., Srbska Crnja) and then were buried in such places as Krušedol and Nova Ravanica. Nova Ravanica, which means "New Ravanica," came to represent the original Ravanica and illustrates the historical ties that South Slavs of the Vojvodina and Srem had with Serbia Proper. Prince Lazar's body, his shroud, and Jefimija's golden prayer were moved to Nova Ravanica in 1683 and they stayed there until the Second World War (Holton and Mihailovich 1988, 23). The Vojvodina and Srem were also the first of the Serbian-inhabited regions to have schools, publishing houses, theaters, and literary societies on a large scale. In essence, the South Slavs who moved to the Vojvodina and Srem reshaped the regions into the image of Old Serbia and became emotionally attached to them as much as they were to Old Serbia. In other words, the Vojvodina and Srem became Serbia.

By the early seventeenth century, the Vojvodina and Srem became not only the preserve of South Slavic culture but major centers for the cultivation of a modern Serbian national identity. With the center of the Serbian church in the region, towns such as Sremska Mitrovica (named after Kosovska Mitrovica in Kosovo), Novi Sad, Pančevo, Sremski Karlovci, Sombor, Vrdnik, and Zemun, as well as monasteries such as Novo Hopovo, Krušedol (in Novi Sad), Nova Ravanica (or Sremska Ravanica in Vrdnik), and Šišatovac began to flourish. Even places as far to the east as Kikinda, Vršac, and Temišvar (at the time Temesvár, Hungary, now Timişoara, Romania) achieved some significance.

The involvement of Serbs from the Vojvodina and Srem in the universal education system that emerged in the nineteenth century not only enhanced their influence but allowed them to dominate. Thus, when Serbia Proper began to exert its independence from the Ottoman Empire, Serbs from the Vojvodina and Srem were recruited as administrators and teachers. By the end of 1835, of the twenty-eight school teachers in Serbia Proper, twenty were from the Vojvodina, Srem, and other Austrian controlled lands, two were from other places outside Serbia Proper, and only six were from Serbia Proper (Petrovich 1976, 1: 222). The overwhelming influence of Serbs from the Vojvodina and Srem in the literary fields and the arts, coupled with their anti-Turkish sentiments, resulted in a Serbian national myth that was anti-Turkish. It also totally glossed over the fact that many Serbs, whether in Bosnia-Herzegovina, Serbia Proper, or Macedonia, lived peacefully and prosperously under the Ottomans and were decidedly anti-Austrian and even anti-West European. Prince Marko was made into a national hero, though he was a vassal of the Turks. Clan leaders, from medieval to modern times, were depicted as Serbs with a clear Serbian national consciousness, though many of them were primarily concerned with their own familial clans and often betrayed other so-called Serbian leaders to the Ottomans.

If Serbian national history had been written by Serbs of Serbia Proper, Serbian national identity would have been much different. The Serbs of Serbia Proper generally found life under Ottoman rule to be much more tolerable than life under Austrian rule. When the Austrian armies first crossed over the Sava-Danube Rivers and pushed the Ottoman armies farther to the southeast, the Serbs of Serbia Proper welcomed the Austrians with enthusiasm. However, after living under Austrian rule for only a short time, they found life to be unbearable. The Austrians were less tolerant than the Ottomans and pursued vigorous policies of forced conversion to Roman Catholicism in comparison to the Islamicization policies of the Ottomans. While the Austrian armies had reached as far as Skopje, the continuing loss of support of the Serbs south of the Sava-

Danube meant that the Austrian armies were eventually pushed back over these rivers. The Serbs of Serbia Proper decided to push for independence without Austrian aid. However, the anti-Austrian and even anti-West European feelings of many Serbs are not clearly noticeable in Serbian national identity. Only in times of crises with the West have they expressed themselves.

Old Serbia (Raška and Kosovo)

Old Serbia falls within the core area of Serbian sense of territory primarily as a result of its historical significance. Because modern Serbian national identity is a product of the Romantic period, history and historical regions cannot be underemphasized. When the Serbs of the Vojvodina and Srem wrote the history of Serbia and the Serbian people, they brought to life a multitude of historical sites.[20] Old Serbia not only contains one of the densest concentrations of places significant to modern Serbian national identity, it contains some of the most significant places (Dragnich and Todorovich 1984, 29). In addition, Old Serbia is the oldest territory that any Serb can possibly claim as a place that is distinctly Serbian.[21]

Old Serbia was the early center of the Nemanjid Dynasty as it arose in the twelfth century (Clissold 1966, 91). The Lim River is in the center of the region; however, the region extended as far west and southwest as the Drina and Tara rivers, and to the northeast as far as the Ibar and Morava rivers (Temperley 1919, 19). The major towns of the territory were Raška, Novi Pazar, and Peć (Ipek). While the town of Raška has not survived into modern times, the significance of this early capital city led to the establishment of a town with the same name in the nineteenth century (Tomasević and Rakić, 1983, 388). Novi Pazar has remained important through the centuries and is a large city today. To the northwest of Novi Pazar is Goleš Mountain. It is often cited in epic poems and songs and considered to be the "very heart and royal fortress of Old Serbia" (Holton and Mihailovich 1988, 74).

Many of the earliest places of great religious significance are also in Old Serbia. In the thirteenth century, the autocephalous Serbian Church was centered on Žiča (in Kraljevo) (Peić 1994, 62). Later, under continual threat of Tartar raids, the religious center was moved to Peć (Clissold 1966, 93); Peć eventually became the patriarchate of the Serbian Orthodox Church in 1346 (Peić 1994, 88–105). Peć, however, was not the only significant religious center. Dečani (Peić 1994, 155–74), Gračanica, Mileševa (Peić 1994, 64–84), Sopoćani, Studenica (Peić 1994, 39–61, 123–39) and Sušica were important religious centers as well. When Stephen Nemanja abdicated his throne in 1196, he retired to Studenica and was later buried there (Fine 1987, 39; Koljević 1980, 98). Sušica is associated with Prince Marko, who

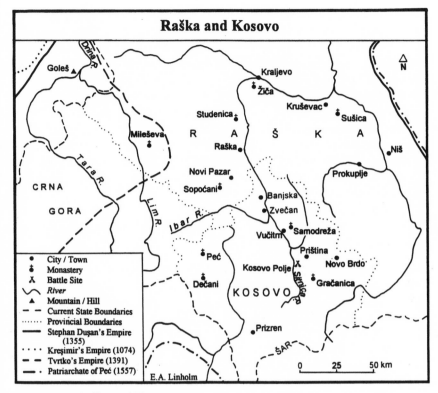

Figure 6.11 Raška and Kosovo.

founded it. In many ways, these monasteries are tangible elements in the landscape that testify to the existence and greatness of these historical figures and of the Serbian nation.

Of all the places in Old Serbia, not to mention all of Serbia, Kosovo Polje is the most significant. It was on Kosovo Polje, "the field of blackbirds," in 1389, that the combined Christian forces of the Balkans were defeated by the Ottomans. The battle was one of many military campaigns of the Ottomans during their occupation of southeastern Europe. In fact, it was only one of several battles that determined the fate of Serbia. The earlier battle of Marica (1371), three more battles (1402, 1448, 1689) on Kosovo Polje, the battle of Smederevo in 1459, the conquering of Bosnia in 1463, the fall of Herzegovina in 1482, and the defeat of Montenegrin forces in 1499 were crucial as well, not to mention several other battles in the Balkan peninsula fought by other Christian armies that could have halted the Ottoman advance. Some historians and other researchers argue that the battle of Marica in 1371 was the most significant (Fine 1987, 379–88; Judah 1997, 26). If the Ottomans had lost the battle, they may have never entered Europe. Moreover, half of the forces from Dušan's Empire were annihilated; the empire was defenseless afterwards. Over time, however, the significance of the Battle of Kosovo in 1389 mushroomed in importance. Serbian national identity has focused on and become preoccupied with this event and place more than any other event or place in Serbian history (Matthias and Vučković 1987). More epics have been written about Kosovo than any other event. One of the most famous Serbian paintings is called the "Kosovo Girl" (1919), a girl holding Prince Lazar and offering him a drink of wine as he dies at the Battle of Kosovo (Judah 1997, 69, between pages 110 and 111; Peić 1994, 192–93). Serbian identity also has been molded by this battle more than any other event in Serbian history (Emmert 1990, 1; Kotur 1977, 131–39).

The significance of Kosovo to the Serbian nation cannot be understated. On the 500th anniversary of the battle in 1889, Serbia's foreign minister, Čedomil Mijatović, stated:

> An inexhaustible source of national pride was discovered on Kosovo. More important than language and stronger than the Church, this pride unites all Serbs in a single nation. . . . We bless Kosovo because the memory of the Kosovo heroes upheld us, encouraged us, taught us, and guided us. (Emmert 1990, 129; Judah 1997, 68)

In 1939, Orthodox bishop Emilijan, while at another anniversary celebration, stated that "Beside the name of Christ, no other name is more beautiful or more sacred" (Kostić and Vuksanović, 1991, 12). By the 600th anniversary in 1989, the battlefield of Kosovo had become a national meeting place, with more than a million people attending the celebrations that year (Silber and Little 1997, 71). Kosovo is also where Slobodan Milošević incited Serbian nationalism on more than one occasion with his incendiary speeches.

Besides Kosovo Polje itself, other places are mentioned with reverence in the Kosovo epics. Most of these places fall within the state of Prince Lazar, one of the Serbian leaders who began to act independently after Stephen Dušan's death. Lazar organized Serbian resistance to the Ottomans and led the Christian armies at the Battle of Kosovo, where he died in battle. Lazar's state was in the northern part of Dušan's realm with its capital in Kruševac. Besides Kruševac, towns such as Banjska, Niš, Prizren, Priština, Prokuplje, Vučitrn, and Zvečan are often mentioned in the Kosovo epics (Emmert 1990; Koljević 1980, 97–176; Matthias and Vučković 1987; Pennington and Levi 1984, 1–29; Subotić 1976, 51–93). The monastery of Samodreža is where Lazar's army took communion before the battle (Holton and Mihailovich 1988, 23). The Sitnica River is mentioned often in the epic poems and songs of Kosovo. The Ottoman leader first pitched his tent along the banks of the river. By the end of the battle many bodies were thrown into the river. Even King Vukašin's body was supposedly thrown into the river after his participation in the battle, though he died at the Marica River eighteen years earlier (Noyes and Bacon 1913, 128).

The prosperous mining town of Novo Brdo is heralded as a great Serbian town because it continued resistance after the Ottoman victory at the Battle of Kosovo; however, it eventually fell too. Not long after the defeat at Kosovo, many of the Balkan Slavs began migrating to the north and northwest. Although modern-day Kosovo is primarily inhabited by Albanians with only a few Serbs, Kosovo is included within the core area of Serbian territories. By simply looking at the current distribution of ethnic groups, it would seem that Serbs do not consider Kosovo to be a very important place. However, with the application of the three indicators of a nation's sense of territory, Kosovo is identified as very important because it is used to define modern Serbian national identity.

The Core: The Tenacity Factor

The Balkans have witnessed many wars in the last twelve hundred years as South Slavs have fought to exert their independence. Although Romantic nationalist historians have written about these events as nationalist struggles, most of these struggles took place before the rise of nationalism some two hundred years. Those involved in struggles before the end of the eighteenth century did not see their causes as national ones. Instead, they fought for reasons related to familial and clan ties, or just to exert and maintain some control over their own lives. That many of these early so-called Serbs fought with one another, and even allied with Ottomans, Russians, Austrians, etc., to conquer one another, demonstrates that the people that we now label the Serbs did not share this common identity that we now impose upon them as suggested by our writings of history. Indeed, these various peoples more often identified themselves in any number of different ways, as Rascians, Montenegrins, Bosnians, Pravoslavni, etc. Not until the beginning of the nineteenth century did a common Serbian national identity begin to develop among these peoples. Only then did they begin the quest to unite politically a common, yet to be defined, Serbian national territory.

In the tenacity factor, Serbia Proper, Montenegro, the Vojvodina and Srem, and Old Serbia (Raška and Kosovo) are all core territories because they are the regions where the struggle for independence of the Serbian nation began. Actually, the Slavs of Montenegro were never completely conquered by the Ottoman Empire. However, it was not until 1799, after Montenegrin forces soundly defeated Ottoman troops, that the Ottoman Empire recognized Montenegro's independence. The independent territory was small at the time, but the Montenegrin government was able to annex more territories after the war with the Ottoman Empire in 1878 and the Balkan Wars of 1912–13. Interestingly, although Serbia proper achieved independence in 1878, and Montenegro shared a border with the Serbian state from the conclusion of the Balkan Wars of 1912–13, the Montenegrins did not decide to join their "Serbian" state with Serbia Proper until after the end of the First World War.

Serbia Proper has the status of a core territory because it was here that the struggle for independent Serbian statehood began and was successful. The struggle began with two insurrections, now known as the First (1804–13) and Second (1815–17) Serbian Insurrections. Serbian national identity was not yet fully developed. The insurrections were initially reactions to the oppressive policies of the Ottoman Empire and the actions of the janissaries, who were part of the Ottoman military. Because many of the insurrections' leaders were landholders who derived their authority and power from the Ottoman Empire, they were not anxious for radical change. On the contrary, they merely wanted the oppressive policies to end and the opportunity to return to the time when they could act with a high degree of independence and simply pay tribute to the Sultan. Likewise, many Serbian peasants simply wanted to return to a time when they could cultivate their land in peace and pay tribute to their landlords. However, neither the Serbian landlords nor the Serbian peasants had any means to reverse the repressive policies of the Ottoman authorities, other than to rebel. Insubordination, however, brought nothing but harsh reprisals from the Ottomans. In time, the rebels wanted more than a restoration of earlier privileges; they wanted autonomy and then independence. Only then did a Serbian national consciousness develop, and concurrently a sense of territoriality.

Despite the desires and actions of the rebels the First Insurrection was suppressed in 1813. On the other hand, the Second Insurrection was marked by quick military victories but achieved only modest political gains after the Russian government pressured Ottoman authorities into making concessions. It ended in 1817 when the leader of the insurrection, Miloš Obrenović, secured a number of concessions from the Ottoman government. These successes, however, were restricted to the territory of the Paşalik of Belgrade (see Figure 6.1). Coupled with new rights of governing, the leadership of a growing Serbian nation was able to focus its attention on defining and obtaining a territory for itself.

The newly developing Serbian nation, however, was not content with partial autonomy over its territory; nations must have political independence to be truly free. Thus, following the Second Insurrection, Miloš Obrenović and other Serbian leaders pushed for greater independence. The achievement of full autonomy, however, did not require the bloody battles of the First and Second Insurrections. This time Serbian leaders could use the course of international events to push their demands. Most noteworthy, the European powers, particularly Russia, were aggressively pursuing expansionist policies in the Balkans. With every military success of Russia, Serbian leaders obtained more concessions from the Ottoman Empire. In 1830, the Sultan recognized the full autonomy of Serbia, and Miloš Obrenović became prince. The Serbian government was then allowed to build its own schools, hospitals, and postal system, and even to maintain its own printing establishments (Petrovich 1976, 1: 128)—all institutions that were necessary to the cultivation of a unique Serbian national identity. In 1833, Miloš Obrenović saw an opportunity to forcibly take the six *nahies* (districts) (see Figure 6.1), and thereby gained more control over Serbia Proper.

The struggle to free the Vojvodina and Srem began on April 12, 1848, in conjunction with the revolutions that took place that year in Europe. The Austrian Empire was politically and militarily very strong, much stronger than the Ottoman Empire. Consequently, although the Serbs in Serbia gave much aid to their fellow nationals in the Vojvodina and Srem, the uprising there was crushed by mid-1849 (Petrovich 1976, 1: 243–46). Despite great efforts to free the Vojvodina and Srem, the military strength of the Austrian Empire throughout the nineteenth century precluded the Serbian nation from gaining control over these territories for decades, until the end of the First World War.

The opportunity to gain control over greater areas of Serbia Proper as well as other core territories did not come until the late 1870s. With an insurrection that erupted in Bosnia-Herzegovina in 1878, the Serbian government saw an opportunity for Balkan Christians to revolt everywhere in the Ottoman Empire. With such a regional revolt, Serbian and Montenegrin forces could successfully occupy the long-desired territories of "Old Serbia" such as the Sanjak of Novi Pazar, the area around the city of Niš, and the area around the Timok River. However, despite national enthusiasm, the Serbian army was ill-prepared for undertaking any military campaigns. The Bulgarians, Romanians, and Greeks also did not revolt. Consequently, after Ottoman forces defeated the Serbian army, they began advancing to Belgrade. By November 1876, the Great Powers became concerned about the situation and issued an ultimatum to the Ottoman government, which ended the Ottoman advance (Jelavich and Jelavich 1977, 145).

Negotiations for peace failed, and the Russian government declared war on the Ottoman Empire in 1877. In early 1878, the Ottoman government agreed to an armistice, and the Russian government submitted a settlement known as the Treaty of San Stefano. The Treaty had many ramifications for Serbia, but most important was the recognition of Serbia's independence. Montenegro would triple in size, and Serbia would expand south to Niš (see Figure 6.3). However, Serbian leaders were disappointed because they wanted to exert their control over much more of the Serbian nation's core territories. The Great Powers of Central and Western Europe also were disappointed by the Treaty of San Stefano. The proposal for a Greater Bulgaria meant too much Russian influence in the Balkans. The Austrian government was also disappointed that its interests in the Balkans were not satisfied in any way. Consequently, the Great Powers wanted a new settlement. A conference was held in Berlin in June and July of 1878 and a new treaty drafted (Petrovich 1976, 2: 399–401) (see Figure 6.3). The Treaty of Berlin included no plan for a Greater Bulgaria. Serbia, however, achieved full independence and expanded to Niš but more in a southeastward direction, gaining 200 square miles, including the town of Pirot, instead of the 150 square miles proposed in the Russian proposal of San Stefano. Montenegro gained some territory, but not as much as was called for in the San Stefano Treaty. To the disappointment of Serbian leaders, Austrian forces were allowed to occupy the Sanjak of Novi Pazar, areas of the core territory of Old Serbia; however, these lands remained under Ottoman sovereignty.

The opportunity to gain Old Serbia came in the Balkan Wars of 1912–13. Out of fear that the Austro-Hungarian Empire would annex Old Serbia for itself, the leaders of Serbia began forging a series of alliances with the governments of Montenegro, Bulgaria, and Greece after 1903 in the event of any new crisis in the Balkans. Following two brief wars, Serbia and Montenegro were able to extend their boundaries into the Sanjak of Novi Pazar and create a common border (see Figure 6.4).

By 1914, the only core territory that the Serbian nation had incorporated into the Serbian nation was the Vojvodina and Srem. Obtaining of this core territory had to wait until after the First World War. Indeed, the war itself dealt a major blow to Serbian national identity as the Serbian nation lost control over all of its territories. Both the Serbian army and the Serbian government had to flee the country. When the tide of the war changed toward the end of 1918, the Serbian army set out to reclaim the nation's core territories. At the beginning of October, the Serbian army broke through enemy lines in Macedonia and moved northward, reaching Belgrade on November 1. The Serbian government intended to liberate the Vojvodina and Srem, not to mention other territories, with the Serbian army as well; however, the establishment of a National Council in Zagreb precluded such action when it declared independence for a state of Slovenes, Croats, and Serbs. The existence of a Slavic state in the northwestern area of the Balkans created an obstacle for creating a Greater Serbian state. While the Serbian government in Belgrade and the National Council in Zagreb were debating the issues, an assembly in the Novi Sad voted to unite the Vojvodina with Serbia. At the same time, a National Council in Podgorica (Titograd), after dethroning King Nicholas, voted to unite Montenegro with Serbia. As time progressed, the National Council in Zagreb found itself in a precarious position. It had no international recognition and no means of protecting its territory from neighboring states; Italy particularly was a threat. Consequently, the National Council in Zagreb decided to hasten its declared intention of uniting with Serbia. Negotiations were brief with the National Council acquiescing to the demands of the Serbian government. With negotiations complete, the Kingdom of the Serbs, Croats and Slovenes came into being at 8:00 P.M. on December 1, 1918 (Petrovich 1976, 2: 680–81).

With the creation of a new state, Serbia ceased to exist as an independent entity. However, the Serbian nation was either directly controlled or shared control of all of its core territories; the Srem was officially in the Croatian part of the kingdom. Nevertheless, despite being in a new state and having to share it with other nations, Serbian leaders were successful in pressing their demands from the outset. Consequently, the new state, ostensibly a "Yugoslav" state, functioned as a Greater Serbian state (Singleton 1985, 143–44). With the partial exception of Slovenia and Croatia, Serbian leaders considered all regions of the kingdom to be Serbian. The state became centrally organized in Belgrade with Alexander Karadjordjević, the Serbian king, as the constitutional monarch. In fact, Alexander swore an oath to the constitution on the anniversary of the Battle of Kosovo in 1921 (Jelavich 1983, 2: 151). Political power remained in the hands of Serbian politicians throughout the interwar period; for example, Serbs occupied 92 percent of the important ministry positions despite comprising only some 38 percent of the population (Pusich 1991, 28; Banac 1984, 58). In 1926, all but four of the 165 generals in the new kingdom were Serbs (Dedijer and others 1974, 538). Any opposition to Serbian rule was treated as treason (Jelavich 1983, 2: 151–52). In fact, in many regions, citizens could be beaten for not using the term Greater Serbia as a substitute for Yugoslavia (Banac 1984, 158).

Although the Serbian nation enjoyed unprecedented control over its core territories during the interwar period, it lost total control over these territories again in the Second World War. Following a German and Italian invasion on April 6, 1940, and the subsequent armistice on April 17, Yugoslavia was dismantled (see Figure 6.5) as the countries surrounding it annexed territories that had long been claimed. Montenegro, Serbia Proper, Old Serbia and the remainder of the Vojvodina[22] came under direct Axis occupation.

From the Serbian perspective, the objective was to begin an effort of resistance and then liberation of Serbian territories. Colonel Dragoljub-Draza Mihailović and a group of Serbian officers retreated to the mountains to form the Chetnik Detachments of the Yugoslav resistance. *Chetnik* was a resurrection of a term applied to fighters who resisted Ottoman rule. The new chetniks were loyal to the exiled Yugoslav government, long dominated by Serbs with a Greater Serbian philosophy. They blamed the Croats for the destruction of Yugoslavia and sought to rebuild Yugoslavia as it had been. With their narrow Serbian view, the chetniks had limited appeal throughout the former Yugoslav territory and its various national groups. The other major resistance group, the Partisans, led by Josip Broz Tito, appealed to a much broader spectrum of ethnic groups and nations within Yugoslavia. Croats, Albanians, Muslims, and Macedonians, for example, were much more willing to fight with the Partisans for a Yugoslavia in which everyone had equal rights rather than fight with the chetniks, who wanted to create a Serbian dominated Yugoslavia. The Partisans even had the support of Serbs who suffered under the rule of the *Ustaša* regime in Croatia and Bosnia-Herzegovina. Over the course of the war, the Partisans grew in strength while the chetniks lost influence.

As the Nazi forces withdrew from Yugoslavia, the Serbian nation regained control of its core territories; even Srem was transferred from Croatia to Serbia (specifically to the Vojvodina), but the Partisans prevented Serbian nationalists from turning Yugoslavia into a Greater Serbian state. In fact, many such leaders either fled the country, were imprisoned or executed, or simply barred from many activities. The rise of Tito and the communists changed the nature of conflict between the South Slavs. Tito was the first leader of a government in Belgrade who was not imbued with the idea of creating a Greater Serbia. He reorganized the internal political geography of Yugoslavia into a federal state with six republics (see Figure 6.6). Macedonia, its people and its language, was recognized as separate and distinct from Serbia, its people and its language. Within Serbia, the autonomous regions of the Vojvodina and Kosovo were created. This latter move was not ideal for the Serbian nation, but resistance was initially limited because these core territories remained within the Serbian Republic.

Tito was a charismatic leader with much popular support but he encountered many difficulties as he piloted the post-war Yugoslav state through the minefield of Balkan ethnic relations. As time progressed, Tito found himself in the position of granting each group more rights as he tried to keep any one group from dominating. However, such actions led to further divergence within Yugoslav society. For example, with the constitution of 1974, Vojvodina and Kosovo were upgraded from autonomous regions to autonomous provinces. Subsequently, Albanians and Hungarians were given more freedom to develop culturally along pathways that deviated greatly from a common Yugoslav identity. Serbs in Serbia were likewise dissatisfied with the growing independence of the Vojvodina and Kosovo. In response, Tito forcibly squelched any opposition to his policies. A vicious cycle began that eventually would tear the Yugoslav state apart. Tito found that he could only smooth over tensions by allowing the various elements of Yugoslav society to follow ever more diverging paths of development. To compensate for growing differences, Tito had to exert more and more personal control over the state. In the end, all that was left of Yugoslavia was Tito. When Tito died in 1980, the Yugoslav state lost much of its *raison d'être*.

Despite Tito's power and charisma, he was never able to alter fundamentally the basic Serbian belief that Serbia was the Piedmont of the Balkans and Serbs were destined to rule the South Slavs. Therefore, to most Serbs, particularly Serbian leaders, Yugoslavia and Greater Serbia were essentially the same. Following Tito's death, Serbian nationalism (not to mention the nationalisms of other groups) began to assert itself again. Significantly, the reemergence of Serbian nationalism was tied to the core territory of Kosovo. Over the preceding decades, the economy in Kosovo was in serious decline. One of the consequences of this decline was the emigration of Serbs from the region, leaving the region more ethnically Albanian. The Albanians had suffered greatly from the poor economy and began agitating as early as 1991 to upgrade Kosovo from an autonomous province to a full-fledged republic (Magaš 1993, 15). Such an act, which would have separated Kosovo from the Serbian Republic, was unacceptable to the Serbian nation. Constituting a plurality in Yugoslavia and in control of many of the state institutions, particularly the military, Serbian leaders successfully implemented policies that were in the interest of the Serbian nation. Not surprisingly then, the Yugoslav government responded to the Albanian demonstrations in Kosovo with force. The Yugoslav army was sent into the region with tanks, and martial law was declared. Over the years that followed, the government systematically removed Albanians from public office and any positions of authority.

The issue and status of Kosovo also touched other segments of Serbian society. In 1986, prominent Belgrade intellectuals sent a petition to the Yugoslav and Serbian assemblies claiming that the government had done nothing to stop the genocide in Kosovo. In essence, they claimed that the emigration of Serbs was the result of Albanian persecution (Magaš 1993, 49). As the Serbian public continued to vent its anger over the issue of Kosovo, individual Serbian politicians saw the opportunity to enhance their political authority. Of these, Slobodan Milošević is the most noteworthy. As early as 1987, Milošević began making trips to Kosovo Polje and making incendiary speeches that reminded the Serbian nation of its historic right to Kosovo (Silber and Little 1997, 37–47). On March 28, 1988, the Serbian constitution was amended to abolish the autonomous rights of the two core territories of Kosovo and the Vojvodina. Significantly, the Serbian government insisted on holding onto the two seats that these now-dismantled provinces held within the Yugoslav presidency. Thus the Serbian nation possessed four of the eight seats of the federal presidency (Lampe 1996, 344).

As Serbs took control of more and more federal institutions, the other nations and ethnic groups of Yugoslavia became alarmed. Lacking the political power to resist Serbian leaders in the federal government, many non-Serbian leaders saw it in the best interests of their peoples to move towards independence. The governments of Slovenia and Croatia declared their independence in June 1991, and within months the government of Macedonia was seeking recognition of its independence. Finally, the government of Bosnia-Herzegovina declared its independence in April 1992. The desire for independence was a severe blow to Serbian national identity. Fighting and bloodshed has ensued with many territories successfully breaking away from Yugoslavia. The Serbian nation, however, has successfully held onto its core territories of Serbia Proper, Montenegro, the Vojvodina (and Srem), and Old Serbia (Kosovo and Raška).[23] Proof that Serbian nationalists cannot see the difference between the Greater Serbian and Yugoslav ideas is shown by the Serbs continuing to call their country Yugoslavia even though it is composed only of two republics: Montenegro and Serbia, with Kosovo and the Vojvodina being undifferentiated components of Serbia.

The Semi-Core: Site Identification and Landscape Description

The semi-core of Serbian sense of territory consists of Macedonia, Bosnia-Herzegovina, the central areas of the Banat, and western areas of Bulgaria. While these regions contain relatively fewer places of great importance than the core territories, the semi-core territories, nonetheless, are very important to Serbian identity. Significant aspects of Serbian identity are shaped by the semi-core, and many Serbs have a strong emotional bond to the semi-core territories. The semi-core territories, however, are inhabited by many peoples who do not consider themselves to be Serbs. Consequently, the issue of control over the semi-core territories has resulted in much conflict between the Serbian nation and these other peoples or between the Serbian government and other governments. The efforts of the Serbian nation to gain or maintain control of the semi-core territories is in many ways a testament to just how important these territories are.

Macedonia

Round the Struma and the Vardar
a lovely flower blooms,
it is the flower of the Serbian tsar:

the holy blossom of Tsar Dušan.
Round the Struma and the Vardar
bloom the flowers of the Serbian tsar.
—Stevan Kaćanski, 1885
(Quoted in Banac 1984, 307)

When the Romantic nationalists of the Vojvodina and Srem constructed a history for the Serbian people, Macedonia figured prominently. Macedonia and the many sites within it served as the power center of Dušan's Empire, heralded as the greatest political-territorial achievement in Serbian history, according to Serbian Romantic nationalists. As a result, many of the specific places within Macedonia that were important in the medieval empire became important to modern Serbs. For example, under King Uroš II (1282–1321), Skoplje (once Üsküb, now Skopje, the modern capital of Macedonia) became the capital of the Nemanjid dynasty. Dušan had himself crowned emperor here on Easter 1346. In addition to Skoplje, Seres, the location of Dušan's second residence, became a center of power in the empire (Dedijer and others 1974, 87). During Dušan's rule, towns such as Bitolj (now Bitola), Debar, Prilep, and Strumica were important. Also during Dušan's reign, monasteries such as Andrejaš, Gračanica (Peić 1994, 109–11, 140–53), Psača, and Ohrid flourished.

After Stephen Dušan's death, his empire began to disintegrate. His son Uroš V could not hold the empire together as the various leaders of the regional substates began to act independently. The activities of these leaders or the exact nature of their states is unclear. What emerged over time among the Balkan Slavs, after living under Ottoman rule for centuries, was an interest in the demise of the medieval Serbian Empire of Dušan. Much was written, even fictitiously, of those southern states, which were the first ones to be threatened by the advance of the Ottoman Turks. King Vukašin's state, with the capital in Prilep, became one of the most popular subjects of Serbian epic poetry (Petrovich 1976, 1: 15).

After King Vukašin died, his son Prince Marko (Marko Kraljević) inherited his lands and became even more popular than his father. Of all the medieval historical figures, Prince Marko probably has been written about the most in folk epics (Low 1968; Pennington and Levi 1984; Popović 1988). Other than the Šar Mountains in the northwest (the current boundary between Macedonia and the autonomous region of Kosovo in Serbia), the exact limits of Marko's state are unknown in any detail. The epic song "Prince Marko and Mina of Kostur" indicates that Marko's state extended as far south as Kostur (now Kastoria, Greece) (Popović 1988, 108–9). Fewer, less precise references suggest that the Vardar River gorge was cut by Marko's sword (Popović 1988, 41) and that a number of huge rocks in the area of Kičevo were thrown by Marko. Urvina Mountain is the supposed location of Marko's death, however, the location of the mountain

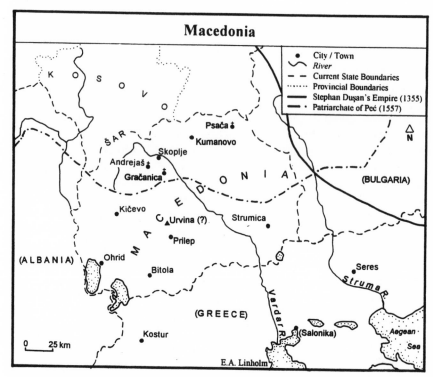

Figure 6.12 Macedonia.

is uncertain. Epic poetry suggests that the mountain is near Skoplje, near the sea! (Holton and Mihailovich 1988, 114; Popović 1988, 168). In reality, Marko probably died at the Battle of Rovine in Walachia in 1395. The word *Urvina* may very well be a derivation of the word *Rovine*. Interestingly, instead of becoming emotionally attached to some far away place as Rovine, Prince Marko's death was moved to a more familiar location. Urvina is not the only incident of moving locations associated with Prince Marko. After South Slavs moved to the northwest into Serbia Proper, Bosnia-Herzegovina, Dalmatia, Croatia, and Slovenia, poets began writing works that spoke of Marko being in specific places in those territories.

Bosnia-Herzegovina and Dalmatia

Bosnia-Herzegovina and Dalmatia, like Macedonia, are territories that have been closely associated with the core territories of Serbia, even at times sharing in the same predicaments. Close associations were likely, given that substantial numbers of Balkan Slavs migrated to and from these semi-core territories and the core territories. From the Serbian perspective, Bosnia-Herzegovina is indeed a Serbian land. Areas of eastern Bosnia, paralleling the Drina River, and most of Herzegovina were within the medieval state of Dušan or the states of his predecessors. In fact, the great leader Dušan lost a portion of Bosnia when he tried to incorporate all of it into his state. Despite the failure to gain complete control of Bosnia, it was and still is considered to be a Serbian land by many Serbs. Indeed, the famous King Tvrtko of Bosnia is simply considered to be one of the many Serbian rulers of one of the numerous Serbian lands (Jelavich 1990, 189). His close ties with places in Montenegro only further convinces Serbian nationalists that he was a Serb.

Serbian leaders and their Slavic predecessors have expressed great interest in Dalmatia for centuries. Dalmatia provides an outlet to the sea for many of the Serbian lands which otherwise would be landlocked. Of course, Montenegro has had periodic access to the sea, but such access has always been problematic. Even during favorable times, the coastal cities of Montenegro never reached the level of prominence of those in

Figure 6.13 Bosnia-Herzegovina and Dalmatia.

Dalmatia. Again, early interest by South Slavic leaders existed as far back as medieval times when the Nemanjids ruled the southern areas of Dalmatia. During that time, Dubrovnik (Ragusa) served as the major trading center for Nemanjid goods, particularly for the silver and other precious metals mined in their territory. The Nemanjids depended heavily on Dubrovnik and its navy for building their wealth and power (Koljević 1980, 33). Great leaders such as Emperor Stephen Dušan, Prince Lazar, and Prince Marko visited Dubrovnik. However, Dubrovnik was able to maintain a high degree of autonomy during medieval times despite the attempts of many outside rulers to subjugate the city. Dubrovnik even expressed its strength and independence by its control of the major mining town of Novo Brdo.

Dalmatia and Bosnia-Herzegovina, like Montenegro, became symbols of Ottoman resistance. The rugged terrain prevented the Ottomans from achieving complete control of these regions. In addition, the entire coast of Dalmatia remained a zone of conflict between the Ottoman, Austrian, and Venetian empires for centuries. The continual waxing and waning of imperial boundaries gave many South Slavs the opportunity to find refuge, usually from the Ottomans, in such Dalmatian cities as Dubrovnik, Split, Zadar, and Senj. These cities even became the bases from which South Slav refugees could launch raids, particularly on the Ottomans. The villages around Srebrenica and Ljubovija, which are in eastern Bosnia-Herzegovina, are heralded in an epic poem as refuges for Serbs from the Ottomans (Morison 1942, 3, 32). Ljubovija is actually across the Drina River from Bosnia-Herzegovina but the mentioning of the town in conjunction with Srebrenica illustrates the close ties that eastern Bosnia has with Serbia Proper.

The anti-Ottoman, Romantic nationalists in the Vojvodina and Srem glorified the raiders of the Dalmatian coast and the *hajduks* and *uskoks* of Bosnia-Herzegovina. The difficulties that these people created for the Ottomans were heralded as examples of a greater Serbian struggle against the Ottoman Empire. Dalmatia and Bosnia-Herzegovina, with their rugged terrain, were seen as protectors of the Serbian nation. The people and these regions worked together to overcome the Ottomans. Subsequently, Dalmatia and Bosnia-Herzegovina were viewed as important Serbian lands. The stories of these raiders were then used to write the history of the Serbs in these lands. For example, Vuk Karadžic collected many of his poems from Filip Višnić, who was from Bjeljina. Those places within Dalmatia and Bosnia-Herzegovina that were important to these raiders became important to the Serbian nation. For example, during the periods of favorable weather, particularly summer, the *hajduks* and *uskoks* would camp in the mountains (Koljević 1980, 219–20). One of the mountain ranges most cited in epic poetry is the Romanija, on the eastern side of Sarajevo. In times of prolonged bad weather, the *hajduks* and *uskoks* were forced to seek refuge in the villages. Interestingly, and important to note, the *hajduks* rarely sought refuge in villages in Bosnia, not even the Serbian villages. Instead, they traveled back to villages in Serbia Proper.

In many epic poems and songs, the enemy is referred to as the Bosnians, not the Ottomans or the Turks. Indeed, many of the native Slavs of Bosnia, whether converts to Islam or continuing Catholic or Orthodox Christians, did not oppose Ottoman occupation as much as the Slavs in Serbia Proper. On the contrary, many Bosnians not only adjusted to Ottoman rule but adapted to it and accepted it. Consequently, while Bosnia as a whole, and even many specific places within it, came to be viewed as a refuge for Serbs, these same areas were viewed as something foreign and hostile. Towns such as Bihać, Livno, Travnik, Sarajevo, and Zvornik (the location of the largest Ottoman fortress in what was to become Yugoslavia) were of major concern to the *hajduks* and *uskoks*. Many captured *hajduks* and *uskoks* were brought to fortresses in these towns and tortured (Koljević 1980, 243–44). Many of these places are referred to often in epic poetry and song, but in negative terms.

Bosnia-Herzegovina and Dalmatia are also significant to the Serbian nation in language and literature. When Vuk Karadžić standardized the modern Serbo-Croatian language, he used the Herzegovinian dialect as the fundamental basis of the new language (Naylor 1980, 72–73). Therefore, any Serbs who want to study their language in its "pure" form must travel to Herzegovina. Although Karadžić strongly resisted mixing dialects when he developed the Serbo-Croatian standard, he did incorporate some phonological practices from the Dubrovnik dialect (Katičić 1984, 278). Thus modern Serbo-Croatian is also tied to the Dubrovnik area. In fact, the entire region of Dalmatia has played a large role through history in language and literature. For example, folk epics of Dalmatia were recorded as early as the fifteenth and sixteenth centuries in such places as Dubrovnik, Hvar, Split, and Kotor. These epics of the Dalmatian coast became known as *bugarštice* (Koljević 1980, 31–66). The Dubrovnik area was also known for its literature in the seventeenth and eighteenth centuries (Naylor 1980, 75). By identifying characteristics of Serbian folk epics in the *bugarštice* and by emphasizing that the Dalmatian literature employed the štokavian dialect—the main dialect of the Serbian nation— Serbian nationalists have argued that much of Dalmatia was essentially a region of Serbia. In actuality, however, Slavs from the southern Balkans migrated to Dalmatia. Their storytelling practices simply blended with those of the local peoples and other immigrants; subsequently, a new culture was created. Nevertheless, Romantic thinkers began writing a history for Serbia that not only expressed unity of all the lands but also depicted the Slavs of prenationalist times as having a sense of a unified Serbian national identity and purpose.

Northern Albania, the Central Banat, and Western Bulgaria

Northern Albania, the Central Banat and Western Bulgaria are the remaining areas in the semi-core of Serbian sense of territory. Northern Albania centers on the Drim (Drin) River Basin, with the city of Skadar (Shkodër) at the mouth of the Drim River the major city. The Drim River served as an important transportation route between the Adriatic coast and the interior medieval states centered in Raška and Kosovo (Temperley 1919, 20). The Nemanjid's control initially extended to the city of Skadar. Even after the passing of the Nemanjids, the great economic and strategic value of Skadar is underscored by the fact that the city often served as the capital of leaders who ruled such areas as northern Albania, Zeta, Brda, and Herzegovina. The significance of Skadar is also emphasized in epic poetry. The earliest epic poem of the Serbs, one that stands alone in its prominence in this time period, is called "The Building of Skadar" (Butler 1980, 429–41; Holton and Mihailovich 1988, 86–94). The city is referred to in the phrase "white Skadar on the Bojana [River]." Skadar was built by three great Serbian figures: King Vukašin, Duke Ugljesa, and Gojko, who is actually a fictional character. King Vukašin appears often in Serbian mythology. His son, Prince Marko (also Kraljević Marko) and a greater mythological figure, was supposedly born in Skadar. In another poem, "The Marriage [or Wedding] of King Vukašin" (Low 1968, 1–9), Skadar is once again highlighted. The importance of Skadar is further reinforced by the name of a street and district in Belgrade, Ulica Skadarska and Skadarlija. In the nineteenth century, Skadarlija, a quarter of the city where painters, poets, and writers lived, became a center of Serbian culture (Holton and Mihailovich 1988, 156–57). Although Skadarlija has lost much of its influence in this century, the district remains a distinct area of Belgrade frequented by tourists.

The Central Banat is comparable to the Vojvodina and Srem in terms of its cultural and intellectual importance. The cities of Arad and Temišvar (Timişoara; Temesvár) are the most noteworthy. Historically, these areas were settled by the same peoples of the southern Balkans as those who migrated into the Vojvodina and Srem to escape Ottoman rule. However, fewer of these peoples settled far east into the Banat. Despite the establishment of some institutions in these areas, including the meeting of the Serbian National Congress in 1790 in Temišvar, the Central Banat never became as significant as the Vojvodina and Srem.

Through history, no obvious political boundary has existed between Serbian and Bulgarian states. Moreover, no cultural boundary served as a logical political boundary. In religious, the peoples that we now call the Serbs and Bulgarians called themselves by one name, Pravoslavni, because they were all Eastern Orthodox Christians. Linguistically, the Torlakian

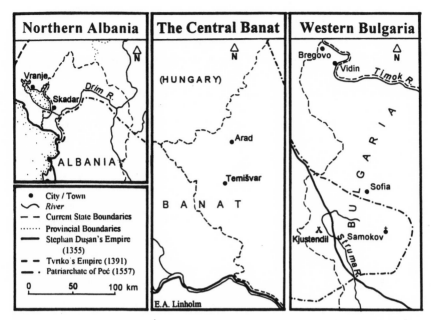

Figure 6.14 Northern Albania, the Central Banat, and Western Bulgaria.

dialect is found on both sides of the modern political boundary. Thus Serbs and Bulgarians along the modern political boundary speak the same dialect. In historical political boundaries, even the exact boundary of Dušan's Empire in this region is uncertain. The Timok and Struma rivers have served as a general boundary but important places such as Bregevo, Pirot, Vidin, Samokov, and Sofia lie east of these rivers. Kjustendil is west of the Struma River but still outside of present-day Serbia. Bregovo and Vidin were even considered to be part of Serbia Proper through the nineteenth century. Bregovo is even associated with the epics relating to Prince Marko, and Pirot is written about in other epics as having been fought over with the Ottomans. The modern Serbian state, however, was never able to gain control of these cities. As a result, Slavs who accepted a Serbian identity left while others developed a Bulgarian identity. At the same time, no significant events for the Serbian nation and no major Serbian institutions were founded in these cities in recent history. Consequently, these cities have lost too much of their significance to be still considered part of the core. Their historical significance, however, keeps them within the semi-core.

The Semi-Core: The Tenacity Factor

Macedonia, Bosnia-Herzegovina, Dalmatia, Northern Albania, the Central Banat, and western areas of Bulgaria are classified as the semi-core of Serbian sense of territory by the tenacity factor as well as by site identification and landscape description. Leaders of the modern Serbian state expressed interest in annexing the semi-core regions early in the nineteenth century though the Vojvodina and Srem, and even Serbia Proper, had not yet achieved independence. Such an early interest by Serbian leaders is clearly seen in such plans as Ilija Garašanin's *Načertanije* of 1844. The plan called for the creation of a Greater Serbian state in which the semi-core figured prominently. Garašanin began laying the groundwork for the construction of a Greater Serbian state by creating a network of agents throughout the Balkans (Petrovich 1976, 1: 233–34). The objectives of the agents were to determine what the secret desires and the most pressing needs of the people were, to ascertain their military preparedness, to compile information about key figures (including enemies), and to discover the attitudes and expectations of the people in question towards the Serbian state (Petrovich 1976, 1: 233). Through the 1840s and 1850s, agents operated all over the Balkans and even received salaries.

Before Serbian leaders would be able to annex any territory to the south, they would have to overcome a major problem. In the centuries following the dissolution of Dušan's Empire in the fourteenth century, the ancestors of most Serbs migrated north out of Macedonia and Old Serbia. During the period of Ottoman rule, Albanians in particular but also Gypsies, Jews, Vlachs, Turks, Bulgarians, and a number of other groups came to dominate the region either by staying behind and increasing in number or through immigration. In fact, it is difficult to talk about these peoples as nations because they lived before the era of modern nationalism. As a sense of modern nationalism developed in the region many of these people accepted an Albanian, a Bulgarian, or even a Macedonian national identity. Only a minority saw themselves as Serbs even though the main body of the Serbian nation saw these regions as integral components of Serbia.

Although the Ottoman Empire was slowly withdrawing from the Balkans, Serbian leaders knew that they would have difficulty taking Macedonia by military force because many Bulgarian and Greek leaders wanted the territory as well.[24] The Great Powers, which were also very concerned about the political status of Macedonia, also presented complications for any Serbian attempts to annex the territory. Therefore, before Macedonia could be successfully annexed, the people of Macedonia had to be convinced that they were really Serbs and that their interests naturally lay with the Serbian state. The annexation of Macedonia would require a monumental effort; however, Macedonia was a territory of substantial importance to Serbian sense of territory. History shows that the Serbian government was willing to implement the programs that would prepare the way for annexation of Macedonia even if a commitment of several decades was required.

Early preparations were undertaken for the annexation when Serbian schools were established in the region in 1868 (Petrovich 1976, 2: 495–501). More than sixty of them functioned until the Serbo-Turkish war in 1876. Afterward the Ottoman government closed most of them. After 1885, the Serbian government set up the supposedly private organization known as the Society of St. Sava. Its main activity was to open schools in Old Serbia and Macedonia. In 1887, the Serbian government created a special department called "Serbian Schools and Churches outside of Serbia" in the ministry of education. In 1889, the department was transferred to the foreign ministry.

Because the Bulgarian and Greek governments also made preparations to annex Macedonia, competition between the three states became fierce; guerrilla groups began fighting, and it was not uncommon for even clergymen to be murdered (Jelavich and Jelavich 1977, 211–12). The Great Powers, namely Austria-Hungary and Russia, intervened and imposed the Mürzsteg Program, which basically called for reforms in order to cool tensions. The intervention of the Great Powers had the effect of smoothing relations between Serbia and Bulgaria. The Serbian government, in particular, was concerned that the Austro-Hungarian Empire would try to occupy more of the Ottoman territories in the Balkans. From 1903, the leaders of Serbia, Montenegro, Bulgaria, and Greece began forging a series of alliances in the event of any new crisis even though they simultaneously watched one another with suspicion.

By the early part of the twentieth century, the Serbian government saw opportunities for military campaigns that could lead to the annexation of Macedonia. In 1912, the Serbian government forged a secret treaty with the Bulgarian government concerning the territorial spoils of a victorious war against the Ottoman Empire. In the agreement, Serbia was to obtain all land north of the Šar Mountain range (Old Serbia) and Bulgaria would receive the areas east of the Rhodope Mountains and the Struma Valley. Because both governments strongly desired Macedonia, no agreement could be reached concerning its annexation. However, the Serbian government agreed not to claim any territory south of a line that extended from the Bulgarian border north of Kriva Palanka to Lake Ohrid in the southwest; the claim ran in a line just north of the cities of Veles and Ohrid (the Kriva Palanka-Veles-Ohrid line) (see Figure 6.4) (Jelavich and Jelavich 1977, 217). Once the war began, the Serbian army violated the agreement when it moved south and occupied areas that included the cities of Prilep, Bitola, and Ohrid. When the war was over, the Serbian government refused to withdraw from the area. The Serbian army even repelled a Bulgarian invasion force when the Bulgarian government started the Second Balkan War in an attempt to obtain its original claims to Macedonia. The Bulgarian defeat resulted in the Treaty of Bucharest, which solidified Serbian control over much of Macedonia.

Up until the early twentieth century, the international community viewed Macedonians as a regional variety of Bulgarians (i.e., Western Bulgarians). However, during the Paris Peace Conference of 1919, the Allies sanctioned Serbian control of much of Macedonia because they accepted the belief that Macedonians were in fact "Southern Serbs." This extraordinary change in opinion can largely be attributed to one man, Jovan Cvijić, a prominent geographer and chairman of the department of geography at the University of Belgrade. He changed western opinion through the publication of a series of maps (see Figure 6.15) over more than a decade that depicted the ethnography of the Balkans (Taylor 1989, 185–88).

Cvijić's first map, published in 1906, depicted only three ethnic groups: Slavs, Albanians, and Greeks. The grouping together of Serbs, Macedonians, and Bulgarians into a single category reflected the long-held, though almost outmoded, belief that all South Slavs were the same. More important, it showed that there was no natural ethnic boundary between Serbs and Bulgarians. In 1909, Cvijić published another map on which he divided the Slav category into three new ethnic categories: the Serbo-Croats, the Bulgarians, and the "Macedo-Slavs." The Serbo-Croat category reflected the Yugoslav movement involving the union of Serbs and Croats. It also strengthened Serbian claims to Bosnia-Herzegovina and Dalmatia. At the time, the separate Bulgarian category illustrated that the Bulgarians were no longer closely associated with the Yugoslav movement. The creation of a Macedo-Slav category was the next step in severing Macedonian identity from Bulgarian identity and fusing it with Serbian identity (Banac 1984, 310–12). Although it was the next logical step, the depiction of a Macedo-Slav category was quite revolutionary because no one before had identified a separate and distinct Macedo-Slav ethnic group (Wilkinson 1951, 163). The distribution of Macedo-Slavs stretched south of Skoplje from the Albanian-inhabited areas in the west to the Bulgarian-inhabited areas in the east. A second category of "Macedo-Slavs under Greek Influence" was shown in what is now northern Greece. Finally, the 1909 map depicted a reduced Albanian presence in Kosovo and western Macedonia.

In 1913, after the Balkan Wars, Cvijić published a map with the Serbo-Croats inhabiting areas much farther to the south than in the 1909 map. Bulgarians were shown inhabiting some areas that were inhabited by Macedo-Slavs on the 1909 map. More important, the Albanian-inhabited areas were dramatically reduced. In particular, the area that is now north-

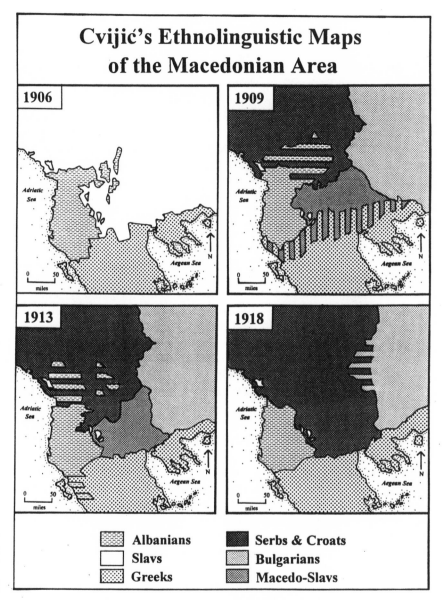

Figure 6.15 Cvijić's Ethnolinguistic Maps of the Macedonian Area.

ern Albania was shown as an area of mixed Serbo-Croat and Albanian population. In 1918, Cvijić published his most important map, one which influenced the decisions made at the Paris Peace Conference in 1919. On this map, Serbs and Macedo-Slavs were grouped into one category, implying that they were in fact the same people. With the publication of the map in the west, in the French *Annales de Géographie* and the *American Geographical Review* (Cvijić 1918), Cvijić was able to legitimize Serbian control of Macedonia on nationalist grounds; he had firmly implanted in the minds of Americans, British, and French the belief that Macedonians were really Southern Serbs. By 1924, with the publication of the first census in Yugoslavia, Macedo-Slav was categorized as a dialect of Serbo-Croatian.

The portion of Macedonia annexed by Serbia in 1913 remained part of Serbia until well into the Second World War. For a brief period during the Second World War, Bulgaria annexed Serbian Macedonia. After the war, Serbian Macedonia was returned to Yugoslavia. Tito gave Macedonia full status as a republic but it stayed firmly under the control of the federal government in Belgrade. With the dissolution of Yugoslavia in 1991, the Macedonian government declared independence. The Yugoslav government, dominated by Serbs, was slow in recognizing Macedonia's independence. It could be argued that recognition was only grudgingly given because Serbian resources were committed to preventing other republics from seceding, such as Bosnia-Herzegovina.

Bosnia-Herzegovina and Dalmatia were initially the primary goals for leaders in the autonomous Serbian state. For example, while Michael Obrenović ruled from 1860 to 1868, he built the Serbian army to a force of 90,000–100,000 men. During that time the phrase "to cross the Drina" (into Bosnia) became a national slogan (Petrovich 1976, 2: 315–16). When Bosnians began an insurrection against the Sultan in 1875, many Serbian volunteers actually crossed the Drina to aid the insurrection. In 1876, the Montenegrin and Serbian governments supported the Bosnians by declaring war on the Ottoman Empire. However, despite national enthusiasm, the Serbian army was ill-prepared for undertaking any military campaigns. The Bulgarians, Romanians, and Greeks also did not revolt as hoped. Consequently, after Ottoman forces defeated the Serbian army, they began advancing to Belgrade. The attempt to gain control of the semi-core territories of Bosnia-Herzegovina and Dalmatia might have resulted in the loss of the Serbian state if the Great Powers had not intervened in the struggle in 1877–78. With the peace treaty of 1878, Bosnia-Herzegovina came under the administration of the Austro-Hungarian Empire, much to the disappointment of Serbian leaders. Disappointment turned to outrage when the Austro-Hungarian Empire formally annexed Bosnia-Herzegovina in 1908. By 1914, Serbian nationalists were fiercely agitating against Austrian control of Bosnia-Herzegovina. Violence erupted with the assassination of Austrian Archduke Ferdinand when he was on a visit in Sarajevo on the anniversary of the Battle of Kosovo (Lampe 1996, 98); however, the issue of Bosnia-Herzegovina's political status quickly became subsumed in a world war.

After the First World War, Bosnia-Herzegovina joined Serbia in the new Yugoslav state, and the government in Belgrade considered Bosnia-

Herzegovina as well as the area around Dubrovnik to be part of the Serbian territories of Yugoslavia. During the Second World War, Bosnia-Herzegovina was annexed by the nominally independent Croatian state. When Yugoslavia was reconstituted after the war, Tito made Bosnia-Herzegovina into its own republic. Tito's act did not please Serbian nationalists, but protests were limited because Bosnia-Herzegovina remained within Yugoslavia with Serbia.

With the dissolution of Yugoslavia in the early 1990s, the government of Bosnia-Herzegovina declared independence in 1992. The Serbian government did not recognize Bosnia-Herzegovina's declaration of independence, however. By supporting militant Serbs within the republic, the Serbian government has prevented the Bosnian government from exercising its sovereignty. The Serbian government and Serbian rebels within Bosnia-Herzegovina claim that they are only trying to maintain control of Serbian-inhabited lands. However, because Serbian forces are attacking non-Serb-inhabited lands and eradicating non-Serbs under a program known as "ethnic cleansing," it seems clear that many Serbs consider all of Bosnia-Herzegovina to be a Serbian territory. After a few years of fighting, Serbian nationalists and their paramilitaries had not succeeded in conquering all of Bosnia-Herzegovina. At the same time, atrocities committed by Serbian nationalists had brought about considerable international pressure on the Serbian government and the Serbian nationalists within Bosnia-Herzegovina. Bosnian Serb nationalists eventually were pressured into a cease-fire, but only after gaining some nominal recognition of the Serbian Republic *(Republika Srpska)* that they founded within Bosnia-Herzegovina. Since then, Bosnian Serb leaders have resisted attempts by the international community to rebuild a single government for Bosnia-Herzegovina, and have instead begun making preparations for having the Serbian Republic annexed to the Republic of Serbia (Serbia Proper), one of the last two remaining republics of Yugoslavia.

Northern Albania was initially occupied in modern times by Montenegrin troops in 1877. However, the Montenegrins were forced to withdraw from the region as stipulated by the Treaty of Berlin in 1878. Montenegrin troops occupied Northern Albania again in 1913 but were forced to withdraw when the Great Powers decided to create an Albanian state. Montengrin troops occupied Skadar in 1915 (Banac 1984, 282), but early Austrian victories in the Balkans forced them to withdraw. At the end of the First World War, Serbian troops occupied the region (Banac 1984, 297–98) and advanced a claim to it at the Paris Peace Conference. However, the Allies decided to recognize the 1913 boundaries of Albania and, therefore, demanded that Serbian troops withdraw from the region (Temperley 1921, 4: 345). After the early 1920s, no serious efforts have been made by the Serbian government to gain control of northern Albania. In the nineteenth and early twentieth centuries, northern Albania was in the core of Serbian sense of territory. However, because Serbs have shown little interest in the region since the early 1920s, northern Albania has lost much of its importance. Its historical significance and the prior efforts of Serbs to gain control of it, however, suggest that it belongs within the semi-core of Serbian sense of territory.

The first attempt to annex the Central Banat was made at the Paris Peace Conference in 1919. In a memorandum submitted on behalf of the Kingdom of Serbia, Croatia, and Slovenia, a boundary line was requested that would run from the Drava River eastward just south of the cities of Pécs and Szeged to a point just south of Arad. The city of Subotica (Szabadka; Maria Theresiopol) would be the kingdom's northernmost city in the Pannonian Plain. From a point south of Arad, a boundary line was requested that would run south to the Danube and include the town of Temišvar (Temesvár; Timişoara). In fact, the Serbian army was occupying Temišvar while the Allies were making their decisions. The Allies approved of the boundary request with Hungary though it excluded many Hungarians from Hungary. However, the Allies modified the proposed boundary with Romania by excluding the city of Temišvar and its hinterland on the grounds that the population of the city was less than 5 percent Serbian (Temperley 1921, 4: 211).

The first boundary disputes with Bulgaria came shortly after the first modern independent Bulgarian state was created in 1878. The ruling Obrenović family of Serbia found that one of their estates lay east of the Timok River in the new Bulgarian state. Difficulties continued until the Bulgarian guard drove Serbian soldiers out of the area in June 1884 (Petrovich 1976, 2: 429–30). Serbian leaders had difficulties accepting a Bulgarian state. The rise of an independent Bulgarian state challenged the view of many Serbs that they were the "Piedmont" of the Balkans, the ones to unify all Balkan Slavs. When Bulgaria declared a union with Eastern Rumelia on September 18, 1885, Prince Milan of Serbia felt threatened. He thought that Bulgaria would annex Macedonia next (Petrovich 1976, 2: 430–33). Within a few months, he declared war on Bulgaria. The war was disastrous for Serbia. Serbs fought with little enthusiasm because they could not understand why they were fighting their brethren. Besides failing to gain any territory or to restore Serbia's position as the "Piedmont" of the Balkans, the war set the Serbs and Bulgarians on two divergent paths.

After the First World War, representatives of the Kingdom of Serbs, Croats, and Slovenes called for the annexation of four small territories along the Bulgarian border: along the northern section, the city of Vidin and its hinterland, Tsaribrod (now Dimitrovgrad) and its hinterland along with Dragoman Pass, an area twelve miles east of the city of Vranje, and the city of Strumica and its hinterland in the south along the Greek border (Temperley 1921, 4: 208). The Allies rejected the claim to Vidin but conceded a strip of land on the east side of the Timok River two kilometers wide and ten kilometers in length. Tsaribrod was granted, but Dragoman Pass just to the east of it was denied. The two southern claims were granted in full (Temperley 1921, 4: 455–56).

The Periphery: Site Identification, Landscape Description, and Tenacity Factor

Western and southern Bulgaria, northern Greece, central and southern Albania, Croatia-Slavonia, and the Pannonian Plain fall within the periphery of Serbian sense of territory. Serbian national identity is only marginally derived from the periphery. Yet the periphery, with its considerable size, delineates a broad geographical range that is important to the Serbian nation. Although each of the individual places within the periphery is relatively unimportant, taken as a whole the periphery illustrates the greatness of the Serbian nation. In addition, the periphery reinforces claims to core and semi-core territories by demonstrating that Serbs have the legitimate right to claim territories beyond the core and semi-core if they desire.

One of the places of significance in the periphery is the site of the Battle of Marica (or Cernomen), which took place just outside Adrianople (now Edirne, Turkey) in 1371. King Vukašin, who had a state in the area, was one of the leading figures of the Balkan forces who engaged the Ottomans. The Balkan forces were defeated, and many leaders were killed, including Vukašin. This particular battle has remained in Serbian national consciousness and with it the place of the battle. Subsequently, many references have also been made to the Marica River in light of the battle that was fought along its banks (Holton and Mihailovich 1988, 74), connecting the Serbian nation with the Marica River as well. However, while it can be argued from a political-strategic point of view that the Battle of Marica signaled the end of Serbian independence and prestige in the Balkan peninsula and the beginning of centuries of Ottoman Turk domination, the battle actually never became that significant in Serbian national consciousness; today it has only peripheral meaning.

The combination of Dušan's Empire and the Patriarchate of Peć are two territorial configurations that contribute to a large periphery and thereby show the greatness of the Serbian nation. Dušan's Empire extended far to the southeast and included such important medieval cities as Durrës, Berat, Vlorë, Janina (Ioánnina) and Seres (Sérrai); during the First Balkan War (1912) the Serbian government tried to claim Durrës but was denied by the Great Powers. Dušan's Empire also included the religious center of Mount Athos with Hilander Monastery (Peić 1994, 175–84), founded

Figure 6.16 Periphery.

by Stephen Nemanja.[25] While Dušan's Empire stretched far to the southeast, the Patriarchate of Peć extended far to the northwest. Orthodox
churches were founded in Kostajnica, Marča, Medak, Orahovica, Pečuj,
Segedin, Budapest, and Szentendre. In addition, one of the earliest teacher
training colleges for Serbs was founded in Szentendre in 1812, and the
first Serbian literary society, *Srpska Matica*, was founded in Budapest in
1826 (Hanák 1988, 111). The Patriarchate of Peć also extended to the east,
to Samokov and the area around it. In addition to the territories of Dušan's

Empire and the Patriarchate of Peć, the Marica River and the battle against Ottoman forces that took place along it attained some significance as well; many passing references to both the river and the battle site exist in Serbian epic history. Nonetheless, while the periphery is significant because it illustrates the greatness of the Serbian nation, few Serbs have developed strong emotional bonds with the periphery. Consequently, little effort has been made to obtain it.

The periphery is also important to the Serbian nation's sense of territory in another context. It helps to create a close link between a Serbian identity and a broader South Slavic, or Yugoslav, identity. All of the significant places to Serbian identity in the periphery are within territories that are significant to other national groups; the most noteworthy of these are the Croatians, Bosnians, Macedonians, and Bulgarians; however, the Hungarians, Romanians, Albanians, and Greeks are worth mentioning as well. The intermingling of Serbs with the other South Slavic peoples in combination with places that are significant to many different groups led to the rise of a few different pan-South Slavic identities.

The Greater Serbian idea has great appeal among Serbs. Many Romantic Serbian nationalists, conscious of the broad geographical distribution of significant Serbian places, particularly Dušan's Empire, developed the belief that all South Slavs were essentially Serbs. They also believed that the Serbian core was the "Piedmont" of the Balkans and that it was the responsibility of the Serbs to unite all South Slavs into a greater Serbian state. Later in the nineteenth century, a second pan-South Slavic idea emerged, the Yugoslav idea. Those advocating a Yugoslav idea believed that a common identity should emerge out of all the South Slavic groups, with no particular group's characteristics dominating. Note that many Serbs did not see a difference between Greater Serbian ideas and Yugoslav ideas. Many Serbs interpreted the willingness of other South Slavs to develop a common identity as a desire of other South Slavs to become Serbs and to be incorporated into a Serbian state.

The emergence of both a Greater Serbian identity and a Yugoslav identity reflected a broader level of the Serbian nation's sense of territory. While most Serbs are not willing to fight tenaciously for control of the periphery, the political status of the periphery is, nevertheless, important to many Serbs; a positive political orientation of the periphery toward Serbia is highly desired. The dissolution of Yugoslavia in the 1990s has been a challenge if not a threat to Serbian national identity from the perspective of sense of territory. The desire of non-Serbs to be independent of Serbs and a Serbian state runs contrary to the Serbian belief that Serbia is the natural "Piedmont" of the Balkans. Much in the same way that many Serbs reacted violently to the rise of a Bulgarian state in the late nineteenth century, many Serbs have reacted violently to the independence movements of Slavs within the Yugoslav state in the 1990s. In both cases, the questioning of the Serbian nation's sense of territory is likewise the questioning of Serbian national identity. While many Serbs will eventually relinquish control of the periphery, many will not be willing to do the same with the core or semi-core.

Notes

1. For example, only a few years ago, the language of the Serbs was considered to be Serbo-Croatian, not Serbian. Serbo-Croatian, of course, was shared by the Croats. The Serbo-Croatian language concept and construct were based on the *belief* that Serbs and Croats were both part of a larger Yugoslav nation. Of course, the Yugoslav nation did not come to fruition even though many individuals subscribed to such an identity. However, that Serbian nationalists abandoned the Serbo-Croatian language concept just a few years ago demonstrates that human identities are very dynamic and ever-changing.

2. The term *Illyrian* in this instance refers to the peoples who inhabited the Balkans prior to the arrival of the South Slavs. It also includes the descendants of those people who still reside in the Balkans, many of whom intermarried with the South Slavs. For a long time, the term *Illyrian* was mistakenly used as a synonym for South Slav. Indeed, many South Slavs thought that they were Illyrians. That Illyrian and South Slavic identities were mistakenly confused with one another illustrates that peoples merged and regrouped, and not in wholes, making the histories of these peoples inseparable even though modern academics will give the impression that the peoples were separate by writing separate histories for them. If Illyrians and South Slavs were unclear about their differences, one can only imagine just how indistinguishable the various forms of South Slavic culture were to people through history. People certainly grouped themselves, but not in the same way as today. It would be absurd to rewrite history by projecting today's definition of Serbian and Croatian nationhood, etc., into the past and forcing every event into the modern matrix.

3. Plural form of *Pravoslav* ("True or Right Believer").

4. During much of the nineteenth century, the beginning of the modern era of nationalism, Serbs in Dalmatia were clearly part of the effort to maintain Dalmatia's territorial integrity within the Hapsburg Empire; along with the other inhabitants of Dalmatia, they even spoke of the Dalmatian nation (Gross 1993). We should be careful how we apply the term *Serb*. The Serbs of Dalmatia were ethnic Serbs, but their national identity was Dalmatian. We should not assume that all ethnic Serbs belong to the Serbian nation, even if many of the ethnic Serbs of Dalmatia have since joined the Serbian nation.

5. The term *Illyrian* eventually was replaced by the term *Yugoslav* (meaning "South Slav"). The term *Yugoslav* is more accurate because the people being referred to are not Illyrians but South Slavs. Intellectuals mistakenly thought that the modern inhabitants of the Balkans were descendants of the Illyrians. Later research demonstrated that the South Slavs were a different people who moved into the Balkans after the Illyrians.

6. The Macedonian language came into being from the mid-1940s to the mid-1950s, after Tito recognized Macedonia as a separate substate unit within Yugoslavia. Previously, Serbian nationalists and the Serbian government had treated Macedonia as South Serbia and the Slavic dialects spoken there as South Serbian dialects (Poulton 1994, 47). Because Macedonia achieved political independence in the 1990s, the Macedonian language is even more on the pathway of being a separate and distinct language.

7. Significantly, Serbian nationalists targeted and destroyed the main library in Sarajevo soon after the war in Bosnia-Herzegovina broke out in 1992. This action was significant because the library contained a lot of material that demonstrated the cultural uniqueness of the Bosnian people, including documents illustrating the linguistic uniqueness of the territory.

8. For example, debate once existed as to whether the *kajkavian* dialect was part of Slovenian or the Serbo-Croatian complex (Katčić 1984, 264; Greenberg 1996, 399). As another example, the *torlak* dialect of Serbian (found in southeast Serbia) is very closely related to western dialects of Bulgarian and northern dialects of Macedonian, to the extent that the souththeastern dialect of Serbian, the western dialect of Bulgarian, and the northern dialects of Macedonian share more in common with one another than they do with the other dialects of their so-called parent languages (Alexander 1976, 310; Naylor 1976). In fact, the *torlak* dialect of Serbian is often considered by some linguists to be Bulgarian and by others to be Macedonian (Greenberg 1996, 399). More commonly known is the dispute over the South Slavic dialects of Macedonia. Some linguists classified the dialects as Serbian, others as Bulgarian. They were eventually recognized as Macedonian after the Second World War, but not by everyone. Language is in constant transition across the Balkans, especially throughout the Slavic complex. The state boundaries are poor linguistic boundaries but unfortunately give the impression that a clear distinction exists between the languages, especially Slovenian, Croatian, Serbian, Bulgarian, and Macedonian. Most sharp differences that exist today between these language are the result of nationalists and state governments, which first imagined the differences and then worked to make them real. The Balkans demonstrate as much as any other region of the world that nations create languages more than languages create nations. Indeed, language classification often depends on the national identity of the linguist.

9. Even after two centuries of much contrived work by nationalists and governments, a one-to-one relationship between language and nationhood still does not exist between Serbs, Croats, and Muslims within the former Yugoslavia. Robert D. Greenberg's recent article on this issue excellently demonstrates the lack of correspondence (1996).

10. *Prečani* means "men from across," that is across the Sava-Danube Rivers. The term is not implicitly derisive, but it illustrates that the Serbs of Belgrade and Moravia considered these Serbs to be so different that they refused to refer to them by the same name.

11. *Nemačkari* derived from the word *nemči*, meaning Germans, but it was very derisive. Because the Serbs from Belgrade and the Morava Valley had lived in the Ottoman Empire for centuries, they had adopted many cultural practices and characteristics of the Ottomans. Indeed, Serbian leaders in the nineteenth century usually wore Turkish clothing (Judah 1997, 69). Thus they found little cultural

affinity with Serbs of the Vojvodina and Srem, who having lived in the Hapsburg Empire had adopted many Germanic traits which the Serbs of Belgrade and the Morava Valley disliked.

12. A *nahie* is a subdivision of a Paşalik.

13. Many of the folk epics of prior times came from *hajduks, uskoks,* and *guslars* (Holton and Mihailovich 1988, 41, 79–85, 114). Significantly, they were mostly from Bosnia-Herzegovina and sometimes from Dalmatia. Depending on one's view, *hajduks* and *uskoks* were bandits or freedom fighters. In any case, they mostly harassed the Ottomans. *Guslars* were storytellers who sang and told glorious stories of great eras of the past. Most of them were illiterate and passed on their tradition orally. Of course the historical accuracy of these stories was highly questionable. However, during the eighteenth and nineteenth centuries, folk epics were the only sources of information about the past for the peoples of southeastern Europe. Consequently, and in true Romantic fashion, as Karadžić recorded folk epics, he also wrote the history of the Serbs. The choice to use the stories of *hajduks* and *uskoks* to write Serbian history made Serbian history characteristically anti-Turkish even though most Serbs preferred Ottoman rule.

14. Serbian Romantic nationalists routinely refer to Dušan's Empire as a Serbian state though it predated nationalism and was inhabited by many different ethnic groups in addition to Serbs. Indeed, Dušan referred to himself as "Emperor and Autocrat of the Serbs and Greeks, the Bulgarians and Albanians" (Clissold 1966, 98).

15. Tvrtko had indeed had himself crowned "king of the Serbs, and of Bosnia, and of the Coast" and later he added "king of Dalmatia and Croatia" (Clissold 1966, 61–63). Tvrtko had also fought at the Battle of Kosovo in 1389. These events, however, predated nationalism. However, as Serbian Romantic nationalists have rewritten history in a nationalist context, Tvrtko, and by extension his territories, has been recategorized as "Serbian."

16. Initially, in 1918, the state was called "The Kingdom of the Serbs, Croats, and Slovenes." It first contained the term *Yugoslavia* in its title when it was renamed "The Kingdom of Yugoslavia" in 1929.

17. For example, Zagreb and Dubrovnik, which are clearly not Serbian cities, were persistently attacked at one point. The only purpose of such attacks would have been to destroy Croatian independence, eventually forcing most, if not all, of Croatia back into the Serbian fold. Serbian paramilitary units also attacked many non-Serb areas within Bosnia-Herzegovina. The only possible outcome of such attacks would have been to prevent Bosnian independence, eventually forcing it back into the Serbian realm.

18. Serbian Romantic nationalists have constructed a "continuous" history for the Serbian nation that traces itself back to the Rascian state. While it is true that Raška occupies the same location as modern Serbia and that modern Serbs are the genetic descendants of these earlier South Slavs, it is important to remember that nationhood is a social and cultural construct and not genetically or biologically defined. Quite simply, the people of that early state did not subscribe to Serbian nationhood as it is understood today, and they did not even conceive of it. Indeed, these people even called themselves Rascians, not Serbs (Judah 1997, 8).

19. Interestingly, Serbian nationalists write a history for their people that implies that the Serbian nation was great under Dušan but was destroyed when the Serbs,

out of a sense of duty to the Christian West, sacrificed themselves and their empire against the onslaught of the Ottoman infidel. In reality, Dušan Empire had disintegrated after his death in 1355, thirty-four years before the Battle of Kosovo. In the period before nationalism, empires like those of Dušan owed their existence to their charismatic leaders. Thus when such leaders died, their empires often disintegrated as the subjects saw no cause to stay together. Dušan's Empire was no exception. Dušan's subjects were not one people, even though modern historians imply that it was by labeling his empire a Serbian state. Thus Dušan's Empire collapsed after Dušan's death when the varying peoples within it fought against one another, including the "Serbs," who did not see themselves as one people.

20. Noel Malcolm recently published a book, *Kosovo: A Short History* (1998), which describes how Serbian nationalist writers transformed the history of Kosovo into Serbian nationalist history.

21. Noteworthy, however, the South Slavs of Raška originally called themselves *Rascians* (Judah 1997, 8). Modern nationhood had not developed yet. Nevertheless, in true Romantic fashion the Rascians are referred to as Serbs because they inhabited the same territory as the modern Serbian nation and shared its genetics. This association is made even though we now know that nationhood is a cultural construct, not a genetic one.

22. The Banat, the portion of the Vojvodina east of the Tisza River, came under direct German administration. Baranya and Bačka, the western portions of the Vojvodina, were annexed by Hungary.

23. Albanians' discontent with Serbian nationalist policies in Kosovo began an independence movement in 1998. At the time of this writing, the Serbian army had just endured 78 days of NATO bombings while it gave no quarter in smashing the movement and systematically "cleansed" Kosovo of ethnic Albanians. Much to the disappointment of members of the Serbian army and other elements of Serbian society, Slobodan Milošević agreed to a withdrawal of Serbian troops from Kosovo but only after obtaining international recognition that Kosovo is still legally part of Yugoslavia and even Serbia—minus a yet-uncounted number of ethnic Albanians!

24. Just as the Serbian national identity was tied to Macedonia, so was Bulgarian and Greek nationhoods. In fact, the national identities of these three groups continue to be called into question and even threatened whenever they are forced into the realization that other groups use the same place to define their identities. Greek national identity seems particularly threatened by a Macedonian national identity. As a result, the Greek government has vehemently denied and even prevented the Macedonians from naming their country Macedonia.

25. Stephen Nemanja lived at Hilander Monastery with his son, St. Sava, after he abdicated the throne in 1196 (Fine 1987, 38).

7

Conclusion

Human identity is intimately bound up in "place" and "territory." Canadian, American, Swiss, Macedonian, Bosnian, and a long list of other place-based names are very meaningful forms of human identity. Even French, German, Japanese, etc., are forms of identity with a salient place component in addition to referring to languages. Indeed, when we speak of the French, for example, we do not mean all the French speakers of the world but rather the people who are from the territory of France, including a number of people who are not French speakers. The same is true when we speak of the Germans, Japanese, etc.

Unfortunately, the close relationship that we as human beings have with the places and territories that we inhabit is generally not recognized. When it is, it is not incorporated into any study or policy in any meaningful way. This lack of appreciation for place and territory stems in large part from the geographical ignorance in society. Consequently, place and territory, and the maps that depict them, are seen as static backdrops, separate from the human experience. When considered, they are treated as nothing more than commodities to be bartered and traded. Little recognition is given to geographical processes such as spatial interaction, diffusion, or any form of spatial relationships. We, however, as human beings, live in places and territories, shape and alter them, and come to think of ourselves in terms of the places and territories we inhabit. These interactions occur with both the physical and cultural environments. The physical environment provides many of the resources for material culture; however, this relationship is not a determinist one, for the physical environment is also altered by humans according to certain cultural values. In many ways, the physical environment becomes tied to human identity from the perspective that individuals and groups simply become accustomed to certain seasonal rhythms, climates, geomorphologies, and vegetation.

The cultural environment, however, is just as important to our senses of identity as the physical environment, if not more so. We as individu-

249

als are born into certain culturally constructed places that are made up of discrete street patterns, buildings of certain architectural styles, and monuments that continually inform and remind us of our history and ideology. These places become ingrained in our minds, shaping our thoughts and actions. Indeed, history and politics, even language and religion, are tied to place and territory because events do not unfold in a spatial vacuum. History is not only of people but of people in places; the two are inseparable. Politics is tied to place too. No less than the others, self-governance requires territory. For although laws inevitably influence and affect the behavior of people, they apply to the people of particularly defined territories. Currently, all laws are tied to specifically defined territories, and because they shape the course of events and the way people think about themselves, territory—with its legal and historical attributes—has become inextricably intertwined with human identity. Laws, in turn, determine what languages can be spoken and what religions can be practiced in each given territory. Thus language and religion are tied to territory as well. Indeed, the languages that we speak and the religions that we practice depend to a large degree on the places that we are from.

Because our identities are so closely tied to place and territory, we are very territorial. Territoriality is a protectiveness of place that we exhibit. It is more emotional than rational, and it can lead to violent conflict. Despite the general geographical ignorance in society, we as individuals are consciously aware of one another's places and spaces in society and are careful not to violate anybody's "space." Territoriality is one realm where the significance of place and territory is easily recognized even though the meaning and significance of it are not understood.

The inseparable bond that we have with places and territories is complicated by the multiple layers of identity humans have. We are husbands, wives, brothers, sisters, bosses, employees, neighbors, friends, etc. Many of these forms of identity are not highly spatially defined; however, it is not unusual for a boss, a neighbor, or even a brother to exert control over certain places and spaces. Other forms of identity are more explicitly spatially defined, and they exist at multiple levels. They range from that of the individual to those of neighborhood, community, region, nation, and even international levels. Unfortunately, the interplay of the many forms of identity that we have often makes it difficult to decipher which form of identity is expressing itself. To understand issues, we must know which form of identity is asserting itself, but also know and understand the source of any given form of identity. Some forms of identity derive more from place and territory than others, and thus express higher degrees of spatiality. Ethnicity, for example, has a lower degree of spatiality than nationalism, and thus ethnic groups are less territorial than nations. In fact, the degree of spatiality distinguishes ethnicity from nationalism.

Unfortunately, many researchers do not consider spatiality at all when examining ethnic groups and nations. Consequently, they confuse ethnicity and nationalism, misidentifying many ethnic groups as nations and vice versa. Sadder still, in their inability to differentiate between ethnic groups and nations, they conclude that nations do not require sovereignty over territory, and also do not recognize that nations struggle for it when they do not have it.

Because levels of human identity have their corresponding territorialities, they must be reconciled with one another. Crisis may ensue, for example, if one's national identity impinges on one's sense of individuality or community. More significant for this study, however, is that territoriality at the broader levels of human identity can be very abstract. We as individuals, although also members of a nation, are unlikely to be as intimately familiar with the national territory as we are with our own individual places. For the most part, the national territory is an image in the mind, created and informed through maps, pictures, the media, and other images. This abstractness at the broader levels of human identity allow these forms of identity to be manipulated. Governments and charismatic individuals, for example, have the ability to intervene in these shared group identities and shape them in particular ways, with specific senses of territorialities. Often the reshaping of such broad levels of identity is not so contrived. It may come about through technological innovations or simply evolving social processes themselves. Modern nationalism and its corollary the nation, only about two hundred years old, came about through a combination of all the forces just identified. Despite its youth, nationalism is currently one of our more salient forms of human identity. Indeed, we now live in the nation-state era, meaning that our national identities have primacy. The nation-state is the ultimate source of political power with no higher level having binding authority. Local and regional laws and actions exist with the consent of national laws and may not contradict them. Thus, some individuals and regional groups act with high degrees of freedom, but only with the consent and tolerance of the nation.

Nationalism is a very pervasive and intolerant force, but it did not wholly supplant the ideologies that came before it. On the contrary, nationalism is in many ways a product of what came before it. Nationalism is simultaneously something very new and yet frequently a reformulation of many older ideas with altered meanings and understandings. Because dynastic-imperialism was the immediate predecessor of nationalism, many elements of this ideology and social system are embedded within nationalism. Significantly, many nations' territorialities are in fact previously existing imperial territorialities reformulated in a nationalist framework. Unfortunately, when ethnic and national conflict is examined, only the current political pattern of states is considered. Prior political geographies, however, are very significant and often underlie conflict. As Alexander B. Murphy points out:

> What lies behind the [current] framework of political territories or formal ethnic regions are spatial constructs with deep ideological significance that may or may not correspond to political or formal constructs. These ideologies are forged in the territorial struggles that produce particular regional arrangements and understandings, and these in turn shape ideas, practices, activities and routines. (1991, 21)

Therefore, to truly understand ethnic and national conflict, one must understand the previously existing spatial framework in which nationalism has cast itself.

Nationalism, of course, has its variations. Initially, when it emerged in Western Europe, it was a product of the Enlightenment, which emphasized rational thought and civic duty to the state. Later, when nationalism emerged in Central and Eastern Europe, it was a product of the Romantic period, which stressed shared language, common religion, and historical continuity. Although the nation as a form of human identity has a territorial component, the nature of any given nation's territoriality depends on when and where the nation developed. In Western Europe, for example, nations defined themselves in terms of the then-existing dynastic-imperial states with their emphasis on loyalty to the state and its territory. To a large degree, nationalism and patriotism were conflated. On the other hand, the evolution of nationalism in Central and Eastern Europe was much more complicated. Those who initially developed national consciousness did not have imperial states that could be redefined as nation-states. On the contrary, they found themselves within dynastic-imperial states of other groups, who themselves were developing national consciousness and were simultaneously viewing their newly defined national minorities with increasing hostility. Thanks to the emphasis that Romanticism placed on language, religion, and history, the emerging nations of Central and Eastern Europe that did not have existing dynastic-imperial territories to redefine as national territories were able to reach back into the past, to some "Golden Age," and resurrect some defunct empire to define the modern national territory. These resurrected empires then gave modern nations not only a defined territory to conquer on behalf of the nation but also the ability to identify the true members of the nation.

Once Romantic nationalists gained control over their resurrected dynastic-imperial territories, they enacted laws to force the inhabitants of these territories to conform to the "national standards," which themselves were defined according to Romantic conceptions of identity, namely that nations are defined by shared language and religion. Histories were rewritten to conform to modern nationalist understandings, with a particular emphasis placed on the autochthonous relationship that the nation had with its territory. That modern nations did not exist prior to the end of the eighteenth century did not daunt Romantic nationalists who countered with the argument that nations needed to be "awakened," or "reawakened" as the case may have been. Many individuals, unaware of who they were, had to be told who they were. Such is the arrogance of Romantic nationalism. Like unskilled or unethical psychologists who plant false memories of childhood experiences into the minds of their patients, Romantic nationalists worked feverishly to implant invented national histories in the minds of individuals, targeted by the territories in which they lived. To legitimize these fabricated national histories, Romantic nationalists used place and territory. By actually pointing to places of historical events and erecting monuments upon them, Romantic nationalists were able to use the tangible qualities of place and territory to convince members of the nation, and indeed themselves, that such historical events were in fact histories of the nation. The places were real; therefore, the events and all their fabricated nuances must have been real too. Because these events occurred in places and territories of the modern inhabitants, historical events that played out in the same places and territories were taken as the histories of the current inhabitants. Such is the character of the bond between people and place.

The processes just delineated were described in detail in earlier chapters for three nations in southeastern Europe: the Hungarian, Romanian, and Serbian nations. The Hungarian nation is one of the few in Central and Eastern Europe which had its own imperial state on the eve of modern nationalism. Thus as Hungarian nationhood developed, it syncretized with the existing imperial territory, reformulating the imperial territory as a national one. At the time, most Hungarians did not conform to the Romantic belief that nationhood is derived from a unique language; most Hungarians did not speak Hungarian. With the rise of nationalism, however, most Hungarians shifted over to speaking Hungarian and subsequently expected all of those within the kingdom's territory to speak Hungarian as well. Hungarian leaders even crafted Magyarization policies to facilitate, even force, the language shift. Although many of the kingdom's inhabitants adopted Hungarian identity, regardless of their ethnicity,[1] many did not, instead adopting other forms of nationhood that were emerging at the time; some of these were Slovak, Romanian, Croatian, and Serbian nationhoods. The number of the kingdom's inhabitants who adopted other national identities was large. Consequently, as Hungarian nationalists tried to Magyarize the kingdom's population, intense conflict with other nationalists ensued. In the end, that is after the

First World War, Hungarian nationalists were unable to assimilate the large numbers of those who refused to adopt Hungarian nationhood before these peoples successfully seceded from the kingdom, of course taking with them many of the kingdom's territories. The loss of territory was a violation of the Hungarian nation's sense of identity. Despite many failed attempts on the part of the Hungarian nation to regain control over its self-defined national territory, the Hungarian nation still defines itself in terms of the kingdom's territory and many places within it.

Romanian national identity is more complicated than the Hungarian one because, as it emerged on the eve of nationalism at the beginning of the nineteenth century, it did not have a single unified political state onto which it could graft itself. It had three separate and distinct political units that were meaningful: Walachia, Moldavia, and Transylvania. Having three Romanian territories, however, did not conform to the nation-state ideal, which insisted that every nation have a single state territory. Moreover, the Hungarian nation was firmly in control of Transylvania at the time and would not relinquish control of it because significant aspects of its national identity were derived from it. Furthermore, Romantic philosophy sided with the Hungarian nation until Romanian nationalists could demonstrate (that is rewrite history to show) that the Romanian nation predated the Hungarian kingdom's annexation of Transylvania. Thus Romanian nationalists were forced not only to find a historical state to legitimize a modern Romanian nation-state which included Transylvania, but also to find a historical state that predated the Hungarian kingdom's annexation of Transylvania. In their quest, Romanian nationalists found the Dacian and the Daco-Roman states of two thousand years ago. These states, which more or less had the same spatial dimensions, were particularly attractive because they allowed the new Romanian nation of the nineteenth and twentieth centuries to use the earlier accomplishments of the Dacians and Romans to claim greatness for itself. More important, the Dacian and Daco-Roman states defined a national territory over which the Romanian nation could begin a struggle to control. Once, the goal was accomplished by the end of the First World War, the Romanian government was able to implement policies to force individuals to conform to Romantic definitions of Romanian nationhood. Most notably, the Romanian government crafted language policies to force individuals within the new Romanian state territory to speak Romanian. Other policies were designed to expel those who would not adopt Romanian nationhood. After the Second World War, the Romanian nation lost control of some of its self-defined national territory and has thus far been unable to regain it. Nevertheless, the Romanian nation still derives its identity from its perceived territory and the individual places within it.

Serbian national identity is the most complicated of the three nations examined in this book. When Serbian nationhood emerged at the beginning of the nineteenth century, it had no existing state onto which it could graft itself. Lacking any state, the Serbian nation defined itself in terms of an Ottoman administrative unit, the Paşalik of Belgrade. In its early stages, the Serbian nation also expanded its sovereignty within the framework of Ottoman territorial understandings. Because anti-Ottoman sentiments were a catalyst for Serbian nationalism, the Serbian nation's initial territorial definition of itself in terms of Ottoman territorial conceptions was a contradiction. However, once the Serbian nation moved from its initial stages of development, Serbian nationalists searched for a previously existing state that could define the territorial component of Serbian national identity. This process too was very problematic because many medieval states existed within the Balkans (see Figure 6.2). Because these states were personal dynasties, their boundaries fluctuated greatly with each passing ruler. Serbian nationalists, however, were able to focus on one leader whose territory could be used to frame the Serbian nation. Stephen Dušan had created one of the greatest empires in the Balkans, meaning that the Serbian nation could derive great national pride by attaching its identity to Dušan's state territory. At the same time, Dušan's state and the preceding and succeeding dynasties were politically and spatially intertwined with other states of the region, especially to the northwest, namely with those of Trvtko and Tomislav. Moreover, in the intervening time, many specific places of significance had also emerged to the northwest. Thus the territorial component of Serbian national identity was framed not only by Dušan's state but by a spatial fusion of Dušan's state with other medieval states. Because these other medieval states form the basis of other Balkan identities (e.g., Croatian, Bosnian, Yugoslav, etc.), Serbian nationhood is joined to and even confused with these other forms of identity and their territorialities. Consequently, many Serbian nationalists do not, for example, recognize a Bosnian national identity, and they cannot see the difference between a Yugoslav identity and a Greater Serbian national identity. Despite any inherent difficulties, the Serbian nation remains firmly bound to the amalgam of Dušan's Empire and other medieval empires. Subsequently, the Serbian government and nationalists have struggled over the last two centuries to gain control over these territories and integrate them into a single Serbian nation-state. As they have done so, they have also forced the inhabitants within these territories to conform to Romantic notions of Serbian nationhood, namely that all inhabitants of Serbia should speak Serbian (Serbo-Croatian, if you please) and adhere to the Eastern Orthodox faith. The Serbian nation's response to the secession movements of a number of the Yugoslav Republics in the early 1990s shows how closely Serbian nationhood is attached to particular territories and the places within them. To thwart the attempts of secession and prove the Serbian nation's right to possess these territories, Serbian nationalists began an "ethnic cleansing" campaign. This campaign not only involved the expulsion of non-Serbs from territories perceived to be Serbian, it included acts of forced assimilation. Thus Serbian nationalists were using territory to define Serbs and not vice versa.

Contrary to the Romantic belief that the number of nations which exist was fixed at the beginning of time and is unchanging, new nations are continually forming. As they do, they too cast themselves in terms of previously existing dynastic-imperial territories. Two of these newer nations in southeastern Europe are Bosnia and Macedonia. These nations have exhibited the characteristics of nationhood only in the last few decades. Unfortunately, many imbued with Romantic ideals refuse to recognize them because they obviously did not exist since the beginning of time. These new nations, however, qualify for nationhood according to the commonly accepted definitions of the concept, demonstrated in Symmons-Symonolewicz's definition of nation:

> a territorially-based community of human beings sharing a distinct variant of modern culture, bound together by a strong sentiment of unity and solidarity, marked by a clear historically-rooted consciousness of national identity, and possessing, or striving to possess, a genuine political self-government. (1985, 221)

Nothing in this definition or other definitions of nation precludes a nation from being multiethnic. Therefore, the many ethnic Serbs, Croats, and Muslims who held together in the recent war and fought for the independence of the Bosnian state demonstrate the existence of Bosnian nationhood. Similarly, the many ethnic Albanians, Vlachs, Greeks, Bulgarians, etc., who have held together and have continued to struggle for an independent Macedonian state demonstrate the existence of a Macedonian nation. Those who argue that Bosnia and Macedonia are just "geographic regions" do not know what geography is,[2] do not recognize the difference between ethnicity and nationhood, and do not understand how ethnic groups evolve into nations as ethnicity fuses with territory. Indeed, territorial understandings have been instrumental in the emergence and evolution of both the Bosnian and Macedonian nations. In addition, both of these nations derive their being more from territory than from any other cultural characteristic.

The territorial components of the Bosnian and Macedonian nations are not simple ones because they derive from layered territorial understandings. On the surface, both nations frame themselves in terms of modern politically organized territories, in these cases within the territories of the republics of the former Yugoslavia. This sense of nationhood is not surprising because these territories represented particular fields of spatial interaction that framed the thinking and behavior of individuals and social groups within the broader region. In addition to the daily reality of this territorial organization, both of these nations also derive aspects of their identities from deeper, more sublime, understandings of territory. In essence, the Bosnian nation derives much of its identity from the medieval kingdom of Tvrtko, and the Macedonian nation derives significant aspects of its identity from classical Macedonia. The importance of these previously existing territories is seen in the Bosnian flag, the coat of arms of King Tvrtko, and the Macedonian flag, that of the classical state.[3] These flags also show that the Bosnian and Macedonian nations have a "clear historically rooted consciousness of national identity." Moreover, these flags, and the overall characters of Bosnian and Macedonian national identities, demonstrate once again, and with consistency, the territorial component of nationhood.

Territory is important because it frames nations' identities, even making it possible to identify who does and does not belong to any given nation. Sovereignty over territory allows nations to cultivate and protect their cultural characteristics (e.g., language, religion, etc.). This aspect of territory, however, represents only one aspect of the significance of the territory. The concept of *place* embodies another aspect of the territorial component of nationhood. Place refers to the individual locales within broader territories which have significance to the nation. They are commonly locations of historical events or of national institutions. The locations themselves are not insignificant because the continued existence of these locations reaffirms, makes real, and even proves the historical events. Place, with its tangible qualities, even allows national institutions to function by bringing people together in one location. Indeed, institutions, although formed to develop ideas and policies and even regulate behavior, are effective only if they exist in time and place. Any institution that exists only on paper is meaningless to the human experience.

The places significant to nations are numerous, filling nations' territories and giving them full dimension. One of the purposes of this book is to map out the spatial dimensions of places of three nations to elucidate the full context of nationhood, and thus provide a basis for a greater understanding of the conflicts that arise between nations. This was done through "site identification" and "landscape description." Because the significance of places and territories themselves varies, not only in meaning but over time, it was important to measure the willingness of nations to assume the costs of maintaining control over places and territories when threatened, or of establishing control over them when sovereignty was not in effect. This need of nations to have sovereignty over places and territories was called the "tenacity factor." It was measured by the examination of peace treaties entered into and alliances forged by nations in wars with regard to territorial allocations that would ensue in the event of particular outcomes. In this analysis, it became clear that the desire of nations to control particular territories dictated the course of international relations. It also became clear that territories and the places within them had varying degree of significance for the nations examined. Thus territories and the places within them were classified into a core, semi-core, and periphery. The core represented the most fundamental aspects of the nation's identity; a nation would not be what it is today without the core territories. The semi-core supported some aspect of the national identity but by no means all of the national characteristics. While the core had been important throughout time, the semi-core usually had been important only for a limited time. The periphery contained none of the fundamental components of the national identity. It primarily confirmed the importance of the core and semi-core territories and helped to define the nation's role in the world.

The analysis of the core, semi-core, and periphery helps us to gain a broader understanding of a nation's identity. The analysis helps us understand an important element of conflict as well as the potential for future conflict in particular places. A nation will struggle more intensely for a core territory than for a semi-core or peripheral territory. For example, the Serb nation will struggle more intensely for the core territory of Kosovo and the semi-core territory of Bosnia[4] than it will for the peripheral territories of Croatia and Slovenia, though these latter territories are economically and strategically more valuable. The analysis of the core, semi-core, and periphery of a nation's sense of territory also broadens our understanding of national identity when it is compared to spatial distributions of national groups based on conventional notions of language and religion. Notable differences in the importance of places arises when the different methods of analysis are employed. Many places sparsely inhabited by a nation, and therefore seemingly unimportant, fall within the core or semi-core of a place analysis. In such cases, the potential for conflict is very high as nations seek to maintain or extend their control over places that they do not inhabit but, nevertheless, are very important to them. Such is the case with Kosovo for the Serbian nation. Conventional studies, which emphasize that approximately 90 percent of Kosovo's population is ethnic Albanian, suggest that the Serbian nation does not value the territory of Kosovo. The place and territory analysis in this study shows otherwise. The territory of Kosovo, and the numerous places within it, has great significance to the Serbian nation. In fact, the Serbian nation would not be what it is without Kosovo. Therefore, the place and territory analysis indicates that the Serbian nation will fight tenaciously to maintain sovereign control over this territory. Recent events support the validity of this assertion.

The case of Kosovo, not to mention Bosnia-Herzegovina, also debunks other conventional theories. Geographically ignorant studies, the ones that treat place and territory as mere commodities, greatly emphasize the location of resources and the strategic value of territories ("geostrategy") when analyzing conflicts. The beauty of such an emphasis is that even those who are the most ignorant of corresponding and relevant facts cannot go wrong because every territory contains some resource and is situated relative to some other location. In many ways, no one can lose with such arguments. On the other hand, such analyses are quite lacking. For example, in the recent dissolution of the Yugoslav state, an inverse relationship existed between the strategic and economic value of territories and the willingness of the Serbian nation to hold on to particular territories. Slovenia had the highest such value, but the Serbian nation put the least effort into maintaining control over it. Croatia ranked lower than Slovenia, but the Serbian nation put more effort into maintaining control over it. Kosovo and Bosnia-Herzegovina have the least value in terms of resources and geostrategy, yet the Serbian nation has fought tenaciously to maintain control over these territories. Resources and geostrategic concerns are not unimportant. However, such concerns are smaller aspects of larger issues. Unfortunately, many appraisals rely too much on resources and geostrategy and never explain the real, underlying conflict. Subsequently, such assessments are not able to predict the occurrence of many conflicts or their outcomes.

Place and territory have always been important aspects of the human condition, but they express themselves differently with every form of human identity. Since the rise of nationalism about two hundred years ago, place and territory have taken on new meanings. Sense of place and territory projected through the prism of nationalism has resulted in great human loss, which has come about from the combination of two phenomena. First, the ideology of nationalism requires that nations have full sovereignty over their territories. Second, nations are historically developed forms of identity which were cast in multiethnic imperial territories. Thus nations delineate their territories in terms of previously existing imperial territories that are still multiethnic. Because the nation-state ideal implies that nations have the right to control territories only inhabited by their members, most nations are confronted with either the problem of having national territories with nonmembers or the problem of needing control over territories which have nonmembers. The nation-state ideal implies that nations must relinquish control over territories inhabited by nonmembers. However, many of these territories have great significance to nations because they derive crucial aspects of their identities from them.

In many ways, then, the bond that nations develop with particular territories becomes threatened by nonmembers. Instead of relinquishing control over the territories from which they derive their identities, many nations find it more palatable to "ethnically cleanse" their territories. Ethnic cleansing can take on three forms: assimilation, expulsion, or extermination. With any of the forms, or any combination thereof, nations are able to conform to the nation-state ideal, that is one nation–one nationally pure state territory. Since the rise of nationalism, history has witnessed all three forms of ethnic cleansing numerous times.

Ethnic cleansing testifies to the meaning and significance of territory. Indeed, ethnic cleansing refers to the cleansing of territory. Unfortunately, many who analyze conflicts, including many policy makers, do not recognize the simple fact that ethnic cleansing is fundamentally tied to territory. They see only that people of differing religions and ethnicities are fighting with one another and, therefore, fallaciously conclude that people of differing faiths and ethnicities will fight and kill one another simply because they are different. If such were the case, then one has to ask, for example, why all Roman Catholics and Protestants are not fighting with each other all over the world as they are in Northern Ireland. The answer is that the Northern Ireland conflict is not a religious one but a territorial one. It is between those who believe that Northern Ireland should be part of the Irish nation-state and those who want it to remain in the United Kingdom. Initially, Roman Catholics and Protestants were on both sides of the issue. The evolution of the conflict has forced most Catholics onto one side and Protestants onto the other, but the correlation is not perfect and the rhetoric still does not revolve around issues of religion. As a further example, if Jews and Arabs have an innate inability to get along with each other, then why do they not always come into conflict when they encounter one another? Why, for example, did a Jew go all the way from New York to Hebron, Israel, when he felt the need to kill Arabs? Why did he not simply kill Arabs in New York if he hated Arabs? The answer is that he did not simply hate Arabs. He could not accept Arabs worshiping in a *place* that was sacred to Judaism, namely the shrine to Abraham in Hebron, where he killed Arabs. Thus the meaning and significance of territory were at the crux of this issue as well. Not all nationalists employ extermination; some prefer assimilation or expulsion. Ethnic Jews and ethnic Arabs who subscribe to other national identities will not commit such acts against each other because territory is not so fundamental to ethnicity. However, they may commit such acts in the context of the national identities to which they subscribe. Indeed, all humans who subscribe to a national identity narrowly defined in terms of specific cultural characteristics will support some form of ethnic cleansing, even if it is some seemingly innocuous policy related to language practice, or to school curriculum.

The significance of place and territory does not always mandate ethnic cleansing. Ethnic cleansing is the result of the significance of place and territory expressed through the prism of nationalism, especially Romantic nationalism with its heavy emphasis on monolingualism and the single religion of nations. In the absence of ideologies such as nationalism, place and territory can be a binding force for human beings. For example, after the Second World War, the Soviets annexed the northern half of East Prussia and renamed it Kaliningrad oblast. They cleansed the territory of Germans through expulsion and replaced them with Russians and other ethnic groups. They also destroyed all the places within the territory tied to the German nation. Most notably, they destroyed the royal castle in the city of Kaliningrad (formerly Königsberg) and demonstrated their authority over the territory by building a twenty-two-story building on the same site for the Communist headquarters (Vesilind 1997, 115–16). Interestingly, many of the young Russians who grew up in Kaliningrad have taken Prussian history as their own, even laying flowers on Immanuel Kant's grave as other Russians once did on Lenin's tomb (Vesilind 1997, 116). Many members of the German nation have had difficulty coping with the loss of such an important territory to German history and identity. However, the Germans who are actually from East Prussia have bonded with the Russians there on their return. Their shared experience of living in East Prussia, though during different times, has brought them together and fostered peace, not conflict. It remains to be seen if the peace will sustain, but it depends in many ways on German and Russian nationalists outside the territory. If they cannot accept the multiethnicity of the territory, they will force the German and Russians within Kaliningrad oblast to come into conflict with one another. Such was the case when the Nazis interfered with and upset the harmonious relationship that many ethnic Germans had with their neighbors in Eastern Europe prior to the Second World War. Such has also been the case in many places and territories around the world, such as Bosnia-Herzegovina, where nationalists from the outside could not accept the harmonious relationship that existed at local and community levels between differing ethnic groups that shared the same places and territories; it was a harmonious relationship derived from the shared experience of living together in a place.[5]

Whether positive or negative, place and territory are fundamental components of human identity. Indeed, geographers and other researchers complain that the terms nation (a people) and state (a place) are conflated and confused. Japan and France are commonly called nations when in fact they are nation-states. The nations in question are the Japanese and the French. Many geographers view this conflation and confusion of terms as another example of the geographical ignorance in society; however, I take it as an example of the close and inseparable bond that humans, in this case nations, have with places and territories. Other examples also demonstrate this bond. For example, the perceived need to impose a single national language throughout the national territory to preserve integrity also illustrates the power of place and territory in shaping human identity. In a similar vein, our willingness as human beings to commit genocide in order to control the places and territories we hold dear likewise demonstrates the significance of place and territory. Place and territory are such fundamental components of human identity that they can also serve as the basis for creating a common group identity among individuals with different languages and religions. The recent Bosnian conflict illustrates this point as well as the previous one of genocide. Individuals from each of the ethnic groups in Bosnia-Herzegovina have shown a determination to stay in their homes and maintain their communities, even in many ethnically diverse communities; Serbs also serve in the Bosnian government and army. Clearly place and territory are as important as language or religion in shaping group identity. Indeed, sense of place and territory is a fundamental basis of what it is to be human.

Notes

1. In fact, some of the venerated Hungarian nationalists were not ethnically Hungarian. Lajos Kossuth, for example, was ethnically Slovak. Miklós Zrínyi was a Croat. The list is actually quite long; these are just two examples.

2. As a professional geographer, I am frequently perplexed by the use of the term *geography* and its many derivations by nongeographers. By the way the term is typically employed, I can only guess that some authors must think that the term is a wholesale reference to rivers, mountains, peninsulas, and other physiographic features. If this is the case, I cannot think of any better example of the *geographical ignorance* in society.

3. The Macedonian nation, after beginning its drive for independence in 1991, chose a design for its flag that is closely associated with the symbols of Philip of Macedon and his son Alexander the Great. Greek nationalists and the Greek government objected to their use because they consider the symbol, which they call the "Vergina Sun," to be of Greek origin and history. Consequently, the Greek government coerced the Macedonian government into altering the design of its flag. The newer version of the flag, however, has the same basic design of the original.

Greek objections, however, have not been limited to Macedonia's flag but to the very name Macedonia, which Greek nationalists consider to be an integral part of the Greek nation's realm, not an independent national realm of its own. Indeed, Macedonia is a very meaningful and significant territory to Greek nationhood. Philip of Macedon and Alexander the Great were from Macedonia. Without Macedonia the Greek nation would not be what it is today, and to admit that Macedonia is not Greek would require the Greek nation to rewrite its history and reconstruct its identity to exclude many of its greatest accomplishments. Not surprisingly, the Greek nation is unwilling to accept the idea of a separate Macedonian nation and is even affronted by the term itself. In many ways, the Macedonian case explicitly demonstrates the significance of place and territory.

4. At the final writing of this book, NATO just finished 78 days of bombing Serbian forces in Kosovo and other strategic targets in Yugoslavia. The Kosovo situation stands in sharp contrast to the one in Bosnia-Herzegovina a few years ago where a few airstrikes brought Serbian paramilitary forces to a standstill and brought Bosnian Serb leaders to the negotiating table. Clearly, Kosovo has more meaning to the Serbian nation than Bosnia-Herzegovina even though the latter is not insignificant. Despite the fact that it took much more intensive bombing to halt "ethnic cleansing" by the Serbs in Kosovo than in Bosnia-Herzegovina, one might still ask why the Serbs did not more tenaciously hold onto Kosovo. First of all, if estimates are correct that 10 percent of Serbian forces were destroyed by NATO, then by definition of the term, Serbian forces were decimated, and the cost of such a loss should not be underappreciated. Second, although Serbian troops withdrew from Kosovo, it was only after Slobodan Milošević received international recognition that Kosovo is still legally part of Yugoslavia, indeed Serbia. Third, even though Milošević secured international recognition that Kosovo is still part of Serbia, his decision to withdraw Serbian forces from the province has lead to a precipitous drop in his support from Serbs. Protests have been occuring daily, and those most dissatisfied with Milošević are members of the military, religious leaders, and Serbian nationalists and ultra-nationalists. The way that Milošević has handled the recent Kosovo situation may be his downfall.

5. At the final writing of this book, the recent conflict in Kosovo brings us yet another poignant example of how people can transcend their religious beliefs, language, and very ethnicity to form a common bond through place. Despite all the emphasis placed on the incidents where longtime neighbors brutalized one another because they were different, we have examples where longtime neighbors protected one another during the recent crisis. Many local Serbs in Kosovo risked their lives to help their Albanian neighbors and now many Albanians are protecting these Serbs from reprisals.

Selected Bibliography

Academia Română: Institutul de Geografie. 1996. *România: Atlas istorico-geografic*. Bucureşti: Editura Academiei Române.

Ádám, Magda. 1993. The Little Entente and Europe (1920–1929). Budapest: Akadémiai Kiadó.

———. 1995. Plan for the rearrangement of Cental Europe, 1918. Chap. in *Hungarians and their neighbors in modern times, 1867–1950*, ed. Ferenc Glatz. Boulder, Colo.: Social Science Monographs.

Adams, Wallace E. 1951. Roumania at the 1919 Paris Peace Conference. Ph.D. diss., University of Oregon.

Ajtay, J., B. Janscó, and A. Kovács. 1921. *The Transylvanian question*. East European Problems, nos. 15–18. New York: Steiger.

Akhavan, Payam, and Robert Howse. 1995. *Yugoslavia, the former and future: Reflections by scholars from the region*. Washington, D.C.: Brookings Institution Press.

Alden, Percy, ed. 1909. *Hungary of to-day*. London: Eveleigh Nash, Fawside House.

Alexander, Ronnelle. 1976. Transitional West Bulgarian dialects: A structural approach. Chap. in *Bulgaria past and present: Studies in history, literature, economics, music, sociology, folklore and linguistics*, ed. Thomas Butler. Columbus, Ohio: American Association for the Advancement of Slavic Studies.

Ali, Rabia, and Lawrence Lifschultz, eds. 1993. *Why Bosnia? Writings on the Balkan War*. Stony Creek, Conn.: Pampleteer's Press.

Alland, Alexander, Jr. 1972. *The human imperative*. New York: Columbia University Press.

Almond, Mark. 1994. *Europe's backyard war: The war in the Balkans*. London: Heinemann.

Almond, Nina, and Ralph Haswell Lutz, eds. 1935. *The treaty of St. Germain: A documentary history of its territorial and political clauses*. Hoover War Library Publications, no. 5. Stanford, Calif.: Stanford University Press.

Alp, İlker. 1988. *Bulgarian atrocities: Documents and photographs*. London: K. Rustem and Brothers.

Alter, Peter. 1994. *Nationalism*. 2nd ed. London: Edward Arnold.

Anchor, Robert. 1967. *The Enlightenment tradition*. New York: Harper and Row.

Anderson, Benedict. 1991. *Imagined communities: Reflections on the origin and spread of nationalism*. Revised edition. London: Verso Edition and New Left Books.

Anderson, James, ed. 1986a. *The rise of the modern state*. Brighton, G.B.: Harvester Press.

———. 1986b. Nationalism and geography. Chap. 6 in *The rise of the modern state*, ed. James Anderson. Brighton, G.B.: Harvester Press.

———. 1988. Nationalist ideology and territory. Chap. 2 in *Nationalism, self-determination and political geography*, ed. R. J. Johnston, David B. Knight, and Eleonore Kofman. New York: Croom Helm.

Andrić, Ivo. 1990. *The development of spiritual life in Bosnia under the influence of Turkish rule*, ed. and trans. Želimir B. Juričić and John F. Loud. Durham, N.C.: Duke University Press.

Apponyi, Count Albert. 1920. *The peace treaty proposed to Hungary*. East European Problems, no. 1. New York: Steiger.

Ardrey, Robert. 1966. *The territorial imperative*. New York: Atheneum.

Armstrong, John A. 1982. *Nations before nationalism*. Chapel Hill: The University of North Carolina Press.

———. 1988. Toward a framework for considering nationalism in East Europe. *Eastern European Politics and Societies* 2 (Spring): 280–305.

Arnakis, George G. 1974. The role of religion in the development of Balkan nationalism. Chap. in *The Balkans in transition: Essays on the development of Balkan life and politics since the eighteenth century*, ed. Charles and Barbara Jelavich. Berkeley: University of California Press.

Arvidsson, Claes, and Lars Erik Blomquist, ed. 1987. *Symbols of power: The esthetics of political legitmation in the Soviet Union and Eastern Europe*. Sweden: Almqvist and Wiksell International Stockholm.

Ash, Timothy Garton. 1990. *The uses of adversity: Essays on the fate of central Europe*. New York: Vintage Books.

Asher, R. E. 1995. The rise and fall of language. *The Geographical Magazine* (August): 18–21.

Baan, Natalie. 1993. The white stag. *Parabola: The Magazine of Myth and Tradition* 18 (Summer): 55–58.

Bachman, Ronald D., ed. 1991. *Romania: A country study*. 2nd ed. Washington, D.C.: Federal Research Division, Library of Congress.

Bačić, Jacques. 1983. The emergence of the Sklabenoi (Slavs), their arrival on the Balkan peninsula, and the role of the Avars in these events: Revised concepts in a new perspective. Ph.D. diss., Columbia University.

———. 1988. Slav, the origin and meaning of the ethnonym. *Slovene Studies* 9 (1–2): 33–41.

Bakić-Hayden, Milicia, and Robert M. Hayden. 1992. Orientalists variations on the theme "Balkans": Symbolic geography in recent Yugoslav cultural politics. *Slavic Review* 51 (Spring): 1–15.

Banac, Ivo. 1984. *The national question in Yugoslavia: Origins, history, politics*. Ithaca, N.Y.: Cornell University Press.

———. 1984. Main trends in the Croat language question. Chap. in *Aspects of the Slavic language question*, ed. Riccardo Picchio and Harvey Goldblatt. Vol. 1 of *Church Slavonic—South Slavic—West Slavic*. New Haven, Conn.: Yale Concilium on International and Area Studies.

———. 1992. Historiography of the countries of Eastern Europe: Yugoslavia. *The American Historical Review* 97 (October): 1084–1104.

Bantock, Granville, ed. 1913. *Sixty patriotic songs of all nations*. Boston: Oliver Ditson.

Barany, George. 1968. *Stephen Széchennyi and the awakening of Hungarian nationalism, 1791–1841*. Princeton, N.J.: Princeton University Press.

———. 1990. The age of royal absolutism, 1790–1848. Chap. 11 in *A history of Hungary*, ed. Peter F. Sugar, Péter Hanák, and Tibor Frank. Bloomington and Indianapolis: Indiana University Press.

Barnard. F. M. 1965. *Herder's social and political thought*. Oxford: Clarendon Press.

Barnes, Trevor, and Derek Gregory, eds. 1997. *Readings in human geography: The poetics and politics of inquiry*. New York: Arnold.

Barth, Frederik, ed. 1969. *Ethnic groups and boundaries*. Boston: Little, Brown.

Bartók, Béla, and Zoltán Kodály. 1906. *Magyar Népdalok*. Budapest: Karl Rozsnyai.

———. 1923. *Népdalok (Erdély Magyarság)*. Budapest: Népies Irodalmi Társaság.

Bauler, Jean. 1923. *A new danger to the peace of Europe*. Berne, Switzerland: Jean Bauler.

Behr, Edward. 1991. *Kiss the hand you cannot bite: The rise and fall of the Ceauşescus*. New York: Villard Books.

Beissinger, Margaret H. 1991. *The art of lǎuter: The epic tradition of Romania*. New York: Garland Publishing.

Bell-Fialkoff, Andrew. 1996. *Ethnic cleansing*. New York: St. Martin's Press.

Bennett, Christopher. 1995. *Yugoslavia's bloody collapse: Causes, course and consequences*. London: Hurst.

Berend, Iván T. 1987. The cultural identity of Central and Eastern Europe. *New Hungarian Quarterly* 28 (Autumn): 26–36.

Berindei, Dan. 1976. *Independent Romania, 1877*. Trans. Leon Levţchi Bucharest: Meridiane Publishing House.

Berry, James. 1919. Transylvania and its relations to ancient Dacia and modern Rumania. *Geographical Journal* 53 (March): 129–52.

Bethlen, Count Steven. [1934] 1971. *The treaty of Trianon and European peace*. Reprint, New York: Longmans, Green.

Binder, David. 1990. Tearfully, Romanians recall a wartime partition. *The New York Times*, 2 September, A16.

Binder, David. 1993. Romanians and Hungarians building a bit of trust. *The New York Times*, 20 July, A6.

Birinyi, Louis Kossuth. 1924. *The tragedy of Hungary: An appeal for world peace*. Cleveland, Ohio: privately printed.

———. 1938. *Why the treaty of Trianon is void*. Grand Rapids: V.L.R. Simmons.

Biró, Sándor. 1992. *The nationality problem in Transylvania, 1867–1940: A social history of the Romanian minority under Hungarian rule, 1867–1918 and of the Hungarian minority under Romanian rule, 1918–1940*. Trans. Márió D. Fenyő. Boulder, Colo.: Social Science Monographs.

Blanke, Richard. 1981. *Prussian Poland in the German empire (1871–1900)*. Boulder, Colo.: East European Monographs.

Blinken, Donald M., and Alfred H. Moses. 1996. Looking beyond Bosnia. *The New York Times*, 19 September, A31.

Blum, Jerome, Rondo Cameron, and Thomas G. Barnes. 1966. *The European world since 1815: Triumph and transition*. Boston: Little, Brown.

Bobango, Gerald J. 1979. *The emergence of the Romanian state*. Boulder, Colo.: East European Quarterly.

Bodea, Cornellia, and Virgil Cândea. 1982. *Transylvania in the history of the Romanians*. Boulder, Colo.: East European Monographs.

Bődy, Pál, ed. 1989. *Hungarian statesmen of destiny, 1860–1960*. Boulder, Colo.: Social Sciences Monographs.

Bohlen, Celestine. 1991. Neighbors making Budapest uneasy. *The New York Times*, 13 October, A8.

Boia, Eugene. 1993. *Romania's diplomatic relations with Yugoslavia in the interwar period, 1919–1941*. Boulder, Colo.: East European Monographs.

Borsody, Stephen, ed. 1980. *The tragedy of central Europe: Nazi and Soviet conquest and aftermath*. New Haven, Conn.: Yale Concilium on International and Area Studies.

———. 1988. *The Hungarians: A divided nation*. New Haven, Conn.: Yale Center of International Area Studies.

———. 1993. *The new central Europe*. Boulder, Colo.: East European Monographs.

Botsford, Florence Hudson, ed. 1931. *Northern Europe*. Vol. 2 of *Botsford collection of folk songs*. New York: G. Schirmer.

———, ed. 1933. *Southern Europe*. Vol. 3 of *Botsford collection of folk songs*. New York: G. Schirmer.

Bovill, B. Forster. 1908. *Hungary and the Hungarians*. New York: McClure.

Bowman, Isaiah. 1922. *The new world: Problems in political geography*. New York: World Book.

———. 1928. *The new world: Problems in political geography*. 4th ed. New York: World Book.

Bracewell, Catherine Wendy. 1992. *The Uskoks of Senj: Piracy, banditry, and holy war in the sixteenth-century Adriatic*. Ithaca, N.Y.: Cornell University Press.

Breuilly, John. 1994. *Nationalism and the state*. 2nd ed. Chicago: The University of Chicago Press.

Brigham, Albert Perry. 1919. Principles in the determination of boundaries. *Geographical Review* 8 (April): 201–19.

Bringa, Tone. 1995. *Being Muslim the Bosnian way: Identity and community in a central Bosnian Village*. Princeton, N.J.: Princeton University Press.

Brkić, Jovan. 1961. *Moral Concepts in Traditional Serbian Epic Poetry*. The Hague, Netherlands: Mouton.

Bruchis, Michael. 1982. *One step back, two steps forward: On the language policy of the Communist party of the Soviet Union in the national republics: Moldavian: A look back, a survey, and perspectives, 1924–1980*. Boulder, Colo.: East European Monographs.

———. 1984. *Nations—nationalities—people: A study of the nationalities policy of the Communist party in Soviet Moldavia*. Boulder, Colo.: East European Monographs.

———. 1996. *The Republic of Moldavia: From the collapse of the Soviet Empire to the restoration of the Russian Empire*. Trans. Laura Treptow. New York: East European Monographs.

Brunn, Stanley D., and Ernie Yanarella. 1987. Towards a humanistic political geo-

graphy. *Studies in Comparative International Development* 22 (Summer): 3–49.
Burant, Stephen R., 1990. *Hungary: A country study.* Washington, D.C.: Federal Research Division, Library of Congress.
Burg, Steven L., and Michael L. Berbaum. 1989. Community integration, and stability in multinational Yugoslavia. *American Political Science Review* 83 (June): 535–54.
Burghardt, Andrew F. 1958. *The Political Geography of Burgenland.* Washington, D.C.: National Academy of Sciences–National Research Council.
———. 1962. *Borderland: A historical and geographical study of Burgenland, Austria.* Madison: University of Wisconsin Press.
———. 1973. The bases of territorial claims. *Geographical Review* 63 (April): 225–45.
———. 1988. Marxism and self-determination: the case of Burgenland, 1919. Chap. 4 in *Nationalism, self-determination and political geography,* ed. R. J. Johnston, David B. Knight, and Eleonore Kofman. New York: Croom Helm.
Butler, Thomas. 1970. The origins of the war for a Serbian language and orthography. *Harvard Slavic Studies* 5: 1–80.
———. 1980. *Monumenta Serbocroatia: A bilingual anthology of Serbian and Croatian texts from the 12th to the 19th century.* Ann Arbor: Michigan Slavic Publications.
Cabot, John M. 1926. *The racial conflict in Transylvania.* Boston: Beacon Press.
Cadzow, John F., Andrew Lundanyi, and Louis J. Elteto, eds. 1983. *Transylvania: The roots of ethnic conflict.* Ohio: Kent State University Press.
Cahman, Werner. 1949. Frontiers between East and West in Europe. *Geographical Review* 39 (October): 605–24.
Campbell, John C. 1971. *French influence and the rise of Roumanian nationalism.* New York: Arno Press and *The New York Times.*
Canovan, Margaret. 1996. *Nationhood and political theory.* Cheltenham, U.K.: Edward Elgar.
Carr, William. 1969. *A History of Germany, 1815–1945.* New York: St. Martin's Press.
Cartledge, T. M., W. L. Reed, Martin Shaw and Henry Coleman. 1978. *National anthems of the world.* New York: Arco Publishing.
Carsten, F. L. 1980. *The rise of fascism.* 2nd ed. Berkeley: University of California Press.
Castellan, Georges. 1989. *A history of the Roumanians.* Trans. Nicholas Bradley. Boulder, Colo.: East European Monographs.
Ceauşescu, Ilie. 1983. *Transylvania—An ancient Romanian land.* Bucharest: Military Publishing House.
Ceauşescu, Ilie, Florin Constantiniu, and Mihail E. Ionescu. 1985. *A turning point in World War II: 23 August 1944 in Romania.* Boulder, Colo: East European Monographs.
Chamberlin, E. R. 1979. *Preserving the past.* London: J.M. Dent and Sons.
Chazonoy, Mathis. 1987. Hungary, Romania embroiled in centuries-old feud over Transylvania. *Los Angeles Times,* 6 July, p. 10.
Chirot, Daniel. 1996. Herder's multicultural theory of nationalism and its consequences. *East European Politics and Societies.* 10 (1): 1–15.
Ciorănescu, George. 1985. *Bessarabia: Disputed land between East and West.* Munich: Jon Dumitru Verlag.
Ciopraga, Constantin. 1981. *The personality of Romanian literature: A synthesis.* Trans.

Stefan Avadănei. Iaşi, Romania: Junimea Publishing House.

Clark, Charles Upson. 1922. *Greater Roumania*. New York: Dodd, Mead.

———. 1927. *Bessarabia: Russia and Roumania on the Black Sea*. New York: Dodd, Mead.

———. [1932] 1971. *United Roumania*. New York: Dodd, Mead. Reprint, New York: Arno Press and *The New York Times*.

Clark, Robert T. Jr. 1955. *Herder: His life and thought*. Berkeley: Unversity of California.

Clissold, Stephen, ed. 1966. *A short history of Yugoslavia: From early times to 1966*. Cambridge: Cambridge University Press.

Close, Elizabeth. 1974. *The development of modern Romanian: Linguistic theory and practice in Muntenia, 1821–1838*. Oxford: Oxford University Press.

Coakley, John, ed. 1993. *The Territorial management of ethnic conflict*. London: Frank Cass.

Cohen, Anthony. 1985. *The symbolic construction of community*. New York: Tavistock.

Cohler, Anne. 1970. *Rousseau and nationalism*. New York: Basic Books.

Comrie, Bernard, ed. 1987. *The world's major languages*. New York: Oxford University Press.

Connor, Walker. 1978. A nation is a nation, is a state, is an ethnic group is a. . . . *Ethnic and Racial Studies* 1 (January): 377–400.

———. 1990. When is a nation? *Ethnic and Racial Studies* 13 (January): 92–103.

———. 1994. *Ethnonationalism: The quest for understanding*. Princeton: Princeton University Press.

Conzen, Michael P. 1993. Culture regions, homelands, and ethnic archipelagos in the United States: Methodological considerations. *Journal of Cultural Geography* 13 (Spring/Summer): 13–29.

Cornish, Louis C. 1947. *Transylvania: The land beyond the forest*. Philadelphia: Dorrance.

Craig, Gordon A. 1972. *Europe, 1815–1914*. 3rd ed. Hinsdale, Ill.: The Dryden Press.

Crampton, R. J. 1994. *Eastern Europe in the twentieth century*. London: Routledge.

Crişan, Ion Horaţiu. 1978. *Burebista and his time*. Bucharest: Editura Academiei Republiciii Socialiste România.

Cristo-Loveanu, Elie. 1962. *The Romanian language*. New York: Published by author.

Crnobrnja, Mihailo. 1994. *The Yugoslav drama*. Montreal: McGill-Queen's University Press.

Csáky, Stephen. 1921. *The responsibility of the Hungarian nation in the war*. East European Problems, no. 14. New York: Steiger.

Custred, Glynn. 1992. Dual ethnic identity of the Transylvanian Saxons. *East European Quarterly* 25 (January): 483–91.

Cvijić, Jovan. 1918. The geographical distribution of the Balkan peoples. *Geographical Review* 5 (May): 345–61.

Czepeli, György, and Antal Örkény. 1997. The imagery of national anthems in Europe. *Canadian Review of Studies in Nationalism* 24 (1–2): 33–42.

Czigány, Lóránt. 1984. *The Oxford history of Hungarian literature: From the earliest times to the present*. Oxford: Clarendon Press.

Davies, Norman. 1982. *God's playground: A history of Poland*. 2 vols. New York: Columbia University Press.

Dárday, D. 1920. *The solution of the Fiume question.* East European Problems, no. 3. New York: Steiger.

Darvasi, István. 1966. *Is there some change in Hungary?* Trans. István Farkas. Budapest: Pannonia Press.

Dawson, Christopher. 1994. *The making of Europe: An introduction to the history of European unity.* New York: Barnes and Noble.

Dávid, Zoltán. 1988. The Hungarians and their neighbors. In *The Hungarians: A divided nation.* Ed. Stephen Borsody. New Haven, Conn.: Yale Center for International and Area Studies.

Deák, Francis. 1928. *The Hungarian-Rumanian Land Dispute.* New York: Columbia University Press.

———. 1972. *Hungary at the Paris Peace Conference: The diplomatic history of the treaty of Trianon.* New York: Morningside Heights, Columbia University Press.

Deák, István. 1965. Hungary. In *The European Right: A Historical Profile.* Ed. Eugene Weber and Hans Rogger. Berkeley: University of California Press.

———. 1979. *The lawful revolution: Louis Kossuth and the Hungarians, 1848–1849.* New York: Columbia University Press.

———. 1990. Uncovering Eastern Europe's dark history. *Orbis* 34 (Winter): 51–65.

———. 1992. Historiography of the countries of Eastern Europe: Hungary. *The American Historical Review* 97 (October): 1041–63.

De Daruvar, Yves. 1974. *The tragic fate of Hungary: A country carved up alive at Trianon.* 2nd ed. Trans. Victor Stankovich. Pennsylvania: Alpha Publications.

Dedijer, Vladimir, Ivan Božić, Sima Ćirković, and Milorad Ekmečić. 1974. *History of Yugoslavia.* New York: McGraw-Hill.

De Hevesy, André. 1919. *Nationalities in Hungary.* London: T. Fisher Unwin, Adelphi Terrace.

Deletant, Dennis. 1991. Rewriting the past: trends in contemporary Romanian historiography. *Ethnic and Racial Studies* 14 (January): 64–86.

———. 1992. A balancing act—Romania, 1919–40. *History Today* 42 (June): 48–54.

Deletant, Dennis, and Hanak, Harry, eds. 1988. *Historians as nation-builders: Central and South-East Europe.* London: Macmillan Press.

Denich, Bette. 1994. Dismembering Yugoslavia: nationalist ideologies and the symbolic revival of genocide. *American ethnologist* 21 (May): 367–90.

Denitch, Bogdan. 1994. *Ethnic nationalism: The tragic death of Yugoslavia.* Minneapolis: University of Minnesota Press.

Dercsényi, Dezső. 1969. *Historical monuments in Hungary: Restoration and preservation.* Budapest: Corvina Press.

Despalatović, Elinor Murray. 1975. *Ljudevit Gaj and the Illyrian movement.* Boulder, Colo.: East European Quarterly.

Deutsch, Karl. 1966. *Nationalism and social communication.* Cambridge, Mass.: MIT Press.

———. 1969. The growth of nations: Some recurrent patterns of political and social integration. Chap. 17 in *The Structure of Political Geography,* ed. Roger E. Kasperson and Julian V. Minghi. Chicago: Aldine Publishing.

Deutsch, Leonhard. 1967. *A treasury of the world's finest folk songs.* New York: Crown Publishers.

Dima, Nicholas. 1982. *Bessarabia and Bukovina: the Soviet-Romanian territorial dispute.* Boulder, Colo.: East European Monographs.

————. 1985. Daco-Romanians and Aromanians. *East European Quarterly* 19 (September): 337–48.

————. 1991. *From Moldavia to Moldova: The Soviet-Romanian territorial dispute.* Boulder, Colo.: East European Monographs.

DIMAP. 1995. *Erdély (Ardeal, Siebenbürgen, Transylvania).* Budapest.

Djilas, Aleska. 1991. *The contested country: Yugoslav unity and communist revolution, 1919–1953.* Cambridge, Mass.: Harvard University Press.

Dobszay, László. 1993. *A history of Hungarian music.* Budapest: Corvina.

Dominian, Leon. 1917a. *Frontiers of language and nationality in Europe.* New York: Henry Holt.

————. 1917b. *The nationality map of Europe.* Vol. 1 of *A League of Nations.* Boston: World Peace Foundation.

Donia, Robert J. and John V. A. Fine. 1994. *Bosnia and Herzegovina: A tradition betrayed.* New York: Columbia University Press.

Dordevic, Mihailo. 1984. *Anthology of Serbian poetry: The golden age.* New York: Philosophical Library.

Drage, Geoffrey. 1909. *Austria-Hungary.* London: John Murray, Albemarle Street, W.

Dragnich, Alex N. 1983. *The first Yugoslavia: Search for a viable political system.* Stanford, Calif.: Hoover Institution Press.

————. 1989. The rise and fall of Yugoslavia: The omen of the upsurge of Serbian nationalism. *East European Quarterly* 23 (June): 183–98.

————. 1992. *Serbs and Croats: The struggle in Yugoslavia.* New York: Harcourt Brace Jovanovich.

Dragnich, Alex N., and Slavko Todorovich. 1984. *The saga of Kosovo: Focus on Serbian-Albanian relations.* Boulder, Colo.: East European Monographs.

Drăguţ, Vasile. 1973. *Humor.* Trans. Caterina Augusta Grundbock. Bucharest: Meridiane Publishing House.

Dreisziger, N. F. 1975. Count Istvan Bethlen's secret plan for the restoration of the empire of Transylvania. *East European Quarterly* 18 (January): 413–23.

Du Nay, André. 1977. *The early history of the Rumanian language.* Lake Bluff, Ill.: Jupiter Press.

Duncan, W. Raymond, and G. Paul Holman Jr., eds. 1994. *Ethnic nationalism and regional conflict: the former Soviet Union and Yugoslavia.* Boulder, Colo.: Westview Press.

Dyer, Donald L., ed. 1996. *Studies in Moldovan: The history, culture, language and contemporary politics of the people of Moldova.* Boulder, Colo.: East European Monographs.

East, William Gordon. 1961. The concept of political status of the shatter zone. In *Geographical essays on Eastern Europe,* ed. N. J. Pounds. Bloomington: Indiana University.

————. 1966. *An historical geography of Europe.* 5th ed. New York: E.P. Dutton.

Economist. 1989. Soviet Union: Trouble, trouble, trouble. 312 (7618) September 2.

Edroiu, Nicholae. 1978. *Horea's uprising: The 1784 Romanian peasants' uprising.* Trans. Alexandru Bolintineau. Bucharest: Editura Ştiintifică Şi Enciclopedică.

Edroiu, Nicolae, and Vasile Puşcaş. 1996. *The Hungarians of Romania.* Cluj-Napoca, Romania: Fundaţia Culturală Română Centrul de Studii Translivane.

Edwards, John, ed. 1984. *Linguistic minorities, policies and pluralism.* New York: Academic Press.

Egri, Peter. 1988. *Literature, painting and music: An interdisciplinary approach to comparative literature*. Budapest: Akadémiai Kiadó.

Eidelberg, Philip Gabriel. 1974. *The great Rumanian peasant of 1907: Origins of a modern jacquerie*. Leiden: Brill.

Eighty Club, The. 1907. *Hungary: Its people, places, and politics*. London: T. Fisher Unwin Aldephi Terrace.

Einstein, Alfred. 1947. *Music in the Romantic era*. London: J.M. Dent and Sons.

Elteto, Louis J. 1983. Reformation literature and the national consciousness of Transylvanian Hungarians, Saxons, and Rumanians. Chap. in *Transylvania: The Roots of Ethnic Conflict*. John F. Cadzow, Andrew Lundanyi, and Louis J. Elteto. Ohio: Kent State University Press.

Emerson, Rupert. 1960. *From empire to nation: The rise to self-assertion of Asian and African peoples*. Cambridge, Mass.: Harvard University Press.

Emmert, Thomas A. 1981. Kosovo: Development and impact of a national pride. Chap. in *Nation and ideology essays in honor of Wayne S. Vucinich*, ed. Ivo Banac, John G. Ackerman, and Roman Szporluk. Boulder, Colo.: East European Monographs.

———. 1990. *Serbian Golgotha Kosovo, 1389*. New York: East European Monographs.

Engelberg, Stephen, and Judith Ingram. 1993. Now Hungary adds its voice to ethnic tulmult. *The New York Times*, 25 January, A3.

Eppstein, John, ed. 1945. *British survey handbooks*. Vol. 4, Hungary. Cambridge: At the University Press.

Erdei, Ferenc, ed. 1968. *Information Hungary*. New York: Pergamon Press.

Ergang, Robert R. 1966. *Herder and the foundations of German nationalism*. New York: Columbia University Press.

Esman, M., ed. 1977. *Ethnic conflict in the western world*. Ithaca, N.Y.: Cornell University Press.

Fehér, Ferenc. 1989. On Making Central Europe. *East European Politics and Societies* 3 (Fall): 412–47.

Fermor, Patrick Leigh. 1986. *Between woods and water: On foot to Constaninople from the Hook of Holland: the middle Danube to the Iron Gates*. 3 vols. New York: Penguin.

Fine, John V.A. 1983. *The early medieval Balkans: A critical survey from the sixth to the late twelfth century*. Ann Arbor: The University of Michigan Press.

———. 1987. *The late medieval Balkans: A critical survey from the late twelfth century to the Ottoman conquest*. Ann Arbor: The University of Michigan Press.

Fine, John V.A., and Robert J. Donia. 1994. *Bosnia and Herzegovina: A tradition betrayed*. New York: Columbia University Press.

Fischer-Galati, Stephen, ed. 1957. *Romania*. New York: Frederick A. Praeger.

———. 1978. The continuation of nationalism in Romanian historiography. *Nationalities Papers* 6 (2): 179–84.

———. 1991. *Twentieth century Rumania*. 2nd ed. New York: Columbia University Press.

Fishman, Joshua A. 1972. *Language and nationalism: Two integrative essays*. Rowley, Mass.: Newbury House Publishers.

———. 1974. The sociology of language: An interdisciplinary social science approach to language in society. *Current Trends in Linguistics* 12: 1629–1784.

Florescu, R. R. 1967. The Uniate church: Catalyst of Rumanian nationalism. *Slavic and East European Review* 45 (July): 324–42.

Florescu, Radu, and Ion Michlea. 1989. *The city of Histria*. Bucharest: Editura Sport-Turism.

Floto, Inga. 1973. *Colonel House in Paris: A study of American policy at the Paris Peace Conference 1919*. Princeton, N.J.: Princeton University Press.

Floyd, David. 1965. *Rumania: Russia's dissident ally*. London: Paul Mall Press.

Fodor, Francis. 1920. *The geographical impossibility of the Czech state*. East European Problems, no. 4. New York: Steiger.

Fodor, István. 1975. *In search of a new homeland: The prehistory of the Hungarian people and the conquest*. Trans. Helen Tarnoy. Budapest: Corvina Kiadó.

Ford, Franklin L. 1970. *Europe 1780–1830*. London: Longmans, Green.

Foreign, Broadcast Information Service. 1994. *New Serb calls for greater Serbia*. 5 January, 48–52. Washington, D.C.: Foreign Broadcast Information Service.

Forter, Norman L., and Demeter B. Rostovsky. [1931] 1971. *The Roumanian handbook*. Reprint, New York: Arno Press and *The New York Times*.

Fox, Richard G., ed. 1990. *Nationalist ideologies and the production of national cultures*. Num. 2 of the *American Ethnological Society Monograph Series*. Washington, D.C.: American Anthropological Association.

Frank, Tibor. 1990. Hungary and the Dual Monarchy, 1867–1890. Chap. 14 in *A history of Hungary*, ed. Peter F. Sugar, Péter Hanák, and Tibor Frank. Bloomington and Indianapolis: Indiana University Press.

———. 1991. Luring the English-speaking world: Hungarian history diverted. *The Slavonic and East European Review* 69 (January): 60–80.

Friedman, Francine. 1996. *The Bosnians Muslims: The denial of a nation*. Boulder, Colo.: Westview Press.

Fügedi, Erik. 1986. *Castle and society in medieval Hungary (1000–1437)*. Budapest: Akadémiai Kiadó.

Fulbrook, Mary, ed. 1993. *National histories and European history*. Boulder, Colo.: Westview Press.

Fyfe, Hamiltion. 1940. *The illusion of national character*. London: Watts.

Gagnon, V. P., Jr. 1994–95. Ethnic nationalism and international conflict: The case of Serbia. *International Security* 19 (Winter): 130–66.

Gallagher, Michael. 1995. How many nations are there in Ireland? *Ethnic and Racial Studies* 18 (October): 715–739.

Gallagher, Tom. 1992. *Vatra Românească* and resurgent nationalism in Romania. *Ethnic and Racial Studies* 15 (October): 570–598.

———. 1997. *Romania after Ceauşescu: The politics of intolerance*. Edinburgh: Edinburgh University Press.

Gamova, Svetlana. 1994. *Moldova: A three-way split. The Bulletin of the Atomic Scientists*. 50 (1/January/February): 41–43.

Gastony, Endre Bela. 1970. Revisionist Hungarian foreign policy and the Third Reich's advance to the east, 1933–1939. PhD. diss., University of Oregon.

Gates-Coon, Rebecca. 1994. *The landed estates of the Esterházy princes: Hungary during the reforms of Maria Theresia and Joseph II*. Baltimore: Johns Hopkins University Press.

Gellner, Ernest. 1983. *Nations and nationalism*. Ithaca, N.Y.: Cornell Unversity Press.

Georgescu, Vlad. 1991. *The Romanians: A history*. Trans. Alexandra Bley-Vroman. Columbus: Ohio State University Press.

Gerő, András. 1990. *Heroes' Square Budapest: Hungary' history in stone and bronze*. Budapest: Corvina.

Gerth, H. H., and C. Wright Mills. 1948. *From Max Weber: Essays in Sociology.* London: Routledge and Kegan Paul.

Ghermani, Dionisie. 1967. *Die kommunistische Umdeutung der rumänischen Geschichte unter besonderer Berücksichtigung des Mittelalters.* Munich: Verlag R. Oldenburg, Südost-Institut München.

Gilberg, Trond. 1974. Ethnic minorities in Romania under socialism. *East European Quarterly* 7 (January): 435–58.

Gilbert, Felix. 1979. *The end of the European era, 1890 to the present.* 2nd ed. New York: W.W. Norton.

Gildea, Robert. 1987. *Barricades and borders: Europe 1800–1914.* Oxford: Oxford University Press.

GilFillan, S. C. 1924. European political boundaries. *Political Science Quarterly* 39 (September): 458–84.

Gillies, Alexander. 1945. *Herder.* Oxford: Basil Blackwell.

Gimbutas, Marija. 1971. *The slavs.* New York: Praeger Publishers.

Giurescu, Dinu C. 1981. *Illustrated history of the Romanian people.* Bucharest: Editura Sport-Turism.

Glassner, Martin Ira. 1993. *Political Geography.* New York: John Wiley and Sons.

Glauber, Bill. 1997. Britain might leave Scotland to the Scots. *Baltimore Sun*, 25 July, 17A.

Glatz, Ferenc, ed. 1995. *Hungarians and their neighbors in modern times, 1867–1950.* Boulder, Colo.: Social Science Monographs.

Glazer, Nathan, and Daniel P. Moynihan. 1975. *Ethnicity: Theory and experience.* Cambridge, Mass.: Harvard University Press.

Glenny, Misha. 1993. *The fall of Yugoslavia: The Third Balkan War.* New York: Penguin Books.

Godkin, Edwin Lawrence. 1853. *The history of Hungary and the Magyars: From the earliest period to the close of the late war.* New York: Alexander Montgomery.

Golea, Traian. 1988. *Transylvania and Hungarian revisionism: A discussion of present-day developments.* 2nd ed. Miami Beach, Fla.: Romanian Historical Studies.

Gottman, Jean. 1973. *The significance of territory.* Charlottsville: University Press of Virginia.

Graham, Lawrence S. 1982. *Romania: A Developing socialist state.* Boulder, Colo.: Westview Press.

Graubard, Stephen R., ed. 1991. *Eastern Europe . . . Central Europe . . . Europe.* San Francisco: Westview Press.

Greenberg, Robert D. 1996. The politics of dialects among Serbs, Croats, and Muslims in the former Yugoslavia. *East European Politics and Societies* 10 (3): 393–415.

Greer, Thomas H. 1977. *A brief history of western man.* San Francisco: Harcourt Brace Jovanovich.

Grosby, Steven. 1995. Territorialty: The transcendental, primoridial feature of modern societies. *Nations and Nationalism* 1(2): 143–62.

Gross, Mirjana. 1993. The union of Dalmatia with northern Croatia: Crucial question of the Croatian national integration in the nineteenth century. Chap. 11 in *The national question in Europe in historical context*, ed. Mikuláš Teich, and Roy Porter. Cambridge: Cambridge University Press.

Gurr, Andrew. 1981. *Writers in exile: The identity of home in modern literature.* Atlantic Highlands, N.J.: Humanities Press.

Gutman, Roy. 1993. *A witness to genocide*. New York: MacMillan Publishing.

Hall, Brian. 1994. *The impossible country: a journey through the last days of Yugoslavia*. London: Secker and Warburg.

Halsted, John B., ed. 1969. *Romanticism*. New York: Walker.

Hamann-Mac Lean, Richard, and Horst Hallensleben. 1963. *Die Monumentalmalerei in Serbien und Makdonien: Von 11. Bis zum frühen 14. Jahrhundert*. Gießen, Germany: Im Kommissionsverlag Wilhelm Schmitz.

Hamm, Michael F. 1998. Chronology. *Nationalities Papers* 26 (1): 165–75.

Hanák, Péter. 1967. Problems of Eastern European history in recent Hungarian historiography. *East European Quarterly* 1 (June): 123–42.

———, ed. 1988. *One thousand years: A concise history of Hungary*. Budapest: Corvina Press.

Harris, Chauncy D. 1993. New European countries and their minorities. *Geographical Review* 83 (July): 301–20.

Hartshorne, Richard. 1969. The functional approach in political geography. In *The structure of political geography*, ed. Roger E. Kasperson and Julian V. Minghi. Chicago: Aldine Publishing.

Haselsteiner, Horst. 1990. Cooperation and confrontation between rulers and the noble estates, 1711–1790. Chap. 10 in A *History of Hungary*, ed. Peter F. Sugar, Péter Hanák, and Tibor Frank. Bloomington and Indianapolis: Indiana University Press.

Haugen, Einar, J. Derrick McClure, and Derick Thompson, eds. 1980. *Minority languages today*. Edinburgh, Scotland: University Press.

Held, Joseph. 1968. Note to the collapse of Hungarian society between the two world wars. *East European Quarterly* 2 (September): 303–13.

———. 1985. *Hunyadi: Legend and reality*. Boulder, Colo.: East European Monographs.

Herb, Guntram Henrik. 1993. National self-determination, maps, and propaganda in Germany, 1918–1945. Ph.D. diss., University of Wisconsin–Madison.

———. 1997. *Under the map of Germany: Nationalism and propaganda 1918–1945*. New York: Routledge.

Hitchins, Keith. 1969. *The Rumanian national movement in Transylvania, 1780–1849*. Cambridge, Mass.: Harvard University Press.

———. 1977. *Orthodoxy and nationality: Andreiu Şaguna and the Rumanians of Transylvania, 1846–1873*. Cambidge, Mass.: Harvard University Press.

———. 1979. Religion and Rumanian national consciousness in 18th century Transylvania. *The Slavonic and East European Review* 57: 214–39.

———. 1992. Historiography of the countries of Eastern Europe: Romania. *The American Historical Review* 97 (October): 1064–83.

———. 1996. *The Romanians, 1744–1866*. Oxford: Clarendon Press.

Hobsbawn, Eric J. 1962. *The age of revolution 1789–1848*. New York: The World Publishing Company.

———, ed. 1983. *The invention of tradition*. New York: Cambridge University Press.

———. 1987. *The age of empire, 1875–1914*. New York: Pantheon Books.

———. 1990. *Nations and nationalism since 1780: Programme, myth, reality*. 2nd ed. Cambridge: Cambridge University Press.

———. 1992. Ethnicity and Nationalism in Europe Today. *Anthropology Today* 8 (February): 3–13.

Hoensch, Jörg K. 1967. *Der Ungarische Revisionismus und die Zerschlagung der Tschechoslowakei*. Tübingen, Germany: J.C.B. Mohr (Paul Siebeck).

Hoensch, Jörg. 1996. *A history of modern Hungary, 1867–1994*. Trans. Kim Traynor. 2nd ed. New York: Longman.

Hoffman, Eva. 1993. *Exit into history: A journey through the new Eastern Europe*. New York: Penguin Books.

Hoffman, George W. 1963. *The Balkans in transition*. Westport, Conn.: Greenwood Press, Publishers.

———, ed. 1983. *A geography of Europe*. New York: John Wiley.

Hoffman, George W., and Fred Warner Neal. 1962. *Yugoslavia and the new communism*. New York: Twentieth Century Fund.

Holborn, Hajo. 1969. *A history of modern Germany, 1840–1945*. Princeton, N.J.: Princeton University Press.

Holton, Milne, and Vasa D. Mihailovich. 1988. *Serbian poetry from the beginnings to the present*. New Haven, Conn.: Yale Center for International and Area Studies.

———, trans. 1997. *Songs of the Serbian people: From the collections of Vuk Karadžić*. Pittsburgh: University of Pittsburgh Press.

Hudson, R. A. 1996. *Sociolinguistics*. 2nd ed. Cambridge: Cambridge University Press.

Hootz, Reinhardt, and István Genthon. 1974. *Kunstdenkmäler in Ungarn: Ein Bildhandbuch*. Munich: Deutscher Kunstverlag.

Horak, Stephen, ed. 1985. *Eastern European national minorities, 1919–80: A handbook*. Littleton, Colo.: Libraries Unlimited.

Horne, Donald. 1984. *The great museum: The re-presentation of history*. London: Pluto Press.

Horowitz, D. 1985. *Ethnic groups in conflict*. Berkeley: University of California Press.

Horváth, Eugene. 1935. *Transylvania and the history of the Rumanians: A reply to professor R. W. Seton-Watson*. Budapest: Sárkány Printing Company.

Hosking, Geoffrey, and George Schöpflin, eds. 1997. *Myths and nationhood*. New York: Routledge.

House, Edward M., and Charles Seymour. 1921. *What really happened at Paris: The story of the Peace Conference, 1918–1919*. New York: Charles Scribner's Sons.

Hroch Miroslav. 1985. *Social preconditions of national revival in Europe: A competitive analysis of the social composition of patriotic groups among the smaller European nations*. New York: Cambridge University Press.

Hupchick, Dennis, and Harold E. Cox. 1996. *A concise historical atlas of Eastern Europe*. New York: St. Martin's Press.

Hymn of Zrinyi. 1989. Translated by Paula Kennedy. London: Boosey and Hawkes/MCPS.

Iancu, Gheorghe. 1995. *The Ruling Council: The integration of Transylvania into Romania, 1918–1920*. Cluj-Napoca, Romania: Center for Transylvanian Studies, The Romanian Cultural Foundation.

Ignotus, Paul. 1972. *Hungary*. New York: Praeger.

Illyés, Elemér. 1982. *National minorities in Romania: Change in Transylvania*. Boulder, Colo.: East European Monographs.

———. 1988. *Ethnic continuity in the Carpatho-Danubian area*. Boulder, Colo.: East European Monographs.

Ioanid, Radu. 1990. *The sword of the Archangel: Fascist ideology in Romania.* Trans. Peter Heinegg. Boulder, Colo.: East European Monographs.

Ionesco, Grigore. 1972. *Histoire De L'Archictecture En Roumanie: De la préhistoire à nos jours.* Bucharest: Éditions De L'Académie De La République Socialiste De Roumanie.

Iorga, Nicholae. 1925. *A history of Roumania: Land, people, civilisation.* Trans. Joseph McCabe. London: Adelphi Terrace.

Iovine, Micaela S. 1984. The "Illyrian Language" and the language question among the Southern Slavs in the seventeenth and eighteenth centuries. In *Aspects of the Slavic language question,* ed. Riccardo Picchio and Harvey Goldblatt. Vol. 1, *Church Slavonic—South Slavic—West Slavic.* New Haven, Conn.: Yale Concilium on International and Area Studies.

Jackson, J. B. 1994. *A sense of place, a sense of time.* New Haven, Conn.: Yale University Press.

Jackson, Peter, and Jan Penrose, eds. 1994. *Constructions of race, place and nation.* Minneapolis: University of Minnesota Press.

Janics, Kálman. 1982. *Czechoslovak policy and the Hungarian minority, 1945–48.* Vol. 9 of *War and society in East Central Europe: The effects of World War II.* New York: Social Science Monographs, Columbia University Press.

Janos, Andrew C. 1982. *The politics of backwardness in Hungary, 1825–1945.* Princeton, N.J.: Princeton University Press.

Janos, Andrew C., and William B. Slottman, eds. 1971. *Revolution in perspective: Essays on the Hungarian soviet republic of 1919.* Berkeley: University of California.

Jelavich, Barbara. 1983a. *History of the Balkans: Eighteenth and nineteenth centuries.* Vol. 1. Cambridge: Cambridge University Press.

———. 1983b. *History of the Balkans: Twentieth century.* Vol. 2. Cambridge: Cambridge University Press.

———. 1984. *Russia and the formation of the Romanian national state, 1821–1878.* New York: Cambridge University Press.

———. 1988. Mihail Kogălniceanu: Historian as Foreign Minister, 1876–78. Chap. 6 in *Historians as nation-builders: Central and South-East Europe,* ed. Dennis Deletant and Harry Hanak. London: Macmillan Press.

Jelavich, Charles. 1988. Milenko M. Vukičević: from Serbianism to Yugoslavism. Chap. 7 in *Historians as nation-builders: Central and South-East Europe.* Dennis Deletant and Harry Hanak. London: Macmillan Press.

———. 1990. Serbian nationalism and the Croats: Vuk Karadžić's influence on Serbian textbooks. *Canadian Review of Studies in Nationalism* 27 (1–2): 31–42.

———. 1990. *South Slav nationalisms—textbooks and the Yugoslav union before 1914.* Columbus: Ohio State University Press.

Jelavich, Charles, and Barbara Jelavich, eds. 1974. *The Balkans in transition: Essays on the development of Balkan life and politics since the eighteenth century.* Berkeley: University of California Press.

———. 1977. *The establishment of the Balkan national states, 1804–1920.* Vol. 8 of *A history of East-Central Europe,* ed. Peter F. Sugar and Donald Treadgold. Seattle: University of Washington Press.

Jeszenszky, Géza. 1990. Hungary through World War I and the End of the Dual Monarchy. Chap. 15 in *A history of Hungary,* ed. Peter F. Sugar, Péter Hanák, and Tibor Frank. Bloomington and Indianapolis: Indiana University Press.

Johnston, R. J. 1991. *A question of place: Exploring the practice of human geography*. Oxford, England: Blackwell Publishers.

Johnston, R. J., David B. Knight, and Eleonore Kofman, eds. 1988. *Nationalism, self-determination and political geography*. New York: Croom Helm.

Jones, Howard Mumford. 1974. *Revolution and Romanticism*. Cambridge, Mass.: Harvard University Press.

Joó, Ruldolf. 1991. Slovenes in Hungary and Hungarians in Slovenia: Ethnic and state identity. *Ethnic and Racial Studies* 14 (January): 100–106.

————, ed. 1994. *The Hungarian minority's situation in Ceauşescu's Romania*. Trans. Chris Tennant. Boulder, Colo.: Social Science Mongraphs.

Judah, Tim. 1997. *The Serbs: History, myth, and the destruction of Yugoslavia*. New Haven, Conn.: Yale University Press.

Judt, Tony. 1990. The rediscovery of Central Europe. *Daedalus* 119 (Winter): 23–54.

Kaiser, K. 1968. *German foreign policy in transition: Bonn between east and west*. Oxford: Oxford University Press.

Kann, Robert A., and David V. Zdeněk. 1984. *The peoples of the eastern Habsburg lands, 1526–1918*. Vol. 6 of *A history of East Central Europe*, ed. Peter F. Sugar and Donald W. Treadgold. Seattle: University of Washington Press.

Karácsonyi, John. 1920. *The historical right of the Hungarian nation to its territorial integrity*. East European Problems, no. 10. New York: Steiger.

Karolyi, Michael. 1956. *Memoirs of Michael Karolyi: Faith without illusion*. Trans. Catherine Karolyi. London: Johnathan Cape.

Kasperson, Roger E., and Julian V. Minghi, eds. 1969. *The structure of political geography*. Chicago: Aldine Publishing.

Katičić, Radoslav. 1984. The making of standard Serbo-Croat. In *Aspects of the Slavic language question*, ed. by Riccardo Picchio and Harvey Goldblatt. Vol. 1 of *Church Slavonic—South Slavic—West Slavic*. New Haven, Conn.: Yale Concilium on International and Area Studies.

Kellas, James G. 1991. *The politics of nationalism and ethnicity*. Basingstoke, U.K.: Macmillan.

Kemiläinen, Aira. 1964. *Nationslism: Problems concerning the word, the concept and classification*. Jyväskylä: Kustanajat.

Kesaris, Paul L., ed. 1980. *Germany and its allies in World War II: A record of Axis collaboration problems*. Frederick, Md.: University Publications of America.

King, Charles. 1993. Moldova: Independence, unification, disintegration? *Contemporary Review* 262 (June): 281–87.

————. 1994–95. Eurasia letter: Moldova with a Russian face. *Foreign Policy* 97 (Winter): 106–20.

Kinzer, Stephen. 1992. Another Yugoslavia region, Kosovo, is threatened with ethnic conflict. *The New York Times*, 9 November, A6.

Király, Béla K. 1969. *Hungary in the late eighteenth century: The decline of the enlightened despotism*. New York: Columbia University Press.

————, ed. 1984. *East central European society and war in the era of revolutions, 1775–1856*. Vol. 4 of *War and society in East Central Europe*. New York: Social Science Monographs, Brooklyn College Press.

Király, Béla K., Peter Pastor, and Ivan Sanders, eds. 1982. *Essays on World War I: Total war and peacemaking, a case study on Trianon*. Vol. 6 of *War and society in East*

Central Europe. New York: Social Science Monographs, Brooklyn College Press.

Király, Béla K., and Gale Stokes, eds. 1985. *Insurrections, wars, and the eastern crisis in the 1870's*. Vol. 27 of *War and society in East Central Europe*. Boulder, Colo.: Social Science Monographs, Columbia University Press.

Király, Béla K., and Walter Scott Dillard, eds. 1988. *The East Central European officer corps 1740–1920's: Social origins, selections, education, and training*. Vol. 24 of *War and society in East Central Europe*. Boulder, Colo.: Social Science Monographs, Columbia University Press.

Király, Béla K., and Lászlo Veszprémy, eds. 1995. *Trianon and East Central Europe: Antecedents and repercussions*. Vol. 32 of *War and society in East Central Europe*. Boulder, Colo.: Social Science Monographs.

Kirkconnell, Watson. 1947. *A little treasury of Hungarian verse*. Washington, D.C.: American Hungarian Federation.

Klein, George, and Milan J. Reban, eds. 1981. *The politics of ethnicity in Eastern Europe*. Boulder, Colo.: East European Monographs.

Klimaszewski, Bolesław, ed. 1984. *An outline history of Polish culture*. Trans. Jerzy Kepkiewicz. Warsaw: Wydawnictwo Interpress.

Kliot, Nurit, and Stanley Waterman, eds. 1991. *The political geography of conflict and peace*. London: Belhaven Press.

Knatchbull-Hugessen, C. M. 1971. *The political evolution of the Hungarian nation*. 2 vols. New York: Arno Press and *The New York Times*; reprint, London: The National Review Office.

Knight, David B. 1982. Identity and territory: Geographical perspectives on nationalism and regionalism. *Annals of the Association of American Geographers* 72 (December): 514–31.

Koch, H. W. 1978. *A history of Prussia*. New York: Longman.

Kocsis, Károlyi. 1994. Contribution to the background of the ethnic conflicts in the Carpathian Basin. *Geojournal* 32 (April): 425–33.

Kocsis, Károlyi, and Eszter Kocsis-Hodosi. 1995. *Hungarian Minorities in the Carpathian Basin: A study in ethnic geography*. Buffalo, N.Y.: Matthias Corvinus Publishing.

Kohn, Hans. 1955. *Nationalism: Its meaning and history*. New York: D. Van Nostrand.

———. 1962. *The age of nationalism: The first era of global history*. New York: Harper and Brothers.

———. 1967. *The idea of nationalism: A study in its origins and background*. 2nd ed. New York: Collier-Macmillan.

Kolarz, Walter. 1946. *Myths and realities in Eastern Europe*. London: Lindsay Drummond.

Koljević, Svetozar. 1980. *The epic in the making*. Oxford: Clarendon Press.

Komjathy, Anthony, and Rebecca Stockwell. 1980. *German minorities and the Third Reich: Ethnic Germans of East Central Europe*. New York: Holmes and Meier Publishers.

Konnyu, Leslie. 1971. *A condensed geography of Hungary*. St. Louis, Mo.: The American Hungarian Review.

Köpeczi, Béla, ed. 1994. *History of Transylvania*. Budapest: Akadémiai Kiadó.

Kormos, C. 1944. *Rumania*. Vol. 2 of *British survey handbooks*. Cambridge: Cambridge University Press.

Kosinski, Leszek A. 1969. Changes in the ethnic structure in East-Central Europe, 1930–60. *Geographical Review* 59 (July): 388–402.

Kostić, Irena, and Slobodan Vuksanović, eds. 1991. *Pesma o Kosvu: Savremena srpska poezija*. Belgrade, Yugoslavia: Vidici SKZ, Jedinstvo. Quoted in Laura Silber and Allan Little, *The death of Yugoslavia*. (London: Penguin Books, 1997), 72.

Kostya, Sandor A. 1992. *Northern Hungary: A Historical Study of the Gechoslovak Republic*. Trans. Zoltan Leskowsky. Toronto: Associated Hungary Teachers.

Kotur, Krstivoj. 1977. *The Serbian folk epic: Its theology and anthropology*. New York: Philosophical Library.

Kovács, A. 1920. *The establishment of three states of nationalities in the place of one*. East European Problems, no. 2. New York: Steiger.

———. 1921. *The development of the population of Hungary since the cessation of the Turkish rule*. East European Problems, no. 13. New York: Steiger.

Kovács, Zoltán. 1989. Border changes and their effect on the structure of Hungarian Society. *Political Geography Quarterly* 8 (January): 79–86.

Kovrig, Bennett. 1979. *Communism in Hungary: From Kun to Kadar*. Stanford, Calif.: Hoover Institute Press.

Krieg, Hans. 1939. Landkarten als Mittel der politischen Propaganda. *Zeitschrift für Politik* 29: 663–69.

Laffan, R. G. D. 1918. *The guardians of the gate: Historical lectures on the Serbs*. Oxford: Clarendon Press.

Lampe, John R. 1996. *Yugoslavia as history: Twice there was a country*. Cambridge: Cambridge University Press.

Lázár, István. 1996a. *An illustrated history of Hungary*. Trans. Albert Tezla. Budapest: Corvina Press.

———. 1996b. *A brief history of Hungary*. Trans. Albert Tezla. Budapest: Corvina Press.

Leader, Ninon A. M. 1967. *Hungarian classical ballads and their folklore*. Cambridge: Cambridge University Press.

Lederer Ivo J. 1963. *Yugoslavia at the Paris Peace Conference: A study in frontier-making*. New Haven, Conn.: Yale University Press.

Legeza, László, and Péter Szacsvay. 1992. *Bácska és Bánság*. Budapest: Officina Nova.

Légrády Brothers. 1930. *Justice for Hungary: The cruel errors of Trianon*. Budapest: privately published.

Lehrer, Milton G. 1986. *Transylvania: History and reality*. Silver Spring, Md.: Bartleby Press.

Lengyel, Emil. 1958. *1,000 years of Hungary*. New York: John Day.

Levinsohn, Florence Hamlish. 1994. *Belgrade: Among the Serbs*. Chicago: Ivan R. Dee.

Lewin, Percy Evans. 1916. *The German road to the east: an account of the "Drang nach Osten" and of the Teutonic aims in the Near and Middle East*. London: Heinemann.

Littelfield, Frank C. 1988. *Germany and Yugoslavia, 1933–1941: the German conquest of Yugoslavia*. Boulder, Colo.: East European Monographs.

Livezeanu, Irina. 1995. *Cultural politics in greater Romania: Regionalism, nation building, and ethnic struggle, 1918–1930*. Ithaca, N.Y.: Cornell University Press.

Lockridge, Laurence S. 1989. *The ethics of Romanticism*. New York: Cambridge University Press.

Lord, Albert B. 1974. Nationalism and the Muses in Balkan Slavic Literature in the Modern Period. In *The Balkans in transition: Essays on the development of Balkan life and politics since the eighteenth century*, ed. Charles and Barbara Jelavich. Berkeley: University of California Press.

Low, D. H., trans. 1968. *The ballads of Marko Kraljević*. New York: Greenwood Press.

Lowenthal, David. 1961. Geography, experience, and imagination: towards a geographical epistemology. *Annals of the Association of American Geographers* 51 (September): 241– 60.

Ludanyi, Andrew. 1983. Ideology and Political Culture in Rumania: The Daco-Roman Theory and the "Place" of Minorities. In *Transylvania: The Roots of Ethnic Conflict*, ed. John F. Cadzow, Andrew Lundanyi, and Louis J. Elteto. Ohio: Kent State University Press.

Lukic, Reneo, and Allen Lynch. 1996. *Europe from the Balkans to the Urals: The disintegration of Yugoslavia and the Soviet Union*. Oxford: Oxford University Press.

Lukinich, Imre. 1968. *A history of Hungary in biographical sketches*. Freeport, N.Y.: Books for Libraries.

Lyall, Sarah. 1997. With gusto, Scots say yes to their own parliament. *The New York Times* 12 September, A3.

Lyde, Lionel W. 1924. *The continent of Europe*. London: MacMillan.

Lytton, Edward Robert Bulwer, and Owen Meredith. 1861. *Serbski Pesme; or National songs of Serbia*. London: Chapman and Hall.

Macartney, Carlile A. 1937. *Hungary and her successors*. London: Oxford University Press.

———. 1942. *Problems of the Danubian basin*. Cambridge: Cambridge University Press.

———. 1953. *The medieval Hungarian historians: A critical and analytical guide*. Cambridge: Cambridge University Press.

———. 1961. *October fifteenth: A history of modern Hungary 1929–1945*. 2nd ed. 2 vols. Edinburgh: Edinburgh University Press.

———. 1962. *Hungary: A short history*. Chicago, Ill.: Aldine Publishing Company.

———. 1968a. *The Magyars in the ninth century*. Cambridge: Cambridge University Press.

———. 1968b. *National states and national minorities*. New York: Russell and Russell.

———. 1969. *The Hapsburg empire, 1790–1918*. New York: Macmillan.

Macartney, Carlile A., and A. W. Palmer. 1962. *Independent Eastern Europe: A history*. New York: Macmillan, St. Martin's Press.

MacGregor-Hastie, Roy. 1972. *The last Romantic: Mihail Eminescu*. Iowa City: University of Iowa Press.

MacKenzie, David. 1967. *The Serbs and Russian Pan-Slavism, 1875–1878*. Ithaca, N.Y.: Cornell University Press.

———. 1985. *Ilija Garašanin: Balkan Bismarck*. Boulder, Colo.: East European Monographs.

———. 1996. *Serbs and Russians*. Boulder, Colo.: East European Monographs.

MacKinder, Halford J. [1919] 1942. *Democratic ideals and reality*. Reprint, New York: Henry Holt.

Magocsi, Paul Robert. 1993. *Historical atlas of East Central Europe*. Seattle: University of Seattle Press.

Magaš, Branka. 1993. *The destruction of Yugoslavia: Tracing the break-up, 1980–92.* New York: Verso.

Malcolm, Noel. 1994. *Bosnia: A short history.* New York: New York University Press.

———. 1998. *Kosovo: A short history.* New York: New York University Press.

Maliţa, Mircea. 1970. *Romanian diplomacy: A historical survey.* Meridiane Publishing House.

Malmberg, Torsten. 1980. *Human territoriality.* The Hague: Mouton.

Manga, János. 1969. *Hungarian folk song and folk instruments.* Budapest: Corvina Press.

Marczali, Henry. 1910. *Hungary in the eighteenth century.* Cambridge: Cambridge University Press.

Markoff, Milan G. 1918. *Bulgaria's historical right to Dobrudja.* Bern, Switzerland: Paul Haupt, Akademische Buchhandlung vormals Max Drechsel.

Martin, Lt. Col. Lawrence. 1924. *The treaties of peace 1919–1923, Vol I: Containing the Treaty of Versailles, The Treaty of St. Germain-en-Laye and the Treaty of Trianon.* New York: Carnegie Endowment for International Peace.

Matthias, John, and Vladeta Vučković, trans. 1987. *The battle of Kosovo.* Athens: Swallow Press, Ohio University Press.

Mayer, Arno J. 1967. *Politics and diplomacy of peace making: Containment and counterrevolution at Versailles, 1918–1919.* New York: Alfred A. Knopf.

Mayo, James M. 1988. War Memorials as Political Memory. *Geographical Review* 78 (January): 62–75.

McNally, Raymond T. and Radu Florescu. 1994. *In search of Dracula: The history of Dracula and vampires.* New York: Houghton Mifflin.

McNeill, William. 1985. *Polyethnicity and national unity in world history.* Toronto: University of Toronto Press.

Mehendinţi, S. 1986. *What is Transylvania?* Miami Beach, Fla.: Romanian Historical Studies.

Meinig, D. W. 1979. *Symbolic landscapes.* In *The interpretation of ordinary landscapes: Geographical Essays,* ed. D. W. Meining. New York: Oxford University Press.

Mellor, Roy E. H. 1975. *Eastern Europe: A geography of Comecon countries.* New York: Columbia University Press.

Mihnea, Gheorghiu, ed. 1973. *Romania and her cultural policy.* Bucharest: Meridiane Publishing House.

Mikesell, M.W. 1983. The myth of the nation-state. *Journal of Geography* 82: 257–60.

Miletich, John S. 1990. *The Burgarštica: A bilingual anthology of the earliest extant south Slavic folk narrative song.* Chicago: University of Illinois Press.

Miller, David Hunter. 1924. *My diary at the conference of Paris.* 21 vols. New York: Appeal Printing, privately printed.

Milojević, Borivojie Ž. 1925. The kingdom of the Serbs, Croats, and Slovenes: administrative divisions in relation to natural regions. *Geographical Review* 15 (January): 70–83.

Mitton, G. E. 1915. *Austria-Hungary.* London: Adam and Charles Black.

Mocsy, Istvan I. 1983. *The effects of World War I—The uprooted Hungarian refugees and their impact on Hungary's domestic politics, 1918–1921.* Vol. 12 of *War and society in East Central Europe.* New York: Social Science Monographs, Brooklyn College Press.

Montgomery, John Flournoy. 1947. *Hungary: The unwilling satellite*. New York: Devin-Adair.

Moraru, Tiberiu, Vasile Cucu, and Ion Velcea. 1966. *The geography of Romania*. Bucharest: Meridiane Publishing House.

Morison, W. A. 1942. *The revolt of the Serbs against the Turks (1804–1813): Translations from the Serbian national ballads of the period*. Cambridge: Cambridge Universtiy Press.

Morse, David. 1982. *Romanticism: A structural analysis*. New Jersey: Barnes and Noble Books.

Muir, Richard. 1975. *Modern political geography*. New York: John Wiley and Sons.

Murphy, Alexander B. 1988. *The regional dynamics of language differentiation in Belgium: A study in cultural-political geography*. University of Chicago Department of Geography Research Paper no. 227.

———. 1989. Territorial policies in multi-ethnic states. *Geographical Review* 79 (October): 410–21.

———. 1990. Historical justifications for territorial claims. *Annals of the Association of American Geographers* 80 (December): 531–48.

———. 1991a. Territorial ideology and international conflict: The legacy of prior political formations. Chap. 9 in *The political geography of conflict and peace*, ed. Nurit Kliot and Stanley Waterman. London: Belhaven Press.

———. 1991b. Regions as social constructs: The gap between theory and practice. *Progress in Human Geography* 15 (March): 23–35.

Murphy, Dervla. 1992. *Transylvania and beyond*. London: John Murray.

Musicescu, Maria Ana, and Sorin Ulea. 1971. *Voroneţ*. Verlag, Bucharest, Romania: Meridiane.

Musicescu, Maria Ana, and Grigore Ionescu. 1976. *Biserica Domneasca Din Curtea De Argeş*. Bucharest, Romania: Editura Meridiane.

Naylor, Kenneth E. 1976. Transitional West Bulgarian dialects: A structural approach. In *Bulgaria past and present: Studies in history, literature, economics, music, sociology, folklore and linguistics*, ed. Thomas Butler. Columbus, Ohio: American Association for the Advancement of Slavic Studies.

———. 1980. Serb-Croatian. In *The Slavic literary languages: Formation and Development*, ed. Alexander M. Schenker and Edward Stankiewicz. New Haven, Conn.: Yale Concilium on International and Area Studies.

Nelson, D. N. 1988. *Romanian politics in the Ceauşescu era*. New York: Gordon and Breach.

Nemoianu, Virgil. 1984. *The taming of Romanticism*. Cambridge, Mass.: Harvard University Press.

Nettl, Paul. 1967. *National anthems*. 2nd ed. Trans. Alexander Gode. New York: Frederick Ungar Publishing.

The new boundaries of Hungary 1920. *Geographical Review* 10 (December): 408–12.

The New York Times. 1996. Romania and Hungary sign treaty on rights. 17 September, A8.

Njegoš, P. P. 1986. *The Mountain Wreath*. Trans., ed. Vasa D. Mihailovich. Irvine, Calif.: Charles Schlacks Jr., Publisher.

Norris, Robert E., and L. Lloyd Haring. 1980. *Political geography*. Columbus, Ohio: Charles E. Merrill Publishing.

Noyes, George Rapall, and Leonard Bacon, trans. 1913. *Heroic ballads of Serbia.* Boston: Sherman, French.

O'Ballance, Edgar. 1995. *Civil War in Bosnia: 1992–94.* New York: St. Martin's Press.

Oberhummer, Eugen. 1920. Die politische Karte Europas nach serbische Plänen aus dem Anfang des Weltkrieges. *Petermanns Geographische Mitteilungen* 66 (September): 190.

O'Grady, Joseph, ed. 1967. *The immigrants influence on Wilson's peace policies.* Lexington: University of Kentucky Press.

Oinas, Felix J., ed. 1978. *Folklore, nationalism, and politics.* Columbus, Ohio: Slavica Publishers.

Okey, Robin. 1986. *Eastern Europe 1740–1985: Feudalism to communism.* 2nd ed. London: Hutchinson.

Oldson, William O. 1973. *The historical and nationalistic of Nicholae Iorga.* Boulder, Colo.: East European Quarterly.

O'Loughlin, John. 1986 Spatial models of international conflict: Extending current theories of war behavior. *Annals of the Association of American Geographers* 76 (March): 63–80.

Oprescu, George. 1935. *Roumanian art from 1800 to our days.* Malmö, Sweden: A.B. Malmö Ljustrycksanstalt.

Ormos, Mária. 1990. *From Padua to the Trianon 1918–1920.* Boulder, Colo.: Social Science Monographs.

Osborne, R. H. 1967. *East-Central Europe.* New York: Frederick A. Praeger.

Paget, John. 1839. *Hungary and Transylvania; with remarks on their condition, social, political, and economical.* 2 vols. London: John Murray.

Palmer, Alan. 1970. *The lands between: A history of East-Central Europe since the Congress of Vienna.* New York: Macmillan.

Palumbo, Michael, and William O. Shanahan, eds. 1981. *Nationalism: Essays in honor of Louis L. Synder.* Westport, Conn.: Greenwood Press.

Pascu, Ştefan. 1982. *A history of Transylvania.* Trans. by Robert Ladd. Detroit: Wayne State University Press.

Pastor, Peter. 1976. *Hungary between Wilson and Lenin: The Hungarian revolution of 1918–1919 and the big three.* Boulder, Colo.: East European Quarterly.

———, ed. 1988. *Revolutions and interventions in Hungary and its neighbor states, 1918–1919.* Vol. 20 of *War and society in East Central Europe.* Boulder, Colo.: Social Science Monographs.

Pavlowitch, Stevan K. 1988. *The improbable survivor: Yugoslavia and its problems, 1918–1988.* Columbus: Ohio State University Press.

Pearcy, G. Etzel, Russell H. Fifield, and Associates. 1948. *World political geography.* New York: Thomas Y. Crowell.

Pearson, Raymond. 1983. *National minorities in Eastern Europe 1848–1945.* London: Macmillan Press.

———. 1994. *The Longman companion to European nationalism, 1789–1920.* London: Longman.

Pearton, Maurice. 1988. Nicholae Iorga as historian and politician. Chap. 10 in *Historians as nation-builders: Central and South-East Europe,* ed. Dennis Deletant and Harry Hanak. London: Macmillan Press.

Peckham, Morse, ed. 1965. *Romanticism: The culture of the nineteenth century.* New

York: George Braziller.

Pei, Mario. 1965. *The story of language.* New York: J.B. Lippincott.

Peić, Sava. 1994. *Medieval Serbian culture.* London: Alpine Fine Arts Collection.

Pennington, Anne, trans. 1977. *Vasko Popa: Collected poems 1943–1976.* Manchester, Great Britain: Carcanet New Press.

Pennington, Anne, and Peter Levi, trans. 1984. *Marko the prince: Serbo-Croat heroic songs.* London: Duckworth.

Penrose, Jan, and Joe May. 1991. Herder's concept of nation and its relevance to contemporary ethnic nationalism. *Canadian Review of Studies in Nationalism* 28 (1–2): 165–78.

Perjés, Géza. 1989. *The fall of the medieval kingdom of Hungary: Mohács 1526–Buda 1541.* Translated by Márió D. Fenyő. Vol. 26 of *War and society in East Central Europe.* Boulder, Colo.: Social Science Mongraphs.

Péter, Katalin. 1990. The latter Ottoman period and royal Hungary, 1606–1711. Chap. 8 in *A history of Hungary,* ed. Peter F. Sugar, Péter Hanák, and Tibor Frank. Bloomington and Indianapolis: Indiana University Press.

Péter, László. 1992a. The national community and its past: Reflections on the history of Transylvania. *The New Hungarian Quarterly* 33 (Spring): 3–11.

————, ed. 1992b. *Historians and the history of Transylvania.* Boulder, Colo.: East European Mongraphs.

Petrovich, Michael Boro. 1976. *A history of modern Serbia, 1804–1918.* 2 vols. New York: Harcourt Brace Jovanovich.

Piirainen, Timo, ed. 1994. *Change and continuity in Eastern Europe.* Aldershot: Dartmouth.

Pinson, Mark, ed. 1994. *The Muslims of Bosnia-Hercegovina: Their historic development from the Middle Ages to the dissolution of Yugoslavia.* Cambridge, Mass.: Harvard University Press.

Pipa, Arshi. 1989. The situation of the Albanians in Yugoslavia, with particular attention to the Kosovo problem. *East European Quarterly* 23 (Summer): 159–81.

Pipa, Arshi, and Sami Repishti, eds. 1984. *Studies on Kosova.* Boulder, Colo.: East European Monographs.

Pivany, Eugene. 1919. *Some facts about the proposed dismemberment of Hungary.* Cleveland, Ohio: Hungarian American Federation.

Plantinga, Leon. 1984. *Romantic music: A history of musical style in nineteenth-century Europe.* New York: W.W. Norton.

Pleshoyano, Dan V. 1991. *Colonel Nicholae Pleşoianu and the national regeneration movement in Walachia.* Boulder, Colo.: East European Monographs.

Polonsky, Anthony. 1975. *The little dictators: The history of Eastern Europe since 1918.* Boston: Routledge and Kegan Paul.

Popa, Eli. 1966. *Romania is a song.* Cleveland, Ohio: America Publishing.

Popović, Tatyana. 1988. *Prince Marko: The hero of south Slavic epics.* New York: Syracuse University Press.

Popovici, Andrei. 1931. *The political status of Bessarabia.* Washington, D.C.: Ransdell.

Portal, Roger. 1969. *The Slavs: A cultural and historical survey of the Slavonic peoples.* New York: Harper and Row Publishers.

Porter, Roy, and Mikuláš Teich, eds. 1988. *Romanticism in national context.* Cambridge: Cambridge University Press.

Poulton, Hugh. 1994. *The Balkans: Minorities and states in conflict*. London: Minority Rights Publications.

Poulton, Hugh and Suha Taji-Farouki. 1997. *Muslim identity and the Balkan state*. New York: New York University Press.

Pounds, Norman J. G. 1961. *Geographical essays on Eastern Europe*. Bloomington: Indiana University.

———. 1963. *Political geography*. New York: McGraw-Hill.

———. 1969. *Eastern Europe*. Chicago: Aldine Publishing.

———. 1990. *An historical geography of Europe*. Cambridge: Cambridge University Press.

Pounds, Norman J. G., and Sue Simons Ball. 1964. Core-Areas and the development of the European state system. *Annals of the Association of American Geographers* 54 (March): 24–40.

Prodan, David. 1992. *Transylvania and again Transylvania: A historical exposé*. Cluj-Napoca, Romania: Center for Transylvanian Studies, The Romanian Cultural Foundation.

Pusich, Scott Michael. 1991. Political and ethnic nationalism in Yugoslavia, 1918–1990. M.A. thesis, Florida State University.

Pred, Allan. 1984. Place as historically contingent process: Structuration and the time-geography of becoming places. *Annals of the Association of American Geographers* 74 (June): 279–97.

Ramet, Sabrina Petra. 1996. *Balkan babel: the disintegration of Yugoslavia from the death of Tito to ethnic war*. 2nd ed. Boulder, Colo.: Westview Press.

Rácz, István. 1969. *Lieder der Puszta: Balladen von Hirten und Räubern, Ungarische Hirtendunst, Lieder aus der Puszta auf Schallplatte*. Olten and Freiburg, Switzerland: Urs-Graf Verlag.

Rădulescu, A.V. 1977. *The triumphal monument Tropaeum Traiani at Adamclisi*. Constanta, Romania: The Museum of National History and Archaeology.

Rady, Martyn. 1992. *Romania in turmoil: A contemporary history*. New York: IB Tauris.

Rady, Martyn. 1996. Self-determination and the dissolution of Yugoslavia. *Ethnic and Racial Studies* 19 (2/April): 379–390.

Rajchman, Marthe. 1944. *Europe: An atlas of human geography*. New York: William Morrow.

Ramet, Sabrina P. 1992. *Nationalism and federalism in Yugoslavia, 1962–1991*. Bloomington: Indiana University Press.

Ramm, Agatha. 1984. *Europe in the nineteenth century: 1789–1905*. Vol. 1. New York: Longman.

———. 1984. *Europe in the twentieth century: 1905–1970*. Vol. 2. New York: Longman.

Relph, E. 1976. *Place and placelessness*. London: Pion Lion.

Rich, Norman. 1970. *The age of nationalism and reform, 1850–1890*. 2nd ed. New York: W.W. Norton.

Roark, Michael O. 1993. Homelands: A conceptual essay. *Journal of Cultural Geography* 13 (Spring/Summer) 5–11.

Robins, Keith, 1984. *The First World War*. Oxford: Oxford University Press.

Rodman, Margaret C. 1992. Empowering place: Multilocality and multivocality. *American Anthropologist* 94 (September): 640–56.

Romsics, Ignác, ed. 1995. *20th century Hungary and the Great Powers*. Vol. 33 of *War and society in East Central Europe.* Boulder, Colo.: Social Science Monographs.

Ronnett, Alexander E. 1974. *Romanian nationalism: The legionary movement.* Trans. Vasile C. Barsan. Chicago: Loyola University Press.

Rootham, Helen. 1920. *Kosovo: Heroic songs of the Serbs.* Boston: Houghton Mifflin.

Roscin, John. 1991. *Transylvania, the Rumanian cradle.* New York: J. Rocsin.

Rosenberg, Michael. 1990. The mother of invention: Evolutionary theory, territoriality, and the origins of agriculture. *American Anthropologist* 92 (June): 399–415.

Rothchild, Joseph. 1989. *Return to diversity: A political history of East Central Europe since World War II.* New York: Oxford University Press.

Roucek, Joseph S. 1932. *Contemporary Roumania and her problems: A study in modern nationalism.* Stanford: Stanford University Press.

Roumania at the peace conference. 1946. Paris.

Rugg, Dean S. 1985. *Eastern Europe.* New York: Longman.

Rumanian architecture. 1956. Bucharest: Foreign Languages Publishing House.

Rupnik, Jacques. 1989. *The other Europe.* New York: Pantheon Books.

———. 1994. Europe's new frontiers: remapping Europe. *Daedalus* 123 (Summer): 91–114.

Rushdie, Salman. 1991. *Imaginary homelands: Essays and criticism 1981–1991.* London: Granta Books.

Sack, Robert David. 1980. *Conceptions of space in social thought.* Minneapolis: University of Minnesota.

———. 1981. Territorial bases of power. Chap. 3 in *Political studies from spatial perspectives: Anglo-American essays on political geography,* ed. Alan D. Burnett and Peter J. Taylor. New York: John Wiley and Sons.

———. 1986. *Human territoriality: Its theory and history.* New York: Cambridge University Press.

———. 1993. The power of place and space. *Geographical Review* 83 (July): 326–329.

Sahlins, Peter. 1990. Natural frontiers revisited: France's boundaries since the seventeenth century. *The American Historical Review* 95 (December): 1423–1451.

Samary, Catherine. 1995. *Yugoslavia dismembered.* Trans. Peter Drucker. New York: Monthly Review Press.

Samuel, Raphael, and Gareth Stedman Jones, ed. 1982. *Culture ideology and politics: Essays for Eric Hobsbawn.* London: Routledge and Kegan Paul.

Samuelson, James. 1882. *Roumania: Past and present.* London: Longmans, Green.

Satmarescu, Gy. D. 1975. The changing demographic structure of the population of Transylvania. *East European Quarterly* 8 (January) : 425–40.

Schama, Simon. 1996. *Landscape and memory.* New York: Vintage Books.

Schevill, Ferdinand. 1922. *The history of the Balkan peninsula: From the earliest times to the present day.* New York: Harcourt, Brace.

Schieder, Theodor, ed. 1961a. *The fate of the Germans in Hungary.* Vol. 2 of *Documents on the expulsion of the Germans from Eastern-Central-Europe.* Bonn, Germany: Federal Ministry for Expellees, and War Victims.

———, ed. 1961b. *The fate of the Germans in Rumania.* Vol. 3 of *Documents on the expulsion of the Germans from Eastern-Central-Europe.* Bonn, Germany: Federal Ministry for Expellees, and War Victims.

Schöpflin, George. 1974. Rumanian nationalism. *Survey* 20 (Spring/Summer): 77–104.

————. 1978. *The Hungarians of Rumania*. Report no. 37, London: Minority Rights Group, Camera Press.

————. 1980. Nationality in the fabric of Yugoslav politics. *Survey: a Journal of East and West Studies* 25 (Summer): 1–19.

————, ed. 1986. *The Soviet Union and Eastern Europe: A handbook*. London: Muller, Blond, and White.

————. 1991. National identity in the Soviet Union and East Central Europe. *Ethnic and Racial Studies* 14 (January): 3–14.

Schöpflin, George, and Nancy Wood, eds. 1989. *In search of Central Europe*. Cambridge: Polity Press.

Schulze, Hagen, ed. 1987. *Nation-Building in Central Europe*. New York: Berg Publishers.

Sekelj, Laslo. 1993. *Yugoslavia: the process of disintegration*. Trans. Vera Vukelic. Boulder, Colo.: Social Science Mongraphs.

Sells, Michael A. 1996. *The bridge betrayed: Religion and genocide in Bosnia*. Berkeley: University of California Press.

Seton-Watson, Hugh. 1956. *The East European revolution*. New York: Frederick A. Praeger.

————. 1962. *Eastern Europe between the wars 1918–1941*. 3rd ed. New York: Harper and Row, Publishers.

————. 1975. *The "Sick Heart" of Europe*. Seattle: University of Washington.

————. 1977. *Nations and states: An enquiry into the origins of nations and the politics of nationalism*. Boulder, Colo.: Westview Press.

————. 1981a. *The making of a new Europe: R. W. Seton-Watson and the last years of Austria-Hungary*. Seattle: University of Washington Press.

————. 1981b. *Language and national consciousness*. London: Oxford University Press.

————. 1985. What is Europe, where is Europe? From mystique to politique. *Encounter* 65 (July/August): 9–17.

Seton-Watson, Hugh, and Christopher Seton-Watson. 1981. *The making of a new Europe*. Seattle: University of Washington Press.

Seton-Watson, R. W. 1963. *A history of the Roumanians: From Roman times to the completion of unity*. New York: Archon Books.

Seymour, Charles. 1951. *Geography, justice, and politics at the Paris conference of 1919*. New York: American Geographical Society.

Shafer, Boyd C. 1955. *Nationalism: Myth and reality*. New York: Harcourt, Brace and World.

————. 1972. *Faces of Nationalism: New realities and old myths*. New York: Harcourt Brace Jovanovich.

Shea, John. 1997. *Macedonia and Greece: The struggle to define a new Balkan nation*. Jefferson, N.C.: McFarland.

Shelley, Fred M. 1994. Geography, territory, and ethnicity: Current perspectives from political geography. *Urban Geography* 15 (March): 189–200.

Skendi, Stravro. 1980. *Balkan cultural studies*. Boulder, Colo.: East European Monographs.

Sisa, Stephen. 1990. *The spirit of Hungary: A panorama of Hungarian history and culture*. 2nd ed. Ontario: A Wintario Project.

Siklos, Andras. 1988. *Revolution in Hungary and the dissolution of the multinational state, 1918*. Trans. Zsuzsa Beres. Budapest: Akadémiai Kiadó.

Silber, Laura, and Allan Little. 1997. *The death of Yugoslavia.* London: Penguin Books.

Singleton, Fred. 1965. *Background to Eastern Europe.* New York: Pergamon Press.

———. 1976. *Twentieth-Century Yugoslavia.* New York: Columbia University Press.

———. 1985. *A short history of Yugoslav peoples.* New York: Cambridge University Press.

Sinor, Denis. 1959. *History of Hungary.* London: Ruskin House, George Allen and Unwin.

Smith, Anthony D. 1979. *Nationalism in the twentieth century.* New York: New York University Press.

———. 1981a. *The ethnic revival.* Cambridge: Cambridge University Press.

———. 1981b. States and homelands: The social and geopolitical implications of national territory. *Millennium* 10 (Summer): 187–202.

———. 1981c. War and ethnicity: The role of warfare in the formation of self-images and cohesion of ethnic communites. *Ethnic and Racial Studies* 4 (October): 375–97.

———. 1983. *Theories of nationalism.* 2nd ed. New York: Harper and Row.

———. 1984a. Ethnic myths and ethnic revivals. *European Journal of Sociology* 25 (November): 283–305.

———. 1984b. National identity and myths of ethnic descent. *Research in Social movements, Conflict and Change* 7: 95–130.

———. 1985. *Ethnie* and nation in the modern world. *Millennium* 14 (Spring): 127–42.

———. 1986a. Conflict and collective identity: Class, *ethnie*, and nation. In *The theory and practice of international conflict resolution*, ed. E. E. Azar and J. W. Burton. Brighton, G. B.: Wheatsheaf.

———. 1986b. *The ethnic origins of nations.* New York: Basil Blackwell.

———. 1994. The problem of national identity: ancient, medieval and modern? *Ethnic and Racial Studies* 17 (July 1994): 375–99.

Snyder, Louis L., ed. 1964. *The dynamics of nationalism.* New York: D. Van Nostrand.

———. 1976. *The varities of nationalism, a comparative view.* Hinsdale, Ill.: The Dryden Press.

———. 1978. *Roots of German nationalism.* Bloomington: Indiana University Press.

———. 1990. *Encyclopedia of nationalism.* Chicago: St. James Press.

Soja, Edward W. 1971. *The political organization of space.* American Geographers Resource Paper no. 8.

———. 1989. *Postmodern geographies: the reassertion of space in critical social theory.* New York: Verso.

Somogyi, Éva. 1990. The age of Neoabsolutism, 1849–1867. Chap. 13 in *A history of Hungary*, ed. Peter F. Sugar, Péter Hanák, and Tibor Frank. Bloomington and Indianapolis: Indiana University Press.

Sopher, David E. 1967. *Geography of religions: Foundations of cultural geography series.* Englewood Cliffs, N.J.: Prentice-Hall.

Sötér, I., and I. Neupokoyeva, eds. 1977. *European Romanticism.* Budapest: Akadémiai Kiadó.

Sozan, Michael. 1977. *The history of Hungarian ethnography.* Washington, D.C.: University Press of America.

Spencer, Christopher. 1993. *The former Yugoslavia: Background to crisis.* Toronto, Canada: Kings College Circle.

Spinei, Victor. 1986. *Moldavia in the 11th-14th centuries*. Bucharest: Editura Academiei Republicii Socialiste România.

Spira, Thomas. 1982. The Sopron (Ödenburg) plebiscite of December 1921 and the German nationality problem. In *Essays on World War I: Total war and peace making, a case study on Trianon*. Vol. 7 of *War and society in East Central Europe*, ed. Béla Király, Peter Pastor, and Ivan Sanders. New York: Social Science Monographs.

Stalin, Joseph V. 1994. The Nation. Chap. 2 in *Nationalism*, ed. John Hutchinson and Anthony D. Smith. New York: Oxford University Press.

Stavrianos, Leften Stavros. 1941–42. Balkan federation: A history of the movement toward Balkan unity in modern times. *Smith College Studies in History* 27 (October-July): 1–338.

——. 1957. Antecedents to the Balkan revolutions of the nineteenth century. *Journal of Modern History* 29 (December): 335–48.

——. 1958. *The Balkans since 1453*. New York: Rinehart.

Ștefănescu-Draganești, Virgiliu. 1986. *Romanian continuity in Roman Dacia: Linguistic evidence*. Miami Beach, Fla.: Romanian Historical Studies.

Stoica, Vasile, ed. 1919. *The Roumanian question*. Pittsburgh, Pa.: Pittsburgh Printing.

——, ed. 1919. *The Roumanian nation and the Roumanian kingdom*. Pittsburgh, Pa.: Pittsburgh Printing.

Stoicescu, Nicolae. 1983. *The continuity of the Romanian people*. Bucharest: Editura Științifică Și Enciclopedică.

——. 1986. *Age-Old factors of Romanian unity*. Bucharest: Editura Academiei Republicii Socialiste România.

Stokes, Gale. 1997. *Three eras of political change in Eastern Europe*. New York: Oxford University Press.

Subotić, Gojko. 1998. *Art of Kosovo: The sacred land*. Trans. Vida Janković and Radmila Popović. New York: Monacelli Press.

Subotić, Dragutin. [1932] 1976. *Yugoslav popular ballads: Their origin and development*. Reprint, Cambridge: Cambridge University Press.

Suchoff, Benjamin, ed. 1967. *Rumanian folk music*. 4 vols. The Hague: Martinus Nijhoff.

——. ed. 1981. *The Hungarian folk song by Béla Bartók*. Trans. M. D. Calvocoressi. Albany: State University of New York Press.

Sudetic, Chuck. 1991. Another Yugoslavia state breaks ties. *The New York Times*, 22 February, A3.

Sugar, Peter F. 1977. *Southeastern Europe under Ottoman Rule, 1354–1804*. Vol. 5 of *History of East Central Europe*, ed. Peter F. Sugar and Donald W. Treadgold. Seattle: University of Washington Press.

——. ed. 1980. *Ethnic diversity and conflict in Eastern Europe*. Santa Barbara, Calif.: ABC-Clio.

——. 1981. From ethnicity to nationalism and back again. Chap. 5 in *Nationalism: Essays in honor of Louis L. Snyder*, ed. Michael Palumbo and William O. Shanahan. Westport, Conn.: Greenwood Press.

——. 1990. The principality of Transylvania. Chap. 9 in *A history of Hungary*, ed. Peter F. Sugar, Péter Hanák, and Tibor Frank. Bloomington and Indianapolis: Indiana University Press.

Sugar, Peter F., Péter Hanák, and Tibor Frank, eds. 1990. *A history of Hungary*.

Bloomington and Indianapolis: Indiana University Press.

Symmons-Symonolewicz, Konstantin. 1985. The concept of nationhood: Towards a theoretical clarification. *Canadian Review of Studies in Nationalism* 12 (Fall): 215–22.

Szacsvay, Imre, Péter Szacsvay, and László Legeza. 1990. *Kárpátalja*. Budapest: Officina Nova.

Szacsvay, Imre, and Kicsi Sándor Írta. 1993. *Erdélyi Utakon*. 3 vols. Budapest: Officina Nova.

Szendrey, Thomas. 1988. Mihály Vörösmarty and the development of Romanticism in Hungary. In *Triumph in adversity: Studies in Hungarian civilization in honor of Professor Ferenc Somogyi on the occasion of his eightieth birthday*, ed. Steven Béla Várdy and Ágnes Huszár Várdy. Boulder, Colo.: East European Monographs.

Szilassy, Sandor. 1969. Hungary on the brink of a cliff 1918–1919. *East European Quarterly* 3 (March): 95–109.

Tanner, Marcus. 1997. *Croatia: A nation forged in war*. New Haven, Conn.: Yale University Press.

Tatrosi, John. 1920. *The Hungarians of Moldavia*. East European Problems, no. 8. New York: Steiger.

Taylor, A. J. P. 1957. *The struggle for the mastery of Europe: 1848–1918*. Oxford: Clarendon Press.

Taylor, Peter J. 1989. *Political geography: World economy, nation-state, and locality*. 2nd ed. New York: Longman Group.

———. 1993. Contra political geography. *Tijdschrift voor Economische en Sociale Geografie* 84: 82–90.

Taylor, Peter, and John House, eds. 1984. *Political geography: Recent advances and future directions*. London: Croom Helm.

Teich, Mikuláš, and Roy Porter, eds. 1993. *The national question in Europe in historical context*. Cambridge: Cambridge University Press.

Teleki, Paul. 1923. *The evolution of Hungary and its place in European history*. New York: Macmillan.

Temperely, Harold W. V. 1919. *History of Serbia*. London: G. Bell and Sons.

———, ed. 1921. *A history of the Paris Peace Conference*. 6 vols. London: Henry Frowde and Hodder and Stoughton.

———. 1928. How the Hungarian frontiers were drawn. *Foreign Affairs* 6 (April): 432–47.

Thane, Pat, Geoffrey Crossick, and Roderick Floud, eds. 1984. *The power of the past: Essays for Eric Hobsbawn*. Cambridge: Cambridge University Press.

Thernstrom, Stephan, ed. 1980. *Harvard encyclopedia of American ethnic groups*. Cambridge, Mass.: Harvard University Press.

Thomas, Raju G. C., and H. Richard Friman, eds. 1996. *The South Slav conflict: History, religion, ethnicity, and nationalism*. New York: Garland Publishing.

Thuróczy, János. 1991. *Chronicle of the Hungarians*. Trans. Frank Montello. Bloomington: Indiana University.

Tihany, Leslie Charles. 1976. *A history of Middle Europe: From the earliest times to the age of the world wars*. New Jersey: Rutgers University Press.

———. 1978. *The Baranya dispute 1918–1921: Diplomacy in the vortex of ideologies*. Boulder, Colo.: East European Quarterly.

Tipton, Frank B., and Robert Aldrich. 1989. *An economic and social history of Europe, 1890–1939.* Baltimore, Md.: Johns Hopkins University Press.

———. 1989. *An economic and social history of Europe, from 1939 to the present.* Baltimore, Md.: Johns Hopkins University Press.

Tivey, Leonard, ed. 1981. *The nation-state: The formation of modern politics.* New York: St. Martin's.

Tőkés, Rudolf L. 1967. *Béla Kun and the Hungarian soviet republic: The origins and role of the communist party of Hungary in the revolutions of 1918–1919.* New York: Frederick A. Praeger, Publishers.

Tomašević, Nebojša, and Kosta Rakić, eds. 1983. *Treasures of Yugoslavia.* Beograd: Yugoslaviapublic.

Todorova, Maria. 1997. *Imagining the Balkans.* New York: Oxford University Press.

Toynbee, Arnold J. 1915. *Nationality and the war.* Toronto, Canada: J.M. Dent and Sons.

Treptow, Kurt W., ed. 1996. *A history of Romania.* New York: East European Mongraphs.

Tuan, Yi-Fu. 1974. *Topophilia: A study of environmental perception, attitudes, and values.* Englewood Cliffs, N.J.: Prentice-Hall.

———. 1977. *Space and place: The perspective of experience.* Minneapolis: University of Minnesota Press.

———. 1980. The significance of the artifact. *Geographical Review* 70 (October): 462–72.

———. 1991. Language and the making of place: A narrative-descriptive approach. *Annals of the Association of American Geographers* 81 (December): 684–96.

Tunnard, Christopher, and Howard Hope Reed. 1955. *American skyline: The growth and form of our cities and towns.* Boston: Houghton Mifflin.

Turnock, David. 1978. *Studies in industrial geography: Eastern Europe.* Boulder, Colo.: Westview.

———. 1988. *The making of Eastern Europe: From earliest times to 1815.* New York: Routledge.

———. 1989. *The human geography of Eastern Europe.* New York: Routledge.

———. 1989. *Eastern Europe: An Economic and Political Geography.* New York: Routledge.

Urbansky, Andrew B. 1968. *Byzantium and the Danube frontier: A study of the relations between Byzantium, Hungary, and the Balkans during the period of the Comneni.* New York: Twayne Publishers.

Vagts, Alfred. 1959. *A history of militarism, civilian and military.* Revised ed. New York: Free Press.

Vale, Lawrence J. 1992. *Architecture, power, and national identity.* New Haven, Conn.: Yale University Press.

Vambéry, Arminius. 1887. *Hungary: in ancient, mediaeval, and modern times.* 2nd ed. London: T. Fisher Unwin.

Van den Berghe, Pierre. 1981. *The ethnic phenomenon.* New York: Elsevier.

Van Meurs, Wim P. 1994. *The Bessarabian question in Communist historiography: Nationalist and Cummunist politics and history-writing.* New York: East European Monographs.

Vána, Zdenek. 1983. *The world of the ancient Slavs.* Detroit: Wayne State University Press.

Váradi, Péter Pál, and Lilla Lőwey. 1995. *Erdély: Tél a havason.* Budapest: Közdok.

Várdy, Steven Béla. 1976. *Modern Hungarian historiography.* Boulder, Colo.: East European Quarterly.

———. 1985. *Clio's art in Hungary and in Hungarian-America.* Boulder, Colo.: East European Monographs.

Várdy, Steven Béla, and Ágnes Huszár Várdy, eds. 1988. *Triumph in adversity: Studies in Hungarian civilization in Honor of professor Ferenc Somogyi on the occasion of his eightieth birthday.* Boulder, Colo.: East European Monographs.

———. 1989. *The Austro-Hungarian mind: At home and abroad.* Boulder, Colo.: East European Monographs.

Vargyas, Lajos. 1967. *Researches into the mediaeval history of folk ballad.* Budapest: Akadémiai Kiadó.

———. 1983. *Hungarian ballads and the European ballad tradition.* 2 vols. Budapest: Akadémiai Kiadó.

Vasić, Miloš. 1996. The Yugoslav army and the post-Yugoslav armies. Chap. 7 in *Yugoslavia and after: A study in fragmentation, despair and rebirth,* ed. David A. Dyker and Ivan Vejvoda. New York: Longman.

Verdery, Katherine. 1983. *Transylvanian Villagers: Three centuries of political, economic, and ethnic change.* Berkeley: University of California Press.

———. 1985. On the nationality problem in Transylvania until World War II: An overview. *East European Quarterly* 19 (Spring): 15–20.

———. 1989. Homage to a Transylvanian peasant. *East European Politics and Societies* 3 (Winter): 51–82.

———. 1991. *National ideology under socialism: Identity and cultural politics in Ceauşescu's Romania.* Berkeley: University of California Press.

———. 1993. Nationalism and national sentiment in post-socialist Romania. *Slavic Review* 52 (Summer): 179–203.

Vermes, Gabor. 1985. *István Tisza: The liberal vision and conservative stagecraft of a Magyar nationalist.* New York: East European Monographs, Columbia Press.

Verona, Sergiu. 1992. *Romania and Moldova: The issue of reunification.* Washington, D.C.: Congressional Research Service, Library of Congress.

Vesilind, Priit J. 1997. Kaliningrad. *National Geographic Magazine* 191 (March): 110–23.

Vladislav, Jan. 1990. Exile, responsibility, destiny. In *Literature in exile,* ed. John Glad. Durham: Duke University Press.

Vlasto, A.P. 1970. *The entry of the Slavs into Christendom.* Cambridge: Cambridge University Press.

Volgyes, Ivan. 1970. The Hungarian Dictatorship of 1919: Russian example versus Hungarian Reality. *East European Quarterly* 4 (March): 58–71.

———. 1982. *Hungary: A nation of contradictions.* Boulder, Colo.: Westview Press.

Volodin, Viktor. 1992. Iasi conference calls for unification. *The Current Digest of the Post-Soviet Press* 44 (February 26): 24.

Von Reiner Luyken. 1994. Der Denkmalkrieg. *Die Zeit,* 19 August, p. 32.

Vucinich, Wayne S., ed. 1982. *The First Serbian Uprising, 1804–1813.* Boulder, Colo.: Social Science Monographs.

———. 1997. Mlada Bosna and the First World War. In *The Habsburg Empire in World War I,* ed. by Robert A. Kann, Béla K. Király, and Paula S. Fichtner. Boulder, Colo.: East European Quarterly.

Vukadinović, Alek, ed. 1989. *Kosovo 1389–1989: Serbian Literary Quarterly 1–3. Special edition on the occasion of 600 years since the Battle of Kosovo.* Beograd: Association of Serbian Writers.

Wagner, Philip L., and Marvin W. Mikesell, eds. 1962. *Readings in Cultural Geography.* Chicago: University of Chicago Press.

Wagner, Philip L. 1996. *Showing off: The Geltung hypothesis.* Austin: University of Texas Press.

Walicki, Andrzej. 1982. *Philosophy and Romantic nationalism: The case of Poland.* Oxford: Clarendon Press.

———. 1997. Intellectual elites and the vicissitudes of <Imagined Nation> in Poland. *East European Politics and Societies* 11(2): 227–53.

Wallis, B. C. 1917. The peoples of Hungary: Their work and land. *Geographical Review* 4 (December): 465–81.

———. 1918. The Rumanians of Hungary. *Geographical Review* 6 (August): 156–71.

———. 1918. The Slavs of northern Hungary. *Geographical Review* 6 (September): 268–81.

———. 1918. The Slavs of southern Hungary. *Geographical Review* 6 (October): 341–53.

———. 1921. The dismemberment of Hungary. *Geographical Review* 11 (July): 426–29.

Walters, E. Garrison. 1990. *The other Europe: Eastern Europe to 1945.* New York: Dorset Press.

Walworth, Arthur. 1977. *America's moment: 1919—American diplomacy at the end of World War I.* New York: W.W. Norton.

———. 1986. *Wilson and the peacemakers: American diplomacy at the Paris Peace Conference, 1919.* New York: W.W. Norton.

Ware, Kallistos (Timothy). 1964. *The orthodox church.* New York: Penguin Books.

Weber, Eugen. 1976. *Peasants into Frenchmen: The modernization of rural France, 1870–1914.* Stanford: Stanford University Press.

Welsch, Darron Ray. 1992. The Horea-Cloşca uprising of 1784 and nationalist history. Eugene: Honors College Paper University of Oregon.

Whittlesey, Derwent. 1944 *The earth and the state.* New York: Henry Holt.

Wiebenson, Dora, and József Sisa, eds. 1998. *The architecture of historic Hungary.* Cambridge, Mass.: MIT Press.

Wilkinson, Henry Robert. 1951. *Maps and politics: A review of the ethnographic geography of Macedonia.* Liverpool: University of Liverpool Press.

Williams, Colin H. 1985. Conceived in bondage—called unto liberty: Reflections on nationalism. *Progress in Human Geography* 9 (September): 331–55.

———, ed. 1988. *Language in geographic context.* Philadelphia: Multilingual Matters.

Williams, Colin H., and Anthony D. Smith. 1983. The national construction of social space. *Progress in Human Geography* 7 (December): 502–18.

Wilson, Duncan. 1986. *The life and times of Vuk Stefanović Karadžić, 1787–1864: Literacy, literature, and national independence in Serbia.* Ann Arbor: Michigan Slavic Publications.

Wilson, William A. 1973. Herder, folklore, and Romantic nationalism. *Journal of Popular Culture* 6 (Spring): 819–35.

Wixman, Ronald. 1980. *Language aspects of ethnic patterns and processes in the north Caucasus.* University of Chicago Department of Geography Research Paper no. 191. Chicago: University of Chicago.

———. 1993. Dream of Greater Serbia fuels Balkan War. *The Register-Guard* [Eugene, Ore.], 6 June, pp. 1 and 4.

———. 1997. The Bosnian dilemma: The use and misuse of maps. *Mercator's World* 2 (March-April): 36–41.

Wolff, Larry. 1994. *Inventing Eastern Europe: The map of civilization on the mind of Enlightenment*. Stanford: Stanford University Press.

Woloch, Isser. 1982. *Eighteenth-century Europe, tradition and progress 1715–1789*. New York: W.W. Norton.

Wood, Anthony. 1984. *Europe: 1815–1960*. 2nd ed. Essex, England: Longman Group.

Woodward, Colin. 1996. Slips of the tongue can incite lashing by locals in former Yugoslavia. *The Christian Science Monitor*, 13 August.

Woolf, Stuart. 1991. *Napoleon's integration of Europe*. New York: Routledge.

Wright, John Kirkland. 1928. *The geographical basis of European history*. New York: Henry Holt.

Zderciuc, Boris, Paul Petrescu, and Tancred Bănăţeanu. 1964. *Folk art in Rumania*. Bucharest: Meridiane Publishing House.

Zimmermann, Zora Devrnja. 1986. *Serbian folk poetry: Ancient legends, Romantic songs*. Columbus, Ohio: Kosovo Publishing.

Zivojurovic, Dragon R. 1969. The Vatican, Woodrow Wilson, and the dissolution of the Hapsburg Monarchy, 1914–1918. *East European Quarterly* 3 (March): 31–70.

Index

About the Author

George W. White is assistant professor of geography at Frostburg State University.